THE SOUTHERN GARDEN POETRY SOCIETY

THE SOUTHERN GARDEN POETRY SOCIETY
Literary Culture and Social Memory in Guangdong

DAVID B. HONEY

The Chinese University Press

The Southern Garden Poetry Society:
Literary Culture and Social Memory in Guangdong
By David B. Honey

ISBN: 978-962-996-467-2

The Chinese University Press
The Chinese University of Hong Kong
Sha Tin, N.T., Hong Kong
Fax: +852 2603 7355
E-mail: cup@cuhk.edu.hk
Website: www.chineseupress.com

Printed in Hong Kong

Table of Contents

Preface

The following institutions at Brigham Young University were warmly supportive of this work in the form of travel grants, research supplies, and salaries for research assistants: the Department of Asian and Near Eastern Languages, the College of Humanities, and the David M. Kennedy Center for International Studies.

Friends and colleagues at universities in Guangzhou, Hainan, Hong Kong, and Taiwan have been encouraging and helpful at various stages of this project. The late Lin Tianwai, former professor emeritus of Hong Kong University, and Li Te-ch'ao of Chinese Culture University, Taipei, were among the earliest supporters of my work on the poetry of Cantonese literati. Professor Lin was particularly considerate in arranging several professional visits to the PRC and Taiwan to participate in various conferences on subjects of concern to Cantonese history and culture. Sadly, he passed away as I was crafting the first draft of these lines of acknowledgement. Professor Wei Chung-yu of the Department of Chinese, Tunghai University, was instrumental in arranging and participating in an exchange program between my institution and Tunghai University for one semester, where I was fortunate enough to teach a graduate seminar on the belletristic traditions of Guangdong. The literary insights of the participants in that seminar, Wu Ch'iu-lan, Yang Yung-chih, and Ch'en Fu-keng, did much to refine my understanding of many aspects of the works we studied. Professor Wong Man-kang of the Hong Kong Baptist University was solicitous in facilitating several visits to lecture and to conduct research. The faculties of Jinan University (Guangzhou campus), South China Normal University, and Hainan University were fine hosts and interested auditors during several visits to their institutions. Mr. Qin Huanming, librarian of the T'ang Studies Society, helpfully supplied various relevant articles that he located on his own volition and offered many useful suggestions and needed corrections to Chapter Two. I must also acknowledge the contribution to this work by several former research assistants, Scott Galer (now Professor of Chinese at Brigham Young University, Idaho), Kayla Ping Lam McKewen, Zijun Lan Dozier, and Elliot Dozier. Most recently, James

Graff performed yeoman's work in wrestling the manuscript into some semblance of stylistic consistency.

I have especially enjoyed collaborating with two fellow students of Cantonese literati culture, Steven Miles and Lawrence Yim. Their strict fidelity as scholars, Steve in the handling of historical texts and Lawrence in the treatment of poetry, has been a constant prick to my conscience as a literary critic; both have saved me from numerous blunders in interpretation and blind spots in historical understanding. My long-lamented colleague at BYU, Dr. Edward Peng, was untiring in his efforts to improve the manuscript when, at an early stage, it was a large collection of translated poems. Professor Paul W. Kroll lent his enormous erudition to a close reading of the entire manuscript, improving both the accuracy and readability of every chapter. The errors and infelicities that remain, despite the phalanx of experts mentioned above, are inescapably my own.

In memory of the late Edward H. Schafer, I present this work about a region that he loved with the passion of the explorer. His seminal works on many aspects of the natural world and material remains of the tropical South, especially his magnificent *The Vermilion Bird*, were indispensable in informing this work with any degree of ecological insight. Lastly, this book was inspired and sustained by my wife, Yi-chin. Her support and encouragement over many years have made many things possible, among them this poetic tribute.

Introduction

Shakespeare's Ferdinand lamented that all his linguistic learning went to waste on the isle on which he was shipwrecked: "My language? Heavens...I am the best of them that speaks this speech, Were I but where 'tis spoken" (*The Tempest*, act 1, scene 2). Some sentiment approaching this must have been harbored by the many cultivated Cantonese literati as they strove to win careers as scholar-officials in the foreign linguistic environments of the dynastic capitals of imperial China. For all their credible book learning, they labored under the social disadvantage of being stamped as culturally backward and racially distinct southerners by a refined northern coterie of insiders. Ethnic prejudices and cultural barriers, as much as linguistic handicaps, had to be surmounted by the would-be southern entrant to the world of Chinese officialdom.

In spite of all of this, Cantonese literati, especially in the later imperial periods of the Ming and Qing dynasties, produced much scholarship on classical exegesis, bibliography, history, religion, and moral and political philosophy, as well as creative contributions to belles-lettres. In another dimension, the same Cantonese character that fueled the intellect in the world of scholarship was evinced by their common country cousins who contributed much to the opening up of both the American West in the nineteenth century and the closed Chinese society in the early twentieth. This type of character, as manifested in traditional Chinese poetry, is described by Paul W. Kroll as a type of "sharable vitality" through "the force of language."[1]

Cantonese poetry, written in the traditional literary language, is expressed through favorite literary images that form what I call the Southern or Cantonese Muse. This muse in turn informs all of the poetry devoted to the Southern Garden Poetry Society, the subject of this book.

This Southern Muse, as the voice of the collective verse produced about Guangdong, gradually created what we may call an "epic of Guangdong." Viewed historically as a set of poems composed by various authors across time and centered on a particular region, such an epic functioned diachronically much like the geographically linked poems in the *Shijing* did as a more synchronous grouping. It formed, in the words of Pauline Yu, "miniature chronicles of the states from which they were said to originate."[2] Yu suggests that such a regional grouping of poems in the *Shijing* "comes close to creating the functional equivalent of the epic in the West."[3] Her definition of epic is worth applying to the case of poetry on Guangdong: "An epic is an extended narrative that can provide origins, structure, and meaning to a culture."[4] That we have to formulate such an epic by reading these poems as an entirety does not invalidate the way they function as a grouping; it just makes the process of reading a wide-ranging journey of exploration instead of a convenient perusal of an individual text. We may also view these scattered poems as part of the canon of Cantonese literati, for, as Martin Kern queries: "Where is the cultural memory, as a social construction of the past, located? In a text-centered culture, it can be preserved in a canon of writing…."[5]

As an initial foray into an epic of Guangdong, or the poetics of traditional literati from Guangdong, I have chosen to focus on one of the most potent literary themes in the region: the Southern Garden Poetry Society, in all its revivals throughout history.[6] Sun Fen 孫蕡 (1335/38–1390/93), the first major poet of the city-port of Guangzhou, founded this literary club headquartered on the banks of the Pearl River. The circle of like-minded literati he gathered earned a reputation throughout China as one of the five leading schools of poetry at that time. Sun's collection of poetical works was considered fine enough to be published in the imperial compendium of the Qing dynasty, the *Siku quanshu* 四庫全書. In the eyes of informed connoisseurs, then, Sun was the father of poetry in Guangzhou.

The periodic revival of this poetry society through the Ming, Qing, and Republican periods is a feat unique in Chinese literary history. As such a long-lived entity, it forms a convenient and almost automatic framework for focusing attention on worthy exponents of the Southern Muse. Nevertheless, the various problems of social interaction and literary composition call for a bipartite approach; this work is therefore in two parts.

Part One, "Literary Culture," provides an overview of notable Cantonese literati and the prominent themes and imagery that informed their poetry before the founding of the Southern Garden Poetry Society during the late Yuan (Chapter One). This includes most prominently Zhang Jiuling 張九齡 (678–740), Yu Jing 余靖 (1000–1064), Li Maoying 李昴英 (1201–1257), and the Three Great Masters of Lingnan: Qu Dajun 屈大均 (1630–1696), Chen Gongyin 陳恭尹 (1631–1700), and Liang Peilan 梁佩蘭 (1632–1708). Then follows an introduction to historical poetry societies in China, from Tang to Qing, and a broad survey of local Cantonese poetry societies (Chapter Two). This chapter clarifies the mechanics of literary gatherings and illustrates how sociality operates. It also introduces the five founding figures of the original Southern Garden Poetry Society. Part One concludes with an examination of poetry written about the garden and the literary gatherings held within (Chapter Three) and the private use of the garden by individuals (Chapter Four).

Part Two, "Social Memory," examines the historical reconventions of the Southern Garden in the mid-Ming, late Ming/early Qing, late Qing, and Republican periods (Chapters Four, Five, Six, and Seven); the focus is treating the poetics of the Southern Garden. A key element is seeing how time-honored themes and imagery from the mainstream literary tradition are interwoven with the local themes and images isolated in Part One. The result is poetry that both creates a local literary tradition as well as justifies pride in a regional identity.

Let me explain my use of the terms "literary culture" and "social memory." Treating so many revivals of the same literary club over 500 years, I came to realize that often very different modes of social interaction were adopted by the different renewals of the society. The Southern Garden occasionally functioned as no more than an ideal image to stimulate poetic composition or to represent poetic excellence; it did not always have an actual existence in the real world of South China. But the existence of the garden was true for those who actually participated in one of the periodic revivals of the storied poetry society and hence wrote verses recalling actual activities in the garden. The garden was equally true for those who were merely inspired by it to recreate an idealized evening in the literary garden through imaginative verse. Perhaps of equal importance, as a sporadically functioning social entity over time, the Southern Garden Poetry Society today helps to serve as a minor index of social interaction of Cantonese literati at various historical stages. For those who convened in its physical precincts for social entertainment, professional interaction, and poetic composition, it offered a tangible springboard for celebrating the delights of southern history, ecology, and culture. For later readers, it affords an enticing entrée into the world of the Cantonese literary landscapes, real or imagined. For all of these reasons then, I use the term "literary culture" to refer to that nexus of literati who socialized together, to the nature and setting of their socializing, and to the body and texture of literature they created for one another.

"Social memory" refers to how the literary culture of one generation was perceived by later generations of poets and to how it was appropriated for the literary, cultural, or political purposes of these later generations.[7] For literature, again according to Paul W. Kroll, is one means of transferring this "living past" across time:

> A unique frame and field of the living past inheres in each separate mind. And literature is one means—possibly, the most magical—of transferring that impalpable life of one's present pasts to other minds, in the future, thereby ensuring the continued survival of both that specific prospect of actuality—let us call it history—and some portion of one's own intangible pith and essence. Hence the truth of the dictum, that all creation in letters is re-creation, *time out of mind*. That creation is, as we know, continual and contingent on every author, every next reader, so that much of literature proceeds, as it were, "in search of lost time"—or "of a stone, a leaf, an unfound door, and of all the forgotten faces"—of we would add, those made lunacies of private recollections and re-shifted realities that otherwise would go to immemorial dust.[8]

Synchronically and diachronically then, the "living past" of the Southern Garden will reveal much about traditional poetic practice, literary attitudes, and the opportunities and constraints of contemporary social reality.

But, as the editors of a recent anthology of historical essays muse, "Historical memory itself is no simple text to be recalled at will. Individual memory and shared history have no fixed or predictable relationship; they produce one another in configurations that themselves change across time."[9] Wide-angle vision will be necessary to encompass the various "configurations" of the past of the Southern Garden, whether recalled or imagined, all equally valid in terms of how they were utilized to serve the present. For an imaginary garden was just as useful when created from the past as the memory of an actual garden. After all, as Stephen Owen puts it, "the act of remembrance" could often be "more vivid than the object of memory."[10] In this regard, Tobie Meyer-Fong's work on Yangzhou in early Qing is salutary; she characterizes her book as being "about place and memory, at a time when imagined architecture was more important than wood and walls." She continues, "It is about the creation of a sense of connection among local elites....It is thus a study of the self-conscious building of community and culture as expressed through the metaphor of physical reconstruction."[11] My project, even though focused merely on one garden and its historical poetry gatherings, is also an attempt to describe the building of a community of literati and the transmission of culture through the metaphor of the reconstitution of a specific club on a particular, time-honored site. A specific site such as a garden club or an academy creates a sacred space that, to paraphrase Linda Walton, can enable and support an ideal, in this case the ideal of southern literary culture, that focuses on the lives of exemplars of the past in a "landscape of historical memory."[12] Many Cantonese worthies contributed their unique individualities to this southern literary culture that was itself enabled by the prism of the poetry focused on the Southern Garden.

When participating in a poetry society is viewed as a ritual act, another link to the past is uncovered. For, as Paul Connerton says, "All rites are repetitive, and repetition automatically implies continuity with the past."[13] But beyond the generic nature of literary rituals were some actual ritual sacrifices: a shrine to Wen Tianxiang 文天祥 (1236–1283) and other Song martyrs was on the site of the garden, as was one to the Five Masters. The Five Later Masters held a sacrifice in the garden, as did the Later Southern Garden Poetry Society in 1911. These and other specific ritual acts in the garden will be examined in this work.

Regional literature can be approached from various angles, including how regional voices differ from more normative literary voices at the center of political or cultural power such as the national capital; how they attempt to access the center; and how they view themselves in the context of local traditions. Guangdong until the Ming dynasty had been the haunt of demoted and exiled officials, with a miasmatic climate that was positively hazardous to one's health; it offered little of the cultural amenities that made life pleasurable and few of the social connections that made bureaucratic success possible. Cantonese poets lived and most often worked on the very fringes of the Chinese cultural world. Being Cantonese, even for a poet, was to be known as being backward, parochial, and socially inept until proven otherwise. Instead of attempting to analyze how poets from Guangdong attempted to defend, downplay, or entirely discount their southernness, this work concentrates on how poets utilized their local literary traditions to define themselves. The recent work by Stephen B. Miles will prove very useful in this regard, especially in terms of how "localist texts" were produced to create a local cultural identity, and often either stimulated or maintained through trans-local networks of literati.[14] Ultimately, this work focuses on the process of legitimizing local literati culture, even though the reverse process of attempting to overcome cultural marginalization on the part of the national center was equally strong historically and perhaps of more interest for some readers. The irony in studying regional literature is that in the attempt to overcome marginalization, local poets often adopted literary themes of national interest to align themselves so closely with central poetic trends that their most famous literary productions hold scant interest for students of regional literature. To prove themselves poetically, they almost had to abnegate their authentic poetical souls. Their native voices ring truest when they write for themselves and their colleagues at home. It is necessary to point out that the poetry and prose treated in the present work will not necessarily be the most well known in our poets' *oeuvres.*[15] The guiding thread is to trace the Southern Muse, not to align our poets in some sort of pecking order of fame according to national reputations.

My occasional use of the term "Cantonese poetics" refers to the modes, purposes, themes, and especially imagery used by poets from Guangdong to write in the traditional literary language; it does not refer to poetry composed in the Cantonese dialect.

Apart from the usefulness of the Southern Garden for its insights into literary networks and the social use of poetry, it is my hope that the present work will also make a contribution on another, less pragmatic, level. I refer to the many delights of the natural ecology, human presence, and cultural heritage of Guangdong that can be accessed through the medium of English translation and evaluation. The richness and pungency of Lingnan 嶺南—"South of the Ridges"—in all its botanical splendor and geological variety, is too variegated to be encompassed in mere words, even those manipulated by native sons and daughters in such a supple and sensitive language as classical Chinese. Still, it is just such a riot of sensory perceptions, transmitted in poetry, that allows us to access part of the past, for as Paul Cohen notes, "the experienced past is grounded in the senses."[16] Despite the unavoidable gap between poem and English translation, traditional sensibilities and modern assumptions, I offer this work in the attempt to provide access to some of the sensory experience of social poetry in a southern garden as a tribute to a great people and an ever-fascinating local culture.

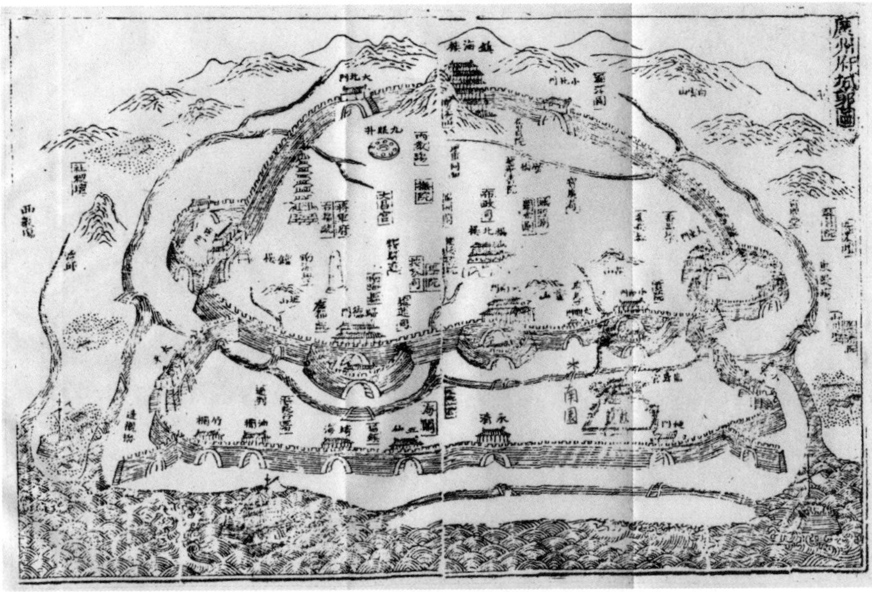

Figure 1. Map of Qing period Guangzhou. From Qiu Juchuan 仇巨川, *Yangcheng guchao* 羊城古鈔. I have added the characters for the Southern Garden on the approximate historical site, indicated by an asterisk marked below the Wenming Gate 文明門. The garden was two *li* south of this gate.

Figure 2. Yuexiu Hill, site of the Terrace of the King of Yue, with the Tower for Quelling the Sea in the background.

Figure 3. Tower for Quelling the Sea

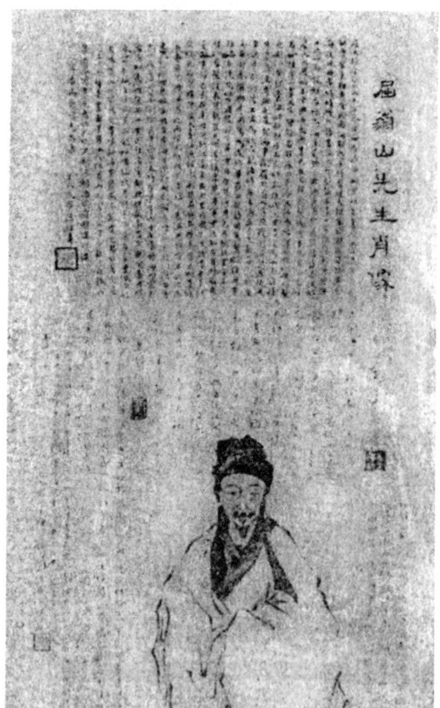

Figure 4. Qu Dajun

Figure 5. Liang Peilan

Figure 6. Sun Fen

Figure 7. Chen Zizhuang

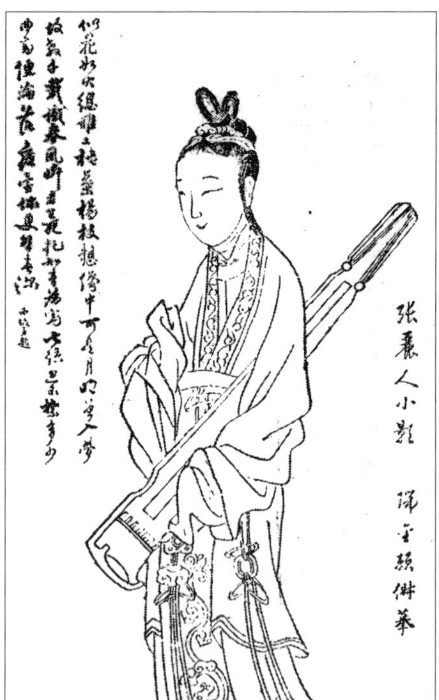

Figure 8. Painting of Zhang Erqiao by Rui Jinlai 瑞金賴, who copied an anonymous original.

Figure 9. Sea of Learning Academy (Xuehai tang), on the site of the Southern Garden, painted by Huang Peifang 黃培芳 (1779–1859).

Figure 10. Zhang Weiping

Figure 11. Chen Li

Figure 12. Qiu Fengjia

Part One

Literary Culture in Guangdong

Chapter One

The Southern Muse

Locality gives art.
—Robert Frost

Six poets from Guangzhou are enshrined in the historical records as having notable reputations during the Han and Six Dynasties periods. Our chief guide in these matters is that master of Cantonese culture and clime, the early Qing poet Qu Dajun 屈大均 (1630–1696) from Panyu 番禺.[1] The title of his great work on local history and lore, *New Tales of Guangdong* 廣東新語, in 28 lengthy chapters, recalls Liu Yiqing's 劉義慶 (403–444) *New Tales of the World* 世說新語. In matters of content, however, Qu expands beyond Liu's seamless and uni-dimensional preoccupation with personalities and interpersonal encounters. The world in the tales of Liu Yiqing is the world of human affairs.[2] The world encompassed by Qu is limited to Guangdong, but, happily, it gains in fullness because of this geographical limitation. Plants and local products, rivers and recreation, foodstuffs and holiday frolics, animals and aromatics all contextualize the many personalities in the work.[3] It is as if the selected characters in "god's plenty," as Dryden described the *Canterbury Tales*, were to be placed in a fully material context so that readers were able to follow not only their movements but also to appreciate the setting in which the action takes place. The inn, the utensils used to banquet and carouse, the weave of the fabrics that clothe the travelers, the accouterments that adorn the horses, and the precise topographical features of the route and historical sites, shrines, and edifices along the way would all be described in intimate detail. Qu's great opus infuses a human presence into such works of economic geography, natural ecology, and ethnobotony of the south as Zhou Qufei's 周去非 (ca. 1178) *Lingwai daida* 嶺外代答, or the earlier *Nanfang caomu zhuang* 南方草木狀 of Ji Han 嵇含 (ca. 300).[4] Such a guide, all-encompassing as it is in a material and tactile sense, is also well-rounded in a historical sense. Therefore, this work will benefit from the company of Qu

Dajun and his book as it surveys Cantonese literati and will benefit greatly from his guidance.

A modern student of the Chinese and Southeast Asian tropics, Edward Schafer, has written widely and deeply on the material culture, natural ecology, and literary images of Guangdong and parts of southwest China. His magnificent study, *The Vermilion Bird*, provides a modern perspective based on both rigorous science and sensitive literary appreciation.[5]

Qu's essay on the genealogy of Cantonese poets is entitled "Poetry Commenced with Yang Fu" 詩始楊孚.[6] It identifies four early versifiers:

> At the time of Emperor He of Han (r. 89–106), Yang Fu of Nanhai, by-name of Xiaoxian, wrote the *Study of the Strange Creatures of the Southern Border*, which was a variant form of poetry. Still, did poetry on Guangdong start with Fu? Rather, at the time of Emperor Hui the Filial (r. 194–87), Zhang Mai of Nanhai, while waiting upon the emperor on a tour of the imperial parks and ponds, hummed a southern tune while beating on an oar in order to admonish His Highness. During the Jin, Feng Rong of Gaozhou attracted a literary gathering and composed poetry and songs. During the Liang, the Marquis of Qujiang, Andou, wrote pentasyllabic verse with refined sounds and sentiments. He frequently invited over men of letters such as Yin Keng and Zhang Zhengjian, commanded them to compose poems and rhapsodies, ranked them, and rewarded them accordingly.[7] All of these men were pioneers who initiated literary refinement in Guangdong. By the time of Zhang Jiuling, poetry was in a flourishing state.
>
> 漢和帝時，南海楊孚字孝先，其為南裔異物贊。亦詩之流也。然則廣東之詩，其始於孚乎？而孝惠時，南海人張買侍遊苑池。鼓棹為越謳，時切諷諫。晉時，高州馮融汲引文華士與為詩歌。梁曲江侯安都為五言詩。聲情清靡。數招眾文士，如陰鏗、張正見之流，命以詩賦，第其高下，以差次賞賜之。此皆開吾粵風雅之先者。至張子壽而詩乃沛然矣。

The work Yang Fu is credited with is more commonly referred to as the *Yiwu zhi* 異物志, or *Monograph on Strange Products*.[8] Perhaps Qu Dajun felt some sympathetic resonance with this earliest ethnobotanist of the south. After all, Yang Fu displayed a kindred spirit and the same intense interest in the local culture; hence Qu assigned him primacy of place in the genesis of Cantonese poetics. But one certainly cannot assess Qu's literary judgment, for, despite the preservation of a handful of prose pieces by Yang Fu, none of his poetry is now extant, nor, strangely enough, does Qu claim that he ever wrote any. Nevertheless, the "appraisals" *zan* 贊 that adorn each entry of *Yiwu zhi* were composed in four-character lines, the earliest poetic meter which, admittedly, is not the best vehicle to display poetic skills. Vestiges of Yang Fu's preface to this work and three short rhymed appraisals—on the cassia, cowry shells, and the gaur—are easily accessed in the *Guangdong wenzheng*.[9] Let us sample one, the appraisal to the cassia, *Cinnamomum cassia Blume*:

桂之灌生	The cassia grows as a bush,
必粹其族	Yet must purify its own species.
何葉不渝	None of its leaves change,
冬夏常綠	Remaining evergreen in winter and summer.
……桂植	…doesn't grow the cassia,
在乎嵩岳	But it is found on Mt. Song.[10]

These sentiments were recycled into later encyclopedias such as the *Guangzhi* 廣志, and were eventually incorporated into Ji Han's flora of Southeast Asia. The opening of Ji Han's entry on this characteristic southern medicinal plant clarifies what Yang Fu only vaguely alluded to: "The Gui is found in Hepu, growing always on the top of high mountains. It is always green in summer and winter. The tree forms uniform forests without mixing with other kinds of trees...."[11]

Daoist and Aquatic Images

Of the four poets isolated by Qu, only one—Feng Rong of the Liang dynasty—is included in Huang Zuo's (1490–1566) important biographical anthology of Cantonese worthies, the *Guangzhou renwu zhuan* 廣州人物傳.[12] However, two of the four, Yang Fu and Zhang Mai, also appear in the major local gazetteers of Guangdong.[13] But not all of these poets were from Guangdong. For instance, one of the poets ranked by Marquis Andou, Zhang Zhengjian, was from Wucheng 武城, Hedong 河東 in Shandong.[14] But only Liu Shan 劉刪 from Nanhai of the Chen era left any poetic remains; he was ignored by Qu Dajun even though included by both the *Liangshu* and *Chenshu* among the poets hosted by Marquis Andou. Liu Shan was known as the "Marvelous Talent from the Left of the Ridges" 嶺左奇才.[15] Eight of his poems are included in a compilation devoted exclusively to verses hitherto overlooked by earlier anthologists, the *Collected Lost Poems from Yue* 粵詩蒐逸 of Huang Zigao 黃子高.[16] One poem concerns boating on a lake by the palace complex in Jiankang (Nanjing).[17] A poem about Jiankang during the Six Dynasties period, even though the place was considered a southern city, scarcely qualifies as literature devoted to Guangdong. Two other poems are typical contemporary products of parlor games: poems composed to assigned topics, a horse and an historical figure, Su Wu 蘇武.[18]

Liu Shan also sings the praises of delicate vines on a pine tree, green grass, and the cicada.[19] Two last poems are of mild cultural interest. One versifies roaming on a famous mountain to seek medicinal herbs.[20] This was a nod to Daoist pursuits, activities that seemed to concern many Cantonese poets, since the region was home to a prominent Daoist holy mountain, Mt. Luofu 羅浮山.[21] The famous Daoist alchemist Ge Hong 葛洪 (ca. 280–ca. 343) once practiced his dark arts in the seventh "grotto heaven" of this mount.[22] It was the presence of Ge Hong that had first brought national prominence to this mountain, despite it having appeared earlier in Han-period historical records.[23] Perhaps it was the fact that Guangzhou had been founded by five holy genies who came riding on the backs of five auspicious sheep that infused the region with more than a passing connection with Daoism. One name of Guangzhou even reflected this Daoist origin: the City of Five Rams 五羊城.[24] Another prominent manifestation of Cantonese interest in Daoism was the construction of a replica of the immortal isle of Penglai during the Southern Han dynasty, when Daoist alchemists were assigned the task of brewing an elixir of immortality for Liu Chang 劉鋹, the last ruler of the Southern Han (r. 958–971).[25] The native preoccupation with local spirits and the ubiquitous presence of popular shrines also helped explain this seemingly pervasive Daoist imagery.[26]

Despite Guangzhou being graced by a notable Buddhist monastery, the Guangxiaosi 光孝寺, and of course numerous lesser ones, Buddhist themes do not seem to overly occupy most native poets, beyond records of occasional visits to the monastery itself to enjoy its famous Myrobalans Grove 訶林.[27] Two examples occurred in 1685, when Qu Dajun took visitor Wang Shizhen 王士禛 (1634–1711) to the grove for an informal gathering, and when Qu returned with Wang Shizhen that same year to the grove when Zhu Yizun 朱彝尊 (1629–1709) was also in town.[28] Of course it was worthwhile for visitors to tour the temple itself just to gaze at the famous painting of arhats by the Tang monk Guanxiu 貫休 (832–912).[29]

The other poem of interest by Liu Shan contains the only direct nod to Liu's southern heritage:

"A Solitary Crane Skips over the Clouds" 獨鶴淩雲去[30]

孤鳴思滄海 Sounding a lonely cry, it longs for the Watchet Sea;
矯翮避虞機 With mighty pinions, it avoids the game warden's traps.
怨別悽琴曲 Grieving at parting, it voices a mournful zither's tune;
淩風散舞衣 Skipping with the wind, it sheds its dancing costume.
五里雖迴顧 Pausing after five miles to glance back,
千年會欲歸 It will return for a reunion after a millennium.
寄語雷門鼓 Charging its words like the drum at Thunder Gate,
無復一雙飛 Never again will it fly in pairs.

The prominent allusion here is to Tao Qian's 陶潛 (365–427) *Soushen houji* 搜神後記:

> Dingling Wei was from Liaodong and studied the Way on Mt. Lingxu. Afterwards he transformed into a crane and returned to Liaodong and perched on the hitching rail of a city gate. A youth drew a bow and was about to shoot it. The crane then flew off, circling around, and said: "A bird, a bird is Dingling Wei,/He left his home a thousand years ago only to return today. The city walls are the same, but the people are not—why not study to be a genie since the grave is all that awaits?" Subsequently he soared straight up into the sky.[31]

> 丁令威，本遼東人，學道于靈虛山。後化鶴歸遼，集城門華表柱，時有少年，舉弓欲射之。鶴乃飛，徘徊空中而言曰：「有鳥有鳥丁令威，去家千年今始歸。城郭如故人民非，何不學仙冢壘壘」。遂高上沖天。

This poem interests us because of its reference to "Watchet Sea," *Canghai* 滄海; this was the ocean surrounding the immortal realm of "Watchet Isle" 滄洲, the home of hermits. It appears in the *Wenxuan* 文選 and was often applied by Cantonese poets, including Sun Fen, to their own region through the association of Guangdong with Daoism.[32] For instance, Qu Dajun poetically describes "candle dragons" *zhulong* 燭龍 as "mouthing the sun, coming from the Watchet Sea" 燭龍銜日來滄海.[33] Yet its coverage was geographically broad enough to include early Ming poets who had been banished to Yunnan, whose collected poems were called "Left-over Pearls from the Watchet Sea,"[34] or a late Qing Hakka poet from Taiwan, Qiu Fengjia 丘逢甲 (1864–1912), known as "Master from the Watchet Sea" 滄海先生. And the manes of three martyrs to the doomed cause of the Southern Song, including Wen Tianxiang, who perished in Guangdong, were urged to "billow across the Watchet Sea" 魂濤滄海.[35]

Edward Schafer describes *Canghai* as one of three Chinese seas:

> Besides Swollen Sea and South Sea, there was the famous northeastern sea, called Ts'ang-hai (canghai). *Ts'ang* means "cold and blue"—it is that iron blue we once called "watchet." This sea washed the shores of the blessed isles of the Taoist transcendents. Swollen Sea was the southern counterpart of Cold-blue Sea. It was "vague and vast, without boundaries," its currents swirling round the rich Indies and carrying the great merchant ships as far as the Red Sea, or to who knows what strange places.[36]

Despite the actual northeastern location of this sea in real geographic terms—it lent its name to a commandery in the region between the old states of Qi and Yan[37]—it will appear frequently throughout this book in its transferred southern setting.

Cantonese poetry often shifts between oceanic images and the aqueous atmosphere of the tropical climate. In a similar vein, early English poetry, although suffused with cold, blustery northern storms instead of steamy southern typhoons, is like the poetry of Guangdong: it cannot be imagined without the lure and life of the sea.[38] Likewise, Guangdong and other southern shores are literally awash with water, whether in the form of sudden squalls, a heavy fall of morning dew, muggy humidity, riverine highways and riparian hideaways, or restful lotus ponds and productive fisheries. Aquatic crops include rice, taro, water chestnuts, and lotuses.[39] The monsoons are seasonal visitors, and, as narrated by Schafer, "The drenching monotonous rains of the sticky 'summer' soon became all too familiar to the tired exiles from the north," for "the incessant wet brought mildew and rot."[40]

If native southerners were more acclimated to the atmosphere, it did not desensitize them to aquatic and oceanic influences.[41] This is entirely natural, given the geographic and topographical realities of the land, as poeticized in a lengthy *fu* on Guangdong by the Ming poet Kong Xun 孔煦 (*juren* 1552):

……	……
巨海環而為池	The huge ocean envelops it and forms ponds:
潮汐之所上下	The morning and evening tides that rise and fall,
江河之所經緯	The rivers and streams that traverse and crisscross it—
北軼乎大庾湘楚	To the north they pierce the Great Yu pass and the Xiang river of Chu,
西界乎蒼梧九嶷	To the west they border on Mt. Jiuyi of Cangwu,

東盡漲海之連天	To the east they terminate in the Swollen Sea that connects to heaven,
南極珠崖之盤黎	To the south they culminate with the intertwinings of the Shore of Pearls.[42]
……	……

The myths of the sea and strange sea-borne apparitions which often appeared in Tang poetry about sea voyages are found in the verse of the Cantonese. For instance, the Fata Morgana, or mirage of a fairy castle, was made the focus of both a long rhapsody entitled "*Fu* on an Oceanic Metropolis" and a short song by the Qing poet Liang Peilan 梁佩蘭 (1632–1708), who shall appear presently.[43]

Such watery imagery is entirely to be expected, given that the original inhabitants, the Man 蠻 barbarians, were, according to Schafer, "themselves incarnate sea dragons and had power over water."[44] The land was itself originally sea-borne, for it seems that Mt. Luofu functioned since earliest times as a "fixatrice" mountain to "anchor" or "fix" *zhen* 鎮 the "isle" of Guangdong and to keep it from floating off with the tide.[45] The mountain itself sometimes was prone to split apart, one side floating off in one direction, the other side in another, as recalled poetically by Liang Peilan: "Pity poor Mt. Luofu,/Its separations and recombinations are set according to time./When it rains, Luo and Fu combine;/When clear, Luo and Fu separate" 可憐羅浮山，離合亦有時。天雨羅浮合，天晴羅浮離.[46] Not to be outdone, Liang's close friend Qu Dajun characterizes the relationship between the two peaks as a conjugal pair.

"Singing About Luofu" 詠羅浮[47]

浮山浮海自東來	A floating hill floated across the ocean from the East,
嫁與羅山不用媒	Married to Mt. Luo she did not need a go-between.
合體真同夫與婦	Joined in one flesh, they truly were the same as husband and wife,
生兒盡作小蓬萊	All the sons they bore became minor Penglais.

Mt. Luofu's role as a "fixatrice mountain" was recalled visually by an imposing edifice erected on Yuexiu Hill 粵秀山 during the Ming, the "Tower for Quelling the Sea" 鎮海樓.[48] It was a favorite destination for picnics and was often celebrated in verse.[49] It was also the best place to see Guangzhou through the panoramic view it afforded. For instance, in 1684 Qu Dajun and several friends "climbed the various peaks to the north of the city and gazed out over the unsurpassed view of Yue. Then they convened for drinks on the top of Yuexiu Hill and deliberated over a suggestion to renovate the Tower for Quelling the Sea. They immediately got to work on composing poems."[50] Even as late as 1911, it was the starting point for visitors to the city to get their bearings, as attested by William Edgar Geil. He commenced his Chinese travelogue in Guangzhou with this historical building: "Sitting on the fifth story of the Five-Storied House [*Zhenhailou*], we survey from this high point Guangzhou…."[51] Back in 1886, the Reverend John Turner, a Wesleyan missionary, had made a similar observation about the view from this edifice: "From the front of the verandah, a very extensive view is obtained, and the city looks well from this elevation especially when the trees in the official parks are 'dressed in living green.'"[52]

One of the earliest military heroes of the south, Ma Yuan 馬援 (14 B.C.–A.D. 49), and his posthumous fame as the "General Who Subdued the Waves" 伏波將軍 also increased the intensity of sea-inspired images.[53] Specifically land-bound associations of water, are, of course, plentiful. The Southern Garden will be placed poetically in the context of many of these watery images, fully in line with this important component of the Southern Muse.

Specific poetic vocabulary carried this imagery along from poet to poet and from period to period. Few such terms were more important than the adjective "watchet." Sun Fen even referred to the Southern Garden Poetry Society as "The alliance of the Watchet Isle" 滄州盟 in one of his longer poems.[54] But a more immediate use of the term in the compound *Canghai* was even reminiscent of the particular literary setting first envisioned by Liu Shan. It occurs in a couplet by the Song poet Mei Pan 梅蟠 (fl. 1085), unfortunately transmitted in an incomplete form. The title indicates that it was composed on the day Mei set off to return home after successfully competing in the regional examinations. What remains of the poem follows: "On wind over the Watchet Sea, the roc's wings are sturdy,/It finds its way through the clouds against the blue—where horse hooves tread lightly" 滄海有風鵬翼健，青雲得路馬蹄輕.[55] Another term in Liu Shan's poem, "Traps of the Game Warden" 虞機, is again connected with a flight over an ocean by Emperor Jianwen of Liang 梁簡文帝 (503–551); instead of a crane or a roc, however, the bird in question is a wild goose: "Loftily soaring, it fears the boundless sea,/Descending below, it shrinks from the traps of the game warden" 高翔憚闊海，下去怯虞機.[56] This example serves to point up the importance of the Cantonese Muse developing from within the mainstream poetic transmission even while focusing on aspects peculiar to its own region and psyche.

The Importance of Zhang Jiuling

The earliest major exponent of the Southern Muse was a national man of letters, the first Cantonese to gain success in the national examinations.[57] Zhang Jiuling 張九齡 (678–740) is praised by the champions of Cantonese culture as being the first poet to hail from Guangdong and is rightly credited as being the "ancestor of Guangdong or Lingnan poetry;"[58] but he was not necessarily a poet who celebrated Guangdong in verse.[59] In three crowded chapters of poetry, only ten of the poems of this famous author and statesman have anything to do with his homeland of Guangdong or hometown of Qujiang 曲江, Shaozhou 韶州 (modern Shaoguan 韶關), and some of these connections are loose indeed. Yet all Cantonese were enormously gratified that as both statesman and poet Zhang Jiuling proved that something good could indeed come out of the miasmatic marshes of the south. The respect accorded him is readily discernable in the preface to Qiu Jun's 邱濬 (1420–1495) printing of Zhang's anthology, *Collection from Qujiang* 曲江集. In this preface Qiu labored to prove that Zhang Jiuling was just as outstanding in literary circles as he was in political ones.[60]

"*Fu* on the Lichee"

Zhang's major manifestation of the Cantonese Muse is found in his justly celebrated rhapsody or *fu* on the lichee, "Lizhi fu" 荔枝賦.[61] With this prose-poem, Zhang, in the words of Paul W. Kroll, "celebrates the unappreciated (by northerners) glories of his native region and attempts to effect a reorientation of traditional geographic prejudice."[62] It was much anthologized and admired by later devotees of this characteristic southern fruit; it also inspired at least two other rhapsodies on the lichee by well-known authors—one by the early Qing poet Chen Gongyin and one by Chen's older contemporary Li Suiqiu 黎遂球 (*juren* 1627).[63] Structurally, Zhang's *fu* divides into seven sections. After the preface in prose, an introduction (I) describes the plant in general terms. The three following sections (II–IV) focus on the natural environment of the lichee, what results when it blossoms, the fruit itself, which is lovingly considered, and an appreciation of the wonderful effects that happen when eaten. After these sections—the heart of the rhapsody—a sequence on the personal and social utility of the lichee follows (V), detailing how this queen of southern flora eases individual retrospection or aids social intercourse. After a short section (VI) comparing it with other fruits used by the court, the piece concludes with a soliloquy addressed directly to the lichee (VII). It ends on a note of ambiguity—is the "truth" to be broadcast by this rhapsody about the lichee or about the author?

"*Fu* on the Lichee, with Preface" 荔枝賦并序

The lichee is produced in Nanhai commandery. Its fruit ripens after the arrival of summer. In shape it is attractively round, with an especially sweet, stimulating taste. Not a single one of the hundred fruits can compare with it. When formerly I was in the central cabinet I happened to fulsomely praise the lichee, but none of my colleagues knew of it, and hence refused to believe me. But my assistant, Liu Hou from Peng City, who had moved around while young and had passed several times through Nanhai commandery, agreed with me. He sighed with delight several times when he heard my words, confirming that it was the most savory of all. But he also stated that a common fruit, the longan, was as notable as the lichee. Even worse, Emperor Wen of Wei compared the longan with grapes. At that time, communication between the two regions (of north and south) was blocked, so such a great error could result from hearsay. Whenever I was consulted on this matter, I thought of composing a *fu* in response; but I was too busy with the daily round of worldly cares, so I never realized my ambition. Now that I am a mere local official with leisurely days, I'll narrate the thoughts that have been on my mind. As for things, they can be slighted if not well known; their taste can be doubted with nothing to compare them to; being distant, they tend to stay unconfirmed, never being appreciated. How much more so with a scholar who has not yet been put to use, who is posted in a nothing position? If one is not well known, how is one different from a lichee? Therefore, to broadcast the truth, I wrote this *fu*:

南海郡出荔枝焉。每至季夏，其實乃熟。狀甚環瑰，味特甘滋。百果之中，無一可比。余往在西掖，嘗盛稱之，諸公莫之知，而固未之信。唯舍人彭城劉侯，弱年播遷，累經于南海，一聞斯談，倍復起歎，以為甘旨之極也。又謂龍眼凡果，而與荔枝齊名。魏文帝方引蒲桃及龍眼相比。是時二方不通，傳聞之大謬也。每相顧閒議，欲為賦述，而世務率率，此志莫就。及理郡暇日，追敘往心。夫物以不知而輕，味以無比而疑。遠不可驗，終然永屈，況礦士有未之用，而身在無譽之間，苟無深知，與彼亦何以異也。因道揚其實，遂作此賦。

菓之美者	Of the finest fruits,
厥有荔枝	There is the lichee:
雖受氣于震方	Although receiving *qi* from the east,[64]
實稟精于火離	Its essence is absorbed from the south[65]—
乃作酸於此裔	Hence its sour aftertaste in this clime.
爰負陽以從宜	Facing the sun, it "follows the proper course";[66]
蒙休和之所播	It receives that which is planted by "the conclusion of peace."[67]
涉寒暑而匪虧	Whether in heat or cold, it still does not wither.
下合圍以擢本	The lower part is as large around as one can hug;
傍蔭畝而抱規	The top forms a circle of shade.
紫紋紺理	It has purple veins and bluish striations,
黛葉緗枝	Green leaves and pale yellow twigs.
蓊鬱而甚	Lusciously luxuriant, deep and dense,
封環合而棼纚	Round and drooping,
如蓋之張	It spreads open like a canopy,
如帷之垂	Sweeping down like a curtain.

II

雲煙沃若	Around it clouds are ethereal and fog is effulgent,
孔翠于斯	Peacocks and kingfishers nest therein.
靈根所盤	Where its numinous root intertwines
不高不卑	Is neither lofty nor low;
陋下澤之沮洳	It loathes the dank and damp of the lower bogs,
惡層崖之崯巇	And detests the sheer heights of stratified cliffs.
彼前志之或妄	Although earlier records might have wronged it,
何側生之見庇	How else could it have survived except by "growing on the side?"[68]

III

爾其勾芒在辰	When its shoots blossom and burgeon,[69]
凱風入律	"The genial wind" matches musical harmonies.[70]
肇允含滋	Commencing with exudations of moisture,
芬敷謐溢	Its aroma swells and overspreads.
綠穗靡靡	Green seed pods cluster together,
青英苾苾	Emerald petals exude fragrance
不豐其華	Its petals are not numerous,[71]
但甘其實	But sweet is its fruit
如有意乎敦本	As if drawing attention to its strong roots—
故微文而妙質	Hence it has delicate veins and marvelous properties.

蔕藥房而攢萃	At the base is the medicinal chamber where pollen gathers;[72]
皮龍鱗以駢比	The rind looks like serried rows of dragon scales;
膚玉英而含津	The skin is like jade petals, mouthing moisture;
色江萍以吐日	The color is that of river duckweed, spouting sunlight.
朱苞剖	When the vermillion fruit pods are cut,
明璫出	The luminous jade appears,
烱然數寸	A gleaming fruit several inches long—
猶不可疋	Nothing can compare with it.
IV	
未玉齒而殆銷	It seems to melt on the approach of "jade-like teeth."[73]
雖瓊漿而可歃	As "marvelous elixir" of the gods, it may be delicately sipped.[74]
彼眾味之有五	One may distinguish five kinds of tastes,
此甘滋之不一	Nor are its degrees of sweetness and moisture all uniform.
伊醇淑之無準	Such an exquisite taste lacks a standard for comparison;
非精言之能悉	Refined words cannot do it justice.
聞者歡而竦企	Upon hearing of it, one waits in joyous anticipation;
見者訝而驚忔	Upon seeing it, one is giddy with amazement.
心恚可以蠲忿	When the heart is enraged, it will dissipate anger;
口爽可以妄疾	While refreshing the mouth, it will dispel disease.
且欲神于醴露	How can you regard it merely as marvelous as sweet spring water,
何比數之相橘	Or place it on a par with mere tangerines?
援蒲桃之見擬	Now some have compared it with grapes,
亦古人之深疾	But this is a great mistake of the ancients.[75]
V	
若乃卑軒洞開	When I open up my humble home,
嘉賓四會	Distinguished visitors gather from the four quarters.
時當燠煜客或煩憒	When suffocating heat greatly troubles my guests,
而斯果在焉	With this fruit at hand,
莫不心侈而體忲	None but are "relaxed in mind and eased in

	body."[76]
信雕盤之仙液	Truly it is a transcendent sauce served in a carved dish;[77]
實玳瑁之綺繢	Verily it is colorfully embroidered silk on bedecked palace beauties.[78]
有終食于累百	Some have eaten up to a hundred at one sitting,
愈益氣而治內	Yet the *qi* is all the more strengthened, and the inner organs bolstered.
故無厭于所甘	Hence one never grows weary of its sweetness—
雖不貪而必愛	Although one is not greedy for it, still it is always welcome.
沉美李而莫取	Even those enamored with fine plums will reject them;
浮甘瓜而自退	Even those mesmerized by sweet melons will shrink from them.

VI

豈一座之所榮	How does it merely claim pride of possession of the feast table—
冠四時之為最	It tops all of the best fruits of the four seasons.
夫其貴可以薦宗廟	Now, as a noble fruit it may be offered at the Temple of the Imperial Ancestors;
其珍可以羞王公	As a prized fruit it will not dishonor kings nor princes.
亭十里而莫致	But even with postal stations every ten miles it cannot be transported north:
門九重兮曷通	Oh, it cannot be presented to the royal family through the nine portals.
山五嶠兮白雲	Oh, the Mountains of Five Peaks are socked in with white clouds;[79]
江千里兮清楓	Oh, the thousand-mile river is girt with pure maple trees—
何斯美之獨遠	How can only this fine fruit be so distant?

VII

嗟汝命之不工	Alas, it is your destiny to not meet with the

	times—
每被銷于凡口	You are always being sullied in common mouths,
罕獲知于貴躬	And seldom appreciated by noble connoisseurs.
柿可稱乎梁侯	The persimmon was praised by the Marquis of Liang;[80]
梨何幸乎張公	And how honored was the pear by Master Zhang![81]
亦因人之所遇	It depends on who happens to champion you:
孰能辨乎其中哉	Who can discern your inner essence?

Zhang Jiuling takes the occasion of celebrating the lichee in this *fu* to symbolize himself and any honest and upright official whose talents are slighted due to ignorance or whose worth is ignored due to jealousy or cliquishness. He seems to feel particularly grieved by the straits of worthy southerners who suffer a regional bias from men of the Central Plains. It is possible that Zhang goes too far, and is guilty of the same blinding prejudice in his whining protestations of superior probity.[82] Yet, despite the moral symbolism and umbrage expressed in this *fu* and Zhang's outright confession of outrage in the preface, his close description of the physical aspects of this fruit seems accurate in terms of both botany and horticulture.[83]

One of Zhang Jiuling's *shi* poems, the most common genre of poetry in traditional Chinese literature, generated an afterlife of its own in its influence on later Cantonese literati. This piece was later mined for themes and specific terminology by Sun Fen:

"Seeing off the Guangzhou Adjudicative Official Zhou" 送廣州周判官[84]

海郡雄蠻落	The commandery by the sea is a stalwart encampment of *Man* (barbarians);
津亭壯越臺	By the kiosk at the ford is the robust Terrace of Yue.
城隅百雉映	At the corner of the city wall one hundred cubits (of the Pearl River) are reflected;
水曲萬家開	At the bend of the river the doors of ten-thousand households open.
里樹桄榔出	Sagwire sugar palms emerge from the trees in the hamlets;
時禽翡翠來	Halcyon kingfishers are seasonal visitors.

觀風猶未盡	Gazing at the scenery I've still not seen everything;
早晚使車廻	Sooner or later I must send my chariot back.

The two sites of civilization in Guangzhou are characterized in literary terms that have traditionally denoted the capital Chang'an—"stalwart" *xiong* 雄 and "robust" *zhuang* 壯.[85] This is a clever but unobtrusive means to bring this rather barbarous region into the pale of Chinese culture. The "commandery by the sea" refers to Nanhaijun 南海郡 or Guangzhou. The "kiosk at the ford" Jinting 津亭 does not fit geographic reality very closely; perhaps it refers to the other extremity of Guangdong in Zhang's hometown of Qujiang. In this way Zhang Jiuling could be characterizing the northern part of the region as being more cultured with its Terrace of the King of Yue, referring no doubt to King of Yue Mountain 越王山 in Qujiang. In this he slights the more reputable Terrace of the King of Yue 越王台 on the hills just north of Guangzhou (to be introduced presently). The southernmost section, on the other hand, merely houses a village of *Man* aborigines. Does Zhang hold the same prejudices against those in the southern part of his own province that his northern colleagues held against those from the south of their state? Alas, it seems likely to be true.

Two prominent natural images of the south appear here, one avian and one botanical. The halcyon kingfisher, *Halcyon smyrnensis*, is commonly called the white-breasted kingfisher, or *feicui* 翡翠 in Chinese. Schafer reminds us that kingfishers, together with pearls, were "both in T'ang times automatically recognizable symbols of Lingnan and Annam, those countries of exotic gems."[86] The kingfisher's blue plumes were favored in costumes for dancers or in jewelry for courtesans.[87] Its presence in this poem infuses a touch of turquoise in an otherwise unrelieved backdrop of greens: the sea, river, and palm trees. The sagwire sugar palm, *guanglang* 桄榔, is either *Arenga pinnata* or *Arenga saccharifera*, depending upon whose classification is accepted. It was a very useful tree; its bark was made into rope and also into edible flour. The veined purple-black wood, which was similar to bamboo, was crafted into chessboards.[88] But most beneficently, it yielded sugar, called jaggery. Palm sugar was highly prized before sugar cane became widely cultivated. The process of deriving sugar from the palm starch was described in detail by Schafer.[89] It was listed as a local tribute product in the late Yuan gazetteer on Nanhai, along with longan, the "rangoon creeper" *shijunzi* 使君子 used in Chinese medicine, *Quisqualis indica*, and turmeric.[90]

These images and related ones will recur over and over in later verses on Guangzhou, and not necessarily only with Sun Fen. But it is true that

Sun is the next major exponent of the Cantonese Muse, and even if Sun's incorporation of southern elements is less elegantly concise than Zhang Jiuling's, he at least presents a more palpable and dense southern persona in his signature piece, "Song of Guangzhou" 廣州歌. Sun's poem is cast as a song, but this is mere convention. Thematically, this poem on Guangzhou is developed in three parts: physical setting, recounting an idealized outing, then a sad conclusion lamenting his separation from the scene of such happy memories. This tripartite division is reflected in the translation by the use of the past tense to recount the outing, while the introductory and concluding portions are couched in the historical present. The debt to Zhang Jiuling's poem in the initial section is evident—*Man* barbarians, the unit of one hundred cubits, ten-thousand households, doors revealed by drawn-back curtains, the verb "to reflect," and the like. When Sun begins to describe his adventure in the city, his personal diction comes through. In terms of rhyme scheme, Sun's song is structured by a series of ten rhyming couplets. Then one un-rhymed couplet transitions to two quatrains, the first rhyming ABCB and ending the outing in Guangzhou, the last rhyming AABA and concluding the song.[91]

"Song of Guangzhou" 廣州歌[92]

I Introduction

嶺南富庶天下聞	Lingnan rich and populous—the world has heard—
四時風氣長如春	The four seasons are as long as spring.
長城百雉白雲裡	Long walls of one hundred cubits lie within white clouds,
城下一帶春江水	Beneath the wall, an entire stretch of the river in spring.
少年行樂隨處佳	Young in age delight in strolling around, every place fine,
城南南畔更緐華	South of the wall the southern bank is even more bustling.
朱樓十里映楊柳	Vermillion towers for ten miles reflect willows,
簾櫳上下開戶牖	Blinds, raised and lowered, open up to reveal doors.
閩姬越女顏如花	Min courtesans and Yue girls have countenances like flowers,
蠻歌野曲聲咿啞	Their southern Man songs and rustic tunes

sound goo-goo ga-ga.[93]

岢峨大舶映雲日
Great argosies, pinnacled and lofty, reflect the clouds and sun,

賈客千家萬家室
Within view a thousand visiting merchants and ten thousand residents.

春風列屋艷神仙
In spring winds the serried dwellings ravishing as genies,

夜月滿江聞管弦
The evening moon fills the river, pipes and strings are heard.

II Outing in Guangzhou

良辰吉日天氣好
Under a fine asterism on an auspicious day, the weather was grand,

翡翠明珠照煙島
Kingfisher blues and bright pearls shone amid the hazy islets.

亂鳴鼉鼓競龍舟
The raucous beating of drums set the dragon boats racing,

爭覩金釵鬬百草
We vied to view the hairpinned girls, competing in beauty with plantlife.

游冶留連望所歸
Indulging in pleasure and reluctant to leave, I forgot to return,[94]

千門燈火爛相輝
Lantern fires of a thousand doorways coruscated, shining on each other.

遊人過處錦成陣
Where the sightseers passed, ranks of brocade were formed,

公子醉時花滿堤
When the dandies got drunk, flowers filled the dikes.

扶留葉青蜆灰白
The leaves of the betel pepper were green, the oyster shells were lime-white,

盤飣檳榔邀上客
Nuts of the betel palm on display tempted clientele to enter.

丹荔枇杷火齊山
Cinnabar lichees and loquats covered the fire-leveled hills,

素馨茉莉天香國
With the pure whiteness of jasmine and sambac, heaven perfumed the state.

III Conclusion

別來風物不堪論
I can't bear to discuss the scenes since my departure,

寥落秋花對酒樽 — Amid the sparse flowers of autumn, I face a wine beaker.
回首舊遊歌舞地 — While turning back to reflect on that land of song and dance,
西風斜日淡黃昏 — Rays of slanting sun and the West Wind turn the dusk pale.

Sun's visit is indicated formally by the reference to time: "Under a fine asterism on an auspicious day." The day was not necessarily a formal holiday, but it was rendered particularly noteworthy since it marked a vigorous competition between crews in dragon boats. Qu Dajun informs us that these races took place in the fifth or sixth month, on a day when the Pearl River was calm and running with a moderate current.[95] On such a day, it is no wonder that Sun Fen described the scenery with such crystal clarity, despite the ever-present haze of humidity. Sun very cleverly sets off the formal competition among crews on the river against a land-based competition among the dandies to view the elegantly coiffured southern belles, themselves holding their own informal competition with the beauties of nature.

Some of the plant images of the poem require explanation. The betel nut palm 檳榔樹, *Areca catechu* L., yielded fruit that is still consumed with great gusto in southern China and Southeast Asia, staining the mouths and cheeks of aficionados black. The name *binlang* was the Chinese transliteration of Malaysian *pinang*, for the tree was native to Malaysia.[96] Also called the areca nut, it was eaten in conjunction with sirih, the leaf of the betel pepper 扶留藤, *Piper betel* L., and oyster-shell lime, as noted by Sun. In the words of Ji Han: "When hung and dried, the fruit becomes hard like dried jujube. By taking it together with betel-leaf and oyster-shell lime, it is slippery and tasty, and it dissolves gases and promotes digestion" 熟如貫之堅如乾棗。以扶留藤古賁灰並食則滑美下氣消穀.[97] Qu Dajun adds that pieces of coconut go well with betel nut; he further supplies the chief reason for its popularity: it makes those who eat it intoxicated.[98] An alternate name betrays its use in entertaining guests, the "medicinal condiment for the use of guests" 賓門藥餞, a function alluded to by Sun, although he uses the term *ke* 客 in the sense of "clientele" rather than "guest."

The lichee, *Litchi chinensis*, evoked fiery images on several levels. First and most obvious was the redness of the fruit. More subtly, it was cultivated on land that had often been cleared with the slash-and-burn technique of cultivation. Most allusively of all, however, was its very nature: "Yue is presided over by the virtue of fire," explains Qu. "All flowers that are mostly purple in color are flowers of fire; all fruit which is mostly purple are fruits of fire, the crystallization of the fiery vapors of the sun. In all there are one hundred varieties of fruits of fire, and the lichee is the most senior: with fire as its mother, the lichee is the eldest son of fire" 粵以火德王。凡花多朱色皆火花，實多朱實皆火實，太陽烈氣之所結。火實之屬凡百種而荔枝為長，火為母，荔支則火之長子也.[99] Qu Dajun admired the lichee enough to dedicate dozens of poems to its various virtues.[100] He differs from Ji Han in describing its flowers as mostly purple, for according to Ji, they were green;[101] modern authorities describe them as yellow.[102] What is at question is obviously a matter of variety.

The loquat 枇杷, *Eriobotrya japonica*, is an ordinary southern fruit, not worthy of mention by either Ji Han or Qu Dajun. Nevertheless, it was chosen by Sun because its yellow color supplied a needed ingredient to combust with the red of the lichee into the fiery imagery that he desired.

The two varieties of jasmine mentioned by Sun were both foreign importations, described by Schafer as follows: "Both the Persian and Indian jasmines had been grown there since long before T'ang times, presumably introduced by Persian seafarers. The scent of the white blooms of *yāsaman* (*Jasminum grandiflorum*), originally of Rome and Iran, which was compared to the delicious odor of *trám* elemi, suggesting the love of beautiful women, filled the air everywhere in Lingnan. The intense Indian *mallikā* (*Jasminum sambac*) was, if possible, even more admired."[103] Sambac, transliterated into Chinese as *moli* 茉莉, renders the Sanskrit *mallikā*; it was more fragrant still than its sister *suxin* 素馨, which was described by Ji Han as resembling a white rose.[104] A cousin of these foreign immigrants is a vine native to China, the cinnamon-leaved jasmine 樟葉茉莉, *Jasminum pentaneurum*, which exhibits white flowers and is noted for the medicinal properties of its bark.[105]

Qu Dajun reveals a connection between the jasmine flower and betel nuts that Sun may have known, which helps to explain the presence of both in this poem:

> Betel nuts expel cold; jasmine expels heat; hence the people of Yue prize these two products. When presenting them to guests, the betel nut comes first; then the jasmine. The sambac is prized while the jasmine belittled. Sambac is suitable for women, the jasmine for men.…Southerners, whether men or women, delight in using flowers as ornaments. Whoever has beautiful tresses inevitably adorns them with sambac; this custom existed back in Han times.[106]
>
> 檳榔辟寒，素馨辟暑故，粵人以二物為貴。獻客者先以檳榔，次以

素馨。素馨貴而茉莉賤。茉莉宜於女子，素馨宜於丈夫。。。。南人喜以花為飾，無分男女。有雲髻之美者，必有素馨之圍。在漢時已有此俗。

Aside from the parallel use of the betel nut and sambac as offerings to guests, another reason for Sun to include them in his poem perhaps is the close connection between men and women represented by these gifts from nature; women and pleasurable assignations seem to lurk just beneath the surface in Sun's poem even though it mentions women openly only twice. But one line is less reticent in revealing the female symbolism of flowers: "*Min* courtesans and *Yue* girls have countenances like flowers." In this line, Sun generously includes neighboring lasses from Fujian—*Min*—along with local Cantonese—*Yue*—girls.

Overall, the density of detail contained in this poem provides a very tactile, sensuous portrayal of early Ming Guangzhou; "reading it," comments Qu Xiangbang, "transports the spirit back to the scenes of yesteryear."[107] And the large body of poetry which Sun composed to sing the praises of his native region earned him the honor of being the "one who initiated poetic elegance in Nanhai."[108] We will have occasion to examine much closer many of Sun's poems on Guangdong in conjunction with his participation in the Southern Garden Poetry Society.

Li Maoying as Prose Stylist

The Song dynasty did not witness any Cantonese poets develop the enormous national reputation of a Zhang Jiuling. Still, several local worthies did rise high in the ranks of officialdom and incidentally produced poetry worthy of notice, at least from the perspective of the Southern Muse. Without this local perspective, I would be constrained to agree with Yoshikawa Kōjirō's assessment that "during the Sung period Canton had no native poet."[109] Li Maoying 李昴英 (*zi* Junming 俊明, 1201–1257) from Panyu was a low-ranking censor and editor in the capital. He rose to be an erudite in the national academy and was granted the honor of directly memorializing the throne concerning policy. He eventually gained the trust of Li Zong 理宗 (r. 1224–1264) who praised his impartiality; his character was defined by unyielding probity and forthrightness. Student of the noted official and poet Cui Yuzhi 崔與之 (1158–1239),[110] Li has more memorials and essays included in the *Guangdong wenzheng* than any other Song-period author except Yu Jing (who will be introduced below).[111] His poetry was locally admired, and his writings were included as the first entry in the *Anthology of the Thirteen Masters of Yue* 粵十三家集.[112]

One *ci* written to the melody of "Preface to the Water Tune" 水調歌頭 yields Li Maoying's general impression of Guangzhou. Instead of treating specific sites or historical events that had occurred in the city, it records the view that any sightseer would enjoy; appreciation—not analytic identification in the "longing for the past" tradition—is the intent of the author. The diction is a little too precious and sappy for it to serve as a direct description of the view; it reads rather like the emotional response of a man of letters to an exquisite natural site captured on the color film of high-flung language:

"Inscribed After Climbing a Terrace in Spring" 題登春台[113]

野趣在城市	Rustic delights are found within the city;
崛起此台高	Loftily does this terrace rise up.
誰移蓬島	Who moved Peng Island here?
馮夷夜半策靈鰲	Does Pingyi spur on his numinous tortoise at midnight?[114]
十萬人家甃碧	Bluish-sided wells—water for a hundred thousand households;
四面峰巒涌翠	Halcyon hills jut up on four sides;
遠岫拍銀濤	Silver breakers beat against distant peaks.
插漢筆雙塔	Twin towers are like the hair pins in the Han fashion;
簸兩葉輕舠	Two skiffs are tossed about like grain in a winnow.
我乘風	I come riding the wind—
時一到	Now is the time
共嬉游	To enjoy a turn with friends.
江山無復偃蹇	The river is no longer arrogant, the hills no longer proud—
彈壓有詩豪	I, the master of poetry, hold them under my thumb.[115]
寶劍孤橫星動	Only I, wielding a precious sword, move the stars.[116]
鐵笛一聲雲裂	With one sound of my iron flute clouds split apart;[117]
寒月冰宮袍	Cold moonlight is frozen over by

the force of my palace robe.[118]

滄海一杯酒	The Watchet Sea—merely one glass of wine;
世界眇鴻毛	So insignificant, the world—a feather on a swan goose.

Being thus entirely occupied with himself, Li found it difficult to consider the Guangzhou of history.

Although Li was a fine poet, his greatest gifts were reserved for prose. Li once composed the preface to a reprinting of a local gazetteer, the *Nanhai zhi*. Li did not introduce the contents of this gazetteer; rather, he chose to stress the function of this genre of historical *cum* geographical writing to provide salutary examples of worthy conduct for the next generation. Li implies that the virtues of the local southern natural environment were responsible for nurturing excellence in the Cantonese character. This belief is perhaps promoted more directly and advocated more vigorously by other Cantonese authors, but it seems to find the earliest local expression here.[119]

> When compiling gazetteers, the most important thing is to present the virtues of local worthies in order to allow later generations to take them as models for study. This is the general principle in writing this work. During the Tang there were three worthies who rose up in the fiery south, Zhang Jiuling from Shao, Jiang from Rinan, and lastly Liu Zhan from Huang;[120] Fujian can not equal this! Yet all of these talents came from inferior regions in Guangdong. Dongguan, for instance, is renowned near and far; its hills are magnificent and its sea is vast. Talented scholars gathered there in droves....[121]

> 志州之土地風氣，莫先於表其產之良以矜式生乎後之士。此一書大綱領也。唐賢相起炎方者三：曰韶之張，曰日南之姜，最後得劉瞻于湟。是閩聚猶未有此。然皆奇拔于支郡。莞府以廣名甚大，山偉海鉅。秀靈鳩凝。。。。

Another author who picked up these same sentiments was Li Zhen 黎貞 (*zi* Yanhui 彥晦, ca. 1346–ca. 1405), a disciple of Sun Fen. In his introduction to a painting on the so-called "Eight Natural Wonders of Yangcheng" 羊城八景 by Liu Gui 劉貴 (fl. 13), Li Zhen exclaimed that in Guangzhou, "because of the blending of mountains and rivers, the collecting of spiritual potency and the nurturing of blooming talent, extraordinarily eminent persons emerged" 以其山川融結，鍾靈孕秀，故俊傑由是出焉.[122] Li Zhen even attributed the development of Cui Yuzhi and Li Maoying, together with the many *jinshi* and other notables from Guangdong, to the "numinous blooming" of the Eight Wonders. The process also worked in reverse, as local worthies could impact the environment. A subtle example is Republican poet Guo Gongjie 郭公接, who wrote: "I presume to ramble on in describing this latent virtue,/ The hills and streams in Guangdong have suddenly broken out in color" 敢以卮言述潛德，百粵河山頓生色.[123] These lines are found in Guo's lengthy poem "Song on Ten Worthies of Guangdong" 廣東十賢歌, which attributes such worthiness to the gathering of "subsidiary qi" 間氣 in the South, which also causes the flowering of "pristine pines." Zhang Xiyuan 張熙元 (1803–1865), father of Zhang Jingxiu 張敬修 (1823–1864) who built the famous Ke Garden 可園 in Dongguan 東莞, even attributed creative power to the natural surroundings of a poetry society, the Mengshan Poetry Society 孟山詩社: "In life the sound of reading books is the best,/Our poems are completed by drawing aid from the rivers and mountains" 人生讀書聲最佳，吟成得借江山助.[124]

From Li Maoying and his admirable essays attention now turns to an earlier compatriot who was more famous both nationally and locally, Yu Jing. Tangible aspects of the Cantonese Muse are embodied in his imaginative verse, which sought to find a blending of mountains and rivers.

Yu Jing: Blending Water and Rock

Like Zhang Jiuling, Yu Jing 余靖 (*zi* Andao 安道, 1000–1064, *jinshi* 1024) was from Qujiang, Shaozhou. And like Zhang, he rose to high office, once serving with Ouyang Xiu 歐陽修 (1007–1072) as an advisor to Ren Zong 仁宗 (r. 1023–1063), and participated in the important work of collating the three earliest histories.[125] He is considered the second patriarch in the poetic genealogy of Guangdong, behind Zhang Jiuling and in front of Sun Fen.[126] His collected works, *Wuxi ji* 武溪集, 20 *juan*, have been evaluated by Kusano Yasuchi in *A Sung Bibliography* as containing "nothing of unusual value."[127] Yet from the narrow perspective of poetry on Guangzhou, his work is filled with noteworthy items. Of two *juan* of poems included in *Quan Song shi*, seventeen are devoted to Guangdong. Most notable are his seven descriptions of the wonders of his hometown, Shaozhou. This place derived its name from the music once performed there by the legendary sage Shun, Shao-music 韶樂.

One lengthy poem about Shaozhou treats what Edward Schafer has described as "[a] magical gateway…for which Shao County was named.

These were two great craggy rocks standing opposite each other on the road leading down from the pass. They made a magical and ceremonial portal.... The crags themselves were gray blue, and, in Sung times at least, fragments of Shao stone were taken from the river which flowed between them to make attractive miniature mountains, much desired by collectors."[128] Li Maoying introduces the legend behind these stones:

"On the Shao Stones, to send off Zhao Guangwen from Qujiang"
韶石說送曲江趙廣文[129]

> Cultivated Shao is music of perfect goodness; it is a fine thing to name a prefecture after it. This name goes back to the early Tang period, which is very far removed from the time of Shun. There are strangely shaped stones on the mountains; according to a legend handed down by the elders, it was here that Shao music was played nine times, hence the shape. How absurd and groundless is this belief! It was not until the Qin period that the Yue range was opened up to communication with the outside, even if the southern inspection tour of the First Emperor did not necessarily reach this far. But the teachings of the Sage were spread as pervasively as the shining of the sun and the moon and were promulgated as extensively as the falling of the frost and the dew. Was Yue the only land at the time of Shun that was not included within his polity? Profound was the virtue of the sage, and how penetrating and long-lasting its influence....It has been more than a thousand years since the time of Shun, yet his thoughts and traditional practices still remain in the hearts of the local people. Why can they still remember Shun, and why are they unable to forget him? Who says that the locals are not the descendants of Shun? It is doubtless that these stones are a sort of stimulus for the local people to remember him by. This is something that need not cause doubt.

> 文韶，盡善之樂也，以名州，嘉矣，名之則昉于唐初，去舜之時如此其遠也。山有異狀石，耆老相傳，嘗於此九成焉。故石之形肖之。其説甚荒唐無稽。粵嶺秦始通，南巡狩故未必至此。然聖人聲教之溥，如日月所照，霜露所墜。粵當舜之世，獨不在舜之天地中乎。甚矣聖人之德，感人之深且久矣。。。。至於今又千有餘歲，而後其思，廟其依，常隱然在人心。舜何以得此於州之人。州之人何以不能忘於舜也。孰謂州之人非其遺民乎。則此石特人心感觸之一機，不必致疑可也。

Yu Jing now provides a poetic picture of these natural monuments of stone:

"Wandering Between the Shao Stones" 遊韶石[130]

世務常喧囂	Worldly affairs constantly clamor for attention,
物外有真賞	But beyond this physical realm is found true reward.[131]
結友探勝槩	Meeting a friend I seek out surpassing vistas,
放晴諧素想	This fine day matches my pristine thoughts.
韶山南國鎮	Shao Mountains, anchors of the southern kingdom,
靈蹤傳自曩	Numinous traces transmitted from the past.
雙闕倚天秀	Paired portals bloom, leaning on the sky,
一徑尋雲上	A single path ascends, probing the clouds.
長江遠縈帶	Long rivers coil distantly like ribbons,
眾巒疑負襁	Mountain ranges seem to be swaddling clothes.
千里眇平視	Across a thousand miles staring out over the reaches,
萬形羅怪象	Over ten thousand formations serried marvelous visages.
日影避崑崙	Shadows from the sun avoid Mt. Kunlun,[132]
鼇頭冠方丈	A turtle's head crag wears an abbot's cap.[133]
青螺佛髻高	A whirled green peak juts up like the Buddha's topknot,
群玉仙都敞	A jade transcendent capital opens up in the foreground.[134]
霞城晴煜輪	A city in the clouds appears like a wheel on this clear day,
桃溪春浩蕩	A peach stream rushes on in the spring.[135]
仰攀霄漢近	Looking up, I clamber closer to the Milky Way,
俯瞰神魂怳	Glancing downward, I am scared witless.
澗深溜如織	Down the fathomless ravine—a waterfall slick as a pearl curtain,
巖虛動成響	Throughout the vacant cavern—movement brings echoes.[136]
造化與真質	The creator lent it pristine quality—
妙畫胡能倣	Who can imitate such a marvelous painting?
賤子生海隅	This poor wretch was born in a corner of the sea;
逢辰辱朝獎	Despite an auspicious birth, I wasted courtly rewards.
靡成彝鼎勳	I cannot hope to accomplish the merit recorded on Shang tripods,

甘從丘壑往	Preferring instead to wander among these vales.
驚禽戀故林	Though frightened, birds long for their home woods,
困驥畏羈鞅	Being haltered, how can fine steeds fear bridles and saddles?
茲遊得幽深	On this trip we found a secluded spot,
同懷樂清曠	With a common aspiration we delight in this pure expanse.
世言帝有虞	For generations legends tell of Emperor Shun,
朔南聲教廣	Whose "fame and influence" spread "to the utmost limits of the north and south."[137]
丹冥卜巡幸	The spirit of cinnabar cliffs foretold the favor of his inspection,[138]
翠華臨蒼莽	A floral banner over greenish haze announced his arrival.[139]
簫韶曾此奏	Once before pipes performed the Shao music here,[140]
鐘石無遺像	But the stalactites have left no residual image.[141]
但覺薰風存	Yet I feel the residual gentle winds,[142]
翛然天籟爽	Untrammeled, the sounds of nature are clear and resounding.
姬公著治典	Duke Ji composed canons for ordering the world,[143]
歷代所遵仗	Adhered to and relied on by every age.
九野奠山川	Across the Nine Regions are demarcated mountains and rivers,
萬靈通肸蠁	All spirits have full reign, permeating everywhere.
醫閭與吳嶽	Mt. Yiwulü and the marchmount of Wu,
半列戎夷壤	Were ranged as barricades against the Rong and Yi peoples.
四時迎氣祠	All four seasons welcome incense from Buddhist shrines,
猶煩禮官掌	But we must still bother the ritual officials.
況乃祝融區	Even more so because this is the region of Zhu Rong,[144]
羣物資含養	And all things do depend on human care.[145]
來儀威鳳居	The "Come to Pay Homage" and "Awesome Phoenix" kiosks command the peaks,
樂有菁莪長	I delight that the aster-southern wood grows,[146]
膚寸起成霖	Even an inch of ground spawns mists that turn

	to drenching rains.[147]
崇高一方仰	All quarters look up to the lofty eminence of Mt. Song,[148]
躋之佐衡霍	And ascend its aide, Mt. Heng the presider—[149]
無慙公侯享	Shao should not be ashamed to receive dukes' and marquises' sacrifices!

Besides Yu Jing, other Cantonese poets naturally mentioned the Shao Stones in passing.[150] A notable instance is when Chen Gongyin characterized these two great stones as follows: "The paired portals of the Shao Mountains are open,/Both sheer and rugged, the outstanding monuments for a thousand leagues" 韶石之山雙闕開，拔地千仞俱崔嵬.[151] But Yu Jing was not limited to mineral imagery alone to record his impressions of the South. Like Zhang Jiuling before him and Sun Fen after him, southern flora figure prominently in Yu Jing's poetry. An imaginary Cantonese beauty in one poem, shyer than Sun Fen's *Min* courtesans or *Yue* girls, hesitates to "contend with the flowers in allurement." Still, like the personification of the lichee, she is conscious of her ultimate superiority. The location of her reticence is revealed in the title:

"Kiosk of Fragrant Lichee" 荔香亭[152]

虛亭何所賞	What to admire at the empty kiosk?
為愛果中奇	The most marvellous of fruits that I love.
氣稟南方秀	Endowed with *qi*, it is the southern quadrant's bloom,
生當火王時	Created at the time of the king of fire.
渡淮嫌橘變	Crossing the Huai, she resents the change to tangerines,[153]
經庾笑梅衰	Passing the Yu Pass, she laughs at the grief over plums.
不共花爭豔	She does not contend with flowers in allurement,
殘鶯莫傍枝	But wounded orioles will have no other perch.

Yu also celebrates the sambac: "With pristine allurement, it alone stands out from others in the south" 素艷南方獨出羣.[154] In another verse, Yu returns his attention to rocks, which really is his forte. He combines several elements already familiar to us from Sun Fen's poem "The Song of Guangzhou" to highlight what is notable to him about the south, its rocks and—not surprising given the above verses—its flowers: "At dawn, the earth embodies spring vapors,/The moon reflects the evening tide when it rises./Stones are the simulacra of the mass of stars,/And many of the flowers carry names of foreign countries" 地含春氣早，月映暮潮生。石有

羣星象，花多外國名. Yu adds his own exegetical gloss, explaining several obscure points: "The stones are set around the corners of my yard....These strange flowers were all brought over on argosies; there are none north of Guangdong."[155] Later he reveals that the attraction of stones to him was natural, given the environment of the region. In the preface to a lengthy poem on "Roaming Great Dong Mountain" 遊大峒山, he notes that "The borders of Shao are rich in mountains and rivers, and Buddhist monasteries occupy the best sites" 韶之境富於山水，而佛刹占勝. So he did not hesitate, as he continues in verse, "To creep up vines and scale lonely peaks,/To sit as one with the clouds on secluded stones" 攀蘿躡孤峰，和雲坐幽石.[156] The very next poem commences with "Sheer ridges coiling into distant climes,/Secluded springs inducing rents in the rocks" 峭嶺盤遠郊，幽泉生石罅. It goes on to vent feelings typical of Song philosophical self-introspection.[157]

Mineral imagery, we should again stress, is not Yu's exclusive preoccupation. For in one simple quatrain, he celebrates the dragon boat races held on the *Duanwu* festival celebrating Qu Yuan 屈原:

龍舟爭快楚江濱	Dragon boats vie to be fastest by a river bank in Chu;
弔屈誰知特愴神	Lamenting Qu Yuan, who knows his grieved spirit?
家釀寄君須酩酊	I'll send homemade brew—you must get dead drunk:
古今嫌見獨醒人	In past or present, it is detestable seeing only one man sober.[158]

Nonetheless, Yu made his greatest contribution to broadening the scope of the Cantonese Muse through his many celebrations of the marvels of southern mountains and stones, for "The strange resources of the southern quadrant are worth prizing and cherishing" 南方異產足珠珍.[159]

Protestations of Patriotism

Sun Fen well deserves his exalted status as father of Cantonese poetics. This is true because his verses on the Southern Garden and Guangzhou are more laden with local details and flavor than the poetry of the other members of his circle and of the later poets who were to reconstitute the Southern Garden Poetry Society over the next five centuries. Sun's exalted status holds true if we are talking about theme, but not necessarily technique. More on this will appear below.

Sun incorporated yet another strand in the tapestry that made up the Cantonese Muse—a long tradition in Guangdong of patriotism to the ruling house. The element of loyalty to the dynasty was very common in Cantonese poetry; it was so pervasive over the ages from Tang to Qing that it forms a convenient organizing theme for tracing the development of an individual Cantonese poetic voice.[160] Isolated nods of loyalty that prefigure Sun Fen's treatment of this theme are apparent in the verse of Yu Jing. For instance, one line in a poem celebrating the Great Yu Pass states, "If I want to cleanse the way that will restore order,/I cannot shirk difficulty, thereby expressing my loyalty and sincerity" 為要澄清歸治道，不辭艱險表忠誠.[161] However, Sun's adoption of a patriotic stance in his poetry was initially merely a preemptive protestation of innocence. It is widely known that the erratic founder of the Ming, Zhu Yuanzhang 朱元璋 (r. 1368–1398), saw the seeds of sedition at every hand. Sun Fen himself was eventually caught up in one of the emperor's vast purges and executed. But the entire group of Sun and his friends, the famous Five Masters of Guangzhou, had served the ephemeral Chinese authority, He Zhen 何真, who had held the region for the Yuan over its last decade. Therefore, the need to voice sentiments of loyalty and patriotism through the vehicle of poetry must have been an urgent imperative. Sun Fen had earlier drafted the memorial of surrender to the Ming general Liao Yongzhong 廖永忠 (1323–1375), so it is not surprising that loyal sentiments safely salt the poetry of this group. For instance, one poem by Sun, "Southern Garden" 南園, points up the beneficence and humaneness of the Ming monarch with tendentiously chosen classical allusions to the verse of Li Yuan 李淵 (r. 618–626), the founder of the Tang. Li's poetry abounds in depictions of the glories of his golden age. Sun therefore describes the pleasures to be enjoyed in the Southern Garden's Veranda for Screening the Wind 抗風軒 through the means of several obvious allusions to Li Yuan's verse. Such citations confirm the direct connection between the Tang dynasty house of Li and the new Ming dynasty house of Zhu, equally legitimate and glorious. All these details will be examined presently. But for now, to better illustrate this aspect of the Cantonese Muse, let us turn our attention to an early Qing group of poets.

The Three Great Masters of Lingnan

If Sun Fen and his group initiated loyalty to the Ming, the early Qing patriotic poets in Guangdong fought hard to preserve it, even after the foreign Manchu regime had consolidated control. The most famous of these was Qu Dajun. Qu Dajun 屈大均 (1630–1696) was born in Nanhai;

he was among the three most prominent poets from Guangdong during this era. Qu, Liang Peilan, and Chen Gongyin together were known as the *Lingnan Sandajia* 嶺南三大家, or Three Great Masters of Lingnan.

Qu was 14 years old at the fall of Beijing in 1644, and he became involved with other Cantonese patriots in an uprising against the new Qing administration in Guangdong. Barely escaping with his life, he took the tonsure in 1650 at age 20 under the influence of an old acquaintance, the famous monk Han Shi 函昰 (1608–1685) and lived in seclusion in Panyu at the Leifeng Haiyun 雷峯海雲 monastery. His identity was safely hidden as he assumed the name of Jinzhong 今種 while residing in a studio called the "Hermitage of the Dead" 死庵. In 1653 he lived on Mt. Lu 廬山, which sojourn generated much poetry on its many monasteries and natural wonders. From 1656 to 1659 he traveled throughout Jiangxi and Zhejiang, composing poems on various notable sites. He resumed a secular life in 1659, and for the next decade or so he experienced both periods of quiet retreat at home in Dongguan, south of the Pearl River from Guangzhou, and periods of hiding for his life. In 1673 he allied himself with the rebellion of Wu Sangui 吳三桂 (1612–1678) but abandoned it three years later, retiring to Foshan 佛山, just east of Guangzhou. From 1679 until 1681 Qu resided in Nanjing. He subsequently returned to Guangzhou where he remained socially active but untroubled by the authorities until his death in 1696.

Qu Dajun had began his formal studies at age 15 in 1645 on Yuexiu Hill with Chen Bangyan 陳邦彥 (1603–1647) after Han Shi recognized Qu's talent and urged him to follow the famous Cantonese master.[162] In addition to his work on the *Zhouyi* 周易 and *Maoshi* 毛詩, he also studied maneuvers and tactics, swordplay, and geography. It was natural during this period that he met Chen Gongyin, the son of his master. (He must have met Liang Peilan at a later date, for poems from Liang do not start appearing in Qu's *nianpu* until around 1662). He seems to have finished the *Guangdong xinyu* 廣東新語 in 1678. Because of his anti-Qing activities, his works were proscribed by the literary inquisitions of the Yongzheng 雍正 (r. 1723–1735) and Qianlong 乾隆 emperors (r. 1736–1795), and hence he received scant attention in traditional biographical sources.[163] For example, none of his works were mentioned by the *Siku quanshu zongmu* 四庫全書總目 catalogue, let alone included in that massive library. Still, he became well-known to his contemporaries through his friendship with such luminaries from classical scholarship and literary circles as Zhu Yizun 朱彝尊 (1629–1709), Gu Yanwu 顧炎武 (1613–1682), Qian Qianyi 錢謙益

(1582–1664), Mao Qiling 毛奇齡 (1623–1716), and Wang Shizhen 王士禎 (1634–1711), all of whom exchanged verses with Qu. In fact, before his regression from Buddhism, he was regarded by Wang Shizhen as being the greatest monk-poet since the Tang and Song dynasties; and Qian Qianyi said that his poems were unapproachable by contemporary practitioners.[164] His chief prose collection was the *Wengshan wenwai* 翁山文外, 14 *juan*; his collection of poetry was the *Wengshan shiwai* 翁山詩外 in 20 *juan*.[165]

As author of the *Guangdong xinyu*, Qu was as famous for his prose as for his poetry. He wrote numerous prefaces and epitaphs and owned a notable collection of books, all stored in his library named after one of the titles that his supposed ancestor Qu Yuan had borne, the Sanlü shuyuan 三閭書院.[166] This was not the only manifestation of Qu Dajun's self-conscious effort to identify with Qu Yuan, the first so-called patriotic poet of China. A more literary effort at justifying a direct genealogical link with this storied poet was Qu's lengthy old-style ballad entitled "Piece on Linking up the Emperors" 維帝篇.[167] A poem on his ancestress Beauty Qu 屈美人, who was one of the numerous consorts of Ming Taizu, states that "The distant progeny of the Sanlü Minister exists in Panyu" 三閭苗裔在番禺.[168]

Another member of the group, Chen Gongyin 陳恭尹 (*zi* Yuanxiao 元孝, *hao* Duluzi 獨漉子, 1631–1700), was the son of Chen Bangyan, as noted above. He was only 16 when Guangzhou was attacked by Qing forces; he was the only male member of the family to survive the subsequent resistance, led in the main by his father. In 1650, when Qu gave up the secular life to take refuge in a monastery, Chen lived in hiding among the hills of Xiqiao 西樵. He could not long remain out of the fray, however, and journeyed to Fujian in 1651 and thence to Zhejiang, Jiangxi, and finally Nanjing. After failing to become involved in the local resistance movements there, he returned to Guangdong in 1654. Open military struggle against the Qing gradually lost steam, and in 1660 he began to live in isolation as one of the "Five Masters of the Northern Field" 北田五子. All members were from Shunde 順德, Guangdong, and swore not to serve the new dynasty. Therefore, both Chen Gongyin and Qu Dajun were regarded not as subjects of the Qing but rather as loyal "left-over" citizens of the defunct Ming.[169] As another outlet for his literary talents, Chen participated in a local poetry association, the "Orchid Lake Society" 蘭湖社.[170]

Liang Peilan 梁佩蘭 (*zi* Zhiwu 芝五, *hao* Yaoting 藥亭, 1632–1708), a poet of exquisite taste and singular imagination, was the third member of the trio. He was from Nanhai and was the founder of the Orchid Lake society. Additionally, he formed a chanting society 吟社 in his "Western Garden" 西園.[171] Liang did not pass his *jinshi* exams until 1688, even though he had become a *juren* in 1657. Unlike Qu Dajun or Chen Gongyin, he had not participated in any anti-Manchu activities, and his official career had been uneventfully conformist and low-key, rising no higher than district magistrate. Therefore, the *Siku quanshu zongmu* saw fit to catalogue one of his poetry collections, his *Yaoting shiji* 藥亭詩集, 2 *juan*. A selection of his poetry was published in 8 *juan* as part of the *Lingnan sandajia xuan* 嶺南三大家選 (for which see below). A modern compilation of his extant verse and prose was produced in 1992, entitled *Liuyingtang ji* 六瑩堂集. It includes a biographical introduction, an evaluation of his poetry, a detailed chronology of his life, and other biographical material by his contemporaries.[172]

Liang's Western Garden is worth savoring for a moment. Qu Dajun dedicated four verses on the theme of his friend's garden that detail its shady precincts and its setting in the city. It was close to the Chan Monastery in the West [of the city] 西禪寺 and encompassed 10 Chinese *li*. A family of fishermen made use of its extensive pond; it produced longyan fruit and willow trees, and guests stayed in a rustic hut of thatch.[173] But the garden was most renowned for its large kapok trees. The kapok 木棉 is *Bombax malabaricum*. According to Qu Dajun, it was a very tall, thick tree with red or golden red petals around a yellow bud. This reddish hue inspired the first king of the ancient kingdom of Yue, Zhao Tuo 趙佗, to call it the "watch fire tree" 烽火樹. Its popular name derives from the wisps of cotton-like wadding that the tree produces; such wadding is used as a soft stuffing for clothing.[174] Shao Yaonian's 邵堯年 scientific note on the kapok includes a listing of historical notices of this tree and its appearance in poetry over the ages.[175] The tree figured often in verse by local Cantonese poets, including poetry about the Southern Garden.[176] Even in Republican times, two ancient kapok trees still graced the former site of the Western Garden.

Republican poet Huang Rongkang 黃榮康 (*zi* Zhuqu 祝蕖) composed a lengthy reverie on these ancient kapok trees in the West Garden. What follows is just a small sampling: "There are no kapok trees in the world like those in Lingnan,/The Western Garden Restaurant has two of them..../ How the trees and flowers sough in the Western Garden,/Facing the wine we should sing beneath the kapok trees" 嶺南木棉天下無，西園酒家有二株。西園花木何瀟瀟，對酒當歌木棉下.[177]

Of all the poets of this generation, Qu Dajun, Chen Gongying, and

Liang Peilan were singled out by their younger contemporaries as carrying the torch of the Cantonese Muse at this juncture in time. Qu was most skilled in composing pentasyllabic regulated verse; Liang was best at writing heptasyllabic unregulated verse in the old style; Chen acknowledged that he was not expert in any one style, but that he wrote excellent verse in all forms.[178] If Chen was good at any one thing, then perhaps his heptasyllabic regulated verse should be singled out.[179] In terms of mood, Liang never seemed to express a word of protest, while Qu and Chen sometimes gave vent "in their compositions to rebellious words because of long-suppressed feelings of resentment" 文中多悖逆之詞，隱藏抑鬱不平之氣.[180] Speaking in imagistic terms, Chen once characterized their individual poetic styles as different types of natural flowing water: Qu's verse was like a large river, that of Liang a waterfall, and that of Chen a secluded mountain brook.[181]

The Three Great Masters of Lingnan superseded an earlier grouping of Seven Masters of Lingnan 嶺南七子 or Seven Masters of the Early Dynasty 國初七子, who had all been members of the Orchid Lake Society. Along with Liang Peilan and Chen Gongyin, they included Wang Bangji 王邦畿 (*zi* Shuozuo 說作, *juren* 1645), Cheng Keze 程可則 (*zi* Zhouliang 周量, *jinshi* 1652), Fang Dianyuan 方殿元 (*zi* Mengzhang 蒙章, *jinshi* 1664), Fang Huan 方還 (*zi* Mingshuo 蓂朔), and Fang Zhao 方朝 (*zi* Donghua 東華).[182] Representative pieces from the voluminous poetic writings of this later, more memorable grouping of three were anthologized in 1692 in *Selections from the Poetry of the Three Great Masters of Lingnan* 嶺南三大家詩選.[183] In making his selection, compiler Wang Ji 王集 was motivated to promote this trio of Ming-loyalist poets over a triad of turncoat poets from Jiangsu and Anhui known as the Three Masters from the Left of the Jiang (eastern Yangzi region), 江左三家. This last group had turned their backs on the Ming to work for the new Qing regime: Qian Qianyi, Wu Weiye 吳偉業 (1609–1672), and Gong Dingzi 龔鼎孳 (1616–1673).[184] What added insult to injury was the fact that the first two poets had even served in the Southern Ming court in Nanjing for a time. This was an untenable situation for the diehard partisan of the Ming, Wang Ji. Therefore, the guiding principle for the selection of poetry by this new trio was the effort to celebrate the patriotism of these heroic Cantonese Ming loyalists, not to display their poetic art. As admirable as this aim may have been, the unfortunate result was that the Southern Muse is scarcely discernable in the poetry included in this anthology. A new selection, based in part on gathering the best of their poetry on Guangzhou, was made in 1980 with an up-to-date anthology, the *Lingnan sanjia shixuan* 嶺南三家詩選.[185]

These three friends dedicated many poems to each other. Some of these exchanged compliments or celebrated various journeys and anniversaries, and some narrated the progress of excursions to historical sites around the region. Prominent among these are poems about the sacred Daoist Mountain Luofu and its holy sites: White Cloud Mountain 白雲山, where Sun Fen once had a studio; the Cantonese counterpart to the natural wonders of Guilin called Seven Star Caverns 七星巖; the Tower that Quells the Sea; the Lookout of the Five Genies 五仙觀; the Guangxiaosi and other temples, kiosks, and shrines; various creeks, beaches, islets, parks, and gardens around the Guangzhou delta. Qu Dajun must have especially enjoyed Mt. Luofu, for one of his self-chosen *hao* was Luofu Shanren 羅浮山人, and he appears to have lived on this mountain sometime in 1655.[186] Chen Gongyin must have been equally enamored with the mount, for he claimed for himself the designation of the Commoner from Luofu 羅浮布衣.[187]

Local flora already isolated in the verses of Zhang Jiuling, Sun Fen, and Yu Jing were celebrated poetically by the Three Masters of Lingnan. The lichee, sambac, and betel-nut were the subjects of various *ci* by Liang Peilan, Chen Gongyin, and Qu Dajun.[188] Qu in particular was so obsessed with the lichee that he wrote 83 *ci* on this most famous of southern fruit.[189] Su Shi 蘇軾 (1037–1101), when living in exile from 1094 to 1097 in Huizhou 惠州 (in southeastern Guangdong), was also especially fond of this fruit and once ate three hundred at one setting, a feat he recorded in verse to memorialize the occasion. He confessed that the taste of lichee almost persuaded him to be a southerner:

羅浮山下四時春	Beneath Mt. Luofu the four seasons are always spring;
盧橘楊梅次第新	The cumquat and box myrtle keep ripening in succession.
日啖荔枝三百顆	Daily I mouth down three hundred lichee—
不辭長作嶺南人	I wouldn't mind to permanently become a Lingnan man.[190]

One major theme treated by each member of the trio is the Terrace of the King of Yue 越王臺. Originally located just outside the city wall of Guangzhou to the north on Yuexiu Hill, it was one of four terraces built by the first king of ancient Yue, Zhao Tuo 趙佗 (ca. 230–137 B.C.).[191] During the Tang it was a common subject of versification by visitors from the north.[192] It was also a frequent theme of indigenous poets as well, and, in the parlance of Steven Miles, the terrace, "surviving more as an idea than a physical site, occupied an important place in local poetic imagination."[193]

For Sun Fen, the terrace was a tactile image of Guangzhou. He remembered it even through the thick haze of a drunken binge with a Cantonese comrade, who, like Sun, was on duty in far-off Nanjing: "Then in our drunkenness was forgotten the road to Jiangling 蔣陵 (Nanjing),/For in our dreams we still remembered the Terrace of the King of Yue" 醉裏時忘蔣陵道，夢中猶記越王臺.[194] For a Republican poet from Nanhai sojourning in Hong Kong, He Shaozhuang 何紹莊 (*zi* Zhimeng 直孟), the terrace symbolized all of Guangzhou itself: "Thoughts of my homeland are still fettered to the Terrace of the King of Yue" 鄉思尚繫越王臺.[195] The colorful view of the terrace during autumn earned it inclusion among the "Eight Natural Wonders of Yangcheng (Guangzhou)" 羊城八景.[196]

Qu Dajun explains the significance of this terrace in the polished prose of the essayist: "Zhao Tuo had four terraces; the one on Yuexiu Hill (The Hill where Yue Bloomed) in Guangzhou is called The Terrace of the King of Yue.…Since antiquity, the practice of feudal lords and kings constructing terraces to reverence the Son of Heaven started with Zhao Tuo" 趙佗有四臺。其在廣州粵秀山上者，曰越王臺。。。。自古諸侯王築臺以朝天子始自佗.[197] This information underlies the initial couplet of Chen Gongyin's poem "Climbing the Terrace of the King of Yue on a Spring Day" 春日登越王臺: "Flowers issue forth from the lofty terrace, the stone-step road distant,/The King of Yue once before paid obeisance here to the Middle Court" 花發高臺磴道遙，粵王曾此拜中朝.[198] Sojourner officials who had been banished to Guangzhou faced north on the terrace in imitation of Zhao Tuo to express, according to Miles, "their own longings for their northern homes."[199]

Following is Qu Dajun's offering on the theme of the terrace, to the tune of "Flowers in the Rain" 雨中花慢:

"Longing for the Past at the Terrace of the King of Yue" 越王臺懷古[200]

雁翅三城	In the Tri-cities and their wild goose wings,[201]
龍荒十郡	At ten commanderies in the draconic wastes,[202]
秋來不減邊沙	There was no diminishing of sand on the "frontier" since autumn.
恨牛羊有地	What a pity that cows and sheep had places to stay,
雞犬無家	But chickens and dogs were homeless.
雖少諸軍浴鐵	Although few troops were bathed in iron

	armour,[203]
還餘幾隊吹笳	Still several brigades blew on barbarian flutes.
朝臺試望	Attempting to gaze out from the Reverencing China Terrace,[204]
天似穹廬直接京華	The sky was like a yurt, directly connected to the capital.
趙佗箕踞南武	Zhao Tuo sat regally on his throne as the Martial King of the South,
稱雄遺墟	He claimed the title of hero on this heap of ruins,
問取棲鴉	Only perching crows can answer questions about him now.
誰得似斑騅漢使	Who now will act like the Han emissary on his blue bayard,
才藻紛葩	With talent like so many flowers?
湯沐千年	At this imperial hostel for over a thousand years,[205]
錦石文章	Edicts were received as exquisite as finely variegated stones.
五嶺梅花	When plum blossoms lined the Five Ridges,
綵絲女子	Colorfully adorned palace maids
爭看旌節	Vied to view his staff of office,[206]
色映朝霞	Its colors reflected in the morning dawn.

Qu borrows the old literary conceit of the nomadic Xiongnu to portray the invading Manchu forest dwellers. The sands of the "draconic wastes" have not diminished on the "frontier," a term I place in quotation marks to indicate its use as a double entendre, since it also means "side" or in this case, river "bank." Its use here perhaps refers to the sands along the "banks" of the Pearl River that have been building up over the years to make the river recede further and further from Guangzhou.[207] The domestic animals of the nomadic invaders, cows and sheep, are right at home in the foreign land of China, but the typical domestic animals of the sedentary Chinese, chickens and dogs, are set adrift and rendered nomadic. This was a simple but effective evocation of the great suffering caused by this barbarian invasion into China proper and specifically Guangzhou. Nevertheless, as Guangzhou had been a part of imperial China for over a thousand years, as symbolized by the imperial hostel and confirmed by the arrival of royal emissaries over the ages, it would recover from Manchurian desecration.

In fact, Guangzhou had already started to witness the recovery of Chinese authority, perhaps in the person of an emissary from the Southern Ming court that was headquartered at Zhaoqing 肇慶. Regardless of how specifically the literary allusions are linked to particular historical events, this is a bold, polemical poem from a "left-over" citizen of the defunct Ming, who, it should be remembered, had to spend nine years in hiding from the Manchu authorities.[208]

The "*Fu* on the Terrace of the King of Yue," a lengthy rhapsody by Li Minbiao 黎民表 (*zi* Weijing 惟敬, 1515–1581) (a Ming poet to be treated in Chapter Five), conjures up the gleaming image of the storied terrace elevated to a lofty rhetorical plane through the use of high-flung diction and arcane literary allusions.[209] I translate a lengthy excerpt that deals mainly with the historical backdrop leading up to Zhao Tuo proclaiming himself the Son of Heaven in his own right, before he swore allegiance to the house of Han. Concentrating on history—even if it is history obscured by literary embellishments—will at least access some of the flavor of this *fu* while avoiding the overblown pomp and attendant tedium that sometimes besets works in this genre. Still, the physical description of the storied terrace itself is worth lingering over:

……	……
則有強秦定霸	Then there was powerful Qin, which set up its hegemony,
勁越守偏	Sturdy Yue, defences all deployed.
五軍摧而弗利	Five armies were crushed, failing to gain victory,
睢祿卻而生捐	Fan Ju was repulsed, and lives lost.[210]
囂死南海	After Ren Xiao perished in Nanhai,
佗據龍川	Zhao Tuo seized Longchuan.[211]
占王氣於東井	Royal *qi* augured under an auspicious asterism,
規閏位於瀛儒	But it portended an usurper at the seaside.
於是	Thereupon,
思華風	They longed for sinicization,
陋魋結	Rejected barbarian hairstyles.
裒秦餘	Gathering the remnants of Qin,
役徒裂	Ex-convicts excavated the land.
乘黃屋以稱雄	Riding an imperial livery, Tuo proclaimed himself a hero,
改金墉而創制	Renovating the Golden Fortification, he created an administration.[212]

日不重明	The sun does not shine twice,
世無兩帝	Nor can there be two emperors in the same age.
念首邱於故墟	Amid the ruins, he recalled his ancient homeland with nostalgia,
挫確心於遊説	Because of his counsellors, he fixed his aspirations with determination:
循南面之儀	He undertook the ceremony of facing south,
講郊宮之禮	Performed the ritual of the suburban sacrifice,
恢夕室以重摹	Destroyed the "slanted chambers" and emulated them,[213]
擬即臺而增累	He tried to ascend the terrace but only increased his weariness.
埋竇夷山	He buried passes and levelled mountains,
審曲面勢	Examined the land's intricacies and strategic sites.
輦道雲連	The royal road intersected with the clouds,
重軒霞起	Double verandas rose from within the aurora.
赬壤密石之工	There was exquisite work in polished stones and carmine loam,[214]
井榦榮楯之麗	And the beauty of wells and floral balustrades,[215]
鉛墀釦閾之華	The magnificence of steps made of lead and thresholds inlaid with jade and gold,
藻棁雕欒之侈	The splendor of short columns decorated with duckweeds and carved rafter brackets—[216]
固已殫海陸	This terrace has exhausted everything on land or in sea,
而炳炳萬里	With glory that shines beyond ten-thousand *li*.
……	……

Another thorough poetic exploration of the terrace is by He Ruquan 何如銓 (*juren* 1875), "*Fu* on the Terrace of the King of Yue" 越王臺賦.[217] Despite being more concrete and substantial in its evocation, we will not examine it here.

At the opposite end of the rhetorical plane, Liang Peilan uses the charming genre of an aria from a Cantonese opera to describe his own springtime attempt at the terrace. The song, although written in Cantonese, rhymes equally well in modern Mandarin and borrows the rhyme scheme of Zhang Jiuling's earlier poem:

"Song of Yue" 越曲[218]

春風試上粵王台	In the spring wind I attempt to ascend the Terrace of the King of Yue,
錦繡山河四面開	Hills and rivers—damasked and embroidered—open up on all four sides.
今古興亡猶在眼	Ancient declines and modern rises, still apparent to me—
大江潮去復潮來	Receding tides of the great river and tides that return again.

Despite the quaintness of the genre, this poem actually seems thematically indebted to an earlier composition on the same subject by a famous official in Guangdong, Wen Tianxiang; his influence was particularly strong in Guangzhou.[219] After the passing of the first Southern Garden Poetry Society, the site where they met had been turned into a shrine to Wen and two other patriotic Chinese who had resisted the invading Mongols; it was called the "Shrine to the Three Great Loyalists" 三大忠祠.[220] The site was selected by rhabdomancy after an initial location had proved unsatisfactory. Apparently it was not known at the time that the place had been the location of the Southern Garden. It had served for a period as a hostel for the local military authority and his guests 總鎮行館.[221] Wen's poem "Yue Wang tai" 越王臺 perhaps inspired by an earlier line by Yu Jing,[222] contains the following couplet: "Affairs of spring depart into dimness, following the flowing water/The sounds of tides return, vainly chasing the evening sky" 春事暗隨流水去，潮聲空逐暮天回. So even when writing for his fellow Cantonese in their common local dialect, Liang Peilan still built on and developed the Cantonese Muse as transmitted from both native and adopted Cantonese poets of the past.[223] And his song seems the point of departure for a late offering by Qiu Fengjia, who adopted the same rhyme scheme and some of the same diction.[224]

Conclusions

As mentioned above in the introduction, literature is one of the major means of both recording literary culture and transmitting it down the ages. As an important component of Cantonese literary culture then, the Southern Muse of Cantonese poetry is best approached on the visual level—that is, the various images that occupied the minds of Cantonese poets. Sweeping pronouncements as to the essence of Cantonese poetry—such as its heroic breadth, its clarity of diction, or other wooly abstractions[225]—do nothing to separate the Cantonese Muse from, say, the Shandong Muse, the Shaanxi Muse, or the Sichuan Muse, which all may be equally heroic and clear. The important thing to examine is the content treated in verse form, not the delicacies of the surface features of linguistic expression. For, as Corey Andrews puts it, "the unifying function of language is conceived as the 'personal property of quite specific groups—their daily speakers and readers.'"[226] The specific literary images and poetic diction that have made a distinctive "unified language" for Cantonese literati, partially identified above, will be happily noted throughout this work.

What, then, has traditionally been the main matter explored by Cantonese literati? From the earliest poets, the following elements are found in poetry that is authentically Cantonese: oceanic elements, riparian revelries, and aqueous atmospheres contrasted with stunning rocks and majestic mountains; a love for the local, especially plants, products, and lore; Daoist transcendentalism; and, finally, an almost tedious concern for pointing up Cantonese loyalty to the distant throne and a fierce pride in being culturally authentic Chinese. This particular combination of disparate poetic themes was first blended, on a very small scale, by Zhang Jiuling. Yu Jing then infused a blend of watery *yin* with mountainous *yang* elements. Sun Fen was among the first of the Cantonese poets to unabashedly celebrate local sites and scenes, historical worthies, and Daoist immortals. The Three Great Masters of Lingnan were the most famous Qing exponents of the Southern Muse of their times who cannot be included in any of the periodic revivals of the Southern Garden Poetry Society. It will prove instructional to see how the different elements of this Southern Muse became embodied in later Cantonese poetry, shared among literati friends, and transmitted throughout time as later poets played off of these images. Most interesting of all will be to see how this tradition of the Southern Muse became enriched by the infusion of imagery from the Southern Garden.

As we turn to Sun Fen and the founders of this most celebrated of all Cantonese poetry associations in the next chapter, we will first survey poetry societies in China, and introduce some literary associations in Guangzhou. This will help to set the contributions of the Southern Garden Poetry Society in sharper relief.

Chapter Two

Chinese Poetry Societies and the Southern Garden

> I have been thinking how in the olden days even men whose lives were spent amidst the hurly-burly of public affairs would keep some quiet retreat for themselves with its tiny corner of mountain and trickle of running water; and how they would seek, by whatever arts and blandishments they knew of, to assemble there a little group of kindred spirits to share in their enjoyment of it; and how on the basis of such leisure-time associations, rhymers' guilds and poetry clubs were then founded, so that the fleeting inspirations of an ideal hour might often be perpetuated in imperishable masterpieces of verse.
>
> —*The Story of the Stone*[1]

Literary Clubs in the West

Literary clubs have a long tradition in the West. The Greek symposium, literally "drinking together," seems to be the earliest antecedent. According to Timothy Raylor, it was characterized by "the competitive composition of verses on set themes or the parodying of serious activities."[2] One view has it that the symposium was not much more than ritual wine drinking, even above poetizing or philosophizing.[3] Close relatives, the Greek *hetaireia*, were formed by young aristocrats to strengthen social and political ties.[4] The Roman *convivium* often extended common drinking and poetizing to actual communal living; when held by upwardly mobile groups, *convivia* reinforced their sense of status and expanded social contacts.[5]

Literary clubs in London began to appear in the early seventeenth century; they were also known as societies, fraternities, and orders. An example of such a club is the Mermaid group of Ben Jonson, which first met in 1604 and persisted until 1616. Often these groups were associated with particular taverns, which signified the fact that they were formalized clubs. The Order of Fancy, formed to better the social lot of budding wits, was distinguished by a "taste for puns, anecdotes, bawdy jokes, and self-mockery...(an) aptitude for mimicry and the competitive composition of humorous verses."[6] The parlors of such famous *salonnières* as Ninon de Lenclos and Madame de Pompadour in eighteenth-century France were dominated by witty and occasionally politically-oriented conversation.[7] Literary associations along the lines of the clubs founded or co-founded by Dr. Johnson, also in the eighteenth century—the Ivy Lane Club, the Literary Club, or the Essex-Head Club—perhaps come closest to the spirit of the Chinese poetry society in fostering what J. Nelson calls the spirit of "learned amiability" in combining all of the best characteristics of the drinking Greeks, the sociable Romans, the refined French, and the literary-minded English.[8]

Eighteenth-century Scottish poetry clubs further refine our understanding of the nature and purpose of such literary gatherings of the time. Three literary figures represent three disparate functions of Scottish poetry clubs. Allan Ramsey and the Easy Club (founded in 1712) wrote poetry to present its members as part of an imagined Scottish national community; Robert Fergusson and the Cape Club (which lasted from 1764 to 1841) focused on poetic composition for pleasure and conviviality as a source of unity; both clubs helped to assimilate its members to English tastes and manners. But Robert Burns and the Crochallan Fencibles (1780 to 1794) defined a new nationalism through revealing universal Scottish character traits. All in all, in seventeenth-century Scotland, concludes Corey Andrews,

> club poetry served not only to commemorate the occasion of the club's meetings but also to represent the "contemporaneous community" of the club to its members. It is during such imagined moments of national communion like these that particular solidarities are built, which in turn generate imagined national communities. Such moments of national bonding are a key means for the strangers in club, city, town, Lowland, and Highland alike to see each other as fellow Scots.[9]

Substitute the word "Cantonese" for the word "Scots" and "regional" for "national" (and transform "Lowland" into "urban" and "Highland" into "delta") and we have a fair depiction of the cultural and social function of poetry societies in Guangdong over the ages.

Early Chinese Poetry Societies

The earliest specific group which has been singled out as the ancestor of all formal poetry associations in China was the one which gathered around Bai Juyi 白居易 (772–846) in his declining years, the "Assemblage of the Nine Elders" 九老會. Bai once partied with Hu Gao 胡杲, Ji Wen 吉旼, Zheng Ju 鄭據, Liu Zhen 劉真, Lu Zhen 盧真, Zhang Hun 張渾, Di Jianmo 狄兼謨, and Lu Zhen 盧貞, all of whom were retired officials of an advanced age; others admired them, resulting in a painting called the "Illustration of the Nine Elders" 九老圖.[10] Following Bai Juyi's preface and poem on this painting in the *Quan Tang shi* are the poems composed by the six oldest members; they were all entitled "Poetry by an Assemblage of Seven Elders" 七老會.[11] This set of verses is infused with the pleasant mood engendered by elderly gents meeting for relaxed drinking, and the heightened enjoyment of the dancing and singing of geishas in a delightful garden setting. And another poem composed by Bai, his "Chanting leisurely facing wine, presented to fellow oldsters" 對酒閑吟贈同老者, reads like it could have been composed on the occasion of a meeting of the nine: "…/ An hundred cares have all dissolved away,/Still left are wine and poetry./ When inspiration comes I chant a verse,/After chanting comes a beaker of wine" 百事盡除去，尚餘酒與詩。興來吟一篇，吟罷酒一巵.[12] But the fact that Bai drinks alone in this poem reminds us that, contrary to the view of Gong Pengcheng,[13] this gathering only met on a single occasion and hence can scarcely qualify as an active association of poets.[14]

The most famous literary community of Song times was the so-called poets of the Jiangxi school; it was apparently the first to be described as a "poetry society" *shishe* 詩社. However, socially it was scarcely more than an after-the-fact, posthumous grouping of like-minded literati formed in retrospect by Lü Benzhong 呂本中 (1084–1145) who almost created a dead poets' society.[15] Still, in 1110, certain members of this "school of poetry" *shipai* 詩派 did form an actual poetry club in Yuzhang 豫章 (modern Nanchang) to "enjoy the pleasure of poetry and wine with fellow members of the poetry society."[16] Another Song poetry circle based on regional identity was the Xikun 西崑 school, which embodied an ornate poetic style popular at court in Kaifeng that was nevertheless based on the southern literary values of Li Shangyin 李商隱 (813?–858) in the Wuyue area.[17] Groups of live poets were also active, catching the contemporary wave of enthusiasm that swept the Song for convening societies of any social status or professional occupation. For the lively arts, there were the

Xihu Poetry Society 西湖詩社, the Tongwen Society 同文社 for *ci* lyrics, the Feilü Society 緋綠社 of dramatists, and the Luhua Society 露華社 of street rappers.[18] Old poets' societies modeled and named after the "Assemblage of the Nine Elders" also flourished.[19] The professionals and white collar workers themselves formed societies of inspectors, archers, butchers, wine sellers, and merchants—all devoted to informal poetry parties.[20] Although another poet had used the term previously,[21] the great Su Shi was the most notable poet to employ the term "poetry society" in verse: "An assembly at the river bridge is for watching the clouds before parting,/What harm is there if we bring wine along to our poetry society?" 河梁會作看雲別，詩社何妨載酒從.[22]

In 1992, Wang Deming published a valuable overview of Song-period poetry societies. In it he stressed that the first poetry societies which began to appear in the late Northern Song period must be distinguished in quality from those that flourished during the Southern Song. Not only were the former much fewer in number, they were much more casually structured social entities, with more relaxed entertainment programs. The foreign threats and corrupt politics that characterized much of the Southern Song naturally placed the discussion of current events on the agenda of poetry societies, lending them an inescapable political hue.[23] Further stimulating the formation of poetry societies in the Southern Song was the change in academic priorities; under the influence of Wang Anshi 王安石 (1021–1086), scholars had been paying scant attention to history and poetry as they concentrated on the classics in preparing for the exams. With the acceptance by Song Gaozong 高宗 (r. 1127–1162) of the academic priorities of Yuan You 元祐 and his party, composing poetry received a fresh impetus.[24] Wang Deming's treatment of the poetry societies that had been founded during the early Yuan era by "left-over" Song poets has been refined in an article by Ouyang Guang, who rightly points out that these poetry societies differed greatly in content and purpose from those of the Southern Song. Because of the cancellation of the examination system during the early Yuan, large-scale poetry societies filled the void, allowing scholars a chance to compete one with another through composing poetry to set themes and to be graded and ranked by an officiating judge. It is true that small-scale poetry societies also continued to provide a social outlet for poets. Still, the development of *shishe* on a greatly increased scale of operation during the Yuan for the purpose of competition at versification was an innovation of lasting impact.[25] Wine, when it appeared in the non-competitive type of relaxed gathering, provided less inspiration for composing occasional poetry than letting former officials of a lost state cry in their cups over their lost cause.

By Ming times, poetry societies resumed their former reduced scale and entertainment-based *raison d'etre*. The alcoholic element characteristic of most casual *wenhui* 文會 must have been little more than a social backdrop at most, and a literary trope at least, to the convivial gatherings of poets and poetasters, for scarcely a hint of besotted behavior or bohemian excess was attached to them. Nevertheless, a frequent description of the activity of the Southern Garden Poetry Society was of "fierce drinking,"[26] and the name of a late Ming literary society, the Grape Society 蒲萄社, founded by the three famous Yuan 袁 brothers—Hongdao 宏道 (1568–1610), Zongdao 宗道 (1560–1600), and Zhongdao 中道 (1570–1623)—must give us pause.[27] Ultimately then, the presence of wine, whether used as a reason for convening, as a facilitator of social exchange, or as an excuse for early departure, was a common element in all the types of literary gatherings surveyed thus far. *Jiuhui* 酒會, *laohui* 老會, *wenhui* 文會, *shihui* 詩會, and the poetry society all utilized this seemingly inseparable companion of composing and chanting poetry. A verse by Cantonese poet Lin Xijing 林習經 (Republican period) clinches the connection between wine and poetry: "By birth I delight in chanting poetry,/By nature I am also fond of wine./Wine is the hook for angling for poems;/poetry is the broom for sweeping away sorrow" 我生喜哦詩，我性又嗜酒。酒是釣詩鈎，詩是掃愁帚.[28]

An exquisite catalogue published in 1987 by The Asia Society Galleries, in association with the Shanghai Museum, celebrates a traveling exhibition on the Chinese Scholar's Studio. Several of the essays treat poetry societies or literary gatherings to a degree of detail that makes very enjoyable reading. A sampling follows. Wai-Kam Ho translates a memoir of Zhu Yizun on the "Tower for Painting the Mountains" 寫山樓 of Li Zhaoheng 李肇亨(ca. 1592–ca. 1662):

> Literary gatherings accompanied with wine and music were exemplified by the Yuan-she [Mandarin Duck Society], whose membership—based on the contribution of poems—at one time or another numbered thirty-three people in all. No less than one hundred years have passed and elders of the town can no longer remember the names of those people. The picnic ground that once glittered with jade cups and brocaded mattresses is now desolate in entangling weeds and chilling mist. Only a single pavilion, the Xieshanlou of the Li family, has survived in the ruins.[29]

The catalogue contains a joint painting by Wen Jia 文嘉 (1501–1583) and two otherwise unknown artists entitled "Herb-Mountain Cottage."

Composed in 1540, it depicts a literary gathering at a private studio called the Herb Cottage. The colophon contributed by Wen Jia, according to Chu-Tsing Li, is "one of the best surviving descriptions of a typical literati gathering where artists and poets all contributed to the painting, calligraphy, and poetry that were the product of the occasion."[30] A specific poetry society mentioned in the catalogue is the Blue Creek Society 青溪社 organized during the late Ming by immigrants in Nanjing that also met, like the Southern Garden Poetry Society, on the banks of a river, in this case the Qinhuai River.[31]

The Moon Springs Chanting Society 月泉吟社

Several different types of literary gatherings and poetry societies have been introduced so far; Huang Zhimin provides the most comprehensive treatment of the motivations and conventions of these different types. He differentiates three broad categories: first are those convened for the purpose of carefree entertainment, often through poetic competition; second are those that gather around famous literati and devote themselves to serious creative work; third are those that consist of refugee literati from defunct dynasties who flock together to console themselves through the diversions of wine and poetry.[32] Even those groups that were actually termed poetry societies were differentiated by at least two major aspects: the regularity and formality of their meeting. In its earliest and strictest definition, a poetry society was an annual or monthly meeting of poets which convened on an appointed date either to write poetry on a set theme or to examine the verses already composed.

The Ming critic and poet Li Dongyang 李東陽 (1447–1516) offers the following observations on this type of formalized poetry society:

> At the end of the Yuan and the beginning of our state, people of the southeast valued poetry societies. Whenever there was a strong personality to rally around, a poet was invited to act as judge, and each year announce a title among those of poetic ability from the various commanderies. Setting a date for the following spring to collect the poems, he would hold a private examination and rank each name, engraving the superior ones on the announcement placard somewhat like the examination system. Only the "Moon Springs Chanting Society" of Mr. Wu of Pujiang is known to the present generation.[33]

元季國初，東海人士重詩社。每一有力者為主，聘詩人為考官，隔歲封題於諸郡之能詩者，期於明春集卷，私試開榜次名，仍刻其優者，略如科舉之法。今世所傳，唯浦江吳氏月泉吟社。

As far as we know, the Moon Springs Chanting Society was convened only once, but because of its scale of operation, its influence on later societies was profound. In brief, its moment in the sun went as follows. On October 15, 1287, the common topic of versification was announced: "Miscellaneous Impressions of Fields and Gardens on a Spring Day" 春日田園雜興; the completed poems were collected three months later on January 15, 1288. In all, 2,735 poems, limited to pentasyllabic or heptasyllabic *shi*, were presented for examination; the verses of 280 poets were selected as the best, and 74 poems by 60 authors were included in the resultant compilation, the *Yuequan yinshe* 月泉吟社, 1 *juan*.[34] Chen Yan's 陳衍 (1856–1937) anthology of Yuan verse, the *Yuanshi jishi* 元詩記事, includes the winning entries of the top fifty-two poets, commencing with the first-place poet-laureate Lian Wenfeng 連文鳳 (fl. 1288).[35]

Jumping ahead to the Qing dynasty, one poetry society which actually operated year round was the Xuannan Poetry Society 宣南詩社; it was active in Beijing circles from 1814 to the 1820s. This association met annually either on the early August anniversary of the birthday of the great Eastern Han scholar Zheng Xuan 鄭玄 (127–200) or on the birthday of Su Shi, just before the lunar New Year. Hence, a symbolic allegiance to both Han learning and to the poetic values of Su Shi was intended by these dates. Its purpose was to further the bureaucratic careers of its participants; these were thirty-one mid- to low-level bureaucrats from the south who hoped to rise through the ranks together by maintaining a social network and support group.[36]

More relaxed and informal, less career-oriented poetry societies convened with lower social profiles; their inner operations are therefore less easily discerned in the historical record. The Southern Garden Poetry Society itself only occasionally appears in documentary sources; most of the relevant information is preserved in the poetic record. The three functions of poetry societies that flourished during the Ming period as isolated by Huang Zhimin will all be fulfilled by the Southern Garden Poetry Society in one iteration or another, since it ultimately is the combination of all three types of *shishe*.

Poetry Societies in Guangzhou

Sun Fen's Southern Garden association was not the only such literary club of the time in Guangdong; concurrent with it was the Phoenix Terrace Poetry Society of Dongguan 東莞鳳台詩社, based in a town straddling the Pearl River south of Guangzhou.[37] This society met at the site of a Daoist monastery first built at the time of the Martial Emperor of Liang 梁武帝 (r. 502–549), where phoenixes, very appropriately, came to roost on its lofty terrace. Both local literati and visiting luminaries periodically gathered at the base of the terrace and composed poetry while enjoying the panorama. Let us examine a lengthy prose piece that details some of the social and cultural activities that occurred there.

Deng Yunxiao 鄧雲霄, "A Record of the Renovation of the Phoenix Terrace Poetry Society"
鳳臺詩社重修記[38]

> In the southwest corner administered by Dongguan lies Mount Daojia.[39] A Shangqing Daoist monastery straddles its peak; it is said to have been built at the time of the Martial Emperor of Liang. During the Song dynasty, the poet Su Shi inscribed a placard that read, "Hall of Golden Portals and the Solar Energy of the Open Sky"; this tightly connected it with the past.[40] Amidst the verdure of this mountain a terrace stands erect. Oldsters state that formerly phoenixes used to roost on its heights. Ever since, local poets and wordsmiths rose up one after the other and established a poetry society that met at its base; that was a few hundred years ago.[41] The resulting compositions are rich and numerous, often approaching the styles of Han and Tang. The ocean awashes this cultured clime,[42] and the land is made significant because of its people; this connection is of long standing.
>
> As the years mounted up, the terrace toppled over and its pavilion decayed. In my youth I studied at the Xiyuan Academy near the terrace[43] and founded a poetry society next door. In my free time, I leaned out from the terrace and gazed far out. Visible were the smoke from a myriad households and sails in the wind on the ocean far away. We all vied in utilizing these themes in our poetic offerings. The exquisite sight of Mt. Luofu was surely beautiful enough to write about, even to ingest! The sound of the bells, chimes, pipes and flutes from the Daoist monastery was chill, sounding shrill yet circling around like the sound of phoenixes—fading away as it traversed the white clouds and spiraled out beyond the sky. Still, I felt as though Zi Jin and Xiao Shi were both close associates.[44] Inspiration came welling up, and I almost felt like I

was transported to the realm of the genies. I felt regret that brambles and briars had overgrown it; I wanted to renovate it but could not accomplish my resolve....

(The terrace gets rebuilt due to funding contributed by several men).

Lu Junzhen, a member of the old poetry society, made the absurd claim that my poetry led the way at the time in the southeast; he begged for some lines from me to record the scene. I was not clever enough to decline, so with his urging I agreed. But living at home in the hamlet, I was disorganized and slothful and had a depressing air about me and no time to pick up the pen. Until I took up an official position in Jinling, I had forgotten my literary debt; then I tried to sketch a draft to settle up. Mr. Lu often sent me letters to requisition my essay, but I replied that I felt no inspiration and had writer's block.

On day *shangsi*,[45] I dragged along five or six lyricists from east of the Jiang to climb the Phoenix Terrace in Jinling.[46] There we raised our cups and gave vent by singing and shouting, longing for the past in heroic fashion.[47] We sighed that the palaces and steles of the Six Dynasties had all become wild grass in the cold mist. Yet the lines of Li Bai about "three mountains" and "two waters" still flowed [in my memory] along with the Yangzi River;[48] this was thus enough to inspire poetry in me. Therefore, I recalled that my old hometown also had its own Phoenix Terrace which rivaled that of Jinling. I do not know how many were with us that day raising their cups, or how many rhymes were made by the brushes we flourished. "The phoenixes have left and the terrace is empty"—both places are the same in this regard.[49] Yet because of his heroic sentiments and refined diction, Li Bai was the phoenix among poets....

Now I have a strong urge to compose poetry, plus I am tired of hiking. Our poetry society lacks a leader, so we will take turns presiding. Fellow locals together with poets have combined to form this splendid affair, so I send along this writing to record it.

莞邑治西南隅有道家山，上清觀跨其巔。傳建于梁武帝時。至宋，蘇長公題其額曰：金闕寥陽之殿，緊維古矣。當山翠微，有臺屹立。故老言昔鳳凰嘗集其上。邑之詞人墨客，相繼而興，結社台傍，已百餘年。卷帙繁富，往往闖唐而逼漢。海濱鄒魯，地以人重，所繇來也。

歲月深積，台榭圮傾。余髫年讀書西恒書院，興社為鄰。暇日倚台高眺，萬家烟樹，遠海風帆，爭入筆格。羅浮秀色，可綴可餐。觀中鐘磬笙簫，泠然清韻，宛作鳳音，縹緲穿白雲而繞天外。但覺子晉簫史皆來親人。興致翩翩，殆對仙去。猶恨榛蕪枳足。欲新之而志未逮也。。。。

陸君故社中人，謬謂余詩為東南一時領袖，願丐一言以紀其勝。余謝而不敏，勉而諾之。里居紛沓，胸中作惡，無瑕載筆。之官金陵，忘卻文債。以起草奪之也。陸君時移札來徵文。余謂興致不到，終覺騫齒。

偶以上巳之日。拉江左詞人五六輩，登金陵鳳凰臺。揮杯舒嘯，慷慨懷古。

嘆六朝殿碣，盡寒煙野草。而太白三山二水之句，猶與長江共流。詩之足興如此，因憶故鄉亦有鳳臺，與金陵相頡頏。不知此日舉杯者幾人。揮毫者幾韻。鳳去台空，兩地一致。而太白之豪懷逸調，信為詩家鳳皇。。。

余雅有詩癖，今且倦遊。社中其虛右哉，歸將狎主齊盟。與故鄉墨客共成勝事也。因先移文以訂之。

The Phoenix Terrace coterie enjoyed modest local notoriety and was revived in Republican times.[50]

Of course other poetry societies came and went in Guangzhou during the Ming and Qing periods. A poetry society organized along the competitive lines of the Moon Springs Chanting Society operated in Guangzhou during the early Qianlong period. It met in the Shihuaiyu Garden 石懷瑜園 and was inspired by the odd sight of some bamboo stalks growing straight through a paulownia tree. Such a marvelous theme encouraged several thousand poets to submit competition pieces. The most renowned participant was Li Erqiao 黎二樵, whose four old-style pentasyllabic poems dominated the event.[51]

Interesting sidelights on the founding of a poetry society are revealed by the Southern Lake Poetry Society. The poems that resulted from this literary gathering merited a preface by a local worthy, the illustrious writer Luo Tianchi 羅天尺, author of that useful guidebook to Guangdong, the *Wushan zhilin* 五山志林.

"Preface to the Southern Lake Poetry Society" 南湖詩社序[52]

After the Five Masters of the Southern Garden, Huang Zuo was the one who reinvigorated the refinement of Cantonese poetry. Accordingly, those who galloped around the Two Guang regions carrying the banner of Guangzhou to unite poetics with that of the Central Plains were Liang Youyu of the Ministry of Justice, Li Minbiao of the Ministry of Personnel, Ou Daren of the Ministry of Foresters, Hunters, and Fishers; they were all disciples of Huang Zuo.[53] A hundred years later, there were He Yuechao and his son the Oldster of the Southern Pond;[54] they inherited the poetic heritage in Guangdong[55] and convened a poetry society at the Southern Lake.

On the Southern Lake is an island on which were ancient shady banyan trees. A five-jointed bridge was used to cross over to the island. There were several thatched huts that could barely keep out the wind and rain. The master chanted his poems in this setting, accompanied by the cries of cranes and the harmonizing of his son. After the master died, the Oldster of the Southern Pond established a poetry society there with notable literati from within the Guangdong region. They met several times a month, each time printing a volume of ancient style poems and a volume of modern style poems; soon quite a collection was formed.

In the sixth year of the Emperor Qianlong (1741), inspired by the precedent of Shanyin,[56] I met with my colleagues and composed poems with the writing materials provided. He Yu brought out his grandfather's collected works and asked me to compose a preface in a few words. I therefore sighed in admiration that Cantonese poetry before Huang Zuo was stately and courtly; its poetic atmosphere was heavy and serious, majestic and not frivolous. But after the Southern Lake, Cantonese poetry became more bucolic; its thought was secluded and profound, airy yet far-reaching. Poetry before Huang Zuo was close to the ideals of the "Elegentiae"; after the Southern Lake poetry became closer to the spirit of the "Airs of the States."[57] In a word, both followed orthodox principles. Hence it seems that the poetry was the same, but the poets were different. If the imperial envoy were to come in his light carriage to collect poetry to present to the throne, who knows but that bucolic poetry could become court poetry! These poems exist in concrete form; I will wait and see how they are regarded. This is my preface.

粵詩自南園五先生後，風雅振起者為香山黃文裕，故馳兩廣之麾以合中原者，梁比部有譽，黎中秘民表，歐虞部大任，皆宮允弟子也，越百年後，有何越巢先生暨其子南塘翁，接踵小欖，開社南湖。

南湖有島，中多榕蔭古樹，橋五析而渡，茆茨數間，僅蔽風雨，先生吟詠其中，鶴鳴子和，先生死，南塘翁與欖中知名士結社其中，

> 月數舉，舉刻古近詩各一，積成卷帙。

> 予乾隆庚申，乘山陰之興，適同人畢業，授簡為詩，其孫宇出全集命予一言弁首，予因歎宮允以前，為廊廟之詩，故其氣象宏重，莊而不佻，南塘以後，為草野之詩，思則幽而深，淡而遠，宮允以前近雅，南湖以後近風，要之皆風雅之正則也，蓋其詩不異而人異，倘有輶軒下采，陳之黼座。安知草野不廊廟哉。其詩具在，吾將拭目俟之矣。是為序。

Certain precedents were involved here. First was meeting with congenial friends at a specific site that had some history of hosting literary activities in the past. Second was convening at regular intervals over an extended period of time. Both were common enough, and not exclusive to Cantonese poetry societies. Publishing the poems that were produced over time was itself a regular occurrence. What did not happen with the Southern Lake Poetry Society was what the Southern Garden experienced: the periodic revival of the same club over the centuries. This seemingly was a rare phenomenon in the history of poetry societies in China. Yet some evidence suggests that two other poetry clubs in Guangzhou were revived at least once.

Qu Dajun wrote a poem in 1690 to celebrate the founding of a poetry society in terms that demonstrate it was being reorganized: "Written on the Reconvening of the Fuqiu Poetry Society" 修復浮丘詩社作. We may presume that this club was inspired by the poetry society of the same name that Ou Daren had frequented in mid-Ming period Guangzhou (see Chapter Five below). This poem contains the lines: "Both the Southern Garden and the Donggao are covered over with barren grass" 南園東皋總荒草. Wang Zongyan, author of Qu Dajun's *nianpu*, adds two notes to the effect that the Donggao was itself "reconvened" 修復 the next year (1691) and that Qu Dajun was invited to preside over it. The *nianpu* 年譜 (chronological biography) of Liang Peilan 梁佩蘭 (1632–1708) mentions that Chen Gongyin and Liang joined in helping to supervise it.[58] The location was the site of the original poetry society at Donggao ("Eastern Bluffs") in Guangzhou, specifically the Wushen Temple 武神廟.[59] But at what date this original association was formed is unfortunately lost to history. The impetus for forming a poetry society derived from a civic effort to renovate the temple.[60] We may be justified in concluding that such a social activity as a poetry society was a natural extension of a project of urban renewal—both lent splendor to the community as well as the sponsor of the two projects. So perhaps we are safest staying with the assertion that the Southern Garden Poetry Society was the only major poetry society in Chinese history which was reconstituted more than once at regular intervals over 500 years.

The Blue Creek Poetry Society mentioned previously that was founded in Nanjing during the late Ming could provide an interesting entrée for studying the continuity of poetry societies. It was in operation again in the early Republican period, but the type or scale of operation is unknown. An educationalist from Guangdong, Lu Kuangwen 陸匡文, declared in the title of a poem that he "participated in the two societies of Blue Creek and White Gate at Xuanwu Lake to observe the *xi* lustration rites..." 青溪白門兩社玄武湖修禊. The excuse for gathering was a ritual occasion; but the main activity was composing verses according to the rhyme scheme of the "Preface" to Wang Xizhi's "Lanting Collection."[61] The spring lustration festival, according to Tobie Meyer-Fong, was a common occasion for gathering to drink, sing, and compose poetry. She narrates at length the poetry parties sponsored by the famous gallant Wang Shizhen 王士禎 (1634–1711) on two such occasions in 1662 and 1664 at the Red Bridge in Yangzhou; these two events were also associated through poetic imagery with the earlier precedent of Wang Xizhi's founding archetype.[62]

The two reconvened poetry societies of Blue Creek and White Gate met again in a private garden for an autumn reverie; rhymes were again assigned for composing individual verses.[63] Another occasion was the New Year's celebration associated with the fifteenth of the month 上元.[64] The Double Ninth Festival 重陽 was an additional popular excuse for these two clubs to team up, according to one offering by a poetess from Guangdong serving in Nanjing.[65] Another Cantonese poetess from the same era, also living in Nanjing, participated in meetings of the White Gate society when it met on its own and in the Beginning of Summer Society 首夏社 when it met for poetic reverie on White Egret Isle.[66] Interestingly enough, all of the joint meetings of the Blue Creek and White Gate poetry societies occurred in the solitary precincts of secluded gardens.

A variation on the very rare type of poetry society that reconvened over time was the Society of the Purity of Ignorance Tower 拙清樓社 of Huang Zaigun 黃在衮 (*juren* 1555). It met on the site of an earlier poetry club, the Society of Yue 越社, that had been established by one Liang Gongshi 梁公實 together with Huang's maternal uncle Li Ruishi 黎芮史. It was a case, therefore, of one poetry society succeeding another, both on the same site. The physical description of the environs of the tower and the setting of the poetry club are worth examining:

> The Purity of Ignorance Tower lay between the outer walls of the city, but the grounds it occupied were both secluded and spacious. One entered through a side-path that circled around. It was embraced by fine trees that formed a fence. In the middle was a huge stone, more than two *zhang* tall, and weird rocks ringed its base.... A small gallery was encircled by plants, trees, bamboo, and rocks, yet one could chant and versify among them.[67]
>
> 拙清樓在城郭間，而居地幽曠。從一徑盤旋而入，夾以嘉樹，徧次為籬。中有巨石，高二丈許，奇事壖砢。。。。一小閣，草木竹石環之，而身吟誦其間。

Literati Sociality In and Out of Poetry Societies: The Case of Liang Peilan

The life of a Cantonese literatus was enriched by participation in a poetry society, for it provided both an extended social network as well as an opportunity for entertainment; but cultivated sociality was hardly limited to it. The literary lifestyle of Liang Peilan, as known from his *nianpu*, may be typical, at least for a prominent man of letters.[68] The following is drawn from only the first 56 years of his 76-year life.

We know that Liang's social profile as a literatus emerged in 1660, when he began to host his friends, among them Chen Gongyin, to evenings of poetry in Liang's "Grass Hall in the Western Garden" 西園草堂. In 1662, Qu Dajun returned to Guangzhou to resume his secular life. He picked up where he had left off in his socializing with Liang Peilan and Chen Gongyin in the western part of Guangzhou, presumably at Liang's dwelling in the same general location. The next year, before traveling to Beijing for another attempt at the exams, Liang spent time poetizing and feasting with other local literati. One poem that he received from Beijing in the spring of 1665 from an old friend, Cheng Keze, was addressed to Liang and his "friends in poetry from the same society" 同社詩友,[69] indicating that a more formal social relationship existed in the group than mere acquaintanceship through *ad hoc* poetry parties. This was before the founding of the Orchid Lake Poetry Society, so it is unclear just which poetry society was in question. The year 1666 was characterized by socializing with Chen Gongyin and Chen Zisheng (for the latter, see Chapter Five). In 1667 Liang again failed to pass the exams in Beijing, but he did meet an important literatus of national standing, Wang Shizhen, mentioned already in connection with two poetry parties held at the Red Bridge in Yangzhou. In 1671, Liang was found most often in the company of Qu Dajun and Chen Gongyin, et al., for instance boating on the Eastern Lake in Dongguan and banqueting at a local gentry's resort.

It was not until 1680 when Liang was 51 that he formally organized the Orchid Lake Poetry Society, which he officially called the White Lotus Poetry Society at the Orchid Lake 蘭湖白蓮社. The fact that it was called a "reorganization" 重修 signifies that a precedent lost to history inspired his efforts, maybe even an earlier iteration consisting of the same members, including the Cheng Keze mentioned above. Even after founding this poetry association, Liang still managed to find other outlets for his socializing. In 1681 he, Qu Dajun, Chen Gongyin, and others "gathered in Liang Peilan's Grass Hall in the Western Garden to compose poetry and did not sleep for an entire month."[70]

In 1682 Liang was back in Bejing, feasting and poetizing with an entirely different group of friends. That year he was involved in the formal organization of a poetry society, over which he, Zhu Yizun, and Fang Zhongde 方中德 were invited to preside. In the summer he was persuaded by Wang Shizhen to dine and compose poems with Wang's own group. Back in Guangzhou in 1683, Liang and Chen Gongyin accompanied Wang Shizhen to a local poetry soirée. In the second month of 1684, "Wu Qi gathered all of the lyricists within the seas at the Chan Monastery in the West of Guangzhou and organized the Yuetai Poetry Society, versifying and matching rhymes on different themes" 吳綺集海內詞人于廣州西禪寺，結越台詩社，分題唱和.[71] As a local "lyricist" with a national reputation, Liang was almost certainly involved in this society. His national reputation led to an invitation from Nalan Singde 納蘭性德 (1655–1685) in the fall of this same year to join him at Beijing in editing an anthology of *ci* by Northern and Southern Song poets. When he arrived in the eleventh month, Liang and Zhu Yizun both inscribed a painting owned by a member of the local gentry. Liang inscribed another painting a few months later and, naturally, was feted by Nalan Singde. Before setting off for Beijing, he had inscribed a painting owned by an official who had arrived in Guangzhou to administer the local exams. And of course, Liang was busy his entire career composing poems of welcome and send-off for visiting dignitaries or departing friends.[72]

These types of literary activities—composing occasional poems, inscribing paintings, writing prefaces and dedicatory inscriptions, maintaining correspondence through both formal letters as well as exchanging verses, and meeting friends for "feasting and poetizing" 晏集唱和—appear extensively throughout Liang Peilan's life. Needless to say, they occur beyond the formal parameters of a literary society. Still, the formation of an official poetry society must have seemed an important threshold to cross in establishing formal social affiliations, especially among literati such as Liang and Zhu Yizun who shared no geographic or local cultural bonds. That a connection established through literati activity was taken seriously as a token of close ties is seen in the event that led to Sun Fen's execution: he was caught up in the disgrace attached to the Lan Yu case merely because he had inscribed a poem on one of Lan's paintings (see below). Similar literati activity must be accorded equal attention as outward manifestations of underlying social alliances and support. Perhaps those who claimed founding membership in a poetry society were bringing such social connections to the surface, for surely they enjoyed a certain degree of elevated prestige reserved only for those in the inner circle of the society. Such prestige would be passed down in history as their names were recorded and transmitted, while mere participants were often not mentioned at all. Most likely this is why Liang was willing to lend his name to formal poetry societies that were organized later during his lifetime. For instance, as mentioned earlier, he helped not only to "reorganize" the Fuqiu Poetry Society but also to preside over the Donggao Poetry Society. In 1696 at age 67, Liang agreed to judge the poetry produced by the Searching for Plums Poetry Society 探梅詩社 of one Huang Deng 黃登. In 1702, Zhou Dazun 周大樽 published a compilation of the poems that had been produced over the past few years by Liang's White Lotus Poetry Society at the Orchid Lake, a work called "Poems Chanted and Matched at the Dharma Nature Chan Cloister" 法性禪院唱和詩. This proves that, despite the lack of any such indication in Liang's biographies or *nianpu*, he had continued his involvement in the Orchid Lake society even while being busily engaged elsewhere across the years. At any rate, the focus of the present work on the formal socializing in poetry societies is set off in a better light by the extensive cultural career of Liang Peilan and his lower-profile literary activities conducted through a looser social network.

The Fuqiu Poetry Society 浮丘詩社

The Fuqiu Poetry Society is an interesting study from the perspective of literati sociality. According to the *Yuetai zhengya lu* 粵臺徵雅錄,[73] Guo

Fei 郭棐 and fifteen others, including Chen Tang 陳堂, Liang Shichu 梁士楚, Chen Lü 陳履, Yuan Changzuo 袁昌祚, and Wang Xuezeng 王學曾, founded a poetry society on this hill during the middle of the Wanli era (1573–1620). The motivation was to "continue the Southern Garden" 續南園.[74] The *Guangzhou chengfang zhi* 廣州城坊志 records that around this same time an official, one Zhao Zhigao 趙志皋, was demoted in office and transferred to Guangzhou; he formed a poetry society on Fuqiu Hill in order "to chant poems with the gentry in Yuezhong."[75] If this story is true, one important impetus behind this cultural activity is the need to form local connections on the part of a non-native official.[76]

Fuqiu Hill itself, some four *li* west of Guangzhou, was named after an eponymous Daoist sage of the Zhou era who had gained enlightenment at the site;[77] a shrine 社, a Daoist monastery, and a Buddhist temple all competed in lending luster to the hill. It was said that Ge Hong had practiced alchemy here. Another tradition associated with this hill hints at another derivation of the name, for legend has it that the hill was once an island that came floating over the sea. Another variant claims that it had once been attached to Mt. Luofu but became detached and floated over to Guangzhou, hence its name of "Floating Hillock."[78] This explains the fact that Ge Hong was able to cultivate his alchemical prowess at both this site and Mt. Luofu, for he was known to have worked at his craft on the latter mountain.

This overview of Chinese poetry societies and numerous Cantonese exempla will conclude with a short quote from an essay by Qu Dajun in his *Guangdong xinyu.* In it he treats a number of Cantonese literary clubs, their founders and habitués, and some of the distinguishing personality traits that render the Cantonese particularly eager to gather together for the sake of poetry:

"Poetry Societies"[79]

> The Southern Garden Poetry Society in Guangzhou was initiated by the Five Masters at the beginning of our dynasty.[80] The Yueshan Poetry Society was initiated by the Grand Master of Splendid Happiness Wang Jiankui[81] and Lun Yixun, President of the National Academy.[82] The Fuqiu Poetry Society was initiated by the Grand Masters for Splendid Happiness Guo Fei and Wang Xuezeng.[83] The Pure Society of the Myrobalan Grove was initiated by the Minister of Rites Chen Zizhuang; he also reestablished the old Southern Garden Society, and twelve notable literati from Guangzhou matched rhymes together.[84]

Ye Shidong stated: "The people of Guangdong are fond of literature. For instance, after resigning a post and returning home, a Cantonese gentry will not ask after his family or finances; rather, he will hold parties for composing poetry or celebrating seasonal festivals. Accordingly, most Cantonese are refined and sensitive towards literature."[85] This sensibility was restored by the Five Masters and reinvigorated by Huang Zuo….

廣州南園詩社，始自國初五先生。越山詩社，始自王光祿漸逵，倫祭酒以訓，浮丘詩社，始自郭光祿棐，王光祿學曾。訶林淨社，始自陳宗伯子壯。而宗伯復修南園舊社，與廣州名流十有二人唱和。葉石洞云，東廣好辭，縉紳先生解組歸，不問家人生產，惟賦詩修歲時之會。粵人故多高致乃爾。粵詩自五先生振起，至黃文裕而復興……

The Original Southern Garden Poetry Society

In the opinion of Hu Yinglin 胡應麟 (1551–1602), the noted late Ming critic, the early period of his own dynasty was distinguished by five schools of poetry 詩派.[86] These were the circles gathered around five literary luminaries: Gao Qi 高啟 (1336–1374) in Suzhou, Liu Ji 劉基 (1311–1375) in Zhejiang, Lin Hong 林鴻 (b. 1340?) in Fujian, Liu Song 劉崧 (fl. 1370) in Jiangxi, and Sun Fen 孫蕡 in Guangzhou.[87] Indeed, the original printing of the Five Masters of the Southern Garden was justified in terms of these verses being worthy of a place beside the poetry of the Four Eminences of Wu 吳中四傑[88] and the Ten Talents of Min 閩中十才子.[89] As with the literary salons of the Six Dynasties, each of these early Ming schools was centered on an outstanding personality. Among the five founders of the early Ming, Gao Qi was the best poet; Gao Bing, who was closely associated with Lin Hong, is regarded as the best literary critic and theorist.[90] According to Sun's contemporaries, he was noted for his sterling moral conduct and the attractiveness of his personality.[91] This characterization is credible, for of these five schools, only Sun's Southern Garden club functioned socially as more than an occasional association. The other groupings seemed to fall on a descending scale of activity ranging at best from the occasional, *ad hoc* assemblage of local literati for any cultural pastime, to a localized poetical outlook much like the Jiangxi School of the Northern Song. At the very least, these literary associations were analogous to the "Victorians" or "Georgians" of English poetic tradition or the "Four Eminences" of early

Tang, that is, poets grouped together by later critics because they happened to be contemporaries even if they did not work together as colleagues or socialize together as friends.[92] At any rate, Xie Huan's 謝環 painting of 1437, "A Literary Gathering in the Apricot Garden," provides a glimpse into the garden setting of a typical literary association of the leisurely elite, at a time just after the passing of this first generation of early Ming poets.[93]

The Southern Garden Poetry Society was composed of five like-minded friends, called variously the Five Gentlemen of Guangzhou 廣州五先生 or Five Gentlemen of the Southern Garden 南園五先生. Apart from Sun, they were Wang Zuo 王左, Li De 李德, Zhao Jie 趙介, and Huang Zhe 黃哲, who were sometimes themselves separately called the "Four Gentlemen of Guangzhou" 廣州四先生. Their anonymously edited anthology was included in the *Siku quanshu* as the *Guangzhou sixiansheng shi* 廣州四先生詩. Sun Fen was eminent enough to merit the printing of his own collection in the imperial library, the *Xi'an ji* 西庵集, or *Western Hermitage Collection*. His is also the only entry included in the *Dictionary of Ming Biographies*, and only selections of his prose find their way into the late Qing anthology *Guangdong wenzheng* 廣東文徵.[94] Despite his superior reputation, the five were fast friends and shared an intimate association within the poetry society, in the bureaucracy at Nanjing, and posthumously by virtue of both literary reputation and the physical proximity of their consecutive biographies in the "Garden of Literati" entry in the *Mingshi* 明史 and in fascicle 271 of the gazetteer of Guangzhou.[95]

I will examine the formal convening of the Southern Garden Poetry Society in the next chapter. Here an introduction to the lives of the five founders will conclude this survey of Cantonese poetry societies.

The Life of Sun Fen

The biography of Sun Fen has already been admirably outlined by W. Pachow.[96] Rather than construct a new summary, a more worthy enterprise would be to provide the details of his life as contained in his most complete biography, the composite portrait drawn in the *Guangdong tongzhi* 廣東通志, or *Comprehensive Gazetteer of Guangzhou*.[97] This source draws on several local Cantonese compositions, such as the *Guangzhou renwu zhuan* of Huang Zuo and earlier gazetteers, plus the short *Mingshi* biographical sketch and other official records. Although Huang's earlier work forms the basis of the *Comprehensive Gazetteer* account, it does not reveal the outlines of Sun's life very clearly—the lush verbosity of its prose is more panegyric than biographical; hence I opt for the later but more sober appraisal. This profile in staccato prose is translated below:

> Sun Fen, *zi* Zhongyan 仲衍, *hao* Xi'an 西菴, was a man from Nanhai, Guangzhou.[98] By nature he was alert and quick. He seemed to have read everything; he composed poetry and prose effortlessly, and the hue of his diction was scintillating.[99] At first glance his work did not appear very attractive, but its poetic atmosphere was forceful, the imagery deep and its metaphors apt, and it galloped along in the style of Wei and Jin.[100] A man of integrity, he did not rashly make acquaintances.[101]
>
> During the waning season of the Yuan, he avoided the disturbances by lying low amid the hills and lowlands.[102] When He Zhen 何真 (1322–1388) occupied Lingnan, he established a bureaucracy and summoned scholars.[103] Sun, Wang Zuo, Zhao Jie, Li De, and Huang Zuo were all received with ritual courtesy; they were called the Five Gentlemen. When Liao Yongzhong 寥永忠 (1323–1375) campaigned in the south, Sun drafted the memorial of surrender for He Zhen.[104] Liao Yongzhong did not slaughter a single person, and the pacification of the Nanhai region was all due to Fen's efforts. Liao Yongzhong hence summoned him as an Examiner for the Regional Inspector.[105]
>
> In the year *gengxu*, the third year of the reign-period Hongwu (1370), the regular recruitment by examination was held for the first time. Fen participated[106] and was assigned as Commissioner in the Weaving and Dyeing Service in the Ministry of Works. Promoted to Hong District (虹 *xian*, Anhui) as the Assistant Magistrate, he strove to safely gather the people before hardships could spread after the region suffered from military devastation—nine out of ten homes had been left vacant.[107] Many of the people then returned to their occupations.
>
> After dwelling there for one year, he was summoned to be an Archivist of the Hanlin Academy. He was praised by his contemporaries Song Lian 宋濂 (1310–1381), Yue Shaofeng 樂韶鳳 (1355–1380), and Zhan Tong 詹同 (fl. 1350–1374),[108] and his reputation increased. He attended His Highness daily, reporting quickly and responding easily, his appearance stately and his comportment at ease. Song Lian and his contemporaries all felt that no one came up to him.
>
> In the eighth year (1375), he participated in compiling the *Hongwu zhengyun* 洪武正韻.[109] Once he responded to an order to versify with "The Song of the Drunken Scholar" 醉學士歌, which pleased the emperor.[110]

In the ninth year (1376), he was dispatched to oversee official sacrifices in Sichuan. He stayed at the Hanlin Academy for three years, striving to fill an opening outside of the capital bureaucracy. He was sent out to be the Assistant Magistrate of Pingyuan (Shandong), but he was implicated in another's crime and returned to the capital in fetters.

He was transferred to assist in overseeing the construction of battlements. While constructing the city wall at the Gate for Gazing at the Capital in Nanjing,[111] Fen chanted poems and hummed songs in Cantonese. The supervisor memorialized the throne about it; Sun was summoned to appear and ordered to chant what he had sung. Both the poems and the songs were about loyalty and love; thereupon the emperor released him.

In the eleventh year (1378) he resigned and returned to his old stomping grounds. He set his traces among the clouds in indulging his fancies and roamed the forests. He redoubled his efforts in his studies and his perceptions increased in depth; his attitude was that life and death were insignificant, and that there was no difference between self and the world. Once he matched rhymes with the "To Return" 歸去來辭 of Tao Qian (365–427) to express his feelings.[112]

In the fifteenth year (1382) he was recalled to the bureaucracy as the Registrar of Suzhou. Suzhou was considered a troublesome commandery in the eastern Wu region, and all along had the reputation of being hard to govern. Fen was skilled in evaluating and planning; he put these skills to use for the government and realized great peace.

In the twenty second year (1389),[113] once again he was implicated in a crime because of some affair and was sent to serve frontier duty in Liaodong. Cheerfully he set on his way, decanting wine and versifying no different than a normal day. While he was in Liaodong, there was a great purge of the Lan Yu 藍玉 faction.[114] Fen had once inscribed a painting for Lan; consequently he was condemned to die. People all urged him to clear his name by presenting a memorial, but Fen did not respond. Right before being executed he composed a poem and chanted it while expiring.[115] All-under-heaven mourned him; his age was 56.[116] At that time his disciple Li Zhen 黎貞 himself was on frontier duty in Liaodong (d. ca. 1394).[117] He then was allowed to prepare the corpse for burial; Sun was interred on the southern slope of Anshan 安山.[118]

Among Fen's compositions are *Tongjian qianbian gangmu* 通鑑前編綱目, or *Outline and Contents of the First Section of the 'Comprehensive Mirror,'* 7 scrolls; *Xiaojing jishan* 孝經集善, or *A Collection of the Best Commentaries on the Classic of Filial Piety*, 1 scroll; *Lixue xunmeng* 理學訓蒙, or *Lessons for Enlightenment on Rational Learning*, 1 scroll; plus *Xi'anji*, 8 scrolls; *He Tao ji* 和陶集, or *Collection Matching Poems with Tao Qian*, 1 scroll; and *Jigu jushi* 集古句詩, or *Regulated Verse Collected from the Ancients*, 1 scroll. Song Lian wrote the preface to the *Xiaojing jishan*.[119] Much of this is lost and has not been handed down. That of his poetry and prose which is extant was edited by Li Zhen.[120] Zhao Chun 趙純 of Panyu praised his "penetration to the ultimate understanding of heaven and man, human nature and destiny" and called him "the Confucian Patriarch of his times."[121]

Biographical Sketches of the Four Gentlemen of Guangzhou

The following biographical outlines of the Four Gentlemen of Guangzhou are extracted from the *Comprehensive Gazetteer of Guangzhou*, again based on the *Guangzhou renwu zhuan* of Huang Zuo.[122]

Wang Zuo 王左 (*zi* Yanju 彥舉, d. 1375) was an adopted son of Nanhai. During the chaos of the fall of the Yuan dynasty, he was unable to return to his native Hedong 河東 (modern southeast Shanxi). Relocated in Guangzhou, he met Sun Fen, who came to venerate him; together they founded a poetry society which met in the Southern Garden.[123] They built a comfortable outpost, called the Veranda for Screening the Wind 抗風軒, in which "to relax for a time with noted scholars." (The veranda will appear as a central image in the poetry devoted to the society.)[124] In quickness of composing poetic lines he was not as adept as Sun Fen, but Sun could not match him in the profundity of his poetry. He served on the personal staff of He Zhen. When He Zhen surrendered control of Guangzhou to invading Ming forces, Wang Zuo returned to his ancestral home. From there he was recommended for an office, and in 1373 he was named Supervising Secretary at Nanjing, with the duty of helping to keep track of the flow of documents between the throne and the bureaucracy and to check them for accuracy of format and style. He seems to have maintained his association with Sun Fen, who was also serving in the new government, and appears to have had some personal access to the throne. For instance, once when Ming Taizu commanded his heir to present minister Song Lian with a fine horse and himself composed an imperial song entitled "Song of the White Horse" 白馬歌 to celebrate the event, Wang Zuo was among the attending ministers ordered to compose songs to the same rhyme.[125] His song was a success and received a cash prize. The emperor was delighted with one line in particular: "The minister rides a bay horse, facing outward with a red (loyal) heart" 臣騎黃馬當赤心.[126] He also occasionally encountered His Highness while promenading with his retinue and would recite poetry on command. The notable scholar Liu Sanwu 劉三吾 (1312–1399), then attached to the Hanlin Academy, "marveled at his talent, calling his compositions the product of a famous generation."[127] Despite such appreciation of his literary talents, he was unhappy at the capital; he endured it for two years before he died and was returned home for burial. His collection of poetry—named after his private veranda—is called *Tingyuxian ji* 聽雨軒集, or *Veranda for Listening to the Rain Collection*, selections of which appear in the *Guangzhou sixiansheng shi* and *Nanyuan qianwu xiansheng shi*.[128]

Li De 李德 (*zi* Zhongxiu 仲修) was from Panyu and early on became noted for both his eremitic character and for the breadth of his reading. He was especially brilliant in elucidating two of the traditional Five Classics, the *Shijing* and the *Shangshu*. Because of his classical learning, he was summoned to the capital in 1370 and personally examined by the emperor; he was then assigned as an Office Manager in the censorate based in Luoyang. In his spare time he liked to visit the ruins of the imperial mausoleums around Luoyang, often climbing them and versifying to relieve the emotions conjured up by viewing the remains of the past. It is reported that his contemporaries vied in chanting and transmitting these poems. This fondness for poetry started young and remained with him during the early part of his official career. But when older he turned to the study of Neo-Confucianism. He gained a reputation in Guangdong and was inevitably mentioned anytime the topic of rational learning came up. He died after retirement in Guangzhou. His literary anthology is called *Yi'an ji* 易菴詩集 or *Hermitage of Changes Collection*, parts of which are included in the main anthologies devoted to the poetry society.[129]

Zhao Jie 趙介 (*zi* Bozhen 伯貞, 1344–1389),[130] like Li De, was from Panyu and also was known for the breadth of his reading; but he went further than Li by adding the classics of Daoism and Buddhism to his store of knowledge. Although a man of heroic sentiments, he no longer had any ambition for advancement through an official career after his parents died. He liked to compare himself with Tao Qian. Like the Tang poet Li He 李賀 (791–817), he would take a bag with him wherever he went, and whenever a line of poetry would come to mind inspired by a passing scene, he would write it down and toss it in his bag. He refused all recommendations for office and spent his days instead amid the rocks and springs of the Xiqiao

西樵 mountains.[131] It has not been transmitted how he supported his four sons, who were all good at poetry and prose compositions and accomplished in writing the *li* 隸 and *zhuan* 篆 styles of calligraphy. But in 1389 he was arrested and taken to the capital for some unrecorded offense; he was soon released but died in Nanchang aboard ship while returning home. His poetry anthology is called the *Linqing shiji* 臨清詩集, or *Verging over Purity Collection*, after the name of the dwelling in which he studied as a youth.[132]

Huang Zhe 黃哲 (*zi* Yongzhi 庸之, d. 1375) was himself from Panyu, the third member of the quartet to have this distinction. His poetry has the largest number of entries in *Guangzhou sixiansheng shi*, occupying a rather long *juan*. Yet his *Mingshi* biography, aside from the localization of his home in Panyu, consists of one line: "He took service in the provinces and commanderies and was praised for his cultivation and conduct." Fortunately, his biographical entry in the Guangzhou gazetteer is even longer than that of Sun Fen and contains much of interest in revealing the sources of his poetic inspiration. It is worth citing at length:

> He was orphaned at a young age, but exerting himself to read, he mastered the five classics. Once he borrowed someone's *Wenxuan* 文選 and copied it by hand.[133] He delved deeply in it and penetrated its essence. Subsequently he was able to compose poetry, creating the subtleties of Jin and Tang compositions. By nature he was fond of the hills and streams; he bound together rushes and reeds by a creek and took his rest among them. He went back and forth among the cliffs and mountains of Mt. Luofu, Nanhua, and other famous sites. But he did not consider this enough. Thereupon he crossed Yu Pass, traversed the ancient regions of Wu and Chu, roamed amid Ren and Qi, and for a time all of the heroic champions of the lakes and seas roamed together with him.[134]

In Nanjing he met some early associates of the future founder of the Ming dynasty, Zhu Yuanzhang; in 1365 they recruited him into the bureaucracy of Zhu's Kingdom of Wu, where he served in the Hanlin Academy as an Academician Awaiting Instructions, acting as literary and editorial aide to the future emperor. He also assisted the heir-apparent with his studies and became one of his favorites. His literary skills were put to use on several occasions at imperial command. Once he versified to celebrate a victory of General Xu Da 徐達 (1332–1385) in 1366; and when the emperor's prayer for rain on Mt. Zhong received a favorable response, he composed a verse to match a poem written by the emperor in celebration.[135] After the establishment of the Ming, he served in various posts around the country. His hard-working service earned him the devotion of the common people because he cured several non-bureaucratic ills; for example, he banished an evil presence from a spring and invoked rain.[136] After retirement in Guangzhou, he built a hut out in the wilds in which to enjoy nature; his collected works of poetry and prose in ten *juan* is named after it: the *Xuepeng ji* 雪蓬集, or *Collection of the Snowy Hut*.[137]

When the Five Masters began their bureaucratic careers, the Southern Garden Poetry Society was effectually if not formally ended, having existed from the end of the Yuan. But all five friends, except probably Zhao Jie, continued their association in the capital bureaucracy and kept in contact through letters and poems while separated on individual official assignments. For instance, a poem by Huang Zhe is entitled "Delighting in old friend Sun Zhongyan's (Fen) Return." The first line reads: "Ten years after going off to the east and entering the royal capital,/Lyrics and rhapsodies vie in praising the grandee of Chu" 十年東去入皇都，詞賦爭誇楚大夫.[138] Ten years, if not just a poetic trope, tells something of the endurance of this friendship. Huang Zhe also complained about a lengthy separation from another friend in this close circle, Wang Zuo, in a line from his poem, "Wang Yanju's (Zuo) Veranda for Listening to the Rain": "As soon as we parted—twelve years of lonely suffering,/The passes and rivers, wind and rain, separated me from your secluded veranda" 一別淒涼十二年，關河風雨隔幽軒.[139] And Li De mentions an unexpected encounter with Sun Fen and Zhao Jie in Nanjing.[140] But it was in the Southern Garden, whether physically present or remembered as a pleasant image, that the association of these five was most intimate.

Chapter Three

Sun Fen and Socializing in the Southern Garden

> There was a rustle of chirruping sparrows in the green lacquer leaves of the ivy, and the blue cloud-shadows chased themselves across the grass like swallows. How pleasant it was in the garden! And how delightful other people's emotions were!—much more delightful than their ideas, it seemed to him. One's own soul, and the passions of one's friends—those were the fascinating things in life.
>
> —Oscar Wilde, *The Picture of Dorian Gray*

Gardens were popular spots to convene literati gatherings for both the mainstream tradition as well as for the five early Ming poetry schools.[1] For instance, Yu Jing celebrated a "Western Garden" in Shaozhou;[2] Gao Qi and his coterie frequented the numerous gardens that made Suzhou famous, among them the "Green Tea Garden" 綠茗園, "Green Water Garden" 綠水園, and the "Gazing at the Imperium Garden" 顧辟疆園, reconstructed from an Eastern Jin dynasty original; Lin Hong and his decade of comrades were headquartered at a generalized "Eastern Garden."[3] And even when a literati gathering was created out of whole cloth, it was localized in a garden, such as the famous Literary Gathering in the Western Garden that Su Shi, Huang Tingjian, et al., supposedly convened in Kaifeng in 1087.[4]

We do not know why Sun Fen and his associates decided to form a poetry club; no indication is preserved in either the historical or literary records. We may conjecture such simple motivations as the need for safe socializing and congenial poetizing.[5] In the introduction, three different types of poetry societies were isolated from the work of Huang Zhimin; each one was concluded for a different purpose.[6] All three of these types could have proven attractive to our five friends. But competition, especially not the broad, county-wide competition open to all comers, does not characterize the verses of these men. And it is questionable whether Sun Fen had attained any wide degree of fame, except for being an accomplished local poet and essayist, before leaving Guangzhou for his career as an official of the Ming government. The third type of poetry society—that of mutual socializing for consolation and support at the end of a defunct dynasty—therefore seems to fit this group best.[7]

Historically, many gardens have graced Guangzhou.[8] Sun Fen and friends either selected the Southern Garden for their use or had it built. Formerly, the site had been an animal park and a traveling palace of the Southern Han dynasty.[9] As already noted, one source claims that that the Veranda for Screening the Wind was originally the dwelling of Sun Fen.[10]

The Southern Garden was located in the south of the city two *li* beyond the wall;[11] today the original Zhongshan Library occupies this site on Wende Road 文德路 outside the old Wenming Gate 文明門. A library on the site was entirely appropriate, since after the last iteration of the Southern Garden Poetry Society of Liang Jie'an, et al. in 1911, the place had been taken over by a bookseller.[12] Meetings of Sun and his friends were held in the Veranda for Screening the Wind and were open to others as well.[13] And there is some evidence that the physical Southern Garden survived into the next generation.[14] According to Qu Dajun, the veranda got its name from Sun Fen.[15] At that time, the waters of the Pearl River reached close to the garden—riparian retreats being one of the six possible sites for gardens, according to a Ming-period authority.[16] It was "nestled next to the river and was an unsurpassed site."[17] The river has receded and is not even visible now: it takes a leisurely ten-minute stroll to reach the bank; alas, intervening buildings block the view anyway.

Two of Sun Fen's poems best combine both physical setting and typical activities:

Sun Fen, "The Southern Garden" 南園[18]

詩社良讌集	Our poetry society is a gathering for fine conviviality:
南園清夜游	At the Southern Garden we roam in the clear evening.
條風振絡組	An ordering wind shakes the gauze tassels,
華月照鳴騶	The florescent moon shines on a neighing *Zouyu*.
高軒敞茂樹	A high veranda opens up on flourishing trees,
飛甍落遠洲	Flying rafters descend on distant islets.
移筵對白水	Rearranging the feast-mats, we face the white current;

列燭散林鳩	Spacing the candles, they flicker like forest doves.
雅興殊未央	Refined pastimes surely have not yet peaked—
旨酒詠思柔	With fine wine our poetry is sentimental.
玉華星光燦	Jade flowers—the starlight glistens,
錦彩雲氣浮	Damasked silk—the cloudy vapors float.
麗景不可虛	This gorgeous scene must not be missed,
眾賓起相酬	The assembled guests rise up in salute.
長吟間劇飲	Extended chanting alternates with fierce drinking,
楚舞雜齊謳	Chu dances are intermixed with Qi ballads.
陵陽杳仙駕	But Lingyang has lost his genie carriage,
韓眾非我儔	And Han Zhong does not become my companion.
聊為徇時序	Indifferently, we celebrate the order of the season,
娛樂忘百憂	In amusement, all our cares are forgotten.

Sun's poem flows from themes found within the mainstream literary tradition, for he illustrates that Guangzhou is a place ruled by civilized virtues through the use of standard allusions. A "gathering for fine conviviality" 良宴詩 is a variation on the title of the fourth poem in the anonymous series *Nineteen Old Poems*: "Today is a Meeting for Fine Conviviality" 今日良宴會; the activities described in this early poem portend what the reader may expect to find in Sun's gathering.[19] Sun utilizes more of the themes of the *Nineteen Old Poems* in his own variations to the titles of the original series, called "Imitating the Ancient Poems" 擬古; one of them, "The Pleasant Banquet Tonight," is set in the literary garden itself: "There is a beauty in the Southern Garden,/With a face as sweet and shy as a peach or plum flower" 南園有佳人，窈窕桃李顏.[20]

Next, a line from Cao Zhi's "Poem on the Duke's Banquet" 公讌詩 is borrowed to set the scene in the garden-park of the royal Wei palace compound.[21] "Florescent moon" 華月 is capitalized to reflect the major connotation of this term, China; here it implies the "Chinese moon."[22] Parallel to it is the "ordering wind," said to blow from the northeast, regulating and nurturing, symbolic of the order emanating from the authority of the sovereign who rules over creation.[23] Other hints of the civilizing virtues of Chinese culture in this formerly frontier region are the presence of the beneficent *Zouyu* beast, said to appear when the Son of Heaven reigns with humaneness and sincerity,[24] and the movements of silken gauze tassels 絡組, suggesting the existence of an elegantly-appointed gallery—the famous Veranda for Screening the Wind. The *Zouyu* beast also foreshadows the appearance of the doves—and by extension women—in the next stanza, for the "Zouyu" poem, Mao #25, is said by Mao to be the "proper sequel" of Mao #12, "Magpie's Nest" 雀巢, which refers to doves (and magpies). The flourishing of Chinese civilization in Guangdong is an understated yet very real undercurrent fed by various allusions and literary tropes that seem to appear often in the poetry of those Cantonese who had to fight against age-old prejudices for their cultural identity as Chinese.[25]

The second quatrain of the poem provides a sense of spaciousness, as the perspective gazes out from within the high veranda observing the view of the Southern Garden. A vista of flourishing trees is seen. From under the flying rafters, their edges seem to be set on distant islands on the river.

The action commences when the poets arrange themselves on mats near the banks of the Pearl River, lighting candles and versifying.[26] The flickering candles, reminding the guests of scattering doves, perhaps should serve to recall for readers the presence of serving women and entertainers.[27] The term "high veranda" 高軒 adds support to the association with imperial beneficence, for the term was used in a *fu* of Zuo Si 左思 (ca. 250–ca. 305), "Rhapsody on the Shu Capital." He describes the litany of virtues of the newly-founded imperial palace complex: "They…erected hostels just like those of Received Brilliance,/Attached long galleries at Yangcheng,/ Set belvederes and terrace halls soaring into the clouds./They opened high Verandas to look down on the hills;/They arranged ornate windows to gaze at the rivers" 結陽城之延閣，飛觀榭乎雲中，開高軒以臨山，列綺窗而瞰江.[28] Furthermore, the term "high veranda" commences a poem from the royal hand of the Tang dynastic founder Taizong, "New Year's Day" 元日: "The high veranda is warmed by spring colors,/The capacious gallery is flattered by the morning light" 高軒暖春色，邃閣媚朝光.[29] Sun's nod to Taizong's poetry is more definite when we read the first two lines from another imperial composition: "The high veranda looms over the cyan islet,/Flying eaves are racks revolving in space" 高軒臨碧渚，飛檐迴架空.[30] The connection between a high veranda, flying rafters/eaves, and islets seems too purposeful to be coincidence. And the term "ordering wind" also appeared in another poem by Taizong.[31] It must be remembered that Sun and Wang Zuo had served on the staff of He Zhen, who had held out against the Ming for a time. Hence it was important for them to stress their loyalty to the new regime. Allusions to the imperial splendor of Liu Bei's capital, as well as the more direct evocation of the founding monarch of Tang, would naturally recall the splendor of the current emperor and would have seemed innocent enough concessions to political reality without burdening the poem with phrases that fawn or flatter outright. This was initially merely a preemptive protestation of innocence on their part, since the erratic founder of the Ming, Zhu Yuanzhang, seemed to see the seeds of disloyalty on every hand.[32]

The third quatrain takes the reader well into the action; refined pastimes are engaged in, namely the composing and enjoyment of poetry and perhaps displays of calligraphy or musical performances, and fine wine is imbibed to accompany the nostalgic versification. Since the term "jade flowers" in line 11 is not only a poetic name for the white chrysanthemum but is also the name of a Daoist goddess,[33] we may be justified in treating it and its parallel, polychrome damask 錦, as metonymy for "Jade-flower geishas and damasked-robed houries." Hence we may retranslate these lines to reflect this female presence more openly: "Jade-Flower maidens glisten like star light,/Geishas in damasked silk float like cloudy vapors." Other poems on the Southern Garden are less reticent about mentioning female presences, who attended both to serve the repast and to entertain the guests. The gastral aspect of the evening's activities, epitomized by arranging the feast mats, reminds us of the importance of this social element, which must surely have had ritual significance in its ancient origins, even if by now it was no more than an introduction to the night's more hearty pastimes.[34]

In the next quatrain, the exotic southern dances from the storied Chu region, together with the more refined ballads from Qi, are cited, perhaps to conjure up the spirits of the two Daoist gentlemen who are evoked in the final quatrain. For the *Chuci*, it must be remembered, was based on the lyrics of shamans and shamankas who endeavored to summon their spirit-lovers. "Chu dances" must recall this tradition, along with the sense of southern exoticism and the wildly rustic. Daoist elements, as both literary tropes and precedents to justify slightly excessive behavior, are common in this and other poems about the garden soirees.[35] In this poem, Lingyang Ziming 陵陽子明 and Han Zhong 韓衆, two Daoist worthies from the Han period, do not appear at the party despite being invited through both song and dance.[36] Nevertheless, the celebration goes on, providing solace from worldly cares amid the pleasures of the party, which was held on the occasion of a holiday.[37]

A second poem is longer but less allusive. It reads more like the factual recollection of a party in the garden than a fanciful re-creation.

Sun Fen, "The Song of the Southern Garden
Presented to Wang Yanju, Supervising Secretary, Preface in Pentasyllabic Lines"
南園歌贈王給事彥舉, 五言詩序[38]

昔在越江曲	Formerly on a bend of the river in Yue,
南園抗風軒	In the Veranda for Screening the Wind at the Southern Garden:
群英結詩社	A group of gallants formed a poetry society—
盡是琪琳仙	All of them were genies from the jade-gem heavens.

(The narrative commences in heptasyllabic verse)

南園二月千花明	Second month in the Southern Garden, a thousand flowers brilliant,
當門綠柳啼春鶯	Gate-side on green willows, orioles chirped at the spring.
群英組絡照江水	The tassels of the group of gallants illuminated the Pearl River,
與余共結滄州盟	Together you and I formed the alliance of Watchet Islet.

(Change to historical present to recount a vision of a bacchanal in the garden)

滄州之盟誰最雄	In the alliance of Watchet Islet who is most heroic?
王郎獨有謫仙風	Only Squire Wang has the air of an exiled genie.
狂歌放浪玉壺缺	Crazed singing, wanton and wasteful—jade jars crack,
劇飲淋灕宮錦紅	Fierce drinking, getting soaked and sudsy—palace brocade reddens.
青山日落情未已	The sun sets over the green hills, but passions still not waned,
王郎拂袖花前起	Squire Wang, grasping a sleeve, rises up in front of the flowers.
歡呼小玉彈鳴箏	With a cry of welcome, Little Jade strums a ringing zither,
醉倚庭痦按宮徵	Drunkenly leaning on the courtyard pawlonia, she plays the notes of do and sol.
哀弦泠泠樂未終	Sorrowful strings, crisp and clear—the music

	has not yet ended.
忽有華月出天東	Suddenly the florescent moon emerges from the eastern sky,
裁詩復作夜游曲	Again composing poems to a set theme—tunes for an evening stroll.
銀燭飛光白似虹	The drifting light of the silver-candle moon is as white as a nimbus,
當時意氣淩寰宇	At this time our ambitions skip throughout the world.
湖海詩聲萬人許	The sounds of poetry within the lakes and seas are praised by all,
酒徒散落黃金空	The drunkards stagger home, their yellow gold spent.

(The vision closes, the persona muses again on the past)

獨卧茅檐夜深雨	Lying in solitude underneath the eaves, it rains deep in the night,
分飛幾載遠離群	Scattering in different directions for several ages, we left the crowds behind.
歸來城市還相親	Coming back to our hometown, we call on our kin,
閒來重訪舊遊處	When at leisure we visit again the place where we roamed of old.
蒼煙萬頃波粼粼	Where grayish mist over myriads of waves forms flitting light,
波粼粼兮日將夕	Oh, the sun is about to set over the waves of flitting light.
西風一葉淩虛舟	A single leaf in the western wind rises up like an empty boat,
猶可題詩寄青壁	We can still write a poem and inscribe it onto the bluish wall.

Since Wang Zuo is addressed by the office he assumed after leaving Guangzhou for Nanjing, Sun must have written this in the capital and personally presented it to Wang. Therefore it idealizes the memory of the Southern Garden; at least it was not written on the occasion of the memorable event recounted here.

The first distich is written in rhymed pentasyllabic meter and functions as a kind of poetic preamble; the rest of the poem follows in heptasyllabic verse. The first part recalls the history of the formation of this poetry society; it gets repeated in more roughhouse terms in the preface to a later linked-verse jointly composed with Wang Zuo: "Together we formed a poetry society in a corner of the Southern Garden; we chanted heroically and drank fiercely, alternating singing with harmonizing verses" 共結詩社南園之曲，豪吟劇飲更唱和.[39] A literary name locates the society in Guangzhou: *Yue* 越 was the archaic name for this region; the specific setting is within the Veranda for Screening the Wind at the Southern Garden.

"Jade-gem heaven" 琪琳 is metonymy for the Daoist heavens, one of which was called "Heaven of Jade-Clarity" 玉清. Elsewhere in Sun's corpus the term seems to refer to a Daoist tower within Guangzhou proper.[40] The "Watchet Islet" 滄州 of lines 8 and 9, an important item in the poetic vocabulary devoted to Guangzhou, was the fairytale homeland of hermits, a literary trope in the *Wenxuan*.[41] As demonstrated in Chapter One, it was often applied by Cantonese poets such as Sun Fen to their own homeland.[42]

Next, the poet presents his vision of the society recounted in the historical present. Squire Wang, the co-founder with Sun Fen of the poetry society, is the champion of the group and hence acts without inhibitions: he breaks wine jars and spills red liquor on the brocade garments of attending geishas dressed in finery befitting the imperial palace. But his behavior meets the norms of Daoist decorum, for he acts out of creative spontaneity, not besotted mischief. Wang was often fondly remembered as a drinking buddy. Once while in office in Nanjing, Sun Fen wrote that he longed "To decant wine in the Southern Garden,/And with you, sir, laugh and sing as one" 酌酒南園上，與君同笑歌.[43] Just as often, however, Sun missed him for the elevated companionship he provided. Again, in a poem sent to Wang from Nanjing: "In a dream I enter the Southern Garden and listen to the evening rain,/Not knowing that my body remains west of Jiang Ridge (Nanjing)" 夢入南園聽夜雨，不知身在蔣陵西.[44]

He next invites a musical performance from a lovely lass from the past, Little Jade. She was the bewitching daughter of Fuchai, King of ancient Wu 吳王夫差, sometimes paired with the temptress Xishi 西施 of the enemy state of Yue.[45] The presence of other elegantly dressed women has already been noticed through figurative language. The climax of the evening comes with the sudden emergence of the moon; it inspires the guests to compose poems devoted to this common theme of literature, using such trite tropes as "silver candle" and "flying light." This is the moment when the poets wax most lyrically, feeling in harmonious unity with all poets of the Chinese realm. Finally the party breaks up.

One evening long after the soiree idealized above, Sun Fen listens in thoughtful contemplation to the rain on the roof. He then recalls the separation from Squire Wang after the friends had gone their individual ways. A return to Guangzhou to call on family and a visit to the old stomping grounds ensue; the vista of the tropical landscape provides the inspiration for yet another poem, which was preserved on the wall of the old veranda.

Another poem provokes a more palpable feeling of the sights, sounds, and tropical climate of the garden; poetizing is not mentioned, but other enjoyable pastimes are indulged in, including fishing and drinking. But beneath the surface narration of events in the garden lurk several allusions that reveal Sun's clever attempt at elevating the social status of the participants by confirming them as "notable gents" 名士 and honored officials who were socializing in the loyal clime of Guangzhou:

Sun Fen, "Toasting the Two Squires Wang Zuo and Zhao Cheng at the Southern Garden on a Summer Day"
南園夏日酬趙、王二公子澄、佐[46]

郡城多暇日	In the county seat, one of many leisurely days,
公子專幽尋	When gentlemen exclusively probe secluded spots:[47]
招攜無俗士	Among those recruited are no common gentry—[48]
歡宴盡華簪	Those welcoming and feasting are officials.[49]
臨水釣游魚	Looming over the water, we angle meandering fish,
淩風弋高禽	Rising on the wind, we shoot high-soaring fowl.
南園當盛夏	In the Southern Garden during the peak of summer,
顥氣滌煩襟	The aqueous atmosphere saturates our irritating collars.[50]
澍雨朝浥道	Seasonal rain in the morning soaks the road,[51]
流雲豁輕陰	Floating clouds open up the light shade.
芙蕖被曲渚	Lotus leaves cover the bent sand spits,
灌木秀窮林	Shrubs bloom amid dense groves.
展席羅長筵	Unrolling mats to surround the long feast-mat,
美酒對坐斟	We face one another, pouring fine wine.
交交黃鳥弄	Caw, caw—yellow orioles sport,
聒聒玄蜩吟	Click, click—dusky cicadas buzz.
歲時遞遷斡	The year and its seasons revolve in cycled stages,
賢聖皆銷沉	The worthies and sages all sink into oblivion.[52]
於時不痛飲	At this time, if we do not drink with abandon,[53]
負此芳賞心	We would waste this euphoric state of mind.

One final poem by Sun centers again on the garden as locus of literati sociality in Guangzhou even though the garden initially functions as a private retreat:

"Longing for Li De in the Southern Garden" 南園懷李仲修[54]

幽獨攄雅懷　Secluded in solitude, I vent longings for elegant activities,
逍遙步南園　Free and easy, I pace the Southern Garden.
嘉禾秀春暄　Praiseworthy plants bloom in the spring warmth,
繁卉耀陽德　Flourishing herbage is dazzling in the power of the sun.
青暘燠土膏　The haze of dawn heats up earthly moisture,
流澌漲通川　It flows out swelling interconnected streams.
荃蘭揚朱英　Sweetgrass and orchids display vermillion petals,
山磯炫文軒　Hilly crags are dazzling set against the decorated veranda.
垂楊列曲渚　Weeping willows are lined up on crooked islets,
鳴鳥何關關　Cawing birds—how they call!
展席芳醑陳　Spreading open the mats, fragrant spirits are displayed,
開觴群物妍　With the beakers opened, all objects look desirable.
顧瞻失儔侶　Turning to gaze around, I have lost my drinking buddy,
高情寄所宣　My heightened feelings are sent to the one I mentioned.
馳思望遠人　Thoughts rushing, I long for the distant one.
遙在伊洛壖　Who is far off on the flats by the Luo.
賢勞事會計　The worthy who labor over worldly affairs must take note:
日昃不遑安　When the sun sets they will have no leisure for repose!
聊復縱長飲　For the nonce let us give way to long drinking,
引領希令言　And stretch our necks in anticipation of hearing fine words.
何能此會合　But at this particular meeting, how can I
宴樂舒我顏　Wipe away my frowns through indulging in pleasure?

The poems treated thus far recount festive gatherings in the garden whether conjured up from memory or created by imagination. Even if the evening activities are not limited to literary pursuits, the garden is conceived as an actual social setting for a poetry club. But occasionally, the garden is merely the location for individual retrospection and solitary musing, as we shall see in the next chapter.

Chapter Four

Li De and Individual Introspection in the Southern Garden

> In this lone, open glade I lie,
> Screen'd by deep boughs on either hand;
> And at its end, to stay the eye,
> Those black-crown'd, red-boled pine-trees stand!
> Birds here make song, each bird has his,
> Across the girdling city's hum.
> How green under the boughs it is!
> How thick the tremulous sheep-cries come!
> ...
> Calm soul of all things! make it mine
> To feel, amid the city's jar,
> That there abides a peace of thine,
> Man did not make, and cannot mar.
>
> —Mathew Arnold, "Lines Written in Kensington Gardens"

In the extant poetry of the quintet from Guangzhou, only Li De joined with Sun Fen in composing verses dedicated to the theme of the Southern Garden, although the garden does get mentioned in passing in the verse of Huang Zhe and Zhao Jie.[1] But Li De's treatment is much different from the overall thrust of Sun's poems, for Li does not dwell on the garden as social setting; rather, being in office far away from Guangdong, he recalls certain physical aspects as points of departure for either painfully recalled romances or philosophical musings.

In the first poem, the Southern Garden serves as a private spot, conjuring up memories peculiar to Li and a love interest. The translation, though dealing with a recollection from the past, is set in the historical present. Since several of the poems in this introspective mode are rather allusive, I have appended a paraphrase to some of them to attempt to produce a coherent interpretation and added a section of commentary:

Li De, "Recalling the Southern Garden" 憶南園[2]

南園蝴蝶飛	In the Southern Garden butterflies flit,
綠草迷行迹	On green grass are traces of meandering.
青鏡掃長蛾	By green-bronze mirror she sweeps her long moth-like eyebrows,
娟娟弄春碧	Gracefully and winsomely she adjusts the blue of youthful makeup.
錦屏千里夢	By damasked screen her dreams a thousand miles away,
寂寞愁芳色	Forlorn and alone, she frets over fragrant beauty.
小字寫長箋	With small characters they write lengthy missives—
鱗鴻坐相隔	But like fish and fowl, they dwell separate from each other.

Paraphrase:

Although the Southern Garden is buzzing with natural life,
He wanders around unheeding, dazed with loneliness.
Meanwhile, far off at her toilet in the seclusion of the boudoir,
She touches up an already perfectly powdered face.
All made up now, she rests in splendor, dreaming of her distant love;
Lonely, she grieves that her beauty is wasted.
They can communicate by sending each other long letters,
But they remain separated by social circumstance.

Commentary:

Images of youth and colors mix together, pervading this pentasyllabic poem. The former include the "green" of the bronze mirror and the "spring" of youthful beauty. The latter consist of the green of natural vegetable dyes 綠; cyan blue 碧; and the hue of sensuous beauty 色. In poetic diction the term *juanjuan*, "graceful and winsome" 娟娟, describes many things: the charm and bloom of youthful beauty, the luster of moonlight, the grace of butterflies in flight, and the brilliance of alluring eyebrows. All of these images resonate throughout the poem with specific references. A reflection of the moon is also indicated by the term "mirror." *Juanjuan* and the interplay of its major connotations, then, contribute to the coherence and tight structure of the poem.

Thematically, Li De has utilized a conventional genre, Palace Poetry 宮題, and its subgenre, Palace Plaint 閨怨, that of the neglected lady in a boudoir; but he utilizes the Southern Garden to localize the lonely male persona who is separated from his love. But the persona remembers her personally as a lover, and not as one of the entertaining geishas commonly present at the social soirees described by Sun Fen. The emphasis is therefore not on public socializing in the garden but the loneliness engendered by its now empty precincts. Perhaps this loneliness is reflected phonetically by the entering-tone internal and end rhymes of sudden, harsh p, t, k finals that, while lost in the Early Mandarin of the Late Yuan period, still registered in Cantonese (*jik* 跡, *bik* 碧, *sik* 色, *gaak* 隔, in Yale romanization).[3]

This piece enjoyed a minor afterlife, for in a poem sent to Qu Dajun by Zhu Yizun in 1657, Zhu seems to be alluding to the first two lines of Li's offering: "Butterflies fly in the spring wind,/Green grass covers the Southern Garden" 春風蝴蝶飛，綠草南園遍.[4] And perhaps a touch of Daoist transcendentalism is hinted at by the presence of the butterflies, for Liang Peilan reminds us that sometimes butterflies are concrete manifestations of magical cloaks. His poem dedicated to the manes of Ge Hong explains it all:

"On Ge Hong's Cenotaph" 葛洪衣冠塚[5]

何代葬神仙	In what age was buried the numinous genie
朱明深洞邊	At the side of the deep Zhuming grotto?[6]
遺衣化蝴蝶	His left-over cloak has transformed into a butterfly,
五色似霞鮮	Its five colors seem to be rainbows in their freshness.

Qu Dajun was equally explicit in making the connection between colorful butterflies and radiant habiliments: "At Luofu the butterflies are as large clouds,/Of old they were the five-colored skirt of Magu" 羅浮蝴蝶大如雲/舊是麻姑五色裙.[7] Chen Sirong 陳嗣容 (*zi* Jusheng 句生), a late 19th century poet from Dongguan, even doubts that the Daoist sages Ge Hong and Zhuangzi were anything but butterflies:

"Butterflies" 蝶[8]

葛洪其仙乎	Was Ge Hong, indeed, a genie?
莊生日夢也	Master Zhuang said that he was only dreaming.
是色即是空	Form is in fact emptiness,[9]
非真亦非假	It is not true, nor is it false.

One Republican-period versifier, Li Yuanshuo 李淵碩, finally was bold enough to lay aside all coyness and directly proclaim in the title of a poem that butterflies were, indeed, Daoist fairies: "Song of the Genie Butterflies of Luofu" 羅浮仙蝶歌.[10] Apparently great men were sometimes characterized in this way; it is unknown whether this was an actual Daoist twist on reincarnation or merely the use of allusive language. In any case, the Three Great Masters of Lingnan, as well as two Song-period Neo-Confucian sages, had all been Daoist butterflies in the discerning eyes of the eminent Cantonese anthologist Wu Daorong 吳道鎔, who shall appear in Chapter Six: "The former matter of genie butterflies is detailed in the *Shanhaijing*,/Continuing the tradition were Qu [Dajun], Liang [Peilan], Chen [Gongyin], Zhu [Xi], and Cheng [Yi]" 仙蝶故事詳山經/繼者屈梁陳朱程.[11]

Edward Schafer provides a rational explanation for the association of butterfly imagery with Daoism:

> By proper breathing, thinking, praying, or eating, these [Daoist] adepts hoped for a transformation of their bodies into a higher and better condition. To adopt the insect imagery (as they often did) they hoped to progress, by means of these thoughts, airs, and reagents, from the larval (or merely human) state, by hidden way of active nymph or quiet pupa, to the ultimate condition of triumphant imago, as winged transcendents or lovely peris—super-human cicadas or butterflies.[12]

The early 19th century Qing poet Chen Jingxin 陳景新 (*zi* Jinchen 錦臣) from Nanhai devoted three poems to the theme "Mourning (the death of) Butterflies"; two of the poems are set in the Southern Garden. The second poem reveals that butterflies in the Southern Garden are probably none other than unfortunate Daoist genies who have met with brigands: "I suspect they are waylaid genies from Luofu—/In front of all the flowers, their tattered clothing is askew./Their lives being fantasies, why should their state be regretted?/Still they die with much passion, thus deserving some pity" 疑是羅浮被劫仙，破衣狼籍百花前，生原是幻何須惜，死為多情合可憐.[13] The poem continues with a nod to the twelve balustrades that mark the presence of the Veranda for Screening the Wind.

Chen Jingxin's first poem recalls Li De's technique of inserting a forlorn courtesan in the garden setting; the imagery in Chen's poem is that of a worldly, worn-out courtesan, a fitting symbol for both the butterflies and of the long-decayed garden:

委頓芳姿淚欲揮	Worn-down but with a lovely gesture, she wipes away tears,
東風無主送君歸	The masterless east wind sends off her lord.[14]
畫欄睡破三更夢	Sleeping by the painted balustrade her dream is shattered during the third watch,
粉徑抛殘五色衣	On a powdered path is abandoned a tattered five -hued cloak.
杏子雨深紅似泣	The rain thick about the apricots like red tears,
紙灰風起白還飛	The wind rises and paper ashes flit about.
賣花聲莫頻頻喚	Don't let calls of the flower sellers keep issuing—
知道南園事已非	By them we know that Southern Garden affairs are all over.[15]

Another Southern Garden poem by Li De continues in this personal and private direction:

"Sent to Sun Zhongyan, Archivist" 寄孫典籍仲衍[16]

南園草色參差綠	In the Southern Garden the color of the herbage would be irregular, uneven green,
忽憶佳人美如玉	Suddenly I recall the high-class lady, fine as jade.
玉堂揮翰事成陳	In a jade hall she wielded a quill, the affair had turned old,
草屋懸燈照幽獨	In a thatched hut, the hanging lantern shone on the secluded one.
江湖狂客未言歸	Amid the wilds of lakes and rivers, the crazed stranger has never spoken of returning.
翹首東南淚濕衣	Raising his head toward the southeast, tears wet his cloak:
何時淨拂青溪石	When will I rub clean the stones in the green brook,
與爾橫竿釣落暉	And fish with you using a drooping pole while the sun sets?

Commentary:

Remembering the secluded and shady precincts of the Southern Garden, the persona suddenly recalls Sun Fen, thinly disguised as a lovely courtesan. "Irregular and uneven" 參差 green refers to the various shades of green of the variegated plants in the garden. The jade hall was one designation of the harem or quarters of the imperial courtesans and concubines, and hence what was symbolically implied in the first poem is here made obvious. The image of a green brook may be more than just a trite description, for it was the name of an actual stream that started in Mt. Zhong 鐘山 immediately west of Nanjing and eventually flowed into the Qinhuai River. So it may be used here to recall an actual experience while both Li De and Sun Fen were serving together in the capital. Both the end rhymes of the first stanza and the internal rhymes throughout the poem are in the same entering series as transcribed in Cantonese above: *sik* 色, *luk* 綠, *fut* 忽, *yik* 憶, *yuk* 玉, *nguk* 屋, *duk* 獨, *haak* 客, *sap* 濕, *fut* 拂, *sek* 石, *lok* 落. But, as the title states and the final quatrain implies, the image of the lovers separated by distance clearly represents the friendship shared between Sun and Li.

The last entry is again dedicated to Sun but is more philosophically introspective, lacking any romantic conceit:

"Sent to Sun Zhongyan from Jinan" 濟南寄孫仲衍[17]

南園虛夜月	The Southern Garden was empty in the moonlight,
風景罷登臨	With such scenery I don't need to ascend heights to sightsee.
鞏洛成塵跡	But now I leave traces in the dust at Luoyang,
青齊入苦吟	I bitterly moan as I enter verdant Qi.
升沉彫壯節	My ups and downs exhaust my steadfast probity,
匡濟負初心	Trying to rectify the age has defeated my initial intentions—
薄宦容身得	Petty officials may find a place for themselves,
寧辭雪滿簪	Better to resign instead of growing old in office.

The rare ten *juan* edition of Sun Fen's *Xi'an ji* preserves three additional poems on the Southern Garden; they form a set devoted to Wang Zuo. An additional poem, found as well in the received version of Sun's *Xi'an ji*, is dedicated to Li De. This poem will be examined first. The relationship to the Southern Garden Poetry Society is perhaps very tenuous in this poem, since it is part of a series imitating the "*Nineteen Old Poems*" and perhaps merely recycles the historical reference to a southern garden contained in the original set. Still, it matches the sentiments of Li De's first two poems translated above:

Sun Fen, "The Pleasant Banquet Tonight" 今日良宴會[18]

南園有佳人	There is a high-class lady in the Southern Garden,
窈窕桃李顏	With a face as sweet and shy as a peach or plum.

容華一何麗	Oh how alluring are her features and deportment!
顧盻生光妍	Favoring with a glance, she radiates a fascinating attraction.
進退禮自防	She restrains her actions with ritual deportment,
秉德幽且閒	Embracing virtue, she is retiring and at ease.
良媒候嘉意	A fine matchmaker awaits one with worthy intentions,
君子希令言	A gentleman expects to hear a positive response.
鴻鴈念儔侶	The swan geese long for their mates,
雎鳩鳴河間	The ospreys caw in the midst of the river.
盛年若流水	While the best years pass like flowing water,
隱處獨長嘆	She heaves a long sigh from her secluded hermitage.

Commentary:

Although the language of this poem is simple and the imagery is straightforward, Sun does employ several classical allusions that should be noted. In line 5, the reference to ritual deportment recalls Kong Yingda's 孔穎達 (574–648) commentary to *Liji*, 6.5a, "Tanggong" 檀公: "The actions (i.e. advances and withdrawals) were all made according to the rites." Two allusions to the *Shijing* link the lovely lass in the Southern Garden with classical love connections in the storied past, lending the sad denouement of solitary spinsterhood an extra layer of pathos: Mao #181, "Hongyan" 鴻雁, where the geese are said to fly together, and Mao #1, "Guanjiu" 關雎, where the ospreys represent conjugal bliss.[19]

The set of three poems by Sun dedicated to Wang Zuo makes the connection to the Southern Garden more explicit, but artfully connects the youthful pastimes of group socializing in the garden with retrospection by elders in quiet solitude. By synthesizing these two major trends, these poems form a fitting conclusion to the poetry by the Five Former Masters on their famous Southern Garden.

Sun Fen, "Longing for Wang Yanju" 懷王彥舉[20]

Poem One:

懷昔南園王給事	I long for Supervising Secretary Wang from the old Southern Garden—
同開書社向滄洲	Together we convened a reading society that

	faced the Watchet Isle.
淩風欲赴三山約	Treading on the wind, he desired to head off for an assignment at Three Mountains,
聽雨還為十日留	But to listen to the rain, he tarried for ten days.
蟻綠新醅浮翠盎	Green froth on new unfiltered wine floats in a kingfisher goblet,
繭黃舊紙試銀鈎	On old yellowed cocoon paper he tried out the "silver hook" style.
別來風物應無恙	The scenery since we parted should not have deteriorated:
幸喜微官未白頭	I am delighted that my hair has not yet greyed, despite my negligible post.

Paraphrase:

I miss my comrade from the good old days,
We co-founded a poetry society that met at the side of the Pearl River.
He should have rushed off to take up his official post at Nanjing,
But he lingered for ten days, not bearing to part.
Here on my own assignment, I listlessly drink new wine by myself,
There in Nanjing, he writes letters to me in an energetic style.
Nothing should have changed in the Southern Garden since he left—
Thank goodness, I don't seem to have changed either, despite my lowly office.

Poem Two:

早歲南園開洛社	At an early age, we convened a "Luoyang Society" at the Southern Garden,
哦詩縱酒野雲邊	And chanted verses and indulged in wine at the edge of the wild clouds.
元龍豪氣三千丈	Your heroic valor, like Primal Dragon, went three-thousand fathoms high,[21]
翰苑文章二十年	For twenty years, you have issued essays from the Hanlin Academy.
春暖翠環歌白雪	In the warmth of spring, young maids with jade pendants intone "White Snow,"[22]
夜闌銀燭颺青煙	Late at night, blue smoke coils around the silver candlestick.

幽期寂寞滄洲裏	Even with my secret assignation, it is lonely by the Watchet Isle—
何日天風泛畫船	When will we ride the winds of Heaven, floating in our gaudy boat?

Paraphrase:

When we were young, we started a poetry society like the one of Ouyang Xiu at Luoyang,
The poetry that we wrote, the wine that we drank, sent our spirits soaring.
Your abilities matched your ambitions, just like that famous worthy Chen Deng,
For twenty years your writings dominated the bureaucracy.
Now that it is spring, refined meetings take place again, graced by educated courtesans,
But in the depths of the night, with smoke circling up towards the moon,
I still long for your companionship in the Southern Garden, despite my delightful date:
When will you return to resume our cultivated pastimes?

The first line overlays the image of Ouyang Xiu's Luoyang poetry society onto the site of the Southern Garden. It is interesting to note that these two images themselves were juxtaposed by a poet from Panyu, Wang Yihe 王亦鶴, at the tail end of the Qing dynasty. In an inscription on a painting of a literary gathering in the Yinshu Garden 因樹園 located in Macao, he drew on this double image to bolster the sheen of his own gathering: "The Southern Garden still has its ten masters;/In Luoyang they still venerate that group of worthies" 南園猶十子，洛下仰羣賢.[23]

Poem Three:

聞道南園華物冷	I have heard that the flowers in the Southern Garden are now cold,
小煙寒雨閉柴門	Slight smoke ascends in the chilly rain from behind a barricaded door.
頻年久負滄洲趣	For many years, the delights at the Watchet Isle have been ignored,
此日誰過杜曲村	Today, who passes by Duqu Village?
肯有文章千載重	Although our compositions will be honored for a

	thousand years,
不知朋舊幾人存	How many of our old companions are still with us?
芳晨樂事成塵跡	The lovely mornings and happy pasttimes are now traces in the dust—
江水江花酒一樽	Waters and flowers of the river remain, but nothing of culture but one beaker of wine.

Paraphrase:

I have been told that the Southern Garden is deserted now,
With just a caretaker trying to stay warm by a small fire in the cold drizzle.
We have not met for many years at our club by the Pearl River,
So who knows today, when one passes by, what great and noble ones had gathered there?
Even though we wrote for the ages, and our poems live on after us,
Who among us is still left among the living?
All that we did, all that we enjoyed, have turned to dust:
The river is there, as are the flowers, but of the Southern Garden club, my single beaker of wine is all that is left.

Out of the Three Great Masters of Lingnan, only Liang Peilan seems to have referred to the Southern Garden in verse. A series of nine poems written to the theme of the "Garden in Autumn" treats a southern garden from various angles; perhaps it was the Southern Garden.[24] The first poem sets the tone of solitary reflection and relaxation that characterizes the entire series:

"The Garden in Autumn" 秋園[25]

秋園吹大海	An autumn wind blows across the great ocean,
海色結寒姿	Ocean colors form patterns in the cold.
入我南園里	I enter inside my Southern Garden
無人獨坐時	And sit in solitude when no one else is around.
陰陽天漸改	The sky gradually turns from dark to light,
景物候新移	The scenery awaits to shift into something new.
一取珠琴拂	As soon as I grasp my pearl zither and give it a strum,
冰流滿地絲	Sounds flow like silken threads of ice, filling the area.

Other images of relaxation include a couplet from poem #2: "Ancient trees encircle the hut in autumn,/Behind the closed door I rest before distant hills" 古樹圍秋屋，閑門歇遠峰.[26] Any socializing was limited to single visitors, like these lines from poem #6:

有時白雲過	Sometimes white clouds pass by,
終日自飛翻	The entire day they circle overhead.
賓主兩不答	Neither host nor guest respond to questions—
往還誰復論	Who in the past is worth discussing?
……	……

Images of seclusion reinforce the mood of relaxed solitude. From poem #5: "Fish in the cold hide deep within the pondweed,/Birds in seclusion silently move to the darkened oaks" 寒魚深在藻，幽鳥暗移柯. A patently southern image, possibly from the Southern Garden, is found in poem #8: "I don't know who on the banks of the Watchet Sea,/Is harmonizing with the oarsman's song" 不知滄海畔，誰和棹歌音?[27]

Despite the thrust of the poems by Li De, a few examples from the poetry by Sun Fen, and these verses of Liang Peilan (if they are even relevant), we can see that the Southern Garden Poetry Society was a cohesive association of friends and guests that functioned socially from time to time. If the site was occasionally used for private purposes, there is no doubt that the garden itself was real, and that the school of poetry located in Guangzhou by Hu Yinglin was not only a poetic outlook and style shared by the local talent but was an integral social unit as well. It seems to have partaken of all three major aspects of poetry societies as isolated by Wang Zhimin: it was a social club for entertainment; it was gathered around a major literary figure (perhaps only notable on the local level at this time), and it was formed at the end of a dying dynasty by "left-over" poet-officials. The technical term used to describe its founding, "to form" 結 a society, according to Wang Zhimin, denoted a more permanent status and social cohesiveness than the more common designation of "to hold, convene" 開, which denoted meetings that were *ad hoc* and occasional.[28]

A further illustration of the social functioning of this group is in the association of the members outside of the garden. For example, a poem again by Li De narrates a group outing to the hills north of Guangzhou: "Touring White Cloud Temple with the Various Members of the Poetry Society, Getting the Graph 'Thousand' When Assigned Rhymes" 同詩社諸公遊白雲寺，分韵得"千"子.[29] One soirée that was convened in the Veranda for Listening to the Rain of Wang Zuo was notable for the sophomoric reveling by the group when inspired by wine: "Sire Sun sang crazily and you sirs all toppled over,/Three days sleeping all a kilter, now drunk now sober" 孫公狂歌君絕倒/橫眠三日醉復醒.[30] And one time in Nanjing, Sun reflected nostalgically on a pleasurable outing with his friends at an historic site in Guangzhou, the Terrace of the King of Yue, 越王台.[31] This social function is important to remember as the history of the Southern Garden Poetry Society is traced in its later manifestations, for it is necessary to distinguish periodicized and localized poets in Guangzhou from those who actually socialized together in formal literary clubs.

Part Two

The Transmission of Social Memory

Chapter Five

Southern Garden, Mid-Ming to Early Qing

> At about the same time I enjoyed a reunion of a different type. Dr. Schlesinger, a highly esteemed man of letters, was accustomed to receive artists, musicians, painters, *littérateurs,* both Continentals and Londoners, in his home on Friday evenings. One went there without special invitation and—once presented by an *habitué* of the salon, or provided with a note of introduction from one of Mr. or Mrs. Schlesinger's friends—could rely on being welcomed. The musicians present played or sang, there were readings and recitations, in accordance with the guests' individual gifts, and it was always grateful [*sic*] to feel that one was contributing to the pleasure of a select audience.
>
> —Leopold Auer, *My Long Life in Music*

The Five Later Masters of the Southern Garden

Sun Fen and his coterie came to be called the "Five Former" masters of the Southern Garden; this distinguished them from a new quintet when the latter achieved local literary fame during the mid-Ming period. Headed by Ou Daren 歐大任 (*zi* Zhenpo 楨柏, 1516–1595), the other four members of this new grouping were Liang Youyu 梁有譽 (*zi* Gongshi 公實, often called Lanting 蘭汀, 1521–1556), Li Minbiao 黎民表 (*zi* Weijing 惟敬, 1515–1581), Wu Dan 吳旦 (*zi* Erdai 而待, *juren* 1537), and Li Shixing 李時行 (*zi* Shaoxie 少偕, 1514–1569). Selections from their poetry were anthologized by Chen Wenzao 陳文藻 in the early Qing compilation *Nanyuan houwu xiansheng shi* 南園後五先生詩.[1] Three of the group, Ou Daren, Li Minbiao, and Liang Youyu, were students of the famous Cantonese scholar-official Huang Zuo 黃佐 (1490–1566), and notable for both their moral cultivation and poetic composition.[2] Following are short biographical epitomes.[3]

Ou Daren was from Shunde. Because late in his career he served as the Director of the Bureau of Forestry and Crafts in the Ministry of Works at Nanjing, his contemporaries also referred to him by this title: Ou Yubu 歐虞部. Ou's tutelage began before the age of five, and by fourteen (1530) he had been accepted as a district-level student. Although he did not take the imperial examination until 1563 (42 years old), his outstanding performance on the exam elicited the label "genius of a generation" from the examination officer. From this point on he was widely known throughout the empire. Despite his superior performance on the exam and his great reputation, however, it was still seven years before he began his bureaucratic career, which led him to posts in Yangzhou, Henan, Fujian, Nanjing, and Beijing. He resigned from official life in 1584, returned home, and died ten years later at the age of eighty. His literary reputation was enhanced by his association with the leading poets of the age. His collected works are preserved in the *Ou Yubu shiwen quanji* 歐虞部詩文全集.[4]

Liang Youyu also hailed from Shunde. Following the family tradition, he earned his *jinshi* in 1550 and was employed as the secretary of the Ministry of Justice. He associated with Li Dongyang and earned inclusion among the "Seven Later Masters." After serving in the capital some three years, Liang was recruited by minister Yan Song 嚴嵩[5] but was loath to accept his offer. Instead, he returned home and withdrew himself from society to read and study. In 1556 he arranged to travel to Mt. Luofu in the company of Li Minbiao and others. While en route, they suffered from the ravages of a hurricane; Liang became ill and died at the early age of 36. Upon his death just over two hundred poems remained of Liang's verse, preserved in an anthology called *Lanting cungao* 蘭汀存稿, alternately *Bibu ji* 比部集, or "Collection of the Adjunct," from one of his official posts. The work is no longer extant.[6]

Li Minbiao was from the Conghua district northeast of Guangzhou, famous today for its hot springs and resorts. In 1559 Li was appointed Clerk of the Hanlin Academy. Two years later his literary notoriety attracted the attention of his superior, and he was promoted to be the Director of Services in the Ministry of Personnel. In 1565 he was again promoted and reassigned to the Ministry of War in Nanjing. He took part in editing the veritable records of both Shizong 世宗 (r. 1522–1567) and Muzong 穆宗 (r. 1567–1573). In 1579 Li retired to Yuexiu Hill in Guangzhou to read and write. (Perhaps his retirement to the site of the former Terrace of the King of Yue is what inspired the composition of the *fu* on this theme that was examined in Chapter One.) He died two years later at the age of sixty-six. In addition to being an accomplished calligrapher, Li was the author of several books, helped edit two local gazetteers, and produced a collection of poetry. The latter, entitled *Yaoshi shanren shigao* 瑤石山人詩稿, is his only extant work.[7]

Wu Dan was born in Nanhai, and spent his bureaucratic life in obscure posts in remote regions; his name, therefore, seldom appears in the poetry of his contemporaries. His collected works, *Langao ji* 蘭皐集, is no longer extant. Today, only eighteen of his poems survive.[8]

Li Shixing came from Panyu, passed the *jinshi* examination of 1541, and served in Zhejiang. Promoted as the Secretary of the Bureau of Equipment and Communications in the Ministry of War, he was slandered by a colleague and resigned, having been unable to clear his name. Wandering around the country, he wrote a great number of poems. After returning home, he engaged in intensive study and wide reading. While accompanying his second son to the national college in 1565, he began another trek. None of Li's original writings are extant; Qing recollections of his *Jiabu ji* 駕部集 and *Qingxia man'gao* 青霞漫稿 contain over 300 poems but are far from comprehensive.[9]

In the Guangdong gazetteer biography of Wu Dan we read that Dan "was friends with Ou Daren, Li Minbiao, and Liang Youyu; they formed a society at the Southern Garden, and later generations called him one of 'the Five Later Masters of the Southern Garden.'"[10] The account further states that they held sacrifices 祀 at the Veranda for Screening the Wind, obviously to the manes of the Five Former Masters.[11] A source preserved in *Guangzhou chengfang zhi*, the *Chuting baizhulu* 楚庭稗珠錄, maintains that they each also "improvised lines of poetry and linked them together in the Veranda for Screening the Wind" 聯吟於抗風軒.[12]

Ou Daren was particularly sensitive to his cultural heritage, for he left a set of highly polished verses about his poetic precursors in Guangzhou:

"Five Poems of Remembrance, with Preface" 五懷詩並引[13]

> Sun Fen, Wang Zuo, Huang Zhe, Li De, and Zhao Jie were the Five Masters of Lingnan. At the commencement of the dynasty they established a society at the Southern Garden, two hundred years ago from the present. Although the society has already disbanded, the garden's ancient components still remain: withered bamboos by an irrigation pond are partly concealed by brambles and vines.[14] The conduct of these men fit the style of the age and may still be imagined. But in no time at all the world has changed, and so I offer these five stanzas in remembrance.

孫蕡，王佐，黃哲，李德，趙介，嶺南五先生也。國初結社南園，去今二百年矣，社已廢而園故在，荒竹淲池，半掩篷藋，其行誼風流，猶可想見，俯仰異日，爰懷五章。

1. 仲衍起南海 Where Sun Zhongyan arose in Nanhai,
滄波湧明月 Watchet waves welled up to the brilliant moon.
蕩蕩魏晉風 Heroic in the style of Wei and Jin,[15]
草昧人文揭 This man of letters transformed the primordial chaos.[16]
畎畝懷靈荃 Among the furrows, he longed for the fragrant lord,[17]
侍從久未達 But long has not been able to reach him.
鵬鷃一逍遙 Once the roc and wren set off in free and easy flight,[18]
邱園竟澌沫 But the barrows are barren and the garden sere.
沉冥古先生 Ancient master, now sunken in obscurity,
詞源在揚粵 The source of your poetics was in Yangyue.[19]

2. 河東有寓公 From Hedong came an exiled squire—
王生仲翔伍 Master Wang was the second of the soaring quintet.
洞鑒蘊九玄 His perspicacity embodied the Nine Obscurities,[20]
深心托千古 The depths of his heart lodged a thousand ages.
辭笏拜夕年 Abandoning tablet of office, he relaxed during his waning years,
懸車抗風侶 Giving up official carriage, he became a companion of the Screening Wind.
黼黻屬興運 In elegance and adroitness, his compositions matched Xingyun,
一時穆修矩 For a time, he was admired like Xiuju.[21]
隱璞縱靡雕 The rock-bound jade, though unpolished,
自不淪幽土 Would not sink into obscurity in a secluded land.

3. 哲也荔灣君 As for Huang Zhe, the Lord of Lichee Bay,
結茅蒲澗下 He built a thatched hut by a reed-filled stream.
薦入侍書閣 Recommended for employment to serve at the gallery of books,
扈蹕鍾山駕 He accompanied the royal retinue to Bell Mountain.[22]
雪篷罔終遁 But Snowy Hut Huang could not escape into seclusion,
世已微法桂 As the age declined in law and order.[23]
郢斤亡堊質 The carpenter of Ying had no materials to plaster,
成風幾悲咤 His wind-like whirling—how often I bellowed in sorrow?[24]

	唯有南浦篇	Only in the verses from southern river banks,
	湘蘭遂凋謝	Were decaying orchids at the river Xiang portrayed as effectively.[25]
4.	楚楚李仲德	Dashing, delightful Li Zhongde,
	南威服猶繭	He overawed the south while still a young buck.[26]
	論都關洛游	He roamed over Luo and Chang'an, noting everything in the capitals,[27]
	友教江湘轉	Taking a turn around the Jiang and Xiang rivers, he became a "friendly instructor."[28]
	賜堪望雲夢	He should have been favored with a view of Yunmeng,[29]
	拜豈及瓜衍	But he was never granted a reward like Guayan.[30]
	鸞嘯遘孫登	Whistling like a simurgh, he encountered Sun Deng,[31]
	牛醫習黃憲	And the cow vet learned from Huang Xian.[32]
	終古蒿廬中	From long ago, even among the reed huts,
	禺陽炳雕篆	South of Mt. Yu his writings shine.[33]
5.	伯貞遁世士	Zhao Zhenbo was a scholar who took refuge from the world,
	深栖向西樵	He settled deep within Mt. Xiqiao.[34]
	潛虬豈不媚	Is not this hidden dragon fascinating?
	永謝弓旌招	Long ago he declined the beckoning of bow and banner.[35]
	清溪撫疏松	The clear creek touches sparse pines,
	心遠趣自超	His mind being distant, his interests were transcendant.[36]
	柴桑臨流潔	At Chaisang he loomed over pure streams,[37]
	句曲聽風遙	On Gouqu, he listened to the distant winds.[38]
	邈載二陶後	After the distant age of the two Taos,[39]
	勒銘寄山椒	I inscribe an inscription to them and entrust it to the mountain peak.

Because of the reconvening of the Southern Garden Poetry Society, adds the biography of Li Minbiao, poetic learning in Lingnan became invigorated, having languished since the time of Sun Fen and the other four.[40]

Physically the Southern Garden was reconstituted at this time, having been transformed into the official garden of the Administration of the Regional Commander in the early Ming period,[41] and the famous veranda was either rebuilt or repaired. But little else in the historical record indicates that these five worthies associated much with each other apart from some of them studying together under Huang Zuo and the one-time sacrifice held in the Southern Garden. Instead, what is stressed is the acceptance of several of these poets in the poetry clubs with dynasty-wide reputations of Li Panlong 李攀龍 (1514–1570) or Wang Shizhen 王世貞 (1526–1590).[42] This is particularly apparent from the poetry included in the *Nanyuan houwu xiansheng shi*. It is to be expected that Liang Youyu, a member, and Ou Daren and Li Minbiao, as associates, of Li Panlong's Beijing circle of the Seven Later Masters, concentrate on poems devoted to its more prestigious membership.[43] The social connections made in Beijing were certainly as practical as they were poetical. But the other members of the Cantonese club also seem to pay most of their attention to associations outside of Guangzhou, probably for the same purpose of maintaining ties with influential officials around the country. Some sources maintain that their social outlet in Guangzhou, before the northward move of the three poets mentioned above, was under the literary rubric of the *Yueshan shishe* 粵山詩社,[44] and that the nickname "Five Later Masters of the Southern Garden" was imparted by later historically minded authorities for the sake of tradition.[45]

Poetizing on the local level must have been inspired by less mundane, less practical, and certainly less materialistic concerns. For instance, a quatrain by Liang Youyu extracted from a longer poem is revealing in this aspect, as it specifically rejects using poetry to further social aims: "A heaven and earth beyond Yanzhou,/Cloudy billows by the side of Swollen Sea./We Confucians spurn worldly affairs,/And form a poetry society to cut ourselves off from dusty karma" 天地炎州外，雲濤漲海邊。為儒嗟世業，結社斷塵緣.[46] Some poetry dedicated to group outings by the Five Later Masters can be localized to the elevated area surrounding Yuexiu Hill, a place at the solar end of the spectrum far from the watery *yin* of the Southern Garden on the banks of the Pearl River.[47] When Ou Daren mentioned feasting with Five Masters from an "ancient garden" located in Nanhai,[48] none of them were the so-called Five Later Masters; one of them was hyperbolically described as being the Lord of Canghai 滄海君.[49] Additionally, another verse by Ou Daren reveals that he participated in the Xiangshan Association 香山社.[50] And the title of a poem by Liang Youyu indicates that he was helping to revive an old poetry society amid the "mountains"; from internal evidence these were located in Guangdong, and the name of the poetry society is mentioned: the "White Society" 白社.[51] Perhaps it should be localized on

Mt. White Cloud, where Master Huang Zuo had his study and where his disciples frequently resorted.[52] Finally, in 1588 Ou Daren, Li Minbiao, and Liang Youyu joined up to form a poetry society that met in the Guangxiaosi called the Pure Society of the Myrobalan Grove, as noted previously.[53] There is no evidence in the poetry of these "Five Later Masters of the Southern Garden" of any verses composed on or in the Southern Garden, a point noted by Wang Zongyan.[54] In fact, there is no mention of the name Southern Garden in the entire *Nanyuan houwu xiansheng shi* other than in Ou Daren's preface to his set of verses "Five Poems of Remembrance." The designation of "Later" masters of the garden, concludes Wang Zongyan, was due to an erroneous assumption first mentioned in the *Mingshi zong* 明詩綜 anthology of Zhu Yizun, who had spent two years in Guangdong from 1656 to 1658 acting as tutor to the son of magistrate Yang Yongjian 楊雍建 (1627–1704).[55] Wang reminds us that the designation "Five Later Masters of the Southern Garden" was never heard of in Yue.[56] He adds that in 1762 one question on the local exam included by a visiting examination official, Huang Yide 黃懿德, concerned the Five Later Masters, thus contributing to the spread of this error. Presumably, Huang was misled by his familiarity with the *Mingshi zong* and eagerness to identify with local culture.[57]

Even if Qu Dajun did not mention that these five friends had any connection with the Five Former Masters of the Southern Garden, he did accord them and their teacher Huang Zuo an important place in the development of a distinct Southern Muse. His essay on poetry societies, which has already been cited, continues as follows:

> Master Huang Zuo rose up in Nanhai and, holding a three-foot sword of the Han line,[58] was masterful enough to give orders to Wei, Jin, and the Six Dynasties literati or to direct poets of the Kaiyuan and Dali periods.[59] All this transformed the barbarians into civilized human beings and cleansed the remote regions of the south. Therefore, his achievements should be ranked with those of Lu Jia[60] and Zong Jun.[61] Ou Daren, Liang Youyu, Li Shixing, and Li Minbiao were all disciples of Huang Zuo. Their poetry was grand and stately, refined and elegant, so rich in *feng* and *ya*. This was all due, it seems, to the teachings of their mentor. Ou Daren and Liang Youyu were constantly praised in the capital because of their poetry. Li Panlong and Wang Shizhen wanted to associate with them and form a coterie called the Eight Talents. But because they detested the fact that two of the members were from Guangdong, and also because Ou Daren had not been through the first exam,[62] they rejected him.[63]

> 泰泉先生崛出南海。其持漢家三尺，以號令魏晉六朝，而指揮開元大曆，變椎結為侑，闢荒薙穢於炎徼。功不在陸賈，終軍下也。楨柏與梁蘭丁，李青霞，黎瑤石皆泰泉門人。其詩正大典麗，澤於風雅，蓋得其師所指授。楨柏，蘭丁常以詩盛稱京師。于麟，元美輩欲連為八才子，旋以八才子中，粵居其二，心嫉之，且楨柏又非甲科，乃舍楨柏。

The essay continues, tracing not the social institution of the poetry society, but the special characteristics of individual Cantonese poets who carried the torch of broadening and refining Cantonese poetics.

In this essay Qu mentions nothing of Ou and his friends participating in a local poetry society. Instead, he outlines their attempt to link up with poets at the capital; in this he supports the conclusion of Wang Zongyan cited above. After all, Qu was very aware of the history of the Southern Garden Poetry Society and would have made any connection explicit if he had known of one.

A biography of Li Minbiao by Ou Biyuan reveals that Huang Zuo originally convened a poetry society on Mt. Pure Spring 清泉山, and there he and his disciples "chanted and harmonized amid the hills, thereby reinvigorating poetry and prose in Lingnan" 唱和其間，嶺南詩書復振. The biography continues: after returning from the north, Li "shut his mouth and no longer spoke of things beyond the pass. Instead, he met daily with his former comrades and disciples and restored the old Pure Spring Society, chanting poetry with them. It seems they held with the attitudes of the airy Daoist genies" 絕口不言關説，日與故人及諸子弟復清泉舊社，吟咏其中，蓋飄飄游神仙想.[64]

Ou Daren, the supposed mainstay of the Southern Garden Poetry Society, convened or attended poetry societies separate from any association with the Southern Garden, as has been mentioned. While living in Nanjing, he convened the "Clear Creek Society" 清溪社 and "could not drink much. Nevertheless, every evening when he attended a convivial gathering, he stayed until dawn without tiring" 公飲不能栢勺，然每夕讌集既達旦不倦. After retirement in Guangzhou, "when not wandering among the four hundred peaks of Luofu, leaving inscriptions and poems at every site, sometimes he attended the Fuqiu society[65]....He was beckoned into the Hasty Garden where he took pleasure in talking about poetry, carrying on with the air of the Bamboo Grove....Whenever he attended convivial meetings of his clan, he would indulge in fierce drinking" 盤桓於四百峯間，遍為題咏，間為赴浮邱社。。。。招入遽園，談詩為樂，大有竹林

風。。。。與宗黨讌會必劇飲.[66] Was the name of the poetry society that Qu Dajun himself organized in the early Qing period, the "Western Garden Poetry Society" 西園詩社, self-consciously patterned after the Southern Garden?[67] This explanation is more reasonable than to suppose that Qu had in mind that famous "Western Garden" of Song-period Guangzhou, a happy combination of fairgrounds, shopping malls, boating lakes, and public parks especially popular with foreign residents, officials, merchants, and missionaries who found lodgings in this bustling quarter of the city.[68] Yu Jing encapsulated the essence of this raucous esplanade in a poem that mentions, among many striking images, the plethora of flowers transplanted from foreign climes that lent Guangzhou much of its charm.[69] Alas, neither explanation is persuasive, for Qu most likely merely claimed the credit for helping to found a poetry society in the Western Garden of his friend Liang Peilan.

The contribution of the Five Later Masters to the Southern Muse can be seen in the occasional verse composed on various visits to the scenic sites around the region, such as the excursions to Mt. White Cloud already noted. Ou Daren frequented the Terrace of the King of Yue, Mt. Luofu, Mt. Xiqiao, Shaozhou, the Great Yu Pass, the Shrine to the Three Loyal Martyrs, the Guangxiao Monastery, the Tower for Quelling the Sea, and the shrine of the famous Neo-Confucian philosopher Chen Xianzhang 陳獻章 (1428–1500). Each of these trips was recorded in verse. Liang Youyu was just as prolific a sightseer, having composed verses on frequent visits to Mt. Luofu, the White Cloud Monastery, the Terrace of the King of Yue, the Tower for Quelling the Sea, viewing plums, Yuezhou 粵州, the city wall around Guangzhou, various local gardens, the Lookout of the Three Genies, and also the Shrine of Chen Xianzhang. When not traversing the length and breadth of China, Li Minbiao rambled around Mt. White Cloud, Luofu, the Terrace of the King of Yue, the Terrace for Reverencing Han, Guangxiao Monastery, the Tower for Quelling the Sea, the Shao Stones, and various local gardens and studios. Yet Wu Dan left no verse on palpably Cantonese sites or themes, nor did Li Shixing except for visiting a local monastery and replying to a letter from home with southern images.[70] It is not surprising, then, that only in the poetry of the first three poets did specifically Cantonese diction occur. For instance, Ou Daren used the term "Watchet Sea" thrice, including the reference to the "Lord of Watchet Sea" mentioned earlier, Liang Youyu also thrice, and Li Minbiao once. Therefore, despite not being particularly active socially as a group other than an occasional pairing up, usually between Liang Youyu and Li Minbiao—and the three seemed to keep in contact socially with their master Huang Zuo—the Southern Muse and thereby literati culture in Guangdong was advanced and transmitted in the verse of at least three of the Five Later Masters of the Southern Garden. Interestingly enough, it was only these three who were renowned as poets.[71]

Chen Zizhuang and the Twelve Masters of the Southern Garden

In the last decade of the Ming dynasty, Chen Zizhuang 陳子壯 (*zi* Jisheng 集生, 1596–1647) revived the Southern Garden Poetry Society.[72] Chen Zizhuang was a noted Cantonese patriot who opposed the Manchu onslaught in the south, ultimately suffering execution along with Zhang Jiayu 張家玉 (d. 1647) and Chen Bangyan 陳邦彥 (1603–1647).[73] Chen served as a Hanlin compiler; but he was dismissed after he was listed as a member of the Donglin 東林 party. Three years later he was rehabilitated and quickly rose to high office in the Board of Ceremonies, serving as its senior vice-president. But he soon ran afoul of the royal family for opposing its practice of nepotism. With the fall of Beijing he participated in the government of the Southern Ming until his capture in the effort to free Guangzhou from the occupying Manchurian forces.[74] His most accessible works are included in the posthumous compilation *Chen Wenzhonggong yiji* 陳文忠公遺集, 16 *juan*.[75]

This eminent official returned to Guangzhou during a period of retirement from office and established the Yunzong Academy 雲蹤書院 on Mt. White Cloud, Yunzong being one of his sobriquets. But turning his sentiments to poetry and wine, he renovated and rededicated the famous Southern Garden literary club around the year 1638. Additionally, he built his own garden of Peiyuan 裴園 a *li* away from the Southern Garden, presumably named for the school he had attended as a child.[76] Chen and his friends who frequented the society came to be called the "Twelve Masters of the Southern Garden" 南園十二子, or the "Later Invigoration of the Southern Garden" 南園後勁.[77]

Among the most noted of these vigorous traditionalists was Li Suiqiu 黎遂球 (1602–1646?, *zi* Meizhou 美周, *juren* 1623) from Panyu.[78] Very precocious at a tender age, Li was recruited to participate in a special exam for youths administered by the county magistrate to develop local talent. He became a provincial graduate in 1623 and moved north to associate with notable scholars in the Jiangsu and Zhejiang regions, including Zhang Pu 張溥 (1602–1641), the founder of the Fushe 復社, and his pupil, the noted poet Wu Weiye 吳偉業 (1609–1672).[79] On the way back to Guangzhou after a thirteen year absence, Li Suiqiu gained some notoriety in 1640 by participating in a poetry competition in Yangzhou called the Yellow Peony Poetry Association 黃牡丹詩會; it was organized by Zheng Yuanxun 鄭元勳 and held in his Ying Garden 影園. Li was awarded first place for his set of ten *lüshi* on the peony. The judge was the famous literatus Qian Qianyi 錢謙益 (1582–1664), who had been invited to both preside over and adjudicate the contest.[80] For his set of prize-winning poems, Li was awarded an engraved gold goblet,[81] and ever after he was teased with the sobriquet of Peony Zhuangyuan 牡丹狀元. Kuang Lu 鄺露 (*zi* Zhanruo 湛若, 1604–1650) from Nanhai, another Cantonese poet noted for his eccentricity, participated with Li in this competition.[82] Kuang's heroic death at the fall of Guangzhou, holding his two treasured zithers while leaping into a lake, provided much matter for later local and national poets.[83] His own set of ten regulated verses on the theme of a "Crimson Parrot" earned him the equally humorous epithet of "Parrot Kuang," most often paired with "Peony Li."[84] After Li's return to Guangzhou, he participated with Chen Zizhuang and Zhang Jiayu in the defense of Guangzhou; he died in battle along with his younger brother Li Suiqi 遂琪 and was honored posthumously with the title of Zhongmin 忠愍, the Loyal and Lamentable.

The other Twelve Masters were little noticed by national historians. Chen Zizhuang's younger step-brother Zisheng 子升 (*hao* Zhongzhou 中洲, 1614–1692) did not even merit a biography in local Cantonese gazetteers. What little is known of him was gleaned by modern researcher Li Jian'er from scattered historical sources.[85] In addition to Chen Zisheng's deep friendship with his bosom buddy Ou Zhuyu (for whom see below), what is stressed is his participation in local administrative affairs under the aegis of the Southern Ming in Fujian and Guangzhou. For instance, he worked under Chen Zizhuang in the effort to raise a militia. Chen Zisheng survived the turmoil in the south, ending his days as a hermit concentrating on expressing himself through poetry. His elder step-brother Zizhuang appreciated his literary talent, once claiming that it surpassed his own skills. Contemporary critic Wang Shizhen praised Zisheng's poetry in lavish terms, stressing his command of the rules of prosody. He was also a skilled player of the zither, as well as a talented painter. He visited Mt. Lu and Mt. Huang and claimed to be a disciple of the teachings of Han Shi, Qu Dajun's Buddhist master. His collected works were printed as the *Zhongzhou caotang ji* 中洲草堂集 in 23 *juan*.

Huang Jiheng 黃季恒 is otherwise unknown. But one untitled poem presented to him by Chen Zisheng is recorded by Li Jian'er.[86] It continues with the tradition first seen in Chapter Four that connects butterflies to Daoism and, peripherally, to the Southern Garden:

秋江楓落雁聲繁	Maple leaves drop over the autumn river, the sounds of geese incessant,
去歲同君深夜論	Last year I discoursed deep into the night with you, sir.
醉倚蠛蠓浮北極	Drunk, I mounted midge flies, floating to the North Pole,
夢驚蝴蝶化南園	Startled awake from my butterfly dream, I transform back at the Southern Garden.
臨文每歎風雲事	Whenever I write essays, I cannot help sighing over stormy events,
作賦能忘筆札恩	Whenever I compose poems, how can I forget that you were kind enough to send me letters?
不見柴桑古人久	Long it's been not seeing my old friend from Chaisang,
幾回煙水限桃源	How many times has the misty river limited the peach font?[87]

Ou Zhuyu 歐主遇 (*zi* Jiake 嘉可, *hao* Hugong 壺公) was from Shunde. In 1627 he appeared on the supplementary list of candidates who had passed the provincial examinations with such distinction that they were immediately awarded *jinshi* degrees, normally reserved for those successful in the metropolitan examinations. As a tribute or "passed" scholar, he was admitted to the national university to prepare for the palace examination. At that time, Chen Zizhuang was still in Beijing, even though he had been dismissed from office in 1625. He so admired Ou's character and learning that he ordered his younger step-brother Zisheng to befriend him. In September of 1653 Ou was back in Guangzhou organizing famine relief. "In his declining years he loved to roam among the woods and vales and kept himself away from public arenas. He built the Southern Park to please himself" 晚歲優遊林壑，絕跡公門，築南圃自娛.[88] The Southern Park was not only built in self-conscious imitation of Chen Zizhuang's earlier Southern Garden where Ou had participated in the revived poetry society, it honored his own heritage, for he was a grand-nephew of Ou Daren, the guiding spirit of the Five Later Masters of the Southern Garden. He authored the *Zigengxuan ji* 自耕軒集, from which an admirable "*Fu* on Bamboo" is extant.[89]

Ou Huairui 歐懷瑞 (*zi* Qitu 啓圖) was from Gaoming, son of the notable official and essayist Ou Daxiang 歐大相 (*zi* Yongru 用儒, *hao* Haimu 海目, 1590 *jinshi*).[90] Ou Huairui obtained his *juren* degree in 1628 and served as district magistrate in Dangyang 當陽 and Pingshan 平山 counties.[91] In Guangzhou, he hung around the younger generation of literati, such as Ou Biyuan 歐必元, a half-brother of Ou Zhuyu, and Kuang Lu; but because of his talent, he was invited to participate with the older generation in forming the Southern Garden Poetry Society. His works include the *Quting gao* 趨庭稿 and the *Kuorantang gao* 廓然堂稿;[92] none of his works are extant. He was trained as a swordsman and was fond of studying military arts. During the chaos attendant to the conquest of the south, he died en route in the service of the Southern Ming in the company of Li Suiqiu and Kuang Lu. He is credited by Wang Shizhen as having continued the new trend in Cantonese poetics originally inaugurated by Kuang Lu.[93]

Ou's younger brother Ou Huainian 區懷年 (*zi* Shuyong 叔永) was ranked at the same level of literary attainment as Huairui himself. Huainian attended the national university as a tribute student and later served as a controller-general. He was appointed as clerk of the Hanlin Academy, but his service was rendered reluctantly, since he preferred to roam around visiting famous mountains and rivers. Back in Guangzhou he joined with Chen Zizhuang to renovate the Southern Garden Poetry Society. After the Ming dynasty collapsed, he retired to live as a recluse. Four of his prose pieces are preserved in the *Guangdong wenzheng*. One notable prose work is "Self-preface to Striking My Poet's Walking Stick" 擊筇吟自序. A "poet's walking stick" 筇吟 or 吟筇 will prove to be an occasional image in Cantonese verse. Ou's integral works included the *Chuting gao* 楚亭稿 and the *Yuanchaotang gao* 元超堂稿, neither extant today.

Huang Shengnian 黃聖年 (*zi* Fengyong 逢永, 1618 *juren*) was from Shunde. He became a cherished intimate of Chen Zizhuang. He served as an instructor at the state-sponsored Confucian school in Dangyang and later became its head, but afterwards he retired to Guangzhou because of problems with his feet. He was fond of learning and proved to be an expert calligraphist and writer. His integral works included *Xueruizai shiji* 薛蕊齋詩集. The *Guangdong wenzheng* includes a *fu* poem devoted to the plant that lent his private studio its name, the Xuerui, a variety of artemisia.[94]

Li Bangjian 黎邦瑊 (*zi* Junxuan 君選, *hao* Shidong 石洞) was from

Conghua, the nephew of Li Minbiao, who was a member of the Five Later Masters of the Southern Garden. After studying as a tribute student in Beijing, he became an instructor in a local academy. He quit to return to Guangzhou and formed a fast friendship with Chen Bangyan. Li was known for his paintings of landscapes, bamboos, and stones, and he was expert in both seal and cursive styles of calligraphy. He seemed a natural as a member of the reconstituted Southern Garden Poetry Society, for, according to Ou's preface, he liked "to nurture his ignorance with wine" 養拙以酒.[95]

Xu Fen 徐棻 (*zi* Muzhi 木之) was from Nanhai; he later changed his name to Rong 榮 to avoid a taboo. We learn from Ou's preface that he was noted for his learning and skill at conversation on current events. It seems he was given to "indulging in pleasure after heroic drinking" 雄飲耽樂.[96]

Little is known of the final member of this poetry society, Seng Tong'an 僧通岸 (*zi* Zhihai 智海), a Buddhist monk. We know at least that he lived in a small retreat called Hermitage Perched Amidst the Clouds 栖雲庵 within the famous woods known as the Myrobalans Grove at the Guangxiao Monastery. That he had a predilection for poetry is indisputable; he once pronounced that "the delights of Zen surpass the written word,/But when I gain enlightenment about something, I sometimes chant verses" 禪悦超文字，解悟或長吟.[97] This monk left enough poems to form his own anthology and named it after his hermitage, the *Qiyun'an ji* 栖雲庵集.

Ou Zhuyu describes a typical meeting of the association in terms reminiscent of its heyday under Sun Fen: "Members came to join the society from Jiangxi, Zhejiang, Hubei, Hunan, and Fujian; many of them were either famous or popular. Although not convening often, on the day of the meeting there were singing geishas urging on the drinking."[98] The presence of these geishas leads to the introduction of the most famous poetess in Cantonese literary history; this was the learned and talented geisha Zhang Qiao 張喬 (1615–1633, originally from Suzhou, called also Zhang Liren 麗人 and Zhang Erqiao 二喬). Li Jian'er wrote: "One notable poetess was Zhang Liren; her singing and dancing were the marvel for a time. She was able to compose minor *ci* and took her ease in serving those in attendance."[99] This praise is quite understated, at least in terms of her literary accomplishments, for her poems numbered enough to make up five *juan*. A portrait of her is still extant, along with several *ci* composed by a friend to describe it.[100] She was also known for her ability to paint orchids and bamboo. One of her paintings of orchids was presented to Qu Dajun by a friend Pang Zuru 龐祖如 in 1687; Qu responded to this kindness by sending him six topical *shi*.

One of Zhang Qiao's charming poems is set in the self-abnegating persona of the Six Dynasties-period poetess Zi Ye 子夜, who peevishly claims to be unconcerned with the imminent departure of a boyfriend:

"Sending Off Li Yanke, the Mountain Man" 送李山人煙客[101]

子夜征歌特底忙	Zi Ye is especially busy, singing requested songs,
奈何花月是離觴	Alas that our romance ends with a farewell drink.
春江千折牽游可	The spring river has a thousand bends, yet the barge can be towed along:
若個津頭柳線長	Will willow thread be long enough to stretch to your next stop?

Zhang Qiao's *ci* were noted for their range of expression. A sample follows with a sentiment strikingly different from the light-hearted lyric just noted.

"Mooring at Dusk, To the Tune of Gazing Out Over Jiangnan" 晚泊望江南[102]

秋風晚	Autumn winds at dusk,
煙草冷斜陽	Mist laden grasses are cold in the slanting sun.
涼透天涯雲浸碧	Cool permeates to the edge of the sky, clouds seep into the blue,
山搖瀫影鏡吞光	Hills' reflections tremble on gauze-like waves, the mirror-surface swallows the light.
孤艇擊垂楊	A solitary skiff is tied to drooping willows.
橫水渡	Crossing against the current,
人去篴聲長	The sound of flutes lingers after his departure.
枕上不知歸是夢	Resting on a pillow I wonder will his return be merely a dream?
衾前空浸淚痕香	The fragrant traces of tears are vainly left on the coverlet,
螢火照漁梁	And the light of fireflies shines on the fish weir.

There is nothing particularly southern about this scene or the sentiments it embodies; still, one modern annotator detected a Cantonese slang expression in the phrase "crossing against the current."[103]

Another *ci* is set in the Southern Garden, identified by an allusion to the twelve balustrades of the original Veranda for Screening the Wind. This *ci* provides a very rare feminine perspective on the atmosphere there, hinting towards the possibly amorous aspect of certain activities:

"Spring Vista" 春景[104]

曉日上簾櫳	The morning sunlight ascends the curtains,
射透青山鏡影重	Shot through with green hills, the images in the mirror double up.
垂柳半池花又落	Weeping willows halfway cover the pond, flowers fall again,
飄紅	Flying reds,
十二闌干度軟風	A soft breeze wafts over the twelve balustrades.
草色錄茸茸	Colors of the herbage are lush greens,
暖水寒煙淡復濃	Warm waters in the cold mist, now thick, now thin.
欲試羅衣還自怯	I am tempted to try a gauze gown but feel too shy,
愁慵	Anxious but indolent,
遠近樓臺望眼中	Towers and terraces, near and far, are within sight of my gaze.

Zhang Qiao's tragically early death at age nineteen from a sudden illness deeply affected the Southern Garden gallants, and indeed, much of polite society, for one hundred mourners accompanied her funeral procession. The members of the poetry society not only gathered her verses for publication but also appended their own eulogies in an anthology entitled *Lianxiang ji* 蓮香集, or *Collection of the Lotus Fragrance*, in five *juan*.[105] Li Suiqiu wrote her funeral inscription, which was still visible if unintelligible in 1891 when her tomb was renovated.[106] Her grave site on Mt. White Cloud, perfumed by an hundred flowers, and the vain attempts to summon her shade for one last visit, are tenderly described in retrospect by Huang Dejun 黃德峻 (*hao* Qinshan 琴山, *jinshi* 1822).[107]

Another literary product of the poetry association was the *Nanyuan huaxin shi* 南園花信詩. This was a short compilation of verses written by the group to match rhymes with Li Suiqiu's ten-poem series "Yellow Peony," recalling his victory in the competition of the poetry society of that name. Alas, no peonies grew in the Southern Garden, but the vagaries of floral variety did not hinder the celebration. This compilation resulted from the verses composed on the day of Li's arrival in Guangzhou and derived its name from the theme of the poems. Two editions of uncertain vintage are still extant today, appended to certain printings of the *Nanyuan qianwu xiansheng shi* and the *Nanyuan houwu xiansheng shi*.[108]

Li Suiqiu is also notable for recording a celebration of the lustration rites in the Southern Garden with his comrades. This was a formal affair which Li characterized as surpassing the Lanting gathering in splendor, since the participants were all drunken genies in exile.[109]

Chen's Zizhuang's sentiments regarding the original Southern Garden society may be approached through the panegyric he wrote to preface the reprinting of the *Nanyuan wuxiansheng shi* in 1638, the same year that he reconvened the Southern Garden Poetry Society. An extract follows:

> The Grand Historian (Sima Qian) said that literary studies in Shandong were due to their heavenly endowed nature; poetry in Yue is then the same. Our country considers the Huai and its tributaries as the capital region; Yue then would correspond to the network of the Jiang and Han rivers. That which capped the "Elegentiae" section are the two "Southern" sections. And the Five Masters, as left-over refugees from a conquered state, together with the Four Eminences of Wu and the Ten Talents of Min, were all exponents of the southern sound. Their contributions to the poetic tradition are still evident today....If this southern sound (of the Five Masters) is allowed to perish, then we might as well eliminate the *Shijing* from the Five Classics, or get rid of Music from the Six Classics. Can we do this?[110]
>
> 太史公謂齊魯文學，其天性。粵於詩，則有然矣。我國家以淮甸為豐鎬，則粵應江漢之紀。風之所為首二南也，五先生以勝國遺逸，與吳四傑，閩十才子並起，皆南音。風雅之功，於今為烈。。。。假如聲音可以盡廢，則是五經當去詩，六藝當綴樂也，而可乎?

Chen Zizhuang's Southern Garden club must have met periodically for a time, stirring up currents of local nostalgia that had staying power, for as late as 1687, the Veranda for Screening the Wind was rebuilt, forty-nine years after Chen had formally reconvened the club.[111] Kuang Lu used to gather with his own set of friends at the Southern Garden, with no apparent connection to the Chen and Li coterie.[112] An unofficial member was Xue Shiheng 薛始亨 (*zi* Gangsheng 剛生, 1617–1686) from Shunde.

He attended a poetry society that met in the Southern Garden, and composed two poems on the Southern Garden, which he termed "a society for literature and wine" 南園文酒社.[113] But what is missing from the literary accounts of Chen's Southern Garden revival is the probable political nature of its meetings.

Here I must present some historical background to the development of literary sociality of this period. Xiao Chi's exquisite study of the garden motif in the *Story of the Stone* outlines the development of a new literati ethos after the mid-Ming period, centered on life in a garden. His chapter entitled "The Two Faces of Literati Culture: Activity and Passivity" contrasts the roles of "diversion seekers" with "political idealists." First he traces the rise of the private garden during the Wei-Jin period to a new type of reclusion, that of *chaoyin* 朝隱 or being reclusive in one's lifestyle while still engaged in government service. According to Xiao, this "made it possible for *shi* to pursue their political ambitions without abandoning the guise of living as dignified recluses at home in nature. In this regard, by Ming times the garden gained a special dimension: it was not officialdom or nature, but somewhere between."[114] By the end of the Ming, literati culture had bifurcated into two camps, the "aesthetes" or reclusives, sometimes called "mountain men" 山人 who were content to lead lives of pleasure-seeking in the safe, shady precincts of private gardens, and the Donglin partisans, who sought to keep engaged in political life to ameliorate the excesses of the age and the corruption of the court.[115] Given this background and the fact that Chen was not reclusive by any means, it is hard to escape the conclusion that the meetings of the Twelve Masters of the Southern Garden Poetry Society had to have had a political coloration to some degree.

Now back to contemporary times. While serving as a Hanlin compiler, Chen had publicly opposed Wei Zhongxian 魏忠賢 (1568–1627), the corrupt eunuch who was the power behind the throne. And Chen's father, Chen Xichang 陳熙昌 (*zi* Dangshi 當時, *hao* Guo'an 果庵, 1616 *jinshi*), had boldly submitted a searing memorial detailing Wei's crimes;[116] as a result both Chen and his father were dismissed from office in 1625. (Chen was recalled in 1631 after Wei fell from power in 1627). Wei had accused him of having been supported by the Donglin party as he worked to supervise the provincial exams in Zhejiang in 1624.[117] Whatever connection the elder Chen had with the Donglin party, it is probable that he had some affiliation, even if unofficially, with the Fushe, the "Restoration Society." This was a group that had been linked with the Donglin party and had as its original aim to provide a literary outlet and support system for young scholars who were preparing for the exams. It soon transcended these admirable parameters and grew to be a national network of allied groups active in political affairs.[118] A list of membership, the *Fushe xingshi lu* 復社姓氏錄, does not contain Chen Xichang's name, but it does include the names of Chen's son Shangyong 上庸, Shangyong's step-brother Zizhuang, and two other members of the Southern Garden, Li Suiqiu and Ou Biyuan.[119] Chen Zizhuang probably participated in local branch meetings in Guangzhou, almost certainly under the sponsorship of the Southern Garden club. The following passage from Chen's biography is better understood with this background: "...Twelve persons restored the old Southern Garden society and were known during the age as the Twelve Masters of the Southern Garden. After this, notable figures from Jiangxi, Zhejiang, Hubei, Hunan, and Fujian all joined the society."[120] And Chen Zizhuang mentioned that in the Southern Garden, besides the chanting of poetry, worldly events had been traditionally discussed.[121] This is entirely in keeping with Naquin and Rawski's evaluation of the function of poetry clubs during eighteenth-century Qing, one hundred years after this iteration of the Southern Garden: "Poetry clubs provided occasions for drinking and conviviality among friends, but, because they were also one of the few acceptable informal associations among the elite, they also provided networks for more serious endeavors—preparation for exams, literary and scholarly discussion, or simply social and political advancement."[122] This type of literary gathering would then provide the same sort of low-key outlet for political expression as did the French literary salons for pre-revolutionary aristocrats, as detailed in a recent work by Steven Kale.[123] Obviously, a local Cantonese poetry society would seem more attractive to famous literati from around the southern provinces of China if it had more than casual local literary connections and facilitated broad political, as well as narrow cultural, exchange. And Benjamin Elman reminds us that "numerous groups of scholars and Ming loyalists in the Yangtze delta continued to meet under the guise of poetry societies that sprang up in the early Ch'ing."[124]

The same could be said for Guangzhou of the period. Once Chen expressed his distaste in verse for such political parties, even those with literary activity as part of their agendas:

……	……
鉤黨舉神名	Forming political parties, they promote their own fame;[125]
招搖學術偽	Swaggering and bragging—their scholarship is all fake.

倡和一至今 They rally round each other even up to the present:
文網密窮治 The net they weave by words is tight with no slack.[126]

Obviously, the political context of the times must be considered when we ponder the chief reasons for the reconvening of the Southern Garden by Chen Zizhuang and his band during the late Ming. Surely in the beginning the prospect of becoming "left-over" poet-citizens of the Ming, and later on the very real fact of having assumed this delicate status, were strong motivations for socializing together; hanging on to a shared but threatened cultural tradition was excuse enough. Perhaps a parallel case from contemporary Yangzhou can be adduced to shed some light on the event from the dual aspects of literati culture and social memory. Recall that the famous Ying garden of Zheng Yuanxun in Yangzhou had been the scene of Li Suiqiu's victory in a poetry competition organized in 1640. In her study of how culture was reconstituted and transmitted in Yangzhou, Tobie Meyer-Fong posits that, after it was burned by the Manchus, this garden became "emblematic of the cultural world that had become lost."[127] It is very plausible to regard the Southern Garden as being similarly "emblematic" of the cultural world of the Guangdong of better days to Chen Zizhuang and his confederates. Reviving and reconstituting a "cultural emblem" during the troubled times of the late Ming/early Qing transition would provide an anchor in the midst of change. It thus became a powerful magnet to rally around, culturally speaking. This is supported from another angle, also suggested by Tobie Meyer-Fong: "Visiting famous sites," in this case the historical site of the original Southern Garden, "allowed the literati to position themselves in settings in which great men of the past had once stood, and thus to celebrate the values represented by those great men."[128] Identifying with the early cultural worthies of Sun and the Five Former Masters, as well as the Five Later Masters, then, was plausibly an equally powerful impulse for reconstituting a poetry society, the same social entity that had graced the very site.

After the final pacification of Guangdong by the Manchus, only four out of the original twelve masters remained alive: Ou Zhuyu, Chen Zisheng, Ou Huainian, and Huang Jiheng. After a long period of chanting poetry and sobbing out his sorrow, Ou Zhuyu set down his thoughts about his fallen colleagues from the garden in the form of eight poems together with a preface, the "Poems Recalling Eight Masters of the Southern Garden" 憶南園八子詩, and sent a copy to each of the three other surviving members.[129] Ou revealed that the purpose of these eight poems was "for promoting their probity, righteousness, and the beauty of their poetic elegance. I did this long chanting in lieu of crying. I post them to you three masters and urge you to match their rhymes" 用揚節義騷雅之美。長歌當哭。 寄三子屬和焉.[130]

Tobie Meyer-Fong notes that matching rhymes is a form of gift exchange among elites. Her full quotation might as well be describing the very anthology that was produced in the Southern Garden to congratulate Li Suiqiu on his victory, the *Nanyuan huaxin shi*: "Composing matched rhyme poems on social occasions functioned as a form of gift exchange, serving to reinforce relationships, which were then rendered public and tangible through the publication and circulation of small anthologies complete with commentary by other well-known friends and associates."[131] But Ou Zhuyu composing verses for his comrades to match was not a normal occasion. Nor was his insistence that his friends compose their own poems in accordance with his original rhyme scheme just an attempt at catharsis through identifying poetically with their lost comrades. Such poetic identification worked just as often diachronically as synchronically, when contemporary poets rhymed with notable poets of the dim past. Instead of emotional venting, such verse matching served more to align the contemporary poet in a cultural continuum; the memory of both the former poet so honored as well as his particular verses were once again renewed. And a not insignificant side benefit for the contemporary poet was surely to be able to bask in the reflected light of the original poet.

Examples of this practice by historical Cantonese poets are presented next. He Feng 何絳, an associate of both Qu Dajun and Chen Gongyin, composed a set of ten poems to match rhymes with an old work of Sun Fen called "Collecting Old Lines About Zhaoyun" 朝雲集古, a pastiche of quotes from ancient poems on the theme of "Clouds in the Morning." This was the name of Su Dongpo's favorite female companion Wang Zhaoyun 王朝雲. She died at age 33 when Su was living in exile in Huizhou, northeast of the Pearl River Delta.[132] He Feng felt it necessary to add a disclaimer in a postface; he admitted that his attempt was not up to the verbal beauty of the original, but still he felt that he deserved some credit for being the first poet to hazard such an attempt over the previous few centuries![133] This practice of matching rhymes with bygone poets was too widespread to require much documentation here, but I might add that it continued well into Republican times.[134] From personal experience, I can attest to its occasional occurrence today. Furthermore, let us recall that Sun Fen, in the attempt to align himself to another cultural tradition, had matched rhymes with Tao Qian's famous work "Lyrics on Returning" 歸去來辭 and had produced a small compilation entitled "Collection of Rhymes Matching Tao," as mentioned in Chapter Two. Li Minbiao had also matched rhymes with Tao Qian, harmonizing with Tao's set of twenty poems on drinking wine.[135] In the case of the "Poems Recalling Eight Masters of the Southern Garden," however, Ou implored his colleagues to match his rhymes as an invitation to work with him to ensure that their fallen comrades would be remembered both as martyred patriots as well as poets, and thus take their rightful place in the local literati cultural tradition.

Although revealing no inside information concerning the motivation for meeting as a poetry society and little about its operational methods, these eight offerings nevertheless contain numerous memorable lines. For instance, Poem Seven, dedicated to Ou Biyuan, praises Ou for having "Made connections with the arena of quills and ink,/Inviting the cranes to fly high to the clouds" 結交翰墨場,/邀鶴雲高飛. This poem concludes with a description of one physical feature of the garden: "I pour a cup of wine in the old park in the woods,/Where a single stretch of water leads to a pond" 斟酌舊林圃/一水引池塘. Poem Five, dedicated to Huang Jiheng, winds down with the following couplet: "He returned from the east to his literature and wine association,/His poems drew aid from the streams and hills" 東歸文酒會,/詩得江山助. Poem Eight about Seng Tong'an observes that "Invoking the bond of the White Lotus Society founded by Master Yuan,/We match rhymes in the south of the City of Genies" 遠公蓮社約,/唱和仙城南.[136]

One poem deserves translation in full. This is Poem Six, dedicated to Xu Fen:

彬彬建安彥	Among the flourishing talents of the Jian'an era,[137]
偉長與等倫	You would be on a par with Xu Gan.[138]
素無仕宦情	You never harbored ambition for office,
疾疫永離羣	But detested it as the plague, forever keeping separate from the crowd.
君自負才藝	You were bestowed with many talents,
蘭藻蘊氤氳	The orchid-like beauty of your writings encapsulated vigor and vitality.
干時時不預	You wanted to engage the times but the times were unfavorable,
絕俗俗隨粉	So you cut off the vulgar for the vulgar followed the

	beauties.
園池小偃仰	At the side of the garden pond you would rest,
靜觀海島均	Quietly observing the sea and islands becoming an equally proportioned mix.
逸爵豈亡酒	You did not touch the jar not because you had no wine,
晨興常鬻文	Only that getting up in the morning you often had to sell your compositions.
石室蒼梧勝	Your stone chamber in Cangwu surpassed any others,[139]
東西游路分	Yet roads for roaming to the east and to the west are separate.
説詩尚中律	As for poetry you emphasized formal rules,
解頤尊所聞	But, cracking a smile, you entertained with light stories.
杳杳尋遠山	You vanished in silence, seeking distant mountains,
悠悠散暮雲	And left in vastness, scattering like evening clouds.
君沒廣未陷	You passed away before Guangdong fell,
却色見兵氛	But it had already been tinted with a military haze.

Poem One, dedicated to Chen Zizhuang the Master of the Grove of Lyricists 詞林師, ends with sentiments that appropriately honor each poet-martyr of the Later Invigoration of the Southern Garden:

……	……
花月無孤影	No solitary shadows of flowers appear in the moonlight,
文酒必先鳴	When meeting for literature or wine, he always led off.
剛風餘涕淚	The steely wind is gone, leaving only lamenting tears behind—
三忠濯厥靈	The Three Loyal Ones cleansed their souls.[140]

Chapter Six

The Southern Garden During the Late Qing

You can still feel the community pack
This place; it's like going into a turfstack,
A core of old dark walled up with stone
A yard thick. When you're in it alone
You might have dropped, a reduced creature
To the heart of the globe. No worshipper
Would leap up to his God off this floor.

Founded there like heroes in a barrow
They sought themselves in the eye of their King
Under the black weight of their own breathing.
And how he smiled on them as out they came,
The sea a censor, and the grass a flame.

—Seamus Heaney, "In Gallarus Oratory"

The memory of the Southern Garden Poetry Society persisted throughout the Qing dynasty, inspiring an occasional poem from local literati. This memory lingered despite the conflagration of the original buildings on the site during the difficult transition from the Ming to the Qing and the subsequent desolation of the spot. Among those affected by this historical memory was Liu Xinlie 劉信烈 (*jinshi* 1699) from Xiangshan; he composed a panegyric at the Southern Garden when a group of poets met there for a quiet retreat, after which they visited an adjacent Buddhist site. When Liu mentions practicing Chan meditation in a secluded corner of the garden, this seems to be the first poem on the Southern Garden to touch on any Buddhist elements.[1] Another local poet to versify on the Southern Garden was Xian Yingyuan 冼應元 (fl. 1795) from Nanhai, otherwise unknown. His *lüshi* entitled "Veranda for Screening the Wind" is preserved by Qu Xiangbang in his *Guangdong shihua*; Qu's comment on this verse is that "Those who discuss the Southern Garden have to be familiar with this poem."[2] It does not appear to be particularly noteworthy, but one memorable couplet stresses the great personalities around whom the original society and its Later Invigoration revolved: "The former badge holders bowed their heads before Sun Xi'an,/Mostly the Later Invigoration relied on the disciples of Chen Zizhuang" 前徽首下西庵拜，後勁多依禮部門.[3]

A visitor from Jiangsu provides an outside perspective on the course of poetic elegance in Guangdong. Pan Lei 潘耒 (1646–1708) graciously accepted the poetic pedigree that started with Sun Fen of the Five Former Masters and ran through Ou Daren and Liang Shixing of the Five Later Masters. But for the Qing of the early seventeenth century, he paired Li Suiqiu with Deng Yunxiao, who appeared above in connection with Deng's founding of the Phoenix Terrace Poetry Society:

Pan Lei, "Miscellaneous Chants on the City of Rams" 羊城雜詠[4]

南園詩社明初盛	The Southern Garden Poetry Society flourished at the beginning of the Ming,
典籍才華最初群	Sun Fen's talent stood out the most from the crowd.
中葉歐梁推秀婉	During mid-dynasty, Ou and Liang promoted delicate gracefulness,
末年黎鄧擅清芬	At the end, Li and Deng monopolized poetic purity and fragrance.
地偏未染諸家病	Being remote, it escaped infection by other schools' failings,
風景堪張一旅旗	With its lovely sites, it could spread one brigade's banner.[5]
韶石淒清珠海濶	The Shao Stones are deserted, the Pearl River and sea broad,
湘靈雅調至今聞	Yet elegant tunes of the Xiang spirit are still heard even today.[6]

A younger contemporary, He Mengyao 何夢瑤 (*zi* Zanzhou 贊周, 1693–1763), mentioned getting drunk with a friend in the same Veranda for Screening the Wind on his way back from a visit to Yuexiu Hill.[7] A later poem about the veranda by Han Hai 韓海 (*zi* Weiwu 緯五, 1677–1736), from Panyu, indicates no hint of sociality of any kind.[8] But Tan Xiang 譚湘 (early 18th century), a poet from Shunde, composed a piece entitled "In Late Spring Convening an Elegant Gathering to Discuss the Matter of Reconvening the Poetry Society" 暮春雅集議修社事, because, as the first line reads, "The airs and elegance of the Southern Garden have long decayed" 南園風雅久凋零. The poem concludes very optimistically: "Anciently or at present, there has never been a better place for versifying and drinking,/Let us sit amid the flowers and chant, drunk like at Lanting" 今古不殊文酒地，坐花吟醉擬蘭亭.[9] There is no hint in recorded history whether the discussion ever amounted to anything.

Chen Dalu 陳大璐 (*gongsheng* 1760) recalled the Southern Garden as both an ideal place for poetry as well as the site of a Shrine to the Sires of the Southern Garden 南園公祠. His poem starts in the garden and then meanders to the shrine as it draws a moral from the transience of life: "Acolytes in the Southern Garden celebrate in the fragrant dawn,/Our pleasure is most genuine with the fraternity among the branches[10]/....May we enjoy a moment of glory until dawn,/With time so long, why should we lodge life's evidence in this edifice?" 南園載酒慶芳晨，棣萼枝頭樂最真。。。。願得須臾光徹旦，漫漫何假宇生陳.[11]

Ye You 葉酉,[12] a onetime associate of Yuan Mei 袁枚 (1716–1798), borrowed the accomplishments of the Five Former Masters to praise the literary talent of a local painter and calligraphist with a national reputation, Li Jian 黎簡 (*hao* Erqiao 二樵, 1747–1799):

"Impressions on Reading Li Erqiao's 'Poetic Compilation from the Hall of Five-Hundred and Four Peaks,' Copied and Sent Off"
讀黎二樵五百四峯堂詩鈔書以寄之[13]

南園盛風雅	The Southern Garden was full of style and elegance,
藉甚五先生	Great was the renown of the Five Masters.
五子後來秀	You bloomed after the Five,
能為正始聲	And are able to write in the style of the "Orthodox Beginning."[14]
詩篇愁漫與	You toss off poems effortlessly in your melancholy,
心跡笑雙清	The sentiments of your heart and laugh are both pure.
見說樵山好	I hear that Mt. Qiao is fine–[15]
相期採藥行	Let us set a time to collect herbs.

Li Jian is worth meeting, if not entirely from the perspective of the Southern Garden, then at least from the angle of the Southern Muse. (A minor connection to the Southern Garden will be noted later). He was born in Nanning 南寧 to a family from Shunde engaged in business in Guangxi. He loved to roam by himself among the local minorities; later biographers credit his skill in painting misty landscapes to his extensive experience out in that tropical clime. By the age of nine he was skilled in composing poems and writing essays. He moved to Guangzhou at 15 and devoted himself to his studies. By age 29 he was living with his wife in the western part of Guangzhou. Despite close involvement with prominent local literati, especially the three poets Zhang Jinfang 張錦芳, Huang Danshu 黃丹書, and Lü Jian 呂堅, Li was uncomfortable with the ceaseless requests for specimens of his poetry, calligraphy, or paintings from the constant stream of admirers. He ignored them as best he could, despite being offered huge sums of money. This earned him the nickname of "Crazy Little Jian" 小子狂簡, which he carved on a seal and used happily. His reputation for eccentricity was reinforced when he refused to see Yuan Mei on the latter's trip to Guangzhou in 1780, going so far as to send him long letters hotly berating him. He never did leave the Lingnan area, but his reputation for brilliance in three major artistic endeavors spread throughout literati circles in China, earning him the sobriquet of the Past Master in Poetry, Calligraphy, and Painting 詩書畫三絕. He is judged by Wu Daorong (one of the participants in the Later Southern Garden Poetry Society to be introduced presently) as the greatest poet in Guangzhou since the Three Masters of Lingnan.[16] His poems were published as *Wubaisifengtang shichao* in 25 *juan* in 1796. The name derived from his love of roaming among the Luofu and Xiqiao mountains, which collectively numbered 504 peaks. This love also led to his *hao* of Erqiao, or "Two Qiaos," since an alternate name of Luofu was "Eastern Qiao," an apt paring with Xiqiao or "Western Qiao."[17]

Like Ye You, local officials also remained cognizant of their heritage. For instance, in 1687 the Veranda for Screening the Wind was renovated by Peng Xiang 彭襄, the country magistrate of Panyu, and the grounds were expanded.[18]

Zhang Weiping as Owner-Caretaker

Much more attention to the Southern Garden surfaces in the nineteenth century with Zhang Weiping 張維屏 (*hao* Nanshan 南山, 1780–1859). Zhang was one of the last Cantonese poets to flourish in Guangdong before conflict with the west and internal rebellion heightened the latent elements of philosophical introspection and brooding pessimism directed towards social and national decline. Like the Cantonese poets of the early Qing, he was considered a "patriotic poet," but his patriotism was devoted to halting the decay in public spiritedness and the national strength of the Qing dynasty, not to restoring the Ming. One level of his patriotism was manifested in his intimate association with such poets, politicians, and thinkers of national repute as Gong Zizhen 龔自珍 (1792–1841), Lin Zexu 林則徐 (1785–1850), and Wei Yuan 魏源 (1794–1856).[19] And while in Beijing he socialized with the members of the Xuannan Poetry Society without apparently being a formal member himself.[20]

As a poet in the Cantonese tradition, Zhang Weiping remained part of the mainstream; however, by virtue of his verbal virtuosity and penetrating vision, he treated time-honored themes from fresh viewpoints, infusing them with new linguistic vigor. But he was much more than a local hero. He had made a splash in the Beijing literary scene in 1807, and poets such as Gong Zizhen highly valued his verse. He also enjoyed a national reputation as a literary critic with the publication of a voluminous work of criticism and biography, the still important *Guochao shiren zhenglüe* 國朝詩人徵略 in 117 *juan*.

Zhang was a prolific poet; his collected works, *Zhang Nanshan quanji* 張南山全集 reach 52 *ce*.[21] The social aspect of his life as a local literatus was manifested by his membership in the Spring of Clouds Poetry Society 雲泉詩社, which met on Mt. White Cloud. He was also further identified with Cantonese poetics as one of the Three Masters of Eastern Yue 粵東三子. The other two masters were likewise members of the Spring of Clouds club, Tan Jingzhao 譚敬昭 (*zi* Zijin 子晉, *hao* Xuanlou 選樓, 1773–1830) and Huang Peifang 黄培芳 (*zi* Zishi 子實, *hao* Xiangshi 香石, Yueyue shanren 粵嶽山人, 1779–1859).[22] Stephen Miles points out that it was an outsider, Weng Fanggang 翁方剛 (1733–1818), who "enhanced" the reputation of this trio by composing a preface to their anthology, the *Yuedong sanzi* 粵東三子.[23] Such a sanction from a non-Cantonese official with a national name not only served to validate their reputations on the local level but also helped to introduce them to a wider, trans-local audience.

Huang Peifang also participated in a group of seven poets called the Seven Masters of the Spring of Clouds 雲泉七子. This set included the original Three Masters of Eastern Yue plus Lin Botong 林伯桐, Huang Qiaosong 黃喬松, Duan Peilan 段佩蘭, and Kong Jixun 孔繼勛. They built a hostel on Mt. White Cloud in 1812, called the Spring of Clouds Mountain Lodge 雲泉山館.[24]

Due to his ancestry, Huang Peifang provides an interesting angle on the process of transmitting social memory in Guangzhou.[25] He was an eighth-generation grandson of Huang Zuo, the mid-Ming teacher of most of the Five Later Masters of the Southern Garden. The need to identify with the cultural continuity that flowed through his ancestral line ran strong in Peifang's psychological makeup. This conclusion is warranted for several reasons. First, he located his Sea Ridge Library 嶺海樓 on the original site of his ancestor's own famous library, the Tower of Precious Books 寶書樓. Of course, the preservation of his ancestor's shrine on the site of the original library was itself a powerful stimulant to remind him of his heritage. Nevertheless, he made a conscious choice to further honor it by locating his own library within this ancestral shrine. The shrine was named for Huang Zuo's posthumous title that had been conferred in 1571, the Shrine to Sire Huang Wenyu 黃文裕公祠.[26] The Cantonese bibliophile Xu Xinfu, who composed a lengthy set of poems as tribute to local book collectors, includes one poem on Huang's library. It indicates that Xu himself was just as cognizant of Huang's exalted ancestry. Note that the name Taiquan 泰泉 that starts off the poem was a *hao* of Huang Zuo, and that "Meditation (i.e. concentration, Sanskrit *samādhi*) on Tang Worthies" 唐賢三昧 was the name of Huang Peifang's poetic anthology:

"Huang Peifang's Sea Ridge Library" 黃培芳嶺海樓[27]

泰泉餘韻有詩孫	Among the residual rhymes of Taiquan is his poetic descendant,
嶺海樓頭世德存	The morality of generations is preserved at the Sea Ridge Library.
參透唐賢三昧訣	Thoroughly peruse the secrets of the *Tangxian samādhi Anthology*—[28]
堂堂大雅振南園	His grand poems of "Great Elegantiae" quality reinvigorate the Southern Garden.

A second reason that Huang Peifang seemed particularly concerned with his bloodlines is demonstrated by the careful way he went about selecting books for his library: he specialized in collecting books by Huang Zuo, by other ancestors, and his own works. He was particularly intrigued by Huang Zuo, as he also composed three *juan* of comments and criticism on his poetry.[29] Third, he also collected works by other, non-related Cantonese authors: he edited an anthology called *A Selection of Three Hundred Poems from Guangdong* 廣東三百首詩選.[30] One exception to the rule of collecting only the Cantonese label proved that he was also a die-hard connoisseur of books: he would also include books that were "stamped with beautiful or exquisite seals."[31] For Huang, then, as a collector of works by Cantonese authors as well as books by himself and his own ancestral line, shared Cantonese ethnicity—as he perceived it—seems to be an important adjunct to shared cultural heritage.

The mention of the Southern Garden in the context of this poem is an odd twist, for it cannot have been referencing any current reconstitution of the poetry club. We may be safe in concluding, therefore, that the Southern Garden symbolized poetic excellence in Guangzhou—the product of historical garden sociality—rather than contemporary socializing itself. This same figurative use of language is found in the frequent use in Cantonese poetics of the name of a section of the *Book of Poetry*, the "Great Elegantiae" 大雅, or its derived use as "poetic elegance" 風雅, metonymy for elegant yet orthodox poetry in general.

One exchange of verses between Zhang Weiping and Huang Peifang centers on the theme of celebrating the richness of Cantonese history; they use the style known as *huaigu* 懷古, or "longing for the past." Both poems are of the *ci* or "lyric" variety, both written to the tune of "Manjiang hong" 滿江紅.[32]

Huang Peifang, "Longing for the Past in Yuedong" 粵東懷古[33]

百粵豪雄	Heroic champions of the Hundred Clans of Yue[34]
人已往撫今追昔	Are all long gone—I now treat the present from the perspective of the past.
憑眺覽九州南盡	Gazing out, I see that the Nine Isles of China proper end in this southern extremity,
衹餘陳跡	But all that remains culturally are traces in the dust:
楊僕樓船寒漲沒	Towered ships of Yang Pu are now inundated by cold tides,[35]
伏波銅柱蒼苔積	Brass columns erected by the Subduing Wave General are buried in moss.
抗古懷想像霸圖空	Confronting the past, my ambitions are vain, like hegemonic schemes,
西風急	But the western wind is urgent as always.
思割據	Longing to partition off an independent regime,
臣陀策	Was the plan of vassal Zhao Tuo.
誇侈靡	Excessively luxuriant
降王宅	Was the mansion of that surrendered king.[36]
悵前朝如夢	While lamenting over former dynasties, now nothing but dreams,

斜陽將夕	The slanting sunlight is about to set.
白草呼鑾亂馳道冷	Withered grass on Calling Bells Way is overgrown, royal roadway deserted.[37]
紅雲宴荔荒煙寂	Red Cloud Banquet dined on lichees, but now lies desolate in the bleak mists.[38]
試登臨但見玉山青	I attempt a sightseeing climb, but only see verdure of jade hills
珠江碧	And the blue of the Pearl River.

Zhang responded with his own version:

Zhang Weiping, "Longing for the Past at the City of Rams" 羊城懷古[39]

此五羊城	This city of Five Rams—
閱多少興亡陳跡	How many dusty traces of rises and falls has it witnessed?
想當初陶唐申命	I ponder the age when Tao Tang first extended the mandate,[40]
南交新宅	And Nanjiao was newly settled.[41]
穀穗種遺周代土	Seeds of grain were planted in residual earth from the Zhou era,
菖蒲香剩堯時石	Fragrance of calamus still lingered on stones from the time of Yao.
看波濤浴出一輪紅	Visible was a red ring bathed by breakers—
扶桑日	The sun from Fusang.[42]
臣陀老	Tuo the vassal grew old,
朝臺寂	Deserted, the "Terrace of Reverencing."[43]
楊僕討	Yang Pu set out in punishment,
樓船入	Towered ships entered the waters.
喜陸郎談笑	They delighted Squire Lu with chatting and laughing,[44]
江山生色	Endowing the rivers and hills with even more vibrancy.
老佛動盤西法立	An old Buddha removed the tribute trays after proclaiming the Law of the West,[45]
降王執梃南強息	The surrendered king brandished his staff and the southern stronghold was pacified.[46]
到於今何物尚依然	Up to the present, what still remains the same as old?
春山碧	Only the green of hills in the spring.

In addition to this evocative *ci* poem, Zhang Weiping wrote much additional poetry on Guangzhou, as much as on any other theme; in fact, he even dedicated entire anthologies to depicting the delights of his private gardens in Guangzhou. He also seemed to have traveled the length and breadth of Guangdong and recorded his impressions in verse. The last years of his life were spent on and off in south-central Guangzhou on the ancient site of the original Southern Garden, apparently his natal site.

The preface to one poem introduces the setting of this storied place:

> My new dwelling at Clear Canal is several hundred paces to the east of my old dwelling;[47] behind is the Quarter of the Assembled Worthies.[48] It seems that the term "Assembled Worthies" refers to the Five Former and Later Masters of the Southern Garden. I hasten to make the following single verse.

> 清濠新居在舊居之東數百步，後有聚賢坊。曰聚賢者，蓋謂南園前後五先生也，率賦一詩:

大有濠梁意	Greatly inspired by the bridge over the canal ditch—
城濠近屋垣	The canal at the city-wall approaches the wall of my house—
前賢餘韻在	Residual rhymes of the previous worthies still remain,
咫尺是南園	An inch and a foot away—there was the Southern Garden.[49]

Other poems concentrate less on the setting than on drawing moral lessons and recounting the past glories of the storied poetry association. But Zhang always seemed to return to his nostalgic evocation of the historical presences that, to his mind, still inhabited the site of his dwelling:

"Poem on the Southern Garden" 南園詩[50]

東園住久住南園	After living long in the Eastern Garden, I now live in the Southern Garden,
咫尺臨街即里門	An inch and a foot away, hard by the street, the hamlet gate.
客館進城仍近水	A guest hostel at the city entrance is close to the water,
人家如畫亦如村	Households of people like paintings, like real villages.
齋前梵字禪心淨	Buddhist writing in front of the hermitage, zen-like minds are pure,
屋後濠梁樂意存	On the canal bridge behind the house, feelings of delight remain:
勸我高吟兼尚友	Inspiring lofty verses and to hold fast to

	esteemed friends,
隔墻便是抗風軒	For only a wall away was the Veranda for Screening the Wind.

The guest hostel was undoubtedly on the site of the former shrine to Wen Tianxiang and other Song-period patriots. The shrine had once housed visiting bureaucrats, but during the late Qing, Buddhist monks lived, studied, and meditated there and in nearby hostels, thus accounting for the Buddhist imagery in Zhang's poems. The pond and pavilion there provided an unsurpassed haven of seclusion for these individual activities of study and meditation. It was also a popular spot for gentry to enjoy a quiet rest while sightseeing.[51]

Close at hand was another Buddhist building, the Hermitage of Benevolent Salvation 慈度菴. It is noteworthy for our discussion, and not only because it was directly connected with the Southern Garden via a gracefully winding waterway. During the Qianlong era Li Jian, the nationally famous painter and calligrapher introduced above, dwelled there; he hosted poetry and painting parties for his friends in his quarters, calling them the Southern Garden Resort 南園別墅.[52]

Li Jian's second son, Yanzu 延祖 (*zi* Fanghui 方回), left an interesting verse describing the sad prospect of his father's ruined hostel. Called "Poem on the Ancient Site of the Southern Garden" 南園故址詩, the first couplet is a reminder of the importance of being physically present at an historical site to effectively identify with the past: "The ancient shrine is still by the eastern corner as of old,/As soon as I read the broken stele, I became inspired" 古祠仍舊在東隅，一讀殘碑覺起予.[53]

The famous veranda, whether whole or ruined, still lived on in the verse of Zhang Weiping's contemporary Huang Dejun 黃德峻 from Gaoyao 高要 (*zi* Jingsong 景崧, *hao* Qinshan 琴山, *jinshi* 1822), who left a dedicatory lyric to the tune "Baiziling" 百字令. In this *ci*, Huang shows himself to be well-informed on the literary tradition associated with the veranda, and he notices the same Buddhist elements in the vicinity that were apparent to Zhang Weiping:

"The Veranda for Screening the Wind" 抗風軒[54]

前賢壇坫	Where previous worthies convened their alliances,
認城勵一帶	Known along the entire stretch of one city hollow.
歸然古屋	Solitary, an ancient edifice,

溯自月泉初結社	Deriving from when the Moon Springs first formed a society.
朋酒番番徵逐	"Comrades in drinking" were passed around with stately dignity:[55]
龍鼎同扛	Needing two to tote these dragon-decorated tripods.
驪珠互索	Black pearls were strung together,[56]
吟鉢聲相促	Sounds of versifying and draining cups urged each other on.
墨花飛處	A place where flowers of ink flew,
一時佳句盈牘	At one time fine verses filled the scrolls.
至今菜錄鋪池	Nowadays floral greenery overspreads the pond,
棉紅堆徑	Reds of brocade pile up on the paths—
景尚供游目	The scene is still worthy of a visit,
大雅扶輪誰繼起	But who will rise up to continue the style of the Great Elegantiae?
漫把五懷詩續	Leisurely I take up the "Five Poems of Remembrance" and add to them,
窗網蛛絲	In calligraphy like spider's silk on a curtain,
壁蜒蝸篆	Or the seal script of snail's spittle on the wall.
時有鄰僧宿	Sometimes a cleric lodges overnight as my neighbor,
瓣香心熱	He burns incense in their honor with passionate intent,
十年人已私淑	But for ten years people have already "privately cultivated themselves."[57]

Note that Huang Dejun recalls the Southern Garden in its role of social setting and depicts it during the heyday when the Five Former Masters would first drink, then chant poetry, and ultimately drink again. He even mentions the famous poetic set by Ou Daren, the "Five Poems of Remembrance." In contrast to this, Zhang Weiping merely mentions the general historical significance of the site, choosing not to dwell on the many refined activities that had occurred there. Perhaps he chose to regard the Southern Garden as he regarded his new home on the site—much like Li De did—as the scene of quiet, private introspection. At any rate, neither Zhang nor the next few poets to notice this place attempted to revive the social ritual of a formal poetry society at the celebrated Southern Garden.

Scholars at the Sea of Learning on the Southern Garden

In 1820, the Sea of Learning Academy (Xuehai tang 學海堂) was established by Ruan Yuan 阮元 (1764–1849). At the time he was based in Guangzhou as the governor-general of Guangdong and Guangxi from 1817 to 1826. As a temporary measure, a plaque with the name Sea of Learning was suspended at the Wenyuan Academy 文瀾書院 in the western part of Guangzhou at Xiguan 西關; examination papers and poems were turned in to the faculty. Some allusions in poetry composed by members of the academy hint at an early relationship between the Southern Garden and the academy. This has led some to conclude that the Southern Garden was the original site of the academy. But most likely these allusions were inspired by unofficial outings to the site by academy members.[58]

The academy itself was built four years later on Yuexiu Hill where the great collection of classical commentaries, the *Huang Qing jingjie* 皇清經解—called originally *Explanations of the Classics from the Sea of Learning* 學海堂經解 — was compiled.[59] The permanent site was on the southern slope of the hill, presently occupied by the Municipal Second Middle School. There were three private academies 書院 in Guangzhou at that time, the Yangcheng 羊城, Yuehua 粵華, and Yuexiu 粵秀 academies.[60] But Sea of Learning was established to fill a specific need: to promote classical learning of the Han school persuasion. This explains the significance of the name, an allusion to He Xiu 何休 (129–182) of the Eastern Han dynasty, who was reputed to possess an "ocean of learning" 學海. It began holding classes in 1821 and operated continuously until it closed in 1903.

The establishment of the academy on Yuexiu Hill was prompted by Ruan's interest in the historical ties of this peak to both the kingdoms of Southern Yue and Southern Han; this is the reasoned conclusion of Stephen Miles.[61] Perhaps this same occupation with history prompted Ruan's consideration of the old site of the Southern Garden for constructing the Academy; alas, it turned out to be unsuitable.[62] Nevertheless, the cultural significance of the first site did not escape the directors of the Sea of Learning. Xu Rong 徐榮 (1792–1855) recalled the Southern Garden in the dedicatory verse composed when the academy moved to the new site in 1824: "The Green-jade Pavilion was high and out of sight,/Southward from the South Garden [linger] desolate weeds."[63] The Cantonese polymath Chen Li 陳澧 (*zi* Lanpu 蘭浦, 1810–1882), served as a teacher or "monitor" 學長 at the Sea of Learning for twenty years. He also noticed in verse a connection between the old garden and the academy, when he reported a meeting on the Double Ninth Festival 重陽 of some Southern Garden gallants at the Sea of Learning.[64] This *ci* suggests that a gathering of Southern Garden poets was active around Chen Li, a gathering only hinted at by history. Fellow monitor Wu Lanxiu 吳蘭修 (*zi* Shihua 石華, *juren* 1808), wrote an ambiguous phrase that could be read as supporting the Southern Garden site: "Long since have we departed the Southern Garden" 南園久別.[65] (Incidently, Zhang Weiping had also served as a monitor for a short while, commencing in 1829; his friend Huang Peifang started his term in 1832.)[66] Chen was the moving force behind renovating the Veranda for Screening the Wind once more and for composing a large placard with the characters "Nanyuan" painted on it. Stone tablets were also engraved and placed next to the door posts. Chen and a certain friend Wang Fusheng 汪芙生 often spent their evenings under the moon versifying in the garden, an activity halfway between the solitary reveries of Li De and Sun Fen and the full-fledged socializing of the Five Former Masters as a formal club.[67]

The activity of moon gazing in the garden by Chen must have been indulged in frequently enough to become widely known, for it was recalled in verse by Huang Shaochang 黃紹昌 (*zi* Yichuan 懿傳), a late 19th century *juren* who had served as a monitor at the Sea of Learning and as an editor at the educational institute attached to the Guangya Publishing House 廣雅文學館, another site associated with the Southern Garden:

"Master Chen Lanpu Visits the Southern Garden to Gaze at the Moon"
陳蘭甫先生過南園看月[68]

明月上池亭	The bright moon ascends beyond pond-side kiosk,
竹樹散清影	Bamboo trees scatter pure reflections.
幽人不能寐	The one in seclusion, unable to sleep,
惜此良夜景	Cherishes the vista of this fine evening.
高言共談塵	With lofty words he discusses this dusty realm,
小飲吸苦茗	And drinks a bit, sipping a bitter brew.
層陰盪孤光	Different strata of shadows waver in the lonely light,
萬動攝一靜	All movement is absorbed into complete stillness.
螢火照不熱	The glow of fireflies shines without any heat,
鶴夢宿方冷	The dreams of cranes grow cold over night.[69]
荷花吹香來	Fragrance is wafted in from lotus flowers,
幽意更誰省	Who can intuit these hidden thoughts?

One of Ruan Yuan's chief aides in compiling the *Gazetteer of Guangdong* as well as the *Huang Qing jingjie* 皇清經解 was Jiang Fan 江藩 (1761–1831), the noted evidential research scholar from Yangzhou. An essay he wrote on the Southern Garden may be authoritative enough to rule out any lingering suspicions that the garden was the original site of the Sea of Learning. Entitled "Record of Repairing the Veranda for Screening the Wind" 重葺抗風軒記, it apparently was an effort at renovation previous to the one headed up by Chen Li. After narrating the history of the Southern Garden Poetry Society in its various incarnations up to Jiang's own time, he turns to his own experience in Guangzhou:

> I once filled a post in this region. Between my editorial duties I perused various records and found out that local residents now occupy the greater part of the old site. All that is left of it now is the single veranda Screening the Wind. Because of some contributions of funds for red paint to decorate it, this site where former worthies drank and sang will not again dare to decay and be obscured by spreading vegetation.
>
> 予承乏是邦，簿書之暇，循覽圖經，乃知舊址大半為居民隱占。今所存者，惟抗風一軒。因捐廉為丹艧塗塈之資，俾昔賢觴詠之地，不敢鞠為蔓草焉.[70]

It is hard to believe that Jiang, who was in residence in Guanghzou from 1818 until 1825 or 1826, precisely the period that the Xuehai tang was being planned and built, would not have mentioned the Southern Garden as the original site of the Sea of Learning had it been the case. A poem by a contemporary at the academy, student Chen Tong 陳同 (*zi* Zhenchang 鎮常, *jinshi* 1826) from Shunde, also describes the scene at the old garden; it is called "On a Spring Day Seeking out the Old Site of the Southern Garden" 春日訪南園故址. The only lines that verify an actual visit read: "Surprisingly, broken tiles and ruined walls appear in this way,/I come to visit the ancient site but the spring shade has changed./The ancient domicile lies vacant in the cold, no one visible" 斷瓦頹垣竟如此，我來訪古春陰變，故宅荒寒人不見.[71] The many allusions to the site of the old garden that appear in the poetry of the period, then, may be nothing more than casual, off-hand allusions to it as the source of poetic power in Guangzhou. In other words, apart from recording specific if low-key visits to the site, other references seemed to use the Southern Garden solely as emblem cited for its cultural authority.

At any rate, subsequent to the move to Yuexiu Hill, poetry composed by Xuehai tang members most frequently treated Southern Han themes when it concerned local history.[72] Chen Li, along with other Xuehai tang members, organized another literary club and named it after what was probably the most prominent local historical theme ever: the Yue Terrace Lyric Association 粵臺詞會. The club met monthly to compose *ci*, most often on local topics.[73]

Chen Li wrote a poignant tribute to the lost glories of Guangzhou, a *ci* to the tune of "On the Phoenix Terrace Remembering a Blowing Flute" 鳳凰臺上憶吹簫. The theme embodied in the subtitle, "Gazing from the Terrace of the King of Yue During Spring," was the one chosen for the first meeting of the Yue Terrace Lyric Society.[74] The first few lines could easily be describing a scene straight from the secluded precincts of the Southern Garden on a spring day, at least as envisioned earlier by Li De:

Chen Li, "Gazing from the Terrace of the King of Yue During Spring"
粵王臺春望[75]

芳樹蹄鴣	Fragrant trees, chirping pigeons—
野花團蝶	Squadrons of butterflies amid wild flowers.
嫩晴剛引吟笻	The clear weather now attracts me and my poet's walking stick.[76]
問故王台榭	Asking after the ancient king's terrace and pavilions—
依約樵蹤	Hazily discerned are footprints of woodcutters.
零落當年黃屋	Desolate and dreary was the Yellow Dwelling,[77]
都分蛋雨蠻風	All exposed to Boat People rain and Man barbarian winds.[78]
添惆悵	Increasing disconsolate
望陀城	I gaze out over the city of Zhao Tuo—
一片海氣冥蒙	Only a single stretch of oceanic atmosphere and dark haze.
青山向人似笑	Verdant hills seem to be laughing at people,
笑淘盡濤聲	But it fades out in the sound of billows.
誰是英雄	Who are the heroes?
只幾堆新壘	Only present are ranks of new ramparts.
鳥散雲空	Birds scatter and clouds disappear—
休說樓船下瀨	Stop mentioning towered ships descending the rapids.
傷心見斷鏃苔封	My heart grieves over broken arrowheads socked in by moss:
還依舊	Just as in the past,

攀枝亂開望點春紅	Myriad drops of red in the spring spread helter-skelter on branches.

The Southern Garden is directly mentioned in another *ci* by Chen Li: "For many years grown used to the sounds of separation,/It is a fine thing to return./Amid the mists and streamlets of the Southern Garden,/ Concluding a league with the gulls" 甚年年慣作別離聲，歸來好。南園煙水，更結鷗盟.[79]

Wu Lanxiu's composition on the theme of the Southern Garden follows:

"Inscribing a Painting by the Female Historian Liang Ruozhu, the Accordion 'Painting of an Hundred Butterflies'"
題梁若珠女史畫百蝶圖冊子

殘春如夢	Tattered spring is like a dream:
翦得生綃摹小鳳	Cut out like raw silk in a small phoenix pattern.
殘夢迷離	This tattered dream is hazy,
圍住東風不放歸	Surrounded by the east wind, I am not released to return.
南園別久	Long since departing the Southern Garden,
苦憶年年春草瘦	Bitter memories year after year, the grass thins in spring.
碧玉回廊	Cyan jade in winding corridors,
誰數花梢五十雙	Who has counted fifty pairs of flower tips?

Jin Xiling 金錫齡, a monitor at the Sea of Learning, took up residence at the Southern Garden for ten years. Under his encouragement, it again became the site of an occasional literary gathering, but nothing regularized came of it.[80] Later, two poets were singled out as the dedicatees of a compilation of verses published in 1874 under the title of "Transcribed Poems from Two Masters of the Ji and Southern Gardens" 寄南園二子詩鈔; I have been unable to ascertain just which two masters are at question.[81]

In 1887, the Southern Garden turned from poetry to printing as the Guangya Publishing House 廣雅書局 took up residence at the site, operating there until 1908.[82] It had been established by Zhang Zhidong 張之洞 (1837–1909), the governor-general of Guangdong and Guangxi, to provide teaching materials for local students, including those enrolled at the Guangya shuyuan, the academy he founded at the same time as the publishing house.[83] The set of 51 poems devoted to Cantonese bibliophiles by Xu Xinfu devotes one to the Ten Peaks Veranda on the grounds of the Guangya printing house complex:

"The Ten Peaks Veranda at Guangya Publishing Company" 廣雅書局十峯軒[84]

六堂輝映十峯軒	The radiance of Six Halls reflected by the Ten Peaks Veranda,
百宋千元豈易言	How can One Hundred Song and Thousand Yuan libraries be mentioned in the same breath?[85]
海水群飛亭榭改	While ocean waters spumed, the pavilions and galleries changed:
不堪老柳憶南園	Can't endure the sight of old willows reminding me of the Southern Garden.

When Zhang Zhidong founded the Guangya Publishing House, he renovated the Veranda for Screening the Wind and inscribed a pair of elegant scrolls to adorn its gate.[86] The first scroll reads: "Their poetry is like the Ten Talents of the Dali period" 詩如大歷十才子;[87] the corresponding line on the other scroll reads: "The garden is similar to the Fifth Bridge of the Great General" 園似將軍第五橋.[88] Zhang also dedicated the veranda as the "Shrine of the Ten Masters of the Southern Garden" and instituted regular sacrifices there.[89] But another flourish of the fading glory of Cantonese poetics was again in the field of socialized poetry.

The Later Southern Garden Poetry Society

The Southern Garden Poetry Society was formally reconvened for the last time in August, 1911, shortly before the revolution on October 10. Eight friends, including most prominently Liang Dingfen 梁鼎芬 (*zi* Jie'an 節庵, 1857–1919), Huang Jie 黃節 (*zi* Huiwen 晦聞, 1873–1935), and Wu Daorong 吳道鎔 (*zi* Yuchen 玉臣, *hao* Dan'an 澹庵, 1853–1936) formed this last iteration.[90] They called it the Later Southern Garden Poetry Society 後南園詩社 and met in the Veranda for Screening the Wind, which was freshly festooned with displays of calligraphy and painting. Wang Zongyan, author of *Guangdong wenwu congtan*, attended the society as a young lad and had some contact with Huang Jie throughout the rest of his life.[91] This time, the poetry society functioned in a variety of ways, covering all three of Huang Zhimin's categories of poetry societies.

The first task of the newly reconstituted Southern Garden Poetry Society was to sponsor a large-scale poetry competition. It is true that verses had been first exchanged between the leading lights that were not competition pieces, but they were composed on the date of the competition in honor of the occasion. One such verse by Huang Jie was sent to the moving force of the literary club, Liang Dingfen, and reiterates what surely must have been the emotional impulse of all who had venerated the original society by reconvening it over the ages:

"Presented to Mr. Liang Jie'an on the Reconvening of the Southern Garden Poetry Society"
南園詩社重開呈梁節菴先[92]

盛時臺笠卻難忘	In their heyday, gentlemen in *tai* leaf caps were unforgettable,[93]
一賦都人已足傷	Now a single intoning of "Capital Men" makes me grieve.[94]
高會及來隨老輩	Attending this lofty assemblage, following the older generation,
雅歌還得共斯堂	I sing elegant songs with you in this hall.[95]
興微國俗詩將廢	When state customs are in flux, poetry will decline,
俯仰前塵地亦蒼	Surveying the dusty affairs of the past, even the earth is grieved.[96]
獨使南園不寥落	If we can only insure the Southern Garden not turning desolate,
蒼天林木起朝陽	The morning sun will rise beyond tree tops against the grey sky.

Another verse written for this occasion was composed by Liao Jingzeng 廖景曾.[97] He must have been especially moved by meeting at the Southern Garden with the newly reconstituted poetry club, for he had studied at both the Sea of Learning and the Guangya Academy; hence, he was certainly very familiar with the many historical predecessors who had versified at the site:

"On Reconvening the Southern Garden Poetry Society, Presented to Jie'an"
南園詩社重開賦呈節菴[98]

神州壇坫衰微日	On this day, even while the alliance of our sacred territory is weakening,
嶺表猶聞雅頌音	Here in Guangdong are still heard sounds of Elegentia and Eulogia.
尚友抗懷千載遠	How they venerated friendships and maintained integrity has lasted a thousand ages,

驚心常凜四夷侵	But my heart grows cold with fear as the Four Barbarians invade.
陽春白雪誰能和	Who can harmonize with "White Snow" and "Warm Spring?"[99]
明月清風喜獨吟	Still delightful to chant alone in the clear wind and bright moon.
珍重昔賢雄直氣	Cherishing and honoring the valor of the former worthies:
三家餘韻未銷沉	The residual rhymes of the Three Masters still have not sunk into oblivion.

The last line contains the first actual connection between the early Qing Three Masters Qu Dajun, Chen Gongyin, and Liang Peilan and one of the iterations the Southern Garden Poetry Society. It is true that it only consisted of their appearance in a poem. Still, their potent image was borrowed for the undying loyalty they had expressed to the Ming dynasty. The negative images betokening rapid dynastic decline and foreign invasion symbolically link the waning days of the Qing with the same period of the late Ming.

Now to the poetry competition that was organized along the lines of the Moon Springs Chanting Society.[100] At least 120 participants submitted entries; Yao Yun 姚筠 and other poet-painters recorded the scene on canvas. Chen Huiqun 陳惠羣 recalled the recent history of the hoary site with his composition on the set theme of "Passing by the Sea of Learning Longing for Ruan Yuan, the Sire of Accomplished Learning" 過學海堂有懷阮文達公; he won first place.[101] Wang Cibo 王慈博 won the prize for a poem on the theme of "Evening Moon over the Pearl River" 珠江夜月.[102] A short compilation, called *Excerpted Lines from the Later Southern Garden Poetry Society, Illustrated* 後南園詩社摘句圖, resulted from this competition, edited by Liang Dingfen.[103]

The host of the event, Liang Dingfen, presented a poem to the large group of competitors:

"Composing a Poem on the Occasion of the Reconvention of the Southern Garden Poetry Society for the Hundred-Plus Participants"
南園詩社重開賦詩會者百數十人[104]

十子芳名尚可鐫	Honorable names of the Ten Masters can still be engraved,
三忠祠屋舊相連	Roof of the Shrine of the Three Loyalists is still intact.
儒生懷抱關天下	Those Confucians' aims encompassed all-

	under-heaven,
詩事銷沉過百年	But their poetic affairs have sunk into obscurity after these hundreds of years.
老柳疏疏人照水	Old willows sparse, men reflected on the water,
山亭隱隱竹成煙	Mountain kiosk indistinct, the bamboos turned to mist.
閒來風物當誰賦	Who should sing of the scenes since their times?
長憶陳黎一輩賢	Long shall we remember those worthies with Chen and Li.

In discussing the revival of the Southern Garden Poetry Society by Huang Jie, Liang Dingfen, and others, Huang's modern editor Liu Sifen insisted that there was no political motivation behind this revival.[105] However, this does not mean that no political tensions were present. For at least two of the members, Huang Jie and Liang Dingfen, were at opposite ends of the political spectrum. Here it would be worthwhile to briefly examine their biographies.

Liang Dingfen was born in Panyu. He earned his *jinshi* degree in 1880 and worked in the Hanlin as a junior compiler. Afterwards he became involved in Zhang Zhidong's educational reforms and presided over a succession of government academies in Guangdong, including becoming the first director of the Guangya Academy. He quit to spend a lengthy period of study on Mt. Xiqiao, then reentered the field of education by serving as Superintendent of the Two Lakes School 二湖學堂. He left education again for mainstream government service by working in the municipal administration of Wuchang; later in Hubei he was promoted to be a Surveillance Commissioner, then a Provincial Administrative Commissioner. He composed a memorial exposing the crimes of Yuan Shikai which brought him widespread notoriety and also forced his resignation out of fear for his personal safety. After the revolution, he served as a Pacification Commissioner. He maintained unswerving loyalty to the Qing house over the years; especially notable was his appointment as tutor to Pu Yi in 1911.[106] This loyalty is evident in the honors he received late in life and by being granted the posthumous title of Wengong 文公. His writings were difficult to find after his demise, but his disciples managed to collect and publish six *juan* of poetry.[107]

Huang Jie hailed from Shunde, and his background was completely different than that of Liang Dingfen. Having studied privately under the Confucian master Jian Zhaoliang 簡朝亮 (*zi* Zhuju 竹居, 1851–1933),[108]

Huang was well-versed in classical literature, yet he did not prepare to take the traditional exams; instead he was fired with enthusiasm to do something for the nation. After a period of travel in the north, he returned home and fell under the spell of the revolutionary literature of such Ming loyalists as Qu Dajun and Chen Gongyin. In striking contrast to Liang Dingfen, this made him ardently opposed to the Qing. In 1906 he participated in the founding of the Association for the Preservation of the National Learning 國學保存會 ("national learning" represented "traditional classical learning"), which took as its purpose the preservation and dissemination of those Ming- and Qing-dynasty works that had been banned by the Qing court for being subversive. In 1908 he helped found the Southern Association 南社 in Suzhou, "which was supported by a group of prominent poets with strong nationalistic sentiments."[109] In 1909 he joined Sun Yatsen's Revolutionary Alliance 中國同盟會 on a boat in Hong Kong, swearing to bring down the Qing house. He participated in local education in Guangzhou, and in 1912 he helped to organize a newspaper and other publications that advocated civil rights. Thereafter he frequently visited Beijing, trying to stem the tide of support among certain literati towards Yuan Shikai. Huang worked for a time in the Bureau of Railways in Beijing but resigned upon Yuan's death in 1916. The next year he began teaching traditional Chinese poetry at Beijing University. In 1923 he worked for a time for Sun Yatsen in Guangzhou but soon left out of frustration with the system and returned to his teaching in Beijing. He gave up his position at Beijing University in 1926 after the university was reorganized and lived in genteel poverty, devoting himself to his studies which focused almost exclusively on Six Dynasties poets. In 1928 he accepted an invitation to be the head of the office of education in Guangzhou as well as the head of the local history bureau. But financial straits made his job in education impossible to fulfill, so he resigned and returned to Beijing, assuming his post as professor at Beijing University where he remained until his death in 1936. His poetry was collected under the title of *Jianjialou shi* 蒹葭樓詩.[110]

These short biographical epitome clearly expose the political leanings of these two Southern Garden participants. Huang Jie was a revolutionary actively working with Sun Yatsen to bring down the Qing house; his revolutionary fervor had earned him a stern rebuke from his former Confucian teacher Jian Zhaoliang way back in 1906, but to no avail.[111] Liang on the other hand, was a confirmed traditionalist, one of the founding members of the Confucian Society 孔教會, inaugurated in 1912 the year after the revolution; he also tutored Puyi, the Last Emperor of the

Qing. His devotion to the Qing earned him the honorary epithet of Grand Minister Who Plants Trees 種樹大臣 (at the royal mausoleum of Emperor Guangxu).[112]

The potential political tensions between these two different men, however, were amenable to being harmonized, if not through the mechanism of their mutual friendship then through the cultural tradition that they shared. Tobie Meyer-Fong comments that often political loyalty should be read in a non-traditional way: "For others, what is now called 'loyalism' represented a cultural, rather than political, commitment."[113] It is true that in the case of Huang and Liang, their political commitments were valid and strong, but obviously their devotion to their common culture was equally strong. Nevertheless, this did not prevent Huang from sending a letter to Liang on October 10 on the occasion of the uprising in Wuchang, only two months after the revival of the Later Southern Garden club, urging him to forsake the cause of the Qing.[114] Perhaps it was this very cultural commitment that persuaded Huang to live close to the Southern Garden in 1923 when he briefly served in Sun Yatsen's administration and took up his residence at 1 Wende Road 文德路, that same short street on which was located the Southern Garden. From Huang Jie's *nianpu* we can tell that his involvement with local Cantonese literati in banqueting and poetizing in 1909 and 1913 bracketed his joining of the Later Southern Garden Poetry Society,[115] so his participation in the revived society was anything but pro-forma politeness to his friends. In light of all of this, perhaps symbols of decline were used and read differently by each poet: for Huang, they were signs of dynastic decline; but for Liang, they were signs of cultural decline. In either case, both men were committed to doing their utmost to turn back this tide of decline.

The third role of poetry societies, that of forming an intellectual refuge for "left-over" scholars from the previous dynasty, is manifested in one rather unique poem from this era. According to Tobie Meyer-Fang in reference to early Qing Yangzhou, "[t]he consecration and maintenance of famous sites enabled elites to articulate new social and cultural identities in reaction to the social flux and political crises of the late Ming and early Qing."[116] Similar conditions certainly prevailed at the end of the Qing as well. Reconvening the Southern Garden Poetry Society surely played such a role for these literati. But articulating "new social and cultural identities" seems a rather understated and coldly clinical way to characterize what must have been a desperate attempt to hold on to both social and psychological realities that were in grave danger of collapse. The following poem, then, reveals just how real and necessary was the haven provided to the group as an ever dwindling closed community of Cantonese literati. This offering, heavy with high-flung phrases from the classics, records a solemn sacrifice performed in the garden to ritually proclaim the beginning of the ineluctable cycle of disaster marked by the March 29th uprising in Guangzhou in 1911.

Ren Shixi 任世熙, "An Autumn Sacrifice in the Southern Garden in Formal Clothing, the Highlight of the Season, Liang Jie'an Presiding"[117]
南園秋祭衣冠極一時之盛梁節庵主其事

忠義拄乾坤	Heaven and Earth suspend from loyalty and fealty,
千秋大節存	Across a thousand autumns great virtue still remains.
莘莘新俎豆	Numerous are the new sacrificial vessels,
肅肅備羔豚	Reverential are the preparations of the lamb and pig.
觸起時賢敬	The respect of contemporary worthies is inspired by the rite—
具瞻斯道尊	All accords with the dignity of the Way.
劫灰燒不盡	The ashes of the apocalypse might burn without end,[118]
此日有南園	But today at least we have the Southern Garden.

This solemn event is reminiscent of the earlier sacrifice made by the Five Later Masters to the manes of the Five Former Masters. At that time, the purpose of the sacrifice was to honor their worthy predecessors. Wang Zongyan notes another sacrifice performed in the Veranda for Screening the Wind in 1683 that had been offered to the souls of the original quintet, with a spirit tablet permanently established for them.[119] And in 1763, a spirit table was set up for the manes of the Five Later Masters; at this time the Veranda for Screening the Wind was given the additional designation of the Shrine to the Ten Masters of the Southern Garden 南園十先生祠.[120] This shrine was repaired in 1867 with fifteen local retired officials contributing funds.[121] Incidentally, in his discussion of Song poetry societies, Wang Deming notes that a chicken was sacrificed as a blood offering to formalize the "social covenant" 盟 of a poetry society.[122] Perhaps the separate sacrifices to the Five Former Masters and the Five Later Masters noted above had something do to with a formal convening of new poetry societies at different times, or at least are dim reflections of a rite directed to such a purpose. However, this last sacrifice by Liang Dingfen and his friends merely required any appropriately solemn and secluded sanctuary. The Southern Garden provided a perfect location. But as the high-class hangout of these friends, it must have been uniquely appropriate as they faced the very real possibility of a tragic change in the mandate of Heaven, thus causing them to join earlier members of the Southern Garden club to become "left-over" citizens, this time of the Qing. In this context, it would be worthwhile to remember what early Qing classical scholars like Gu Yanwu felt about rituals during a time of upheaval: as summarized by Xiao Chi, "ritual practice was to express cultural identity."[123] This leads in turn to the "social solidarity" function of ritual as developed by anthropologists, a notion that explains how ritual aids in cultural cohesiveness, even to the extent of reinforcing group solidarity across time.[124] The sacrifice in the garden, then, surely must have conveyed much more significance to the members of the Later Southern Garden Society than would a pro forma religious act—it must have served as a comforting social rite that served to bind them to their cultural heritage and to each other at this turbulent juncture in time. Of equal importance was its role to both sanctify and transmit cultural memory. We may be justified, then, in reading Liang's poem recording the sacrifice as a performance text in the mode of certain ritual poems in the *Shijing*. For performance texts prescribe the performance of an act rather than merely facilitating the passive reading about an act. Ultimately, as Martin Kern reminds us, "the performance text generates and perpetuates cultural memory."[125]

Chapter Seven

The Southern Garden, Republican Period

> It happened only recently, and you heard it yourself. Rome, the mistress of the world, shivered, crushed with fear, at the sound of the blaring trumpets and the howling of the Goths. Where, then, was the nobility? Where were the certain and distinct ranks of dignity? Everyone was mingled together and shaken with fear; every household had its grief and an all-pervading terror gripped us. Slave and noble were one. The same spectre of death stalked before us all.
>
> —Pelagius, "Epistula ad Demetriadem"[1]

Refuge for a Refugee: Qiu Fengjia in the Southern Garden

One occasional member of the Southern Garden coterie of Liang Dingfen was Qiu Fengjia 丘逢甲 (1864–1912), the Hakka refugee patriot, educator, and reformer from Taiwan. He is included in this chapter to serve as a transitional figure between the late Qing and early Republican times.

Qiu was born in Zhanghua, Taiwan, scion of an old and distinguished Chinese family that had emigrated from Guangdong in the middle of the 17th century. He studied under the famous scholar Wu Ziguang 吳子光 (*juren* 1864), whose capacious personal library provided the foundation for Qiu's erudition. By age 20, Qiu had earned the reputation of being a fine poet. In 1887 Qiu became a student at the Haidong Academy 海東書院, having been personally selected by the official Tang Jingsong 唐景崧 (*jinshi* 1865). Qiu obtained his *jinshi* degree in 1889; in 1891 he followed Tang to Taipei and participated in Tang's Peony Poetry Society 牡丹詩社. When Formosa was ceded to Japan in 1895, Qiu and other petitioners were denied permission from Beijing to resist the Japanese takeover; Qiu thereupon joined Tang, who was president of the newly formed independent Republic of Formosa, as Tang's vice-president.

Fleeing Taiwan in late 1895 after resistance against the invading Japanese troops proved futile, Qiu moved about in various places in Guangdong. He ultimately settled in Guangzhou and actively participated in local educational institutions organized along western lines. His contributions in Guangdong were characterized by one author as being motivated by the "thought of patriotic education."[2] In 1909 he was elected a member of the provincial assembly. Later, he was made head of the education department of the newly established government of independent Guangdong, and he went to Nanjing as one of the delegates representing Guangdong. He was appointed a member of the Administrative Committee of the Chinese Republic but returned home because of illness and died shortly after in 1912.[3]

Several critics considered Qiu the leading Cantonese poet of his times, or at least the leading poet in Yue since ethnically he was Hakka, not Cantonese. Wu Daorong praised him for being skilled at depicting hills and streams 善狀山水, an important component of the Southern Muse; and Qu Xiangbang grouped him with Kang Youwei and Huang Zunxian 黃遵憲 (1848–1905) as one of the three best contemporary Cantonese poets.[4] What makes his poetry especially interesting is that he wrote from dual perspectives: as a refugee political outsider from Taiwan and as a resident poet at home in the local culture.

As a part-time participant in Liang Dingfen's revived poetry club, Qiu wrote occasional verse while attending soirees in the garden. Among his collected poems are ten devoted to the Southern Garden Poetry Society. Two of these, "Mountain Monastery" 山寺 and "Jotting Down My Longings While Traveling at Night" 旅夜書感, read as perfunctory exercises upon assigned rhymes, reflecting merely the social side of his literary talents. To an outsider at least, they have nothing to do with Southern Garden scenery.[5] But one poem, again written on an assigned rhyme, does focus on a concrete aspect of the site: a miniature mound erected in the garden. It sounds rather tongue in cheek, commencing as it does with Su Shi's masterful opening line on Mt. Lu, against which the man-made hillock compares poorly, but it ends ominously.

"Rhyming by Turn on the Miniature Mountain in the Southern Garden, Encountering Rain"
次韻南園小山預雨[6]

橫看成嶺側成峰	Looked at directly it forms a ridge, from the side a peak:
怪石參差地足容	Strange stones in irregular rows—worth having on site.
正喜園林饒氣象	Delighted that the garden is rich in poetic atmosphere,
忽驚雷雨起蛟龍	I start at the thunder and rain pouring down.[7]
半池新水花初落	Fresh water halfway fills the pond, flowers newly fallen,
舊壁殘題蘇未封	Faint inscriptions on the ruined wall, not yet overgrown.
歸去更欣逢夕霽	I return, enjoying even more the post-rain evening,
東南回首海雲濃	But turning back towards the southeast, the clouds over the sea are gathering.

Another poem focuses on the natural environs and greater outdoor setting of the garden:

"Southern Garden" 南園[8]

玉帶河邊萬柳絲	Bank side at Jade Belt River, silken strands of ten-thousand willows,
跨河樓閣鬱參差	Straddling the river, towers and galleries densely packed in irregular rows.
重來祗恐風光異	Returning once more I only fear the strangeness of new scenery—
再為南園住少時	But I shall stay again in the Southern Garden for a time.

A final poem devoted to the contemporary Southern Garden treats the garden merely as the site of a solitary reverie. Although reminiscent of the lonely longings of Sun Fen or Li De when they enjoyed the garden in solitude, this poem has a pathetic tone and tragic aftertaste scarcely imaginable in the usually sunny Ming poets:

"Facing the Moon in the Southern Garden" 南園對月[9]

南園一片娟娟月	In the Southern Garden, a slice of lithesome moon
曾照詩人更美人	Once shone on poets, and even more on beauties.
窮海未應人物盡	But the empty ocean does not respond, the men all gone,[10]

中天還見月華新 Still seen in the sky, the light of the moon grows.
百年耆舊誰高詠 Who will celebrate in lofty verses the elders of hundreds of years ago?
萬劫光明此法輪 Myriads of disasters or glorious brilliance—it all depends on the Dharma Wheel.
應有珊珊環佩影 There should be the images of tinkling jade pendants—
夜歸來弔柳梢春 I will return one night to lament amid spring willow tips.

This poem underscores the site of the Southern Garden as the historical locus of poetic excellence in Guangzhou, as the same moon that shone on those ancient worthies and storied beauties still shines on Qiu. His physical presence hence allowed him to access the cultural memories transmitted by the site and authorized him, in a manner of speaking, to join the historical continuum of caretakers of these memories. Who indeed will once again celebrate in lofty verses the former elders of hundreds of years ago if not Qiu himself?

A set of verses entitled "Five Poems on Being Moved by Events at the Southern Garden, with Preface" 南園感事詩有序五首 seems to have been created from this authoritative stance as it reveals a second perspective in Qiu's poetry on the Southern Garden: reflections on the historical significance of the site.[11] He includes an occasional contemporary reference, most movingly in the following distich that opens poem #3: "How is it only the ancients who wound the heart?/Still evident are the traces of events five years old" 豈獨傷人為古人，五年前事跡俱陳.[12] This refers to the quick succession of deaths that left the poetry society bereft of four members. But the main thrust of this set is nostalgic connection to the past, perhaps the only emotional anchor Qiu could find in the waning years of his life that found him driven from his home and living in exile. Guangdong was hardly unfamiliar to Qiu, and it had hosted his Hakka ancestors for several generations until they resumed their journey to their final destination of Taiwan in the seventeenth century. As a nominal Cantonese, Qiu was quick to versify the personalities, places, events, and natural wonders of the region. In fact, the percentage of his extant poetry devoted topically to various themes of Guangdong is rather high.[13]

Regardless of any internal impulses that may have inspired him, Qiu had an outer, social motivation for composition: a student surnamed Zhang Liushi 張六士 had written a poem on the Southern Garden when the current inhabitant of the site, the provincial Bureau of Education, vacated it. In responding to this poem, Qiu concentrates on past associations and connections of the Southern Garden, revealing his intimacy with its storied history. His preface encompasses the entire sweep from Ming to late Qing: the Five Former and Later Masters, the Shrine to the Three Loyal Ministers of the Song, the Guangya Publishing House, and the Bureau of Education. One poem, #2, even mentions the celebrated houri Zhang Qiao associated with Chen Zizhuang's generation of the poetry society:

> The Southern Garden is outside of Wenming Gate; its waters are bright and trees are clean. It was the site of the lofty assemblage for composing poetry of the Former and Five Later Masters of the previous Ming dynasty in Yue. Later persons then offered up sacrifices on the old altars. On one side was the Shrine of the Three Loyal Ones of the Song; hence Yi Moqing had inscribed on its gate "Three Great Exemplars of the Relationship Between Lords and Ministers" and "Ten Masters who Composed Poetry."[14] Chen Li rewrote them to make the inscriptions visible. On another side was the Guangya Publishing Company; all of this was on the grounds of the Southern Garden. The Ministry of Education for Guangdong and Guangxi had already taken it over for its administrative operations. The Public Affairs Office of the Ministry of Education for Guangdong succeeded it.
>
> The many masters, former and later, who attended would always gather for poetry games when they were at leisure. When the taper of incense had just burned down to an inch and the sound of a bell was clanging, the competitive spirit bred much boasting in vying to grasp the bull's ear.[15] Later a system was formalized to keep score and rank members from high to low. Although detailed and overly refined, still participants were highly motivated and inspired to make their best efforts. All felt that this pleasure was not even surpassed by the ancients. Over the years I grieved at having left and sighed over the passage of time, and so my inspiration is not what it was before. Nevertheless the old events have never ceased—I remember them even today. This year the public affairs office has moved away, so the images of old multiply before my eyes, and I dejectedly ponder them. A student, Zhang Liushi, wrote a poem. In order to explain his intentions, I have matched rhymes with it and have sought out as co-authors all the former masters who were in the Garden.
>
> 南園在文明門外，水木明瑟，為前明粵中前後五子賦詩高會地。後人即供俎斗于舊壇坫間。旁有宋三忠祠，故伊墨卿以君臣三大節，詞賦十先生題其門，陳東塾為重書以揭之。其旁復有廣雅書局，皆

南園地拓也。兩廣學務處已借以治事。廣東學務公所仍之。前後在事諸子，暇輒為詩鐘之會。當其寸香甫燼，鐘聲鏗然，鬪捷誇多，爭執牛耳。復創為表格，以積分法高下之，體制雖纖瑣乎而與會者皆興高采烈，以為此樂不滅古人。年來傷離歎逝，意興非昔。然其事尚不輟至今。今年公所始遷地，重重影事。思之憮然。張生六士有詩，為廣其意和之，并索前在園諸子同作。

1. 一代風騷起海湄 — In one generation, stylish poetry originated at sea edge,
千秋忠憤剩荒祠 — Over a thousand autumns, outraged loyalty remains in the deserted shrine.
興亡併作斜陽色 — Rises and falls create the hues of slanting sunlight—
如此江山合賦詩 — In this way the rivers and mountains combine to versify.

2. 五百年間幾劫灰 — How many ashes of apocalypses have piled up in 500 years?
南園非復舊池臺 — The Southern Garden will not restore its old pond and terrace.
溶溶玉帶河邊水 — The current of the full-flowing Jade Belt River
曾見張喬照影來 — Has seen the reflected image of Zhang Qiao floating by.[16]

His term "ashes of apocalypses" 劫灰 is the exact diction that Ou Zhuyu had employed at the end of the Ming; it appears in Ou's set of poems dedicated to the memory of eight of his fallen comrades who participated in Chen Zizhuang's iteration of the Southern Garden, treated in Chapter Five.[17] The phrase literally means the "ashes of the *kalpa* of fire," *kalpa* being the Buddhist term for a great eon of time. The phrase connotes the ashes caused by the fire of this destructive era and came to represent the destruction attendant on any age as it died and was replaced by a new one. Ou also described his era as "times of great upheaval" 滄桑變.[18] Both of these terms, and similar ones, are frequently employed by Qiu throughout his poetry.[19] This is not surprising, since his times seemed to him to be a replication of the tragic events attendant upon the fall of an earlier dynasty, the Ming. Still, in addition to his chosen theme of the Southern Garden, his choice of diction ensconces him even deeper within the cultural continuum transmitted by learned literati in Guangdong.

3.	豈獨傷心為古人	How is it only the ancients who wound the heart?
	五年前事跡俱陳	Still evident are the traces of events five years old.
	青青幾樹河橋柳	How many green willows are still by the river bridge?
	不待飛花已送春	Not waiting for flying blossoms, spring was already sent off.[20]
4.	女墻殘月度鐘聲	The waning moon crosses over battlements to bell sounds,
	捉鼻微吟笑洛生	Covering my nose I chant and laugh at Luoyang students.[21]
	不信風流今歇絕	Do not believe that heroic valor is all vanished today—
	夜烏啼雨過春城	A bird calls in the night rain, passing over the wall in spring.

This poem dimly evokes Liu Yuxi's 劉禹錫 (772–842) poem "Stone Head Fortress" 石頭城 in Nanjing with its moon passing over battlements in the depths of night.[22] Poem #5 finishes off the set with a rhetorical flourish that includes a literal nod to Li Bai's "Ascending the Phoenix Terrace in Jinling" 金陵鄧鳳凰台 ("The phoenixes have departed, the terrace is empty" 鳳去臺空江自流):[23]

5.	春潮欲上水松陰	Spring tide rising under the shade of the waterside pines,
	春夢迷離不可尋	But spring dreams are confused, and cannot be recalled.
	人去堂空簾不捲	All departed, the hall empty, curtains left unrolled:
	碧闌干外晝沈沈	Beyond the azure balustrade, the day seems dark and dim.[24]

A contemporary poet from Dongguan, Luo Genshen 駱根深, composed a verse in the style of "longing for the past" that, curiously enough, celebrated the past history of the Southern Garden from the ancient precincts of the old Phoenix Terrace Poetry Society in Dongguan. This poem cleverly combines interchangeable imagery from both poetry associations, thus informing his memory of them both. Of course, the poet could be merely comparing the meetings held at the Phoenix Terrace with those of the more storied club. But as the poem unfolds it initially focuses on the Phoenix Terrace, the site of an ancient Daoist monastery; the second half of the poem is obviously devoted to the Southern Garden:

"Longing for the Past at Phoenix Terrace" 鳳台懷古[25]

荒臺落落莽寒秦	Desolate, the terrace is overgrown with winter hazel,
巢鳳栖仙跡並陳	But nesting phoenixes and perching genies left visible traces.
丹灶至今飛野蝶	Even now, wild butterflies flit around the cinnabar cauldron,
青山終古屬詩人	As in ancient times, the verdant hills belong to poets.
琴樽花底南園會	Zithers and goblets placed under flowers at Southern Garden assemblies,[26]
亭院榕陰北宋春	Northern Song springs spent under banyans in the courtyard.[27]
十二闌干明月冷	Bright moonlight reflects coldly off the twelve balustrades:
斗壇誰為薦溪蘋	Who will offer up watercress at the Square Rostrum?

The "Square Rostrum" 斗壇, literally a rostrum constructed of square wooden planks, refers to the Phoenix Terrace. The "twelve balustrades" 十二闌干 was an authentic feature of the Veranda for Screening the Wind; for instance we saw it earlier in the *ci* devoted to the garden by the poetess Zhang Erqiao.[28] Strangely enough, twelve balustrades also appear in a poem devoted exclusively to the Phoenix Terrace, so both locations are unified through this particular image.[29] With the final scene transforming from the deserted environs of the Southern Garden back to the sacred site of the Phoenix Terrace, our initial impression is confirmed: both poetry societies have coalesced in the mind of the poet who, being a loyal son of Dongguan, was honoring all socialized poetry in Canton over the ages. If he felt that his native poetry society at Dongguan needed strengthening by association with the Southern Garden, he could not have found a more potent and authentic source for the Southern Muse.

Chen Rong, the Old Man of Yong Garden

During the Republican period before the Japanese invasion of Guangzhou in 1937, five friends were the last to inherit the mantle of the

Southern Muse, earning them the title of the Five Modern Masters of the Southern Garden 南園今五子. As they were all informal followers of Chen Rong 陳融 and frequently socialized in Chen's Yong Garden 顒園, they will be treated after an introduction to their patron.

Chen Rong (*zi* Xiezhi 協之, *hao* Yong'an 顒菴, 1876–1955) was from Panyu.[30] After studying law in Japan, he returned home and turned his house over to the revolutionary committee for use as their headquarters. He participated in the uprising at Huanghuagang in 1911, served as the head of the college for training police officers, and later practiced law. After the founding of the Republic, he served in the Guangdong Provincial Judicial Bureau and then in Nanjing in the Administrative Yuan as a Bureau Chief; late in life he was recruited as advisor to the president. Because of the success of the Communist revolution, he fled to Macao and then moved to Hong Kong, where he ultimately died. His private library collected over many years in the Yong Garden specialized in the verse of Qing poets; he gathered the anthologies of over two thousand of them. His ambition was to write a *jishi* 紀詩, a chronological record of poems with historical background, along the lines of Chen Tianming's *Mingshi jishi*; alas, all that resulted was a collection of comments on poetry entitled *Qiumenglu shihua* 秋夢廬詩話.

Of great interest, however, are 3,000 regulated verses composed over a lifetime of reading Cantonese poets. In the first published installment of these poems, some five hundred items,[31] Chen referred several times to the different reasons for writing these verses. The first poem queries rhetorically, "Who preserves the sounds of the Orthodox Beginnings in the south" 南服誰存正始音?[32] Chen seems to be trying to isolate just those poets in Guangdong who preserved the true poetic voice of the motherland, not necessarily just those who transmitted an authentic Southern Muse. He apparently desired to link himself up with past worthies by comprehending their grief: "Reading poetry we can understand the minds of sorrowing people" 讀詩知有憂民意.[33] At another point he confesses that "[b]ecause of poetry, the loneliness of isolation can be relieved despite much illness" 多病因詩解寥寂.[34]

The name Southern Garden is mentioned seven times in these poems. But probably twice as many verses are devoted to the historical habitués of the garden, from the first installation under Sun Fen through the Five Later Masters down to Chen Zizhuang's generation. And since these poems are devoted to important poets broadly conceived, Zhang Jiuling, Huang Zuo, and Qu Dajun figure prominently. Such Song masters as

Yu Jing and Li Maoying as well as Qing personalities Liang Peilan and Chen Gongyin, including many lesser lights, also make their appearance. In keeping with the theme of recording the "Orthodox Beginning" in the south, Wang Shizhen and Zhu Yizun, among other visitors to Guangzhou of national prominence, are featured by Chen. The Ying Garden where Li Suiqiu triumphed is treated twice. It should be noted that Chen names the dedicatee, and often the crucial identifying allusion, of each poem in notes that he appends to the majority of the verses.

When the Southern Garden is first mentioned, it is in conjunction with Ou Shiheng, a member of the Later Southern Garden Poetry Society:[35]

過眼安危髮已翁	Personally experienced, danger after stability turned their hair white,
詩因老病詎求工	Because of age and illness, how could they expect expertise?
南園諸子論風雅	The various masters of the Southern Garden discoursed on poetic elegance—
嘉祐清名在九峰	By heavenly commendation, their pure names resound among the nine peaks.[36]

The following offering to the Five Former Masters is more historically oriented:[37]

南園先後五先生	Of the Five Masters of the Southern Garden, former and later,
首數西庵氣象橫	We first count Sun Fen, whose poetic atmosphere soared.
閩十才人吳四傑	Add the Ten Talents of Min and the Four Eminences of Wu,
同時風雅輔休明	Sharing poetic elegance to support virtuous brilliance.[38]

Another poem mentions the garden in general terms, not tied to any particular time, as seen in the first couplet: "News from the Southern Garden is once again sunk in obscurity,/But the seas south of the ridges still gather spiritual potency—the treasure of the state" 南園消息又湮沉，領海鍾靈此國琛.[39] Another couplet is reminiscent of Li De's solitary soliloquies, yet is generic in its melancholy: "Chanting poetry alone in a white gallery is too bitter,/In my dreams I can tell that plums in the Southern Garden are still fragrant" 白閣獨吟詩太苦，南園梅訊夢魂香.[40]

A final poem reveals the symbolic potency of the garden to inspire any poet from Guangdong who happens by. It was dedicated to an otherwise unknown official from Panyu, Pan Shaocheng 潘少承:

白首微官任去留	With white hair and a negligible post—stay or leave at will,
二樵山裏足忘憂	Being among the Two Qiao mountains is enough to forget sorrow.
往來情興南園客	His inspiration while traveling is heightened by a stay at the Southern Garden,
蓮社風騷占一籌	Poetry at this Lotus Society—let's rhyme according to the word 'marker.'

Chen was very historically minded, and not only in terms of remembering so many Guangdong poets lost to history, or even the places and things already described in this work such as the Terrace of the King of Yue, the Sea of Learning, or the two sites versified as follows: "Conversations about Mt. Xiqiao and *fu* poems on the Three Cities" 西樵話與三城賦.[41] I refer rather to his command of the poetic diction of the Southern Muse, for his verses are filled with the terms and diction already isolated above. For instance, Watchet Sea frequently is used to symbolize Guangzhou: "In the autumn wind, a fishing boat on the Watchet Sea is tiny,/In the spring rain on Mt. Luofu, wine cups are capacious" 滄海秋風漁艇小，羅浮春雨酒杯深 or "Much sorrow on the Watchet Sea and grief on the forked roads" 滄海多憂歧路悲.[42] This term is also used to symbolize great changes in the mode of Qiu Fengjia: "How have vicissitudes changed in the Watchet Sea" 桑田滄海變如何?[43] Other terms encountered before, such as "wine-bringing acolytes" 載酒, "poet's walking stick" 吟筇, and the like gladden the heart of readers with an interest in Cantonese poetics! But more importantly, they provide a comfortable sense of belonging to a literary tradition stretching back in time in Guangdong and outward throughout China, accessible passively if one learns the language and actively if one composes with the same imagery. Given that Chen is first and foremost a poet, he cannot help mentioning the pleasures of pure poetry: "Discoursing on marvels of verse one should use the metaphor of zither strumming" 論詩妙以彈琴喻; or "With a zither and wine to chase after pleasure, I will not forget you sir" 琴酒追歡不忘君; or "In Mister Li poetry and wine are mandated to stick together" 李生詩酒命相依.[44] And Chen is quick to mention various poetry societies, not just the Southern Garden variety; for instance, "Another endeavor of the Myrobalan Grove Society was to convene the Lotus Society" 訶林別業開蓮社.[45] Nonetheless, most often Chen celebrated poetic sociality in Canton through the emotive vehicle of the Southern Garden.

Witness the following couplet which recalls Ou Zhuyu, one of the four masters who remained alive after Chen Zizhuang, et al. had been killed off by the Manchus: "Three or four masters at the old poetry society, by light of morning stars/Sang long and cried, unable to overcome their feelings" 舊社晨星三四子，長歌當哭不勝情.[46]

Chen Rong did not just idle about, versifying about poets and poetizing; he was renowned as a very active host. Wu Daorong describes Chen Rong's generosity of spirit in the following terms: "During his life he delighted in getting together with guests. Notable scholars who came south were lodged by him" 生平喜結客，名士南來者館之.[47] Among the fortunate locals who were hosted by Chen were the Five Modern Masters of the Southern Garden. Wu Daorong continues: their talent "was appreciated by the Master of Yong Hermitage, and [they] often came as guests at the Yong Garden....They had the reputation of being the Modern Five Masters of the Southern Garden" 為顒菴師所賞識。常為顒園座客。。。。有南園今五子之譽.[48]

The Five Modern Masters of the Southern Garden

These modern masters were Yu Xinyi 余心一,[49] Li Guang 李洸, Tong Shaobi 佟紹弼, Xiong Runtong 熊閏桐, and Zeng Xiying 曾希穎.

Yu Xinyi (*zi* Yinke 印可) from Chao'an 潮安 graduated from the forerunner of Zhongshan University, the Guangdong Higher Education Normal University; together with 11 other concerned citizens, he founded the Knowledge for Utility Academic Association 知用學社, which started a school of this name. As the head of Nanhai county, Yu took the lead in building the Zhongshan Bridge and the swimming pool in the Zhongshan Park, and in expanding the county hospital. In 1936, the year before Guangzhou fell, he built some 16 roads and connected them with the Guangsan Railroad to create the first transportation network in Guangzhou. He died comparatively young, leaving two unpublished works, the *Gankulu* 甘苦錄 and the *Quesizhai shiji* 闕思齋詩集.

Li Guang (*zi* Lü'an 履菴) from Zhongshan 中山 also graduated from the Guangdong Higher Education Normal University; he became a middle school principal. He delayed fleeing from the Japanese and died subsequently in Guangzhou out of despair. His anthology is the *Chuiwanlou shizi* 吹萬樓詩梓.

Tong Shaobi (original name Lixun 立勳, 1911–1969) from Nanhai

won some renown for his calligraphy, which he modeled on that of Kang Youwei; later in life he turned towards the study of rubbings. His calligraphy is often displayed in Guangzhou among Cantonese masters of the art. He fled to Hong Kong in 1937 after Guangzhou fell to the Japanese and participated in a poetry club called the Elegant Gathering of A Thousand Springs 千春社雅集. Once when drunk he fell down a well; ever after he had a bum leg. His anthology is the *Lazhai shicao* 臘齋詩草.

Xiong Runtong (*zi* Luke 魯柯, *hao* Ze'an 則菴) from Dongguan also settled in Hong Kong and participated with Zeng and others in a poetry society that convened every month with local poets and recent refugee poets. One such society in Hong Kong was called the Ocean Sound Lyricist Club 海聲詞社. His anthology is the *Dongguan Xiong Luke xiansheng shiwenji* 東莞熊魯柯先生詩文集.[50]

Zeng Xiying taught poetry in Guangzhou. Separate from his association with the other Modern Five Masters of the Southern Garden, he socialized with one Li Yanshan 李研山 in their own "literary and wine association" 文酒會; he favored Song-style poetry in his own approach to versifying. Zeng also made it to Hong Kong and taught poetry. A primary school is named after this beloved figure.

It is unclear whether the physical Southern Garden existed in pre-war Guangzhou; at any rate, another garden took the lead in refined sociality, for as contemporary poet Zhan Antai 詹安泰 (*zi* Zhunan 祝南, *hao* Wu'an 无菴) wrote, "A famous garden, at dusk, can always be delightful" 名園臨夜可常歡.[51] Chen's Yong Garden was just such a setting. It was located on the slope of Yuexiu Hill and hence was in the cultural center of the city, at least historically speaking. Another source describes it as being built "as a place to discourse on literature and discuss fine arts, and to meet for literature and wine; it flourished for a time" 以為論文談藝之所，文酒之會，一時稱盛.[52] The garden was quite extensive and included such edifices as the Tower for Pondering the Wind 風思樓, the Chamber of the Stringless Zither 無絃室, the Snowy Buddhist Hermitage 雪迦菴, the Rinsing Sounds Kiosk 浣音亭, the Snowy Park 雪圃, the Hostel for Leaving Traces in the Snow 雪留痕館, the Tower for Lodging the Mind 栖心樓, and the Hostel of Intertwined Mulberries 桑連理館.

A set of eight verses by Li Guang, who also contributed the names of the edifices, describes some of their physical features and, more importantly, evokes the very essence of the feelings inspired there: "Inscribing 'Eight Chants on the Yong Garden' for Chen Rong" 顒園八詠為陳協之題.[53] The poem on the "Rinsing Sounds Kiosk" is worth delving into:

瀑泉照影影成雙	A waterfall shines on its reflection, and forms a pair with it,
歷亂疏花動寶幢	A riot of colors, the sparse flowers move against the treasured stele.[54]
溪畔若耶音不斷	By the banks of Ruoye Stream poetic sounds never cease,[55]
先生歲晚臥滄江	The master late in age lies by the Watchet River.

Calling these five worthies the Modern Five Masters of the Southern Garden may have merely borrowed the name of the most prestigious literary club in Cantonese history to elevate them over other groupings of poets. This was necessary because other poetry societies did operate at this time. For instance, the White Gate Society was active;[56] Zhan Antai participated in both the White Gate and the Blue Creek Poetry Societies.[57] The Liao Poetry Society 聊社 convened with 13 members who were all fast friends.[58] This particular borrowing of the name, therefore, did not necessarily refer to contemporary socializing under the rubric of the Southern Garden, at least not at the old site. I have been unable to examine much of the verse produced by the Five Masters, so the question of the actual degree of their sociality must remain open.

The history of the Southern Garden Poetry Society was a living presence in the person of some of the former members of Liang Dingfen's generation; this can be seen in a set of poems written by Xiong Runtong upon reading recent Cantonese poets. One of these was dedicated to the Southern Garden patriarch himself, Liang Dingfen:[59]

少日聲名慕范滂	During your younger years, longing for the reputation of Fan Pang,[60]
晚年蹤跡近冬郎	Late in life, the course of conduct approached that of Han Wo.[61]
一家興廢曾何有	What remains of the rise and decline of a single poetic lineage?
寥落南園草亦荒	In desolate Southern Garden, even the grass is barren.

I conclude with what to my knowledge is the last poem—and easily the longest—written about the Southern Garden Poetry Society. This lengthy piece, with a prose preface but no title, both traces the history of the hoary club over time and details its recent social functions. It also reveals a degree of contemporary socializing in a literary association in Guangzhou immediately after World War Two. This recapitulation of each historical member of the poetry society also includes distinguished Cantonese officials and literati across the ages; seemingly it is an attempt to link all of them up in a single cultural tradition, a poetic pedigree, thus harnessing their collective literary power for jumpstarting the Southern Muse in a new age.

The author was Sheng Pengyun 盛鵬運 (*zi* Jiuwan 九萬). He was a graduate of the Guangdong Public Legal and Administrative Technical School and held Chen Rong, the Master of Yong Hermitage, almost in awe. It was from his association with Chen Rong that he met the Five Modern Masters of the Southern Garden and became acquainted with the history of this poetry society. (From a reference in the poem it is evident that Sheng was born near the historical site of the Southern Garden). Sheng all along harbored the ambition to compile the collected verse of poets from Panyu. Perhaps the following lengthy poetical panegyric in some way compensated for not having achieved his ambition. He does in this one poem of 80 lines what Chen Rong had done with thousands of regulated verse. His purpose is to identify, praise, and pass on the cultural memory of the major exponents of literati culture in Guangdong in the form of poets in and out of the Southern Garden. Again like Chen, he attempts to validate this tradition on the national level by noting some of the learned poets, Wang Shizhen and Zhu Yizun, who came to Guangdong and felt at ease in its poetic climate. For good measure, he added Han Yu and Su Shi as well. I divide the poem according to change of era or subject:

> After the Japanese pirates surrendered,[62] the literary society in Macao removed to Guangzhou. The Old Man from Yong Garden just happened to have returned from overseas and exhibited three thousand of his regulated verses written about Cantonese poetry that he had read. I was startled but pleased and sighed over them in praise. I also inspected a worn out case that fortunately preserved many manuscripts from the Xinhai-period Southern Garden Poetry Society. I compose this poem to gleefully announce this to my colleagues.

> 日寇既降澳門文社移穗。顒園老人適自海歸，出示讀粵人詩絕句三千首。驚喜讚歎。予檢敝篋亦幸存辛亥南園詩社諸老遺墨多紙，賦此喜告同人。[63]

1	南服聲詩寂寥久	In the South music and song long neglected,
	藝苑荒荒何所有	The Garden of Fine Arts barren,

	nothing inside.[64]
滿目蒼涼盡草萊	Desolation fills the eyes, all turned to weeds,
喪亂淪夷餘惡莠	Noxious sedges remain after upheaval and barbarian aggression.
溯自唐來有曲江	Looking back to Tang there is Zhang Jiuling,
奚袛政事推賢良	How were his contributions limited politically to recommending the worthy?
發姦摘伏膽如斗	He also courageously denounced evil ministers,
氣節文章孰頡頏	Who competes in the vitality and integrity of his prose?
海濱自此騷人集	Poets gathered at seaside ever since,
退之坡老皆來客	Han Yu and Su Shi both came as guests.
戶誦家絃賞妙音	Households chanted their verses, appreciating marvellous tones,
雪香更話楊孚宅	Due to fragrant snow people talk of Yang Fu's residence.[65]
宋興間氣屬文溪	Song arose and subsidiary *qi* concentrated in Li Maoying,[66]
并與剛峰行跡齊	His accomplishments equalled Hai Rui,[67]
簡勁為詩屏靡靡	His compact vigorous poetry swept away decadent verse,
氣盛言宜誰敢詆	Full of *qi*, appropriate in speech, who dared defame him?
逮及南園前五子	By the time of the Southern Garden Five Former Masters:
西庵節槩緊何似	Who compared with Sun Fen in integrity, moral courage?
彥舉仲修早倦遊	Wang Zuo and Li De soon wearied of a roaming lifestyle,
庸之伯貞絕涯涘	Huang Zhe and Zhao Jie expired on water's edge.[68]
繼聞嘉靖五先生	Then was heard the Five Masters of the Jiajing period,[69]
歐稱不貳梁堅貞	Ou Daren was loyal, Liang Youyu firm in his probity.
黎甘淡泊行潔著	Li Minbiao was simple, his behaviour of

renowned purity,

李吳吏治權貴驚
Li Shixing and Wu Dan's governing shocked the powerful and aristocratic.

明季士夫節尤厲
In late Ming officials' integrity was even more lofty,

會值艱虞共延濟
When troubles began, they united to extend aid.[70]

高歌意欲振頹風
Loudly singling to ameliorate decadent mores,

時危社事猶能繼
Poetry society's activities continued, though times were critical.[71]

就中有女張二喬
Among them was a woman Zhang Erqiao,

清辭麗句比瓊瑤
Her limpid diction carbuncle, beautiful lines agate.

可憐蕕忽埋花塚
A pity she is forgotten, buried under a floral barrow,

世變滄桑捲怒潮
The world changed, a raging tide of vicissitudes.

遺民抱恨思填海
Nursing hatred, left-over citizens longed to fill up the sea,

鏡湖託跡緇流滙
Retreating to Mirror Lake, converging like mendicants.[72]

密謀規復聚英豪
Secretly scheming a restoration, gathering heroic bravos,

絕島窮邊耀文采
Their literary splendour shone from isolated islands.

世運終哀莫挽回
But the cycle of the age was doomed, none could save it,

翁山諸老心成灰
Qu Dajun and other elders were utterly disheartened.

漁洋竹垞踰嶺至
Then came Wang Shizhen and Zhu Yizun, traversing the ridges,

寫憂聊與共徘徊
Venting their sorrow, whiling away time with us.

餘哀時落興亡淚
Lamentations lingering, crying over the national rises and falls,

鬱鬱雄奇筆力肆
Their diction richly unrestrained

	and energetic.
欲留正氣在文章	They kept a decent air in literary compositions,
嶽雲湖藻非其類	"Clouds on the marchmount" and "algae on the lake" were not their style.
有清中葉號昇平	Mid-Qing was termed ascendant peace,
魚山二樵競崢嶸	Feng Minchang and Li Jian, competing to be paramount.[73]
吟來盤礴矜錘鍊	Poetry majestic because of meticulous polishing,[74]
海內咸推正始聲	All promoted their sound as the Orthodox Beginning.
芷灣松心繼其緒	Song Xiang and Zhang Weiping carried on this line,[75]
哀樂無端同心許	Sorrow and happiness came from nowhere, both accepted.
雅會雲泉七子壇	Literati once met at the altar of Seven Masters of Cloud Springs,[76]
而今勝地感禾黍	Yet now in this unsurpassed land, moved by 'millet.'[77]
學海堂開得大師	Sea of Learning opened, we gained a great master,[78]
作育人才盛一時	He cultivated talented personnel, the elite of the times.
高第于文沾溉遠	High officials Yu Shimei, Wen Tingshi also influential,[79]
節庵風節最嶔崎	But the integrity of Liang Dingfen loftiest of all.
兩度辭官還理第	Twice resigning, returning to his native domicile,
痛心朝政光宣際	Distressed at the court politics of Guangxu and Xuantong.[80]
勉將吟事續南園	He continued the poetic traditions of the Southern Garden,
草木力微淚沾袂	Status low as grass and strength waning, he could only cry.
我生濠上近比鄰	I was born by canal side close to the site,[81]

園任嬉游眉宇親	And roamed in the garden close to his kindly countenance.
中遭喪亂竄濠鏡	But during the upheaval I fled to Mirror Canal,[82]
普濟禪堂禮哲人	Paid my respects to the wise elders in Charity Zen Hall.[83]
年時復徙湞江畔	That year again removing to the banks of the Zhen River,
風度高樓獨登瞰饍	In a high wind alone I ascended a lofty tower for the view.
情懷激越効謳吟	Full of nostalgia, singly loudly and vigorously,
更喜新詞來遠翰	More delightful to receive new poems from afar.[84]
竟然四面發楚歌	Unexpectedly songs of Chu were heard on four sides,[85]
天縱重瞳可奈何	There was nothing even double-pupils could do.[86]
一朝寇退仙城聚	After Japanese bandits withdrew, literati again assembled in this city of immortals,
顒翁把卷出雲霞	Oldster Yong emerged from the cloudy empyrean with various drafts in his hands.
居夷十載成鉅制	Among the eastern barbarians for ten years, he finished a monumental production,[87]
網羅千古何偉麗	How exquisite is this work, encompassing a thousand ages!
得窺昇降正本源	We can now peruse the correct source of all rises and falls,
文教從玆起衰弊	Culture and education can now escape the defects of decay.
草堂幸亦賸殘叢	Fortunately your thatched hall remains amid ruined shrubs,
金剛歷劫終不窮	Surviving like a diamond, unharmed through many kalpas.
日月重光數流澤	The sun and moon shine again, dispensing favour—
鐘呂心期振瞶聾	I expect Orthodox Sounds to rouse the blind and deaf.[88]

In this lengthy panegyric Sheng documents the collective poetic culture across time and demonstrates how it has culminated in the Southern Garden of his age. He does this through adroitly alluding to numerous poets, local places, and historical events in Guangdong. He had another means to help accomplish this, that of wielding the specific diction—in the words of Benedict Anderson, the "unifying language"—of the Southern Muse. But other than "disaster" 劫, a frequent term of Qiu Fengjia, and others such as the late Ming poets caught up in the turmoil of dynastic change,[89] he did not seem to take this route. Instead he elected to employ common allusions from the mainstream literary tradition such as "Orthodox Beginning" 正始, "the orthodox sounds of music" 鐘呂, and the negative image portending the end of a dynasty, "troubles and uncertainties" 艱虞.

Yet many of these universal images were nevertheless closely connected to Cantonese poetics, only at a deeper level. The most prominent example is from line #52, "moved by 'millet'" 感禾黍, a nod to Mao #65, "Shuli" 黍離. It was often used by Cantonese literati to characterize the tragic voices of local poets at the end of the Ming. As an example, Zhuo Erkan 卓爾堪 encapsulates the old age of one of the Twelve Masters of the Southern Garden, Chen Zisheng, with this image: "He only engaged in reciting and chanting to end out his years; much of his poetry was imbued with the feelings of 'Ban,' 'Dang,' and 'Shuli'" 惟事吟詠以終身，詩多板蕩黍離.[90] Two of Chen's own verses confirm this grim appraisal by revealing a melancholy tone; one states "For three years now I have overcome ghosts,/ In China there now is no lord" 三年曾克鬼，諸夏乃無君; or "Naturally I hate that there is no place for me,/Who will return and travel with me to Heaven?" 自恨無容地，誰還共載天?[91] Qu Dajun himself used the allusive image of millet in a set of verses dedicated to Mt. Hua: "How can any grief be comparable to that of millet" 禾黍哀何及.[92] Another instance is by the Old Man of Yong Garden, Chen Rong, in his *Yongyuan shihua*. He refers to the diction of He Shi, the founder of the "Heart of the Lake Poetry Society," as revealing the "sentiments" of the poem "Shuli" 黍離之感.[93] Finally, Zhang Weiping wrote an essay defending the traditional classification of the poem "Shuli" among the "Daya" section of the *Shijing* against those who suggested placing it within the less prestigious "Guofeng" section.[94] A tradition of attention to the diction, imagery, and cursory scholarship on this poem was thus part of literary culture in Guangdong. By noting this, even if ever so innocuously through a single allusion, Sheng Pengyun demonstrates himself to be as thoroughly conversant with the ins and outs of poetic imagery related to Guangdong as he was with the rises and falls, people and places, of its history.

Envoi

Approximately four hundred years after the first efflorescence of the Southern Garden as a literary club, an ex-official from Zhejiang who was teaching in Guangzhou visited the site of the garden. By this time it had been turned into a shrine for the worship of Wen Tianxiang and other Song-period patriots. Even if fallen into ruin, the shrine could not hide the latent physical traces of the famous five poets nor mask their spiritual presence:

Hang Shijun 杭世駿 (1696–1773), "Southern Garden"[95]

五子風流歇	The heroic valor of the five masters is exhausted,
南園跡尚存	But the Southern Garden still preserves their traces.
靈風吹葯樹	Numinous winds blow over the medicinal trees,[96]
冷月照詩魂	A cold moon illuminates the manes of the poets.
下馬空憑弔	Descending my horse, I lament in vain,
班荊費討論	Talking about the past, I waste words.
荒祠尋衲子	I seek out the altar boy in the ruined shrine,
畏客早關門	But, fearing visitors, he had early on barred the doors.

Notes

Introduction

1 Paul W. Kroll, "The Memories of Lu Chao-lin," *Journal of the American Oriental Society* 109 (1989), 583.

2 Pauline Yu, *The Reading of Imagery in the Chinese Poetic Tradition* (Princeton: Prineceton University Press, 1987), 70.

3 Ibid, 79.

4 Ibid.

5 Martin Kern, "*Shi Jing* Songs As Performance Texts: A Case Study of 'Chu Ci' (Thorny Caltrop)," *Early China* 25 (2000): 68.

6 For a short overview of this storied poetry club over time, see my "Southern Garden Poetry Society" 南園詩社, in *Lingnan wenhua xintanjiu lunwenji* 嶺南文化新探究論文集, ed. Lin Tianwai 林天蔚 (Hong Kong: Xiandai jiaoyu yanjiushe, 1996), 251–60.

7 Paul Connerton, *How Societies Remember* (Cambridge: Cambridge University Press, 1989), includes a very relevant chapter for our purpose: "Social Memory" (6-40). His notion that "images of the past commonly legitimate a present social order" lead us to concentrate on those images of the past that are preserved and transmitted in poetry. It will also be important to remember that literature can bridge differences in social memory, for, again in the words of Paul Connerton, when "memories of a society's past diverge…communication across generations is impeded by different sets of memories"; *How Societies Remember*, 3.

8 Kroll, "The Memories of Lu Chao-lin," 582.

9 Gail Hershatter, et al., eds., *Remapping China: Fissures in Historical Terrain* (Stanford: Stanford University Press, 1996), 2.

10 Stephen Owen, *Remembrance: The Experience of the Past in Classical Chinese Literature* (Cambridge, Massachusetts: Harvard University Press, 1986), 19.

11 Tobie Meyer-Fong, *Building Culture in Early Qing Yangzhou* (Stanford: Stanford University Press, 2003), 2, 3.

12 See Walton's essay "Southern Sung Academies and the Construction of Sacred Space," in *Landscape, Culture, and Power in Chinese Society*, ed. Wen-hsin Yeh. China Research Monograph, Center for Chinese Studies (Berkeley: Institute of East Asian Studies, University of California, Berkeley), 23.

13 Connerton, *How Societies Remember*, 45.

14 For the production of localist texts in 19th century Guangzhou, see Steven B. Miles, "Rewriting the Southern Han (917–971): The Production of Local Culture in Nineteenth-Century Guangzhou," *Harvard Journal of Asiatic Studies* 62 (2002): 39–75; for the impact played by national figures serving as local officials and sojourner literati on the production of local culture and texts, see Miles, "Celebrating the Yu Fan Shrine: Literary Networks and Local Identity in Early Nineteenth-Century Guangzhou," *Late Imperial China* 25, no. 2 (December 2004): 33–73.

15 This point was discussed at length at the panel entitled "A Contending Voice from the Far South: Lingnan Poetry in Seventeenth Century China," Association of Asian Studies Annual Meeting, Washington, DC, April 6, 2002.

16 Paul Cohen, *History in Three Keys: The Boxers as Event, Experience, and Myth* (New York: Columbia University Press, 1997), 60.

Chapter 1

1 For Qu Dajun, see 31–33 above.

2 Translated by Richard B. Mather, *A New Account of Tales of the World*, 2nd edition (Ann Arbor: Center for Chinese Studies, University of Michigan, 2002); for a short introduction, see Mather in William H. Nienhauser, ed., *The Indiana Companion to Traditional Chinese Literature* (Bloomington: Indiana University Press, 1985), 704–05.

3 Convenient introductions to the *Guangdong xinyu* are Lai Xinxia 來新夏, "Qu Dajun yu *Guangdong xinyu*" 屈大均與廣東新語, in *Lingnan wenhua xin tanjiu lunwen ji*, 127–31; and Liu Zuomei 柳作梅, "Qu Dajun *Guangdong xinyu* de lishi beijing" 屈大均《廣東新語》的歷史背景, *Guangdong wenxian* 5 (1976): 16–21.

4 See Almut Netolitzky, *Das Ling-wai tai-ta von Chou Ch'ü-fei. Eine landeskunde Südchinas aus dem 12. Jahrhundert* (Wiesbaden: Franz Steiner, 1977); Yuan Zhongren 袁鍾仁, "Zhongwai xuezhe zhongshi de *Lingwai daida*" 中外學者重視的嶺外待答, *Lishi wenxian yu chuantong wenhua* 歷史文獻與傳統文化 4 (1994): 170–80; and Li Huilin, *Nanfang caomu zhuang. A Fourth Century Flora of Southeast Asia* (Hong Kong: The Chinese University Press, 1979).

5 Edward H. Schafer, *The Vermilion Bird: T'ang Images of the South* (Berkeley and Los Angeles: University of California Press, 1967).

6 GDXY, 2:345. A modern overview of historical Cantonese literati is Chen Yongzheng 陳永正, ed., *Lingnan wenxueshi* 嶺南文學史 (Guangzhou: Guangdong gaodeng jiaoyu chubanshe, 1993); an introductory survey of pre-Tang poets, prose writers, and classicists is found on 25–37.

7 Qu lifts this language directly from *Liangshu* 梁書, 66.1612, and *Chenshu* 陳書, 8.147. (All citations to the Twenty-Four Dynastic Histories refer to the Beijing punctuated edition, Zhonghua shuju, 1975–77).

8 I have adopted the translation of Edward S. Schafer, *The Vermilion Bird*, 148. A reconstituted version of the *Nan Yi yiwu zan*, a work lost since the Song period, is printed in the *Lingnan yishu* 嶺南遺書 (*Baibu congshu* 百部叢書 ed.), *ji* 集 5. Variant titles are treated in Chen Yongzheng, *Lingnan wen- xueshi*, 33. See also He Guohua 何國華, "Lingnan zuizao de xueshu zhuzuo—Yang Fu *Yiwuzhi*" 嶺南最早的學術著作—楊孚異物志, *Guji zhengli yanjiu tongxun* 10 (1994): 17. Little is known of Yang Fu other than his role as author. The "collected explanations" 集解

commentary at *Hou Hanshu* 後漢書 2.128 at least records that he once held the office of Court Gentleman for Consultation. (All translations of official titles are taken from Charles O. Hucker, *A Dictionary of Official Titles in Imperial China* [Stanford: Stanford University Press, 1985]). Most lore associated with Yang Fu has been gathered in Chen Zehong 陳澤泓, ed., *Guangdong lishi mingren zhuanlüe* 廣東歷史名人傳略 (Guangzhou: Guangdong renmin chubanshe, 1998), 1–4. Other early precursors of what were to become local gazetteers of the south are introduced by Schafer along with the *Yiwuzhi*. A comprehensive listing of local gazetteers, miscellanies, and travelogues is found in Huang Yinpu 黃蔭普, *Guangdong wenxian shumu zhijianlu* 廣東文獻書目知見錄 (Hong Kong: Chong-wen shudian, 1972), 263–80; an exhaustive catalogue of local gazetteers is Guangdongsheng Zhongshan Tushuguan 廣東省中山圖書館, comp., *Guancang Guangdong difangzhi mulu* 館藏廣東地方誌目錄 (Guangzhou: Guangdongsheng Zhongshan Tushuguan lishi wenxianbu, 1986). The earliest extant gazetteer on Guangzhou, Wu Lai's 吳萊 (1297–1340) *Nanhai shanshui renwu guji ji* 南海山水人物古跡記 (SBCK ed.) is translated by Schafer as "A Fourteenth Century Gazeteer of Canton," in *Oriente Poliano*, ed. Étienne Balazs, et. al. (Rome: Istituto italiano per il Medio e Estremo Oriente, 1957), 67–93. Most fortuitiously, it presents the cultural landscape of Guangzhou on the eve of the founding of the Southern Garden Poetry Society. Most of the important local buildings and natural wonders that will appear in this work are introduced in brief by Wu through the medium of Schafer's strictly literal English translation with slim annotation.

9 GDWZ, 1:3.

10 GDWZ, 1:3; Chen Yongzheng, ed., *Lingnan wenxueshi*, 34. An additional "appraisal," on the boa constrictor 蚺蛇, is excerpted in GDSC, 3:1089. "Appraisals" to the banyan tree, the Chinese francolin 鷓鴣, and the cowrie were selected as representive by Chen Yongzheng, ed., *Lingnan wenxueshi*, 34.

11 Li Huilin, *Nanfang caomu zhuang*, 83.

12 Huang Zuo 黃佐, *Guangzhou renwu zhuan* 廣州人物傳 (Guangzhou: Guangdong gaodeng jiaoyu chubanshe, 1991), 36–39.

13 Their biographies in GDTZ are located respectively in 268.6b–8a and 268.4a–5a. Consult Poon Ming-sun 潘銘燊, *Guangdong difangzhi zhuanji suoyin* 廣東地方誌傳奇索引, 2 vols. (Hong Kong: Zhongwen Daxue chubanshe, 1989), for other entries in minor gazetteers.

14 Zhang Zhengjian's verses appear in XQHS, 2:2470–99.

15 Chen Yongzheng, ed., *Lingnan wenxueshi*, 35.

16 Huang Zigao (fl. 1828), *Yueshi souyi* 粵詩蒐遺 (*Lingnan yishu* ed.), 1.1b–2b. Huang was associated with the Xuehai tang and compiled his anthology according to Steven Miles to reconstruct a Guangdong poetic tradition that derived from the Chen dynasty extending all the way up to the Qing; see Miles, "Rewriting the Southern Han," 57.

17 *Yueshi souyi*, 1.1b.

18 Ibid, 1.2a–b.

19 Ibid, 1.2a–b.

20 Ibid, 1.2b.

21 Schafer provides a brief introduction to both Daoist and Buddhist imagery in

Guangdong in *The Vermilion Bird*, 87–92. See also Hu Shouwei 胡守為, "Zaoqi Daojiao yu Lingnan de guanxi" 早期道教與嶺南的關係, in *Lingnan wenhua xin tanjiu lunwen ji,* 111–20 and Liu Can 劉燦, "Daojia yu Lingnan fangzhi xiaoshuo" 道家與嶺南方志小說, *Lishi wenxian yu chuantong wenhua* 2 (1992): 252–67. On the sacred Daoist Mt. Luofu, most accessible among many possibilities are Chen Lian 陳連 (*juren* 1390), *Luofuzhi* 羅浮志, 10 *juan* (*Lingnan yishu* ed.) and Michel Soymié, "Le Lo-Feou Chan: Etude de geographie religieuse," *BEFEO* 48 (1956): 1–139. For a lengthy poetic treatment, the interested reader can do no better than Li Nanzhong 李南仲 (fl. 1078). Li was one of the earliest poets to celebrate the mountain; after years of study on this storied peak, Li composed a lengthy poetic tribute entitled "*Fu* on Mt. Luofu"; GDWZ, 1:84–85. Properly speaking, the name of this mountain should be pronounced Luofou; as indicated by rhyme schemes. But I will accord with modern convention and call it Luofu.

22 See GDWZ, 1:156. Ge Hong's presence at Mt. Luofu among the other patron Daoist saints is substantiated by Soymié, "Le Lo-Feou Chan," 104. For introductions to Ge Hong as alchemist, consult Isabelle Robinet, *Taoism. Growth of a Religion*, trans. Phyllis Brooks (Stanford: Stanford University Press, 1997), 78–113 and James R. Ware, *Alchemy, Medicine, and Religion in the China of A.D. 320: The Nei P'ien of Ko Hung* (1966; rpt., NY: Dover Publications, 1981).

23 Huang Zuo, "Preface to the *Monograph on Mt. Luofu*" 羅浮山志序, GDWZ, 2:400.

24 See, *inter alia*, Fan Duan'ang 范端昂 (*zi* 呂男, fl. 1736–1796), *Yuezhong jianwen* 粵中見聞 (Guangzhou: Guangdong gaodeng jiaoyu chubanshe, 1988), 50; Huang Foyi 黃佛頤, ed. *Guangzhou chengfang zhi* 廣州城坊志 (Yangzhou: Guangling guji keyinshe, 1991), 1.1a–3a; Sun Fen, "Record of the Five Genies Belevedere" 五仙觀記, GDWZ, 2:2, and Zhang Mai 張勱 (fl. 1113), "Record of the Rennovation of the Five Genies Shrine in Guangzhou" 廣州重修五仙祠記, GDWZ, 1:89–90. The fact that the Daoist genies were holding stalks of grain 穗 in their hands provided Guangzhou with another historical name.

25 Miles, "Rewriting the Southern Han," 46.

26 Regarding local belief in spirits, Meng Tianmin 蒙天民 (fl. 1174) commences his essay on a sacred cavern by explaining this part of the Cantonese psyche: "Among the customs of the south, a belief in spirits is highly developed. Between barren hills and rivers in the wilds, local shrines are close enough to be visible one to another"; GDWZ, 1:95.

27 The grove of myrobalan trees (*hezi* 訶子, originally *helile* 訶梨勒 from the Persian and Arabic *halila*) was the reason that site had been selected for the founding of the Guangxiaosi in 435 by Gunabhadra from Central India; it became famous as the home monastery of the Sixth Patriarch of Chan Buddhism, Hui Neng 慧能 (638–713). But the site had been a monastery since the Three Kingdoms era; before that time it had been a royal residence of Zhao Jiande 趙建德, the grandson of the self-proclaimed emperor of Nanyue Zhao Tuo 趙佗 (ca. 230–137 B.C.), and then the private garden of Yu Fan 虞翻 (164–233), an exiled official from Wu. It was first called by its present name in 1137, but only in 1151 was the spelling of Guangxiao 廣孝 codified to 光孝. For the history of this monastery, see Lo Hsiang-lin 羅香林, *Tangdai Guangzhou Guangxiaosi yu Zhong-Yin jiaotong zhi guanxi* 唐代光孝寺與中印交通之關係 (Hong Kong: Zhongguo xueshe, 1960); on Hui Neng's influence,

see Xie Fuya, 謝扶雅, "Guangxiaosi yu Liuzu Huineng" 光孝寺與六祖慧能, *Lingnan xuebao* 4, no. 1 (1935): 175–201. Steven B. Miles, "Celebrating the Yu Fan Shrine: Literary Networks and Local Identity in Early Nineteenth Century Guangzhou," *Late Imperial China* 25, no. 2 (December 2004): 40–46 introduces Yu Fan and the history of this monastery, its role in hosting Cantonese poetry societies, and the development of its literary image in 19th century Guangzhou. For a brief synopsis of the historical development of Buddhism in Guangdong, see Lo Hsiang-lin, "The Southward Expansion of Chinese Civilization and the Advancement of Learning in Kwangtung Province," in *Symposium on Historical, Archaeological and Linguistic Studies on Southern China, Southeast Asia, and the Hong Kong Region*, ed. F. S. Drake (Hong Kong: University of Hong Kong, 1967), 142–45. For the myrobalan tree, *Terminalia chebula* Retz., originally imported from India by way of Indo-China, see Li Huilin, *Nanfang caomu zhuang*, 92–94.

28 Wang Zongyan 汪宗衍, *Qu Wengshan xiansheng nianpu* 屈翁山先生年譜 (Macao: Yujin shuwu, 1970), 152, 203.

29 Several visits to the monastery for the specific purpose of viewing this famous painting by such notables as Su Shi, Zhu Yizun, Qu Dajun, Chen Gongyin, and Liang Peilan (the latter four on the same occasion) are noted by Wang Yu'an 汪杅庵 (Zongyan), "Guanxiu Luohan huaxiang yu Su Dongbo" 貫休羅漢畫像與蘇東坡, *Yilin conglu* 藝林叢錄, vol. 3 (1962; rpt., Hong Kong: Commercial Press, 1975), 28–30; on the painting itself, see Cheng Bozi 程伯子, "Guangxiaosi de Guanxiu hua" 光孝寺的貫休畫, *Yilin conglu*, 26–28.

30 *Yueshi souyi*, 1.2b.

31 *Soushen houji* 搜神後記 (Beijing: Zhonghua shudian, 1981), 1.1a.

32 See, e.g., the commentary at WX, 27.5b. It also is found in a *fu* by the Han poet Feng Yan 馮衍; see *Hou Hanshu*, 28.999. Its appearance throughout Cantonese poetry often will be noted in this work, but see in particular, Liu Xiufen 劉繡芬 (Republican period), "Canghai," GDSC, 2:464.

33 Qu Dajun 屈大均, *Wengshan shiwai* 翁山詩外 (*Xuxiu siku quanshu* 續修四庫全書 ed.), 3.30b–31a.

34 *Canghai yizhu* 滄海遺珠 (SKQS 四庫全書 ed.), *juan* 570.

35 GDWZ, 2:222.

36 Schafer, *The Vermilion Bird*, 138.

37 *Hanshu* 漢書, 24b.1157.

38 *The Cambridge History of English Literature*, 15 vols. (Cambridge: Cambridge University Press, 1963), 1:1–2.

39 Schafer, *The Vermilion Bird*, 182.

40 Ibid, 127.

41 Witness the "*Fu* on Oceanic Tides" 海潮賦 of Liang Qi 梁起 (*zi* Yusheng 庾生, *juren* 1886), GDWZ, 6:281–82.

42 GDWZ, 3:264.

43 Zhao Tianxi 趙天錫 (*juren* 1881), "*Fu* on fata morgana" 海市賦, GDWZ, 6:328–29; Liang Peilan, "Haishi ge" 海市歌, *Liuyingtang ji* 六瑩堂集 (Guangzhou: Zhongshan Daxue chubanshe, 1992), 31.

44 Schafer, *The Vermilion Bird*, 254.

45 On the function of "fixatrice" mountains and Mt. Luofu's role as one, see Soymié, "Le Lo-Feou Chan," 74–77.

46 Liang Peilan, "Song of Luofu," *Liuyingtang ji*, 402.

47 Qu Dajun, *Wengshan shiwai*, 14.45b.

48 This storied edifice was first erected in 1380 by Zhu Liangzu 朱亮祖 (d. 1380), the Marquis of Yongjia 永嘉侯. For a compilation of historical notices, see Huang Foyi, *Guangzhou chengfang zhi*, 2.4a–7b. *Guangzhoushi wenwu zhi* 廣州市文物志 (Guangzhou: Lingnan meishu chubanshe, 1990), 170–71 surveys its numerous renovations over time. See also Xu Xu 徐續, *Lingnan gujinlu* 嶺南古今錄 (Hong Kong: Shanghai shuju, 1984), 110–12.

49 As a mere sampling, peruse *Yueshi souyi*, *passim*; Ou Daren, "Heda Zhu Jiabu Keda deng Zhenhailou jianji" 和答朱駕部可大登鎮海樓見寄, NYHS, 320; Liang Youyu, "Muqiu deng Zhenhailou" 暮秋登鎮海樓, NYHS, 435; Li Minbiao, "Zhenhailou dengwang" 鎮海樓登望, NYHS, 548; Chen Gongyin, "Qiuri deng Zhenhailou" 秋日登鎮海樓, *Dulutang ji* 獨漉堂集 (Guangzhou: Zhongshan Daxue chubanshe, 1988), 222 (and a lengthy party piece on 261); Yang Rongxu 楊榮緒 (*zi* Fuxiang 黼香, *jinshi* 1853), "Zhenhailouming bingxu" 鎮海樓銘並序, GDWZ, 6:23; Qu Dajun, in *Yuedong cichao* 粵東詞鈔, compiled by Xu Yubin 許玉彬 (1849; rpt., Macao, 1965), 12a, and a lengthy pentasyllabic ballad in Qu Dajun, *Wengshan shiwai*, 1.36a–37b. Chen Gongyin also wrote an interesting *fu* on this edifice; his autograph copy of this piece was particularly admired by Wu Daorong 吳道鎔; see Wu's appreciation at his *Dan'an wencun* 澹盦文存, printed in the series Jindai Zhongguo shiliao congkan xubian 近代中國史料叢刊繼編, No. 20. (Taipei: Wenhai chubanshe, 1975), 1.22b–23a.

50 Wang Zongyan, *Qu Wengshan xiansheng nianpu*, 148. The famous building did get renovated between 1687–1688; ibid, 186.

51 William Edgar Geil, *Eighteen Capitals of China* (London: Constable, 1911), 78. A view of the city from the Zhenhailou is found in the photototograph opposite page 80.

52 J. A. Turner, *Kwang Tung or Five Years in South China* (1894; rpt., Hong Kong: Oxford University Press, 1984), 32.

53 Ma Yuan's biography is found at *Hou Hanshu*, 24.827–50; for his storied career and afterlife as a cult figure, see Max Kaltenmark, "Le Dompteur des flots," *Han Hiue* 3 (1948): 1–112; Donald S. Sutton, "A Case of Literary Piety: The Ma Yuan Cult from High-Tang to High-Qing," *Chinese Literature: Essays, Articles, Reviews* 11 (1989): 79–114; and Schafer, *The Vermilion Bird*, 97–99.

54 Sun Fen, "The Song of the Southern Garden, Presented to Wang Yanju, Supervising Secretary" 南園歌贈王給事彥舉, XAJ, 3.1b–2a; NYQS, 47–48. This poem is translated and analyzed in Chapter Three below.

55 *Yueshi souyi*, 2.9a.

56 "Fude longdi yan chufei" 賦得隴坻雁初飛, in XQHS, 3:1950.

57 As stressed by Qiu Rui 邱濬 (*zi* Zhongshen 仲深, d. 1683), "Preface to *Qujiang ji*" 曲江集序, GDWZ, 2:69–70.

58 Miles, "Rewriting the Southern Han," 44. Miles cites Qu Dajun as his authority for this assertion and elicits the positioning of Zhang's works in the first chapter of various prose and poetic anthologies of the 19th century to confirm it.

59 Some preferred to regard him as the first poet of the entire province of Guangdong,

with later poets credited with having initiated the stream of Cantonese poetry in their individual counties. According to this schema, the distinction of being the first poet of Guangzhou was the founder of the Southern Garden Poetry Society based in early Ming Guangzhou, Sun Fen.

60 GDWZ, 2:69–70. For this prolific and influential Ming period Cantonese author, see DMB, 1:249–52.

61 Zhang Jiuling, *Qujiang Zhang xiansheng wenji* 曲江張先生文集 (SBCK ed.), 1.11a–12b; *Wenyuan yinghua* 文苑英華, 6 vols. (Beijing: Zhonghua shuju, 1966), vol. 1, ch. 144, 1a–2b. For Zhang Jiuling's life, see *Jiu Tangshu* 舊唐書, 99.3097–100 and *Xin Tangshu* 新唐書, 126.4424–440; a convenient entrée is the *nianpu* by He Ge'en 何格恩, "Zhang Jiuling nianpu" 張九齡年譜, *Lingnan xuebao* 4, no.1 (1935): 1–21; see further He Ge'en, "Zhang Qujiang shiwen shiji biannniankao" 張曲江詩文事蹟編年考, in *Guangdong wenwu* 廣東文物 (1937; rpt., Shanghai: Shanghai shudian, 1990), 444–515. Zhang's political career is studied by He in his article "Zhang Jiuling zhi zhengzhi shenghuo" 張九齡之政治生活, *Lingnan xuebao* 4, no. 1 (1935): 22–46. Zhang's thought, poetry, and prose are briefly evaluated in Chen Yongzheng, ed., *Lingnan wenxueshi*, 39–50. See also Chen Baozhen 陳寶珍, "Zhang Jiuling yanjiu ziliao suoyin" 張九齡研究資料索引, *Guji zhengli yanjiu tongxun* 3 (1988): 10–11 and Paul W. Kroll, in Nienhauser, ed., *Indiana Companion to Traditional Chinese Literature*, 207–09.

62 Kroll, ibid, 208. This poem may be contrasted with another *fu* on a southern tree, the banyan *rong* 榕, by Li Gang 李綱 (1085–1140). However, this latter piece lacks both the moral point and the literary virtuosity of Zhang Jiuling's piece; see Edward H. Schafer, "Li Kang: A Rhapsody on the Banyan Tree," *Oriens* 6 (1955): 344–53.

63 Chen Gongyin, *Dulutang ji*, 656–58, also in GDWZ, 4:24–25; for the *fu* of Li Suiqiu, see GDWZ, 4:313. In his own work, Chen makes four direct allusions to Zhang's earlier *fu*, once blessing it with the benediction "True, indeed, are the words of Qujiang!" Chen, *Dulutang ji*, 657. Li's rhapsody also alludes to Zhang's *fu* four times.

64 *Zhen* 震 is the name of *Yijing* 易經, 5.23a, hexagram #51; the locution *zhenfang* 震方 refers to the east: "The ten thousand things emerge from *zhen*, *zhen* is the eastern quadrant" 萬物出乎震，震東方也; *Yijing*, 9.5a. All references to the *Thirteen Classics* are to the *Shisanjing zhushu* 十三經注疏 *Thirteen Classics* ed. (Taipei: Yiwen yinshuguan, 1981).

65 The term used for the south 火離 refers to *Yijing*, 3.36a, hexagram #30 *li* 離, which is associated with the sun and, by extension, the south; see the commentary by Guo Jianxun 郭建勳, *Yijing duben* 易經讀本 (Taipei: Sanmin shuju, 2004), 237. It is specifically called "fiery *li*" by Kong Yingda 孔穎達 (574–648) at *Zuozhuan* 左傳, 14.233, "Xi Gong 15th year." In *Zuozhuan*, 14.9b, "Xi Gong 15th year," this hexagram is associated with hexagram #51; see James Legge, *The Chinese Classics*, 5 vols. (1861–93; rpt., Hong Kong: Hong Kong University Press, 1970), 5:169.

66 "Follows the proper course" 從宜 is an allusion to *Liji* 禮記, 1.4a, "Quli shang" 曲禮上: "What is ritually proper follows what is suitable, what is compelled follows what is vulgar" 禮從宜，使從俗.

67 "The conclusion of peace" 休和 is an allusion to *Zuozhuan*, 30.30b, Duke Xiang, ninth year: "If one is able to conclude peace, then those in the distance will come"

若能休和遠人將至. Legge translates this line loosely as "If we can rest and be harmonious they will come to us from a distance"; *The Chinese Classics*, 5:441. This allusion refers to the power of the lichee, by virtue of its very essence, to exert moral influence far beyond normal fruit.

68 "Growing on the side" 側生 is a description borrowed from Zuo Si 左思 (ca. 253–ca. 307) in "*Fu* on the Capital of Shu" 蜀都賦: "On the flank juts out dragon eyes; growing on the side are lichee" 旁挺龍目，側生荔枝; WX, 4.19a; cf. David Knechtges' translation: "Longans shoot up from the sides,/Litchi grow on the edges," in *Wen xuan or Selections of Refined Literature*, Vol. 1 (Princeton: Princeton University Press, 1982), 345. The literal sense of this line denotes the lichee's struggle in obscurity and its willingness to avoid self-promotion, which has assured its self-preservation.

69 Taking *goumang* 勾芒 in the sense of "tender shoot," a term usually written *goumeng* 勾萌.

70 The "genial wind" 凱風 is a southern image, since this nurturing wind originates from the south; Legge records the tradition that it was "said to exert a genial influence on all vegetation"; see *Shijing* 詩經, 2b.1a, Mao #32, "Kaifeng," Legge, *The Chinese Classics*, 4:50.

71 An allusion to Kong Yingda's exegetical note on *Liji*, "Liqi" 禮器, 23.14b, Legge, *Li Chi: Book of Rites*, 2 vols. (New Hyde Park, NY: University Books, [1967]), 1:491: In ritual, "while usages are different, the relations between them as many or few should be maintained." Kong explains that the term *bufeng* 不豐 means that "what should be few must not be numerous."

72 The "medicinal chamber" 藥房 is the pod at the base of the fruit where pollen is produced.

73 "Jade-like teeth" 玉齒 connotes a beauty like Yang Guifei 楊貴妃.

74 "Marvelous elixir" 瓊漿 is the fine wine mentioned in Song Yu's 宋玉 (ca. 298–ca. 223 B.C.) "Summoning the Soul" 招魂; see *Chuci buzhu* 楚辭補註 (Taipei: Yiwen yinshuguan, 1981), 9.10b; David Hawkes translates it as "sparkling wine"; *The Songs of the South* (Harmondsworth, England and New York: Penguin Books, 1985), 228.

75 No doubt referring to Cao Pi's 曹丕 (187–226) disparagement of southern fruit, especially in comparison to grapes. See "Letter to Wu Jian" 與吳監書, in *Wei Wendi ji* 魏文帝集 (BSJJ ed.), 2:20b.

76 "Relaxed in mind and eased in body" 心侈而體忲 is a phrase borrowed from Zhang Heng 張衡 (78–139), "*Fu* on the Western Capital" 西京賦, WX, 2.1b; cf. Knechtges' translation of "His mind was bent on extravagance and his bearing was arrogant"; *Wen xuan*, 1:181.

77 A "carved dish" 雕盤 was a dish carved with floral patterns traditionally used to serve fancy food. See, for instance, Xiao Tong 蕭統 (501–531), "Qixie" 七契, QSGW, 20.4b where it appears in conjunction with a "jasper tray" 瑤俎.

78 "Colorfully embroidered silk" 綺繢 is another allusion to Song Yu, this time to his "*Fu* on a Goddess" 神女賦, WX, 19.9a translated by Knechtges as "damask and fine remnants"; *Wen xuan*, 3:343. The translation "bedecked palace beauties" is a drastic foreshortening and interpretation of a phrase that literally means "those who wear hairpins made of hawksbill tortoise shell," for, according to *Hanshu*, 65.2858, "Palace beauties wear hawksbill shell hairpins" 宮人簪玳瑁.

79 "The Mountains of Five Peaks" 山五嶠 is another locution for "The Five Ridges" 五嶺, five major peaks that make up the mountain range that separates Guangdong—Lingnan South of the Ridges—from Hunan.
80 "The Marquis of Liang" 梁侯 refers to Emperor Jianwen 簡文帝 (r. 550–552) of the Liang Dynasty who wrote a royal commendation entitled "Decree of Gratitude to the Eastern Palace for Presenting Persimmons" 謝東宮賜柿啟, QSGW, 10.1b. He is given the title of "marquis" in the *fu* only for the sake of the rhyme scheme.
81 Master Zhang is alluded to in Pan An's 潘安 "*Fu* on Dwelling in Idleness" 閒居賦; according to the commentary, Pan An grew particularly sweet pears on Mt. Beimang 北邙山 outside of Luoyang 洛陽; see WX, 16b; Knechtges, *Wen xuan*, 3:153 and 152, n. 71.
82 Chen Yongzheng finds Zhang guilty of the same charges he levels at northerners; see *Lingnan wenxueshi*, 50.
83 He draws on the same lore that was included in two later compendia on the lichee, the *Lizhi pu* 荔枝譜 of Cai Xiang 蔡襄 (1012–1067) (*Congshu jicheng chubian* 叢書集成初編 ed. [Shanghai: Commercial Press, 1936]), and the *Lingnan lizhi pu* 嶺南荔枝譜 of Wu Yingkui 吳應逵 (*Congshu jicheng* ed.). Six different parallels with the former compilation are discernable in Zhang's *fu*, and at least ten in the latter, more commodious, handbook.
84 Zhang Jiuling, *Qujiang Zhang xiansheng wenji*, 4.3b; QTS, 2:587.
85 Witness the following couplets: Zhang Zhengjian, "Pieces on Where Imperial Kings Dwell" 帝皇所居篇: "Beyond the Yao and Han passes—a stalwart imperial residence,/At Wan and Luo rivers—a robust royal dwelling," XQHS, 2:2475; and Li Shimin 李世民 (i.e. Tang Taizong 唐太宗, r. 626–649), poem #1 of "Pieces on the Imperial Capital, Ten Poems" 帝京篇十首: "Amid the rivers of Qin—the stalwart imperial residence,/Beyond the Hangu pass—the robust royal dwelling," QTS, 1:1.
86 Schafer, *The Vermilion Bird*, 85.
87 Ibid, 238–39.
88 Li Huilin, *Nanfang caomu zhuang*, 90.
89 Schafer, *The Vermilion Bird*, 175.
90 *Dade Nanhai zhi* 大德南海志, comp. Chen Dazhen 陳大震, in *Song-Yuan fangzhi congkan* 宋元方志叢刊, 8 vols. (Beijing: Zhonghua shuju, 1990), 6.b (8:8415).
91 I wish to thank Paul W. Kroll for pointing out this rather odd rhyme scheme.
92 Sun Fen, XAJ (SKQS *zhenben* ed.), 3.1b–2b.
93 The three italicized proper names in this couplet need defining: *Min* refers to Fujian Province; *Yue* of course indicates the Guangdong region; and *Man* refers to southern aboriginals in general.
94 Reading *wang* 望 as 忘, following the XAJ *shanben* ed., 4.2a.
95 GDXY, 18.487. For an interesting notice on the dragon boat with illustrations and photographs, see Carl Whiting Bishop, "Long-Houses and Dragon-Boats," *Antiquity* 12 (1938): 411–24.
96 Schafer, *The Vermilion Bird*, 175.
97 Li Huilin, *Nanfang caomu zhuang*, 111.
98 GDXY, 25.629.
99 Ibid, 25.621.
100 For instance, Qu's *Wengshan shiwai*, 13.40a–45a, contains 54 "Lyrics to the Lichee in

Guangzhou" 廣州荔枝詞, that were, in fact, heptasyllabic regulated *shi*.

101 Li Huilin, *Nanfang caomu zhuang*, 113.

102 Chen Fenghuai 陳封懷, ed., *Guangdong zhiwuzhi* 廣東植物志 (Guangdong: Guangdong guji chubanshe, 1987), 246; S. L. Thrower, *Hong Kong Trees* (Hong Kong: Urban Council, 1988), 272.

103 Schafer, *The Vermilion Bird*, 198.

104 Li Huilin, *Nanfang caomu zhuang*, 36. One interesting *fu* on this flower by the otherwise unknown Ou Zimei 區子美 is preserved in GDWZ, 1:130.

105 Beryl M. Walden and Shiu Ying Hu, *Wild Flowers of South China and Hong Kong*, Part 2 (Hong Kong: All Noble Co., 1987), 36. Qu Dajun nevertheless notes that it is fragrant; see GDXY, 25.644.

106 GDXY, 27.696–97.

107 Qu Xiangbang 屈向邦, *Guangdong shihua zhengxubian* 廣東詩話正續編 (Hong Kong: Longmen shudian, 1964), 48.

108 Ye Chuchun 葉初春 (1532–1589), cited in Sun Fen, *Sun Xi'an ji* 孫西菴集 (*Zimingchenglou congshu* 自明誠樓叢書 ed.), 1831, preface, 7a.

109 Yoshikawa Kōjirō, "Sung Poets in Canton," in *Symposium on Historical, Archaeological and Linguistic Studies on Southern China*, 135.

110 A lengthy biographical eulogy composed by Li Maoying on his teacher is included in GDWZ, 1:123–24.

111 GDWZ, 1:101–25. For his life, see Huang Zuo, *Guangzhou renwu zhuan*, 9.2a–9a, GDTZ, 270.6b–15b. Modern assessments of his life and writings are by Yang Zhihua 楊芷華, "*Wenxi cungao* zuozhe Li Maoying shengping kaolüe" 文溪存稿作者李昴英生平考略, *Lishi wenxian yu chuantong wenhua* 1 (1992): 147–65; Yang Zhihua, "Li Maoying nianpu" 李昴英年譜, *Lishi wenxian yu chuantong wenhua* 4 (1994): 181–224 and Chen Yongzheng, ed., *Lingnan wenxueshi*, 85–92.

112 *Yue shisanjia ji* 粵十三家集, ed. Wu Yuanwei 伍元薇 (Qing) (*Shixuexuan* 詩雪軒 ed.), 1845.

113 Chen Yongzheng, ed., *Lingnan lidai cixuan* 嶺南歷代詞選 (Guangzhou: Guangdong renmin chubanshe, 1993), 18–19. Another *ci* to the same tune, this time devoted to describing the view from the Dounan lou 斗南樓 erected on a hill close to the seat of the government in Guangzhou, utilizes the same technique of concentrating on the imaginative depiction of scenery divorced from its historical setting; see Li's "Inscription on the Dounan lou to match rhymes with Liu Qi" 題斗南樓和劉齊韵; ibid, 16–18.

114 Pingyi 馮夷, according to the *Zhuangzi*, "Dazong shi" 大宗師, was the God of the Yellow River who straddled a tortoise to tour the river; see *Zhuangzi jishi* 莊子集釋 (ZZJC ed.), 113.

115 "To hold under the thumb" 彈壓 is an expression borrowed from the *Huainanzi* 淮南子 (ZZJC ed.), 6.113, "Benjingxun" 本經訓: "holding the mountains and streams under the thumb" 彈壓山川. The commentary explains this phrase as meaning "to be able to summon forth wind and rain, and then to stop them by applying pressure."

116 This refers to the fact that the Big Dipper was a common decorative motif on swords.

117 An "iron flute" was a typical instrument played by hermits and other eremites; it

produced music that was otherworldly in its clarity and power. The instrument was indeed capable of affecting nature, as witnessed by Zhu Xi 朱熹 (1130–1200) in his "Miscellaneous Chants from the Wuyi Meditation Chamber, Preface to the Iron Flute Pavilion" 武夷精舍雜詠，鐵笛亭序: Hermit Liu "was good at playing the flute; it produced a sound that pierced the clouds and split stones" 善吹鐵笛，有穿雲列石之聲; see *Hui'an xiansheng Zhuwengong ji* 晦庵先生朱文公集, 2 vols., 1:147 (SBCK ed.).

118 An allusion to the Tang poet Yin Yaofan 殷堯藩, "Climbing Phoenix Terrace" 登鳳凰臺: "My five colored palace robe shines on the water, turning it cold" 五色宮袍照水寒, QTS, 17:5570.

119 These sentiments on the utility of gazetteers in presenting the virtues of local worthies apparently became a local truism, for they are repeated verbatim in the "general principles" to *Guangdong wenxian* 廣東文獻, 8 vols, compiled by Luo Xuepeng 羅學鵬 (Luoshi Chunhuitang 羅氏春暉堂 ed., 1864; rpt., Jiangsu: Guangling guji keyinshe, 1994).

120 Jiang from Rinan referred to Jiang Gongfu 姜公輔 (fl. 785), who was born in Aizhou 愛州, part of modern Vietnam; see *Jiu Tangshu*, 138.3787; GDTZ, 299.9b–11b; GDWZ, 1:33. For Liu Zhan 劉瞻 (written 湛 in GDTZ) (*jinshi* ca. 850), see *Jiu Tangshu*, 177.4605; GDTZ, 251.4b–5a; GDWZ, 1:49–50. Both were outspoken in their criticisms of the respective emperors they served. Liu's remonstrance that caused his temporary demotion is included in GDWZ, 4:49.

121 GDWZ, 1:114–15; this piece was the only essay included by Li Maoying in the most important modern anthology of prose authors from Guangdong: Qiu Jiang 仇江, ed., *Lingnan lidai wenxuan* 嶺南歷代文選 (Guangzhou: Guangdong renmin chubanshe, 1993), 39–43.

122 Qiu Jiang, ed., *Lingnan lidai wenxuan*, 67. These eight natural wonders first became codified in the Song dynasty; the Ming and Qing had their own sets, with some overlapping of specific sites; see Lu Ping 路平, *Guangzhou fengwu* 廣州風物 (Guangdong: Guangdong keji, 1991), 70–80 and Xu Xu, *Lingnan gujinlu*, 55–58.

123 GDSC, 2:635.

124 Yang Baolin 楊寶霖, ed., *Keyuan Zhangshi jiazu shiwen ji* 可園張氏家族詩文集 (Dongguan: Dongguanshi zhengxie wenshi ziliao weiyuanhui chubanshe, 2003), 4.

125 See *Songshi* 宋史, 320.10407–415; GDTZ, 288.13b–18a.

126 This trio of poetic founders is mentioned, *inter alia*, by Wang Zongyan 汪宗衍, "Nanyuan shishe zatan" 南園詩社雜談, in *Guangdong wenwu congtan* 廣東文物叢談 (Kowloon: Zhonghua shuju, 1974), 1; this chapter is a revised printing of a piece that had appeared earlier under the pen name of Yu An 杅庵, in *Yilin conglu*, 162–68.

127 Etienne Balazs and Yves Hervouet, eds., *A Sung Bibliography* (Hong Kong: The Chinese University Press, 1978), 382. For a strictly bibliographical study of the editions of the *Wu Wuxi ji*, see Wang Zongyan, *Guangdong wenwu congtan*, 88–92. A modern edition of selected verse, with copious annotations, is Yi Hangguang 易行廣, ed., *Yu Jing shixuan* 余靖詩選 (Guilin: Lijiang chubanshe, 1993). See further, Chen Yongzheng, ed., *Lingnan wenxueshi*, 65–81.

128 Schafer, *The Vermilion Bird*, 24. For Qu Dajun's essay on these rocks, see GDXY, 5.175–76.

129 GDWZ, 1:113.

130 QSS, 4:2663; Yi Hangguang, *Yu Jing shixuan*, 107–17.

131 "Beyond the physical realm" 物外 reminds us of a local trip to Mt. Luofu by the monk Dao Kai 道開: "In the third year of Ascendant Peace (升平, A.D. 259), he arrived in the capital and then proceeded on to Nanhai. He entered Mt. Luofu and dwelt in solitude in a thatched hut, remaining strictly beyond the physical realm. After he was over one hundred years, he died in his mountain cottage"; *Jinshu* 晉書, 95.2492.

132 Implying that the sun shines on the Shao Peaks instead.

133 A "turtle's head" 鰲頭 was the candidate in the final exams who placed first, the Principal Graduate 狀元; here it indicates a rocky formation that appears to be a scholar who is wearing an abbot's green cap.

134 "Transcendent Capital" 仙都 refers to one of the "grotto heavens" 洞天 that are located beneath sacred mountains.

135 A "peach stream" is an oblique way to refer to the storied "peach blossom font" 桃源, symbol of a Daoist utopia. On the secular level, a "peach stream" is a stream that is clear enough for the pebbles on its stream bed to appear like peach blossoms; I opt for the former interpretation.

136 Qu Dajun tells us that the Shao Stones are hollow, which results in the piping quality of the famous Shao music: "The Shao Stones are all hollow in the center, caverns and caves interconnect. When the wind blows through them, large or sometimes small sounds resound" 韶石皆空心，竅穴相通。風入其中，大小聲一時響應; see GDXY, 5.176.

137 An allusion to *Shangshu* 尚書, 6.33b, "Yugong" 禹貢: "His fame and influence filled up all within the four seas" 朔南暨，聲教訖于四海; Legge, *The Chinese Classics*, 3:150.

138 The spirit was the numinous presence of a tree, the *mingling* 冥靈, according to *Zhuangzi*, a southern image; see *Zhuangzi jishi*, "Xiaoyao you" 逍遙游, 1.7.

139 A "halcyon floral banner" 翠華 was a royal banner during the Han dynasty; see Sima Xiangru 司馬相如, "*Fu* on the Shanglin Park" 上林賦, WX, 8.15a, translated by Knechtges, *Wen xuan*, 2:105 as "banners adorned with kingfisher tufts."

140 An allusion to the Shao music performed on pipes for Confucius, who after hearing it, could not perceive the taste of meat for three months; see *Shiji* 史記, "Kongzi shijia" 孔子世家, 47.1911.

141 According to legend, caverns with stalactites are repositories of Shao music; but Yu Jing concedes that there is no actual extant image of Shun performing Shao music.

142 A "gentle wind" 薰風 blows from the southeast, according to *Lüshi chunqiu* 呂氏春秋, "Youshi" 有始, 13.125 (ZZJC ed). But it also alludes to a song once chanted by Shun called "Nanfengge" 南風歌, the lyrics of which are "Oh, the gentleness of the southern wind can resolve the anxiety of my people,/Oh the time of the southern wind can enrich the wealth of my people" 南風之薰兮可以解吾民之慍，南風之時可以阜吾民之財兮; *Liji*, 38.677, "Yueji" 樂記. For doubts about this tradition, consult R. P. Kramers, *K'ung Tzu Chia Yü* 孔子家語, *The School Sayings of Confucius* (Leiden: E. J. Brill, 1950), 16.

143 According to Huangfu Mi 皇甫謐, "Sire Ji" 姬公 refers to the Yellow Emperor; he took Ji as his surname because of having dwelt along the Ji River; see the *Suoyin* 索

隱 commentary at *Shiji*, 1.1, n. 3; see also the discussion at William H. Nienhauser, Jr., et al., trans., *The Grand Scribe's Records, Vol 1. The Basic Annals of Pre-Han China* (Bloomington and Indianapolis: Indiana University Press, 1994), 1, n. 6.

144 These lines imply that, because of the numerous visitors to the five Buddhist temples in these hills, the burning of incense reaches dangerous proportions, especially since this was the region home to Zhu Rong 祝融, the Sage-king of Fire 赤帝; so local officials had to be bothered to deal with the problem. For Zhu Rong, see GDXY, 6.207–08.

145 The human element in this line comes from the word *han* 含, an abbreviation for hanchi 含齒, "those who contain teeth in their mouths": "Those who have bodies of seven feet, distinguish their hands from their feet, who wear hair and contain teeth in the mouth and are partial in their interests, call them human" 有七尺之骸，手足之異，載髮含齒，倚而趣者，謂之人; *Liezi* 列子, 2.26, "Huangdi" 皇帝 (ZZJC ed.).

146 An allusion to *Shijing*, 10a.3a–5b, "Qingqing zhe e" 青青者莪, Mao #176, which "celebrates the attentions paid by the early kings of Chow to the education of talent"; Legge, *The Chinese Classics*, 3:279. The phrase as used by Yu Jing is an allusion to the "Little Preface" associated with this poem: "When the ruler develops and nourishes men of talent, then all under heaven rejoice and are glad there at"; Legge, ibid, 65.

147 This notion is probably indebted to a line by Cao Zhi 曹植 (192–232) in his poem "Presented to Ding Yi" 贈丁儀: "Morning clouds do not return to the mountains,/ Drenching rain forms streams and marshes" 朝雲不歸山，霖雨成川澤; WX, 24.3a.

148 "Lofty Eminence" 崇高 refers to Mt. Song 嵩山; see *Shiji*, 12.474; *Hou Hanshu*, 8.337; but more importantly, it was the place where Zhu Rong, mentioned earlier in the poem, first descended to earth.

149 "To preside" 霍 is used in the *Zhouli* 周禮, 22.345, "Dasile" 大司樂 in the sense of large mountains presiding over hills.

150 See, for example, QSS, 4:2657.

151 Chen Gongyin, *Dulutang ji*, 501.

152 QSS, 4:2656.

153 Alluding to the fact that the sourpeel tangerine which grows south of the Huai gives way to the trifoliate orange north of the Huai; see "In Praise of the Tangerine" 橘頌, *Chuci buzhu*, 4.29b.

154 QSS, 4:2673.

155 Ibid, 4:2658.

156 Ibid, 4:2664.

157 Ibid, 4:2665.

158 Ibid, 4:2681.

159 Ibid, 4:2682.

160 On this theme, see Li Dechao 李德超, "Guangdong zhi zhongyi shige chugao" 廣東之忠義詩歌初稿 in *Lingnan wenhua xin tanjiu lunwen ji*, 7–13 and my "The Southern Muse: Some Cantonese Men of Letters." Paper presented to the Annual Meeting of the Western Branch of the American Oriental Society, Boulder, Colorado, October 2, 1992. Ming dynasty "left-over" poets who heroically but tragically

resisted the Qing onslaught are studied by Huang Haizhang 黃海章, *Mingmo Guangdong kang Qing shiren pingzhuan* 明末廣東抗清詩人評傳 (Guangdong: Guangdong renmin chubanshe, 1987). See also Feng Erkang 馮爾康, "Qingchu Guangdongren yu Jiangsu" 清初廣東人與江蘇, in *Mingmo Qingchu Hua'nan diqu lishiwenwu gongye yantaohui lunwen ji* 明末清初華南地區歷史文物功業研討會論文集, ed. Law Ping-min 羅炳綿 and Lau Kin-ming 劉健明 (Hong Kong: History Department, Chinese University of Hong Kong, 1993), 75–83.

161 QSS, 4:2678.

162 For the biography of Chen Bangyan, see MS, 278.7134–36; GDTZ, 285.13b–18a; copious annotations and corrections are provided by Yan Xuxin 顏虛心, "Mingshi 'Chen Bangyan zhuan' pangzheng" 明史陳邦彥傳旁證, in *Guangdong wenwu*, 551–87, and Lynn A. Struve, *The Ming-Qing Conflict, 1619–1683: A Historiography and Source Guide*, Association for Asian Studies, Monograph and Occasional Paper Series, No. 56 (Ann Arbor, 1998), 294–95.

163 L. Carrington Goodrich, *The Literary Inquisition of Chien Lung* (1935; rpt., New York: Paragon, 1966), 112–35 provides a fascinating look into the process of banning his works; it includes many original case documents—memorials and edicts—translated and thoroughly annotated.

164 Wang Zongyan, *Qu Wengshan xiansheng nianpu*, 27, 35.

165 The most valuable source for Qu's life is the *nianpu* compiled by Wang Zongyan, *Qu Wengshan xiansheng nianpu*; see also the grave epitaph composed by Wu Daorong, *Dan'an wencun*, 2.1a–2a. A convenient entrée in English is ECCP; see also Chen Yongzheng, ed., *Lingnan wenxueshi*, 206–22 for an analytical introduction and the short biographical epitome at Struve, *The Ming-Qing Conflict*, 340–41.

166 This library also serviced the local school; for a poem and introduction to this library see Xu Xinfu 徐信符, *Guangdong cangshu jishishi* 廣東藏書紀事詩, *Jindai Zhongguo shiliao congkan xubian* 近代中國史料叢刊續編, No. 20 (Taipei: Wenhai chubanshe, 1975), 145–46.

167 Qu Dajun, *Wengshan shiwai,* 2.1a–4a.

168 Ibid, 14.23b.

169 See Sun Jing'an 孫靜庵, *Ming yiminlu* 明遺民錄 (Hangzhou: Zhejiang guji chubanshe, 1985), 102, 194–95. The nature of the "Five Masters of the Northern Field" is not clearly stated in the *Qingshigao* 清史稿, where it is mentioned in the biography of Chen Gongyin; but a modern encyclopedia characterizes them as a group of scholars who gathered together to study the classics; see Zhao Yongji 趙永紀, ed., *Qingdai xueshu cidian* 清代學術辭典 (Beijing: Xueyuan chubanshe, 2004), 20. For the life of Chen Gongyin, see GDTZ, 285.8a; ECCP, 1:88–89; Chen Yongzheng, ed., *Lingnan wenxueshi*, 222–30.

170 Lanhu or "Orchid Lake" was one of two original lakes in the center of Guangzhou; the other one was called the Western Lake; because of the growth of the city over time, Lanhu is now towards the north of the city within the Dabei Gate 大北門; Huang Foyi, *Guangzhou chengfang zhi*, 4.7a–b. This source credits the founding of the Orchid Lake Poetry Society to Chen Zizhuang, who had built a garden and pavilion on the site. This easily explains Chen Gongyin's participation in the society; *Guangzhou chengfang zhi*, 4.7b–8a includes two anonymous poems about this poetry society.

171 See Liang Peilan, *Liuyingtang ji* 六瑩堂集 (Guangzhou: Zhongshan Daxue chubanshe, 1992), 455.

172 Other traditional sources on Liang's life include ECCP, 1:502–04, GDTZ, 286.8a–8b and *Shunde xianzhi* 順德縣誌 (Guangzhou: Zhongshan Daxue chubanshe, 1993), *juan* 21, 13120; this is a modern reprinting that combines the Qing Xianfeng 咸豐 (1851–1861) and Republican editions.

173 Qu Dajun, *Wengshan shiwai*, 8.42a.

174 See the long notice at GDXY, 2:615–16.

175 See Shao Yaonian 邵堯年, "The Kapok of Guangdong" 廣東木棉樹, *Lingnan xuebao* 2, no. 1 (1931): 77–83.

176 On Cantonese versification on this tree, see Yu Jing, QSS, 4:2657; two entries by Zhang Jinfang 張錦芳 (*jinshi* 1789), *Yuedong cichao*, 1.3a–b; Huang Danshu 黃丹書 (*juren* 1795), *Yuedong cichao*, 1b–2a; Zhang Weiping, *Yuedong cichao*, 3a–b; and two poems by Qiu Fengjia, *Lingyun hairilou shichao* 嶺雲海日樓詩鈔 (Shanghai: Shanghai guji chubanshe, 1982), 98, where the kapok was again associated with a shrine.

177 GDSC, 2:699–700.

178 *Qingshi jishi* 清詩紀事, 22 vols., ed. Qian Zhonglian 錢仲聯, et al. (Jiangsu: Jiangsu guji chubanshe, 1987–1989), 2:880.

179 Ibid, 881.

180 Ibid, 843.

181 Ibid, 887.

182 Their anthologies are grouped together, along with short biographies, in the large compilation GDWX, 8:535–673.

183 Compiled by Wang Ji in 1692 (for him, see GDTZ, 244.8b). A reprinting by a Mr. Chen of Nanhai 南海陳氏 appeared in 1868. According to *Qingshigao*, 484.13331–3332, the original name of the anthology was *Lingnan sanjia ji* 嶺南三家集.

184 This was first suggested by Deng Zhicheng 鄧之誠, *Qingshi jishi chubian* 清詩紀事初編, 2 vols. (Hong Kong: Zhonghua shuju, 1976), 2:986. A verse by Hong Liangji 洪亮吉 (1749–1783) makes a nod in this direction: "We can still find heroic and stalwart aura from ancient worthies,/It seems that Lingnan surpasses Jiangnan in this regard" 尚得古賢雄值氣，嶺南猶似勝江南; ibid. Incidentally, Wang Zongyan, *Guangdong wenwu congtan*, 14–19, surveys the *Qingshi jishi chubian* for what it contains about poets from Guangdong.

185 Liu Sifen 劉斯奮 and Zhou Xifu 周錫輹, eds., *Lingnan sanjia shixuan* 嶺南三家詩選 (Guangdong: Guangdong renmin chubanshe, 1980).

186 Wang Zongyan, *Qu Wengshan xiansheng nianpu*, 19.

187 *Qingshigao*, 484.13331.

188 *Yuedong cichao*, "Liang Peilan," 1a–b, 2b; "Chen Gongyin," 1a; "Qu Dajun," 3b, 8b, 9a, 11b–12a.

189 Qu makes this claim in a prose piece entitled "On Presenting Lichee to Hua Jiangwen" 以荔子薦華姜文, *Wengshan wenwai* 翁山文外 (Beijing: Wenwu chubanshe, 1982), 13.9b–10a.

190 Huang Yu 黃雨, ed., *Lidai mingren ru Yue shixuan* 歷代名人入粵詩選 (Guangdong: Guangdong renmin chubanshe, 1980), 144. For Su Shi's fondness for Cantonese lichee, see Xu Xu, *Lingnan gujinlu*, 66–69.

191 Zhao Tuo was a young commissioner in Guangzhou when the Qin empire collapsed. He seized power outright after the local Qin governor died and rendered nominal allegiance to the house of Han by accepting the seal of office in 196 B.C. that confirmed him as the King of Nanyue 南越王 (which kingdom lasted from 204–111 B.C.). But in 180 B.C., reacting to an embargo on the sale of strategic goods to his kingdom by the Han, he claimed the title of emperor. He died in 136 B.C. His history is preserved in the monograph on Nanyue in *Shiji*, 113; for modern summaries of his reign and the history of his kingdom, see Jiang Zuyuan 蔣祖緣 and Fang Zhiqin 方志欽, *Jianming Guangdongshi* 簡明廣東史 (Guangzhou: Guangdong renmin chubanshe, 1987), 62–64; He Guangyue 何光岳, *Baiyue yuanliushi* 百越源流史 (Nanchang: Jiangxi jiaoyu chubanshe, 1989), 138–45; and Keith Weller Taylor, *The Birth of Vietnam* (Berkeley, Los Angeles, and Oxford: University of California Press, 1983), 23–27. The second king of Nanyue, Zhao Mei 趙眛, has received some modern notoriety from archaeology, for in 1983 his tomb was discovered at the foot of Yuexiu Hill. See *Xi-Han Nanyuewangmu* 西漢南越王墓, 2 vols. (Beijing: Wenwu chubanshe, 1991), and the specialized studies included in *Yangcheng wenwu bowu yanjiu* 羊城文物博物研究 (Guangzhou: Guangdong renmin chubanshe, 1993). The ancient city of Guangzhou under Zhao Tuo was located between Yuexiu Hill and the hills of Pan and Yu and stretched 10 *li* from east to west; see Tsang Yat-man 曾一民, "Guangzhou Zhao Tuo gucheng kao" 廣州趙佗古城考, *Guangdong wenxian* 8, no. 21 (1978): 30–38. The founding of Guangzhou in the Warring States era is the focus of a very detailed archeological report and convenient historical table by Mai Yinghao 麥英豪, "Guangzhoucheng shijian niandaikao" 廣州城始建年代考, in *Yangcheng wenwu bowu yanjiu*, 64–75.

192 Schafer, *The Vermillion Bird*, 29.

193 Miles, "Rewriting the Southern Han," 54. Still, the terrace had actually existed. Tsang Yat-man has gathered references to its precise location from all relevant traditional sources; see his "Guangzhou Zhao Tuo gucheng kao," 34. During Ming times the site was the home of the Guanyin Gallery 觀音閣 on Dexuan Xilu 德宣西路. Because of a loose association with Sun Zhongshan (he had once stayed in the yamen of the military governor that had been built on the site), a memorial hall dedicated to him was later erected in the close vicinity, known as the Sun Yat-sen Memorial Hall 中山紀念堂, and today forms part of the Yuexiu Park.

194 XAJ, 4.5a.

195 GDSC, 2:711.

196 Qiu Jiang, ed., *Lingnan lidai wenxuan*, 67.

197 GDXY, 17.461.

198 *Lingnan sanjia shixuan*, 282; *Dulutang ji*, 154. Ten other poems on this theme are included in ibid, 453–54.

199 Miles, "Rewriting the Southern Han," 58.

200 *Yuedong cichao*, 21b. A lengthy pentasyllabic poem of the *pailü* 排律 variety treats this theme with greater depth and transparency. See Qu Dajun, "Longing for the Past at Yue Terrace" 粵臺懷古, *Wengshan shiwai*, 11.7b–8a.

201 Tri-cities 三城 was an early reference to Guangzhou; it seemed to appear during the Tang period when the phrase "Prefectural city trice multiplied" 州城三重 was coined in the Buddhist travelogue *Tang daheshang dongzheng ji* 唐大和尚東征記.

The tri-cities included three distinct areas: the main city 主城, the subsidiary city 子城 with the ancient city of Yue 古越城 both off to the east, and the Barbarian Quarter 番坊 out beyond the Western Gate. See the extended treatment by Zeng Zhaoxuan 曾昭璇, *Guangzhou lishi dili* 廣州歷史地理 (Guangzhou: Guangdong renmin chubanshe, 1991), 233–34. The Barbarian Quarter is itself treated on 234–37, including a map. *Guangdong xinyu* records the use of the proper name Tri-cities elsewhere in the verse of one He Duanke 何端恪, who celebrated a meeting of "nine elders" 九老 in Guangzhou in 1554 in which his aged father participated; see GDXY, 9.294. "Wild goose wings" 雁翅 refers to two "wings" or extensions that were built out from the tri-cities towards the southeast and southwest; the enclosed area became known as Wild Goose Wing City; see *Yuan Dade Nanhaizhi canben* (*fu jiyi*) 元大德南海志殘本(附輯佚) (Guangdong: Guangdong renmin chubanshe, 1991), 8.50

202 "Draconic wastes" 龍荒 was a Han period term for the northern deserts, home of the Xiongnu and other nomadic hordes.

203 "Bathed in iron armor" 浴鐵 means to be in full armor.

204 Referring to Zhao Tuo inclining towards the Han.

205 An "imperial hostel" 湯沐 was where visitors to the ancient Zhou capital stayed, fasted, and bathed in preparation for audience with the king.

206 The "banner of authority" 旌節 was held by ancient officers to escort travelers along official highways; it was assigned for a specific trip and had to be returned; see *Zhouli*, 15.12a, "Zhangjie" 掌節 and the commentary by Zheng Xuan 鄭玄 (127–200).

207 See Zeng Zhaoxuan, *Guangzhou lishi dili*, 55–69 for the changes in the banks of the Pearl River throughout history consequent to the build up of sandy flats along the old banks.

208 In another poem by Qu, his "Mourning the Past in Guangzhou" 廣州弔古, Qu recycles many of the same images that appear in this *ci*, including the Terrace of the King of Yue, the Mongol yurt, and cows and sheep; see *Qingshi jishi*, 2:860.

209 GDWZ, 3:99–100.

210 Fan Ju 范睢 was a Prime Minister of Qin; see *Hanshu*, 60.2675, 2676, n. 7.

211 Ren Xiao 任囂 was the prefect of the county of Longchuan, who, while on his deathbed, advised Zhao Tuo to seize power to maintain order during the chaos attendant upon the collapse of the Qin empire; for historical details of the rise and reign of Zhao Tuo, see *Shiji*, 113.

212 This was the name of the fortress where Emperor Ming of the Wei dynasty 魏孝明 (r. 526–528) retired after his abdication; *Weishu* 魏書, 4.154. In the context of the royal pretensions of Zhao Tuo, its use by Li Minbiao is hardly a ringing endorsement of Zhao Tuo's claims.

213 *Lüshi chunqiu*, 6.62, "Mingli" 明理, uses the term a "slanted chamber" 夕室 to drive home a point: commonplace lords who do not understand music and hence lack the substance of a worthy ruler are likened to trying to "sit upright in a slanted chamber." According to the commentary, then, a slanted chamber is a metaphor for a tragic person.

214 "Carmine loam" 赬壤 was used to paint walls; see Bao Zhao, "Wuchengfu" 蕪城賦, WX, 11.14b; Knechtges, *Wen xuan*, 2:257 coined the translation of "carmine loam." The use of the term here may harbor an implied criticism of Zhao Tuo's construction

projects, for a line by Li Shangyin 李商隱 (813?–858) concludes that "It is vain to paint with carmine loam—truly of what use is it?/Desiring to raise the yellow banner, surprisingly it has not been done" 空糊赬壤真何益，欲舉黃旗竟未成; QTS, 16: 6206. Anciently, a yellow banner was used in defensive warfare; see *Mozi* 墨子, 15.342, "Qizhi" 旗幟. The allusion to red carmine earth and the image it recalls of defensive warfare combine to criticize Zhao Tuo's expenditures on building projects at the expense of defensive warfare.

215 "Floral balustrades" 榮楯 appears in Zuo Si's 左思 "Wudufu" 吳都賦, WX, 5.17b; Knechtges, *Wen xuan*, 1:397 translates the relevant line as "affixed with eaves and balustrades intricately joined" 施榮楯而捷獵. However, another negative dig against Zhao Tuo is discernable in how this image was used by a later poet. Yue Ke 岳珂 (1183–1243) wrote "Domiciles with floral balustrades may be dwelled in, and are worth using to adorn my cottage; but how are they worth destroying my homeland for?" 榮楯可居，適足華吾廬，胡足以隳吾之都. See Yue's "Guanwa wuxi" 館娃浯溪 from his *Chengshi* 程史; cited in Luo Zhufeng 羅竹風, ed., *Hanyu dacidian* 漢語大詞典 (Shanghai: Hanyu dacidian chubanshe, 1989), 4:1230.

216 Another negative image is intended by the use of "short columns decorated with duckweeds" 藻梲, *Lunyu* 論語, 5.17: "The Master said, 'Tsang Wan kept a large tortoise in a house, on the capitals of the pillars of which he had hills made, with representations of duckweed on the small pillars *above the beams supporting the rafters*.—Of what use was his wisdom?'" Legge explains in his notes that, despite the reputation of being wise, keeping such a tortoise was an act of usurpation on the part of Tsang Wan (Zang Wen 臧文); Legge, *The Chinese Classics*, 1:179.

217 GDWZ, 6:211–12.

218 Liu Sifen and Zhou Xifu, eds., *Lingnan sanjia shixuan*, 292.

219 For the activities of the Song minister Wen Tianxiang in Guangdong in various official capacities, civil and military, that led to interest still being attached to him in the region, see Lo Hsiang-lin, "Song Wangtai yu Song ji zhi haishang xingchao" 宋王臺與宋際之海上行朝, *Journal of Oriental Studies* 3 (1956): 185–217; see also Xu Xu, *Lingnan gujinlu*, 88–91.

220 The other heroes commemorated by the shrine are Lu Xiufu 陸秀夫 and Zhang Shijie 張世傑; see GDWZ, 2:222. The original memorial by Tao Lu 陶魯 (1434–1498), a local magistrate urging the construction of this shrine, is preserved in GDWZ, 2:139.

221 See Huang Ai 黃哀, "Sanzhong ci ji" 三忠祠記, GDWZ, 2:222; Li Suiqiu, "San Dazhong ci fu you xu" 三大忠祠賦有序, GDWZ, 4:310–11 and *Qingshi jishi*, 4:754–60.

222 Huang Yu, *Lidai mingren ru Yue shixuan*, 282; Yi Hangguang, ed., *Yu Jing shixuan*, 34.

223 This poem adopts the same rhyme scheme of the last ruler of Chen, Chen Shubao 陳叔寶 (r. 583–589), and his poem "Looking Down from a Lofty Terrace" 臨高臺; see XQHS, 2:2505.

224 "Recording my impressions from the Terrace of the King of Yue" 粵王臺書感, *Lingyun hairilou shichao*, 218. Qiu Fengjia will be treated in Chapter Seven.

225 As characterized by Li Dechao 李德超, *Lingnan shishigao* 嶺南詩史稿 (Taipei: Fayansi chubanshe, 1998).

226 Corey Andrews, *Literary Nationalism in Eighteenth-Century Scottish Club Poetry*

(Lewiston, Queenston, and Lampeter: The Edwin Mellen Press, 2004), 10, citing Benedict Anderson, *Imagined Communities: Reflections on the Origin and Spread of Nationalism* (1983; rpt., London: Verso, 1991), 84.

Chapter 2

1 David Hawkes, trans., *The Story of the Stone, vol 2: The Crab-Flower Club* (Harmondsworth, England: Penguin Books, 1977), 214.

2 Timothy Raylor, *Cavaliers, Clubs, and Literary Culture: Sir John Mennes, James Smith, and the Order of Fancy* (Newark: University of Delaware Press; London and Toronto: Associate University Presses, 1994), 71.

3 This argument is made by Francois Lissarrague, *The Aesthetics of the Greek Banquet: Images of Wine and Ritual*, trans. Andrew Szegedy-Maszak (Princeton: Princeton University Press, 1990).

4 Raylor, *Cavaliers, Clubs, and Literary Culture*, 71.

5 Ibid, 72.

6 Ibid, 72–73, 98, 102.

7 For the French literary salon, see now Steven Kale, *French Salons: High Society and Political Sociability from the Old Regime to the Revolution of 1848* (Baltimore: Johns Hopkins University Press, 2004).

8 Consult J. Walter Nelson, "The Literary Club and Gregarious Males." Paper presented to the South Central Society for Eighteenth-Century Studies, 17th Annual Meeting, Lubbock, Texas, Feb. 14, 1992. On the most famous eighteenth-century literary club in England, see Lewis P. Curtis and Harmon W. Liebert, *Esto Perpetua: The Club of Dr. Samuel Johnson and His Friends, 1764–1784* (N.p.: Archon Press–The Shoestring Press, 1963), and Charles N. Fifer, ed., *The Correspondence of James Boswell with Certain Members of the Club* (New York and Toronto: McGraw Hill, 1976).

9 Andrews, *Literary Nationalism in Eighteenth-Century Scottish Club Poetry*, 11.

10 *Xin Tangshu*, 119.4304.

11 *Jiu Tangshu*, 14.5262–65.

12 Gu Xueyi 顧學頡, ed., *Bai Juyi ji* 白居易集, 4 vols. (Beijing: Zhonghua shuju, 1979), 3:825–26. See also QTS, 14:5222.

13 Gong Pengcheng 龔鵬程, *Jiangxi shishe zongpai yanjiu* 江西詩社宗派研究 (Taipei: Wen, shi, zhe chubanshe, 1983), 14.

14 See Zhu Jincheng 朱金城, *Bai Juyi nianpu* 白居易年譜 (Shanghai: Shanghai guji chubanshe, 1982), 329–32.

15 To the introduction and bibliography by J. D. Schmidt at Nienhuaser, ed., *The Indiana Companion to Traditional Chinese Literature*, 261–62, add now Jonathan O. Pease, "Lin-ch'uan and Fen-ning: Kiangsi Locales and Kiangsi Writers during the Sung," *Asia Major*, 3rd series, 4 (1991): 39–85.

16 See Qin Huanming 秦環明, "Lü Benzhong *Jiangxi shishe zongpaitu* chuangzuo shijian kaobian" 呂本中「江西詩社宗派圖」創作時間考辨, *Wenjiao ziliao*, 1989, issue 6: 95.

17 Wong Siu-kit, trans. and annot., *Notes on Poetry from the Ginger Studio* (Hong Kong: The Chinese University Press, 1987), 124, n. 8.

18 Gong Pengcheng, *Jiangxi shishe zongpai yanjiu*, 14.

19 Ibid, 40; consult further Huang Zhimin 黃志民, "Mingren shishe zhi yanjiu" 明人詩社之研究, Master's thesis, Zhengzhi University (Taiwan), 1972, 4–6.

20 Ibid, 40.

21 The poet Lin Bu 林逋 (968–1028) mentions a *shishe* in one of his poems; see QSS, 2:1228. I owe this reference courtesy of Mr. Qin Huanming.

22 Su Shi, "Responding to Ma Zhongyu by following the previous rhyme" 次前韵答馬忠玉, in *Dongpo shiji fenlei* 東坡詩集分類 (SBCK ed.), 19.357. The term *zaijiu* 載酒 was also one of the self-designations of Su Shi, as recalled in Hainan by renaming the "Shrine to Dongpo" 東坡祠 as the Hall to the Wine-Bringer 載酒堂: "The reason that it is named Hall of the Wine-Bringer is because it was a self-designation of the master [Su Shi]"; see Wang Zuo, GDWZ, 2:45. Another reading of this line, then, would be "What harm would there be if I—the wine bearer—came along?"

23 Wang Deming 王德明, "Lun Songdai de shishe" 論宋代的詩社, *Wenxue yichan* 1992, issue 6: 66–72.

24 Huang Baohua 黃寶華, "*Jiangxi shishe zongpaitu* de xieding yu *Jiangxi shipai* zongji de kanxing" 《江西詩社宗派圖》的寫定與《江西詩派》總集的刊行, *Wenxue yichan*, 1999, issue 6: 68–69.

25 Ouyang Guang 歐陽光, "Yumen shiluo de qunti: lun Yuanchu yimin shishe jian yu Wang Deming xiansheng shangque" 鬱漶失落的群體: 論元初遺民詩社兼與王德明先生商榷, *Wenxue yichan*, 1993, issue 4: 83–89. See now his book, *Song-Yuan shishe yanjiu conggao* 宋元詩社研究叢稿 (Guangzhou: Guangdong gaodeng jiaoyu chubanshe, 1996).

26 GZSS, 4.2a. This characterization also appears in a poem by Sun Fen describing a typical gathering of the society; see XAJ, 1.2b.

27 In fact, Iriya Yoshitaka 入矢義高 epitomizes the literary persona exhibited by Yuan Hongtao as a "martyr for wine and women"; see *Mindai shibun* 明代詩文 (Tōkyō: Chikuma shobō, 1978), 93–115. On these three Yuan brothers and their poetry society, consult DMB, 2:1636.

28 GDSC, 3:911.

29 Wai-Kam Ho, "Late Ming Literati: Their Social and Cultural Ambience," in *The Chinese Scholar›s Studio: Artistic Life in the Late Ming Period. An Exhibition from the Shanghai Museum*, ed. Chu-Tsing Li and James C. Y. Watt (New York and London: Thames and Hudson, in conjunction with The Asia Society Galleries, 1987), 25.

30 Chu-Tsing Li, "The Literati Life," in *The Chinese Scholar's Studio*, 41; see plate 7 for the painting.

31 Wai-Kam Ho, "Late Ming Literati," 23.

32 Huang Zhimin, "Mingren shishe zhi yanjiu," 19–37.

33 Li Dongyang, "Huailutang shihua" 懷麓堂詩話, in *Li Dongyang ji* 李東陽集, 3 vols. (Changsha: Yuelu shushe chubanshe, 1984), 2:541.

34 The *Yuequan yinshe* in one *juan* is still extant in various *congshu*, including the *Sikuquanshu* and the *Congshu jicheng*; see *Siku quanshu zongmu tiyao* 四庫全書縱目提要 (Taipei: Hanjing wenhua shiye yuxian gongsi, 1981), 187.1062–63. For further analysis of this poetry society, consult Huang, "Mingren shishe zhi yanjiu," 13–16. Ouyang Guang presents short biographical studies of the participants in the Moon Springs Chanting Society in his two-part series, "Yuequan yinshe zuozhe kaolüe" 月泉吟社作者考略, *Wenxian* 1 (1993), and "Yuequan yinshe zuozhe

xukao" 月泉吟社作者續考, *Wenxian* 3 (1994): 232–45.

35 Chen Yan 陳衍, *Yuanshi jishi* 元詩紀事, 2 vols. (Shanghai: Shanghai guji chubanshe, 1987), 1:94–95; the Moon Springs Chanting Society poets are included on 94–119. After the Xinhai revolution, rather than participate in the new government, the compiler of this anthology Chen Yan himself organized a poetry society with colleagues of similar sympathies and poetic tastes to pass their remaining years in isolation as members of a now defunct-dynasty; see ibid, preface, 1.

36 For the Xuannan Poetry Society, see the discussion by James M. Polachek, *The Inner Opium War*, Harvard East Asian Monographs, 151 (Cambridge, Massachusetts: The Council on East Asian Studies, Harvard University, 1992), 39–59. Yang Guozhen 楊國楨, "Zailun Xuannan shishe yu Lin Zexu" 再論宣南詩社與林則徐, *Zhuanghua wenshi luncong* 13 (1980): 149–58 disputes the characterization of this poetry society as having political motives. He also distinguishes formal members of the society such as Lin Zexu from other poets who happened to socialize with them such as Gong Zizhen 龔自珍 (1792–1841) and Zhang Weiping 張維屏 (1780–1859).

37 GDXY, 12.317. Qu Dajun surveys the major poetical associations of Guangzhou from the Southern Garden until the early Qing period at GDXY, 12.315–17. A similar survey in modern Chinese is by Lu Ping, *Guangzhou fengwu*, 371–73.

38 GDWZ, 4:163–64. Hailing from Dongguan, Deng gained his *jinshi* degree in 1598. He served as an administrative commissioner and as magistrate in Fengyang 鳳陽, Anhui. His short biography at GDWZ, 4:158 indicates that he was upright and acted in the fashion of great ministers of the past. Despite this conservative bent, he socialized almost daily in the capital with the local luminaries discoursing on the great events of the day. Numerous prose pieces are found in GDWZ, 4:158–65; two of his poetic anthologies are noted in the SKQS catalogue. His poems will appear in *juan* 17 of the next reprinting of the *Dongguan shilu* 東莞詩錄 compiled by the Qing scholar from Dongguan, Zhang Qigan 張其淦 (*zi* Yuquan 豫泉, *jinshi* late Qing), a disciple of Chen Li 陳澧. So far only vol. 1 has been published (Dongguan: Dongguanshi zhengxie wenshiziliao weiyuanhuiyin, 2001).

39 A mount located in Dongguan. During the Song dynasty, a Daoist adept named Cui Zixia 崔紫霞 moved from Mt. Luofu and settled there. He dug a well and the spring that resulted was named Zixia Spring. The Phoenix Terrace was located right above this spring. See *Dongguan xianzhi* 東莞縣志 (Jiaqing 嘉慶 ed.), 4.1b.

40 Meaning that these words recall the historical setting of the site as a Daoist monastery. Golden portals 金闕 were a typical feature of Daoist temples, at least those located in the Daoist heavens; see the many entries for this phrase at K. M. Schipper, *Index du Yunji Qiqian: Project Tao-Tsang*, Publications de l'Ecole Française d'Extrême-Orient, No. 131, 2 vols. (Paris: l'Ecole Française d'Extrême-Orient, 1981–82), 1:663–64. It should be recalled that this term features in Bai Juyi's famous "Song of Everlasting Sorrow" 長恨歌: "At the west chamber by Golden Palace Gate he tapped on a door of jade,/transmitted his request to Little Jade" 金闕西廂叩玉扃，轉教小玉報雙成; see QTS, 435:4819, translated by Howard S. Levy, *Translations from Po Chü-i's Collected Works*, 2 vols. (New York: Paragon Book Reprint Corp., 1971), 1:140.

41 The founding figure of this poetry society was Chen Jingji 陳靖吉 (fl. early Ming). Some ten or twenty years older than Sun Fen, this native of Dongguan was a gifted poet; his fellow founders were Huang Shang 黃裳, Zhou Pujing 周溥敬, Zeng

Weizhong 曾惟忠, Pan Zhu 潘翥, He Qianyuan 何潛淵, and Luo Tai 羅泰. Zhang Qigan, ed., *Dongguan shilu*, 125 citing the *Dongguan xianzhi*.

42 "A cultured clime" is an interpretation of the "land of Zou and Lu" 鄒魯, the homelands of Mencius and Confucius respectively.

43 A Confucian school built by Chen Xuanwen 陳絢溫 on Mt. Daojia; *Dongguan xianzhi*, 7.5b.

44 Zi Jin was a fairy figure better known as Wang Ziqiao 王子喬. In human form he was the son of King Ling of Zhou 周靈王, and was known as Prince Jin 太子晉. He was fond of playing the reed pipes 笙 imitating the sounds of phoenixes; a local Cantonese connection exists because of his meeting the Daoist immortal Fuqiu Gong 浮丘公 while both were in Henan. For Wang Ziqiao, see *Liexian zhuan* 列仙傳 (*Zhengtong Daozang* 正統道藏 ed.), HY #294, 1.13b–14a. Xiao Shi 蕭史 was an immortal whose whistling could attract phoenixes; see *Liexian zhuan*, 1.17a.

45 *Shangsi* 上巳 was the third day of the third lunar month, a day traditionally set aside for riparian purgation and lustration rites 祓禊; it soon became the occasion for drinking and feasting, and by Tang times poetry composition became a common element. As a sampling of historical celebrations, see *Hou Hanshu*, 21.671, 61.2028; *Jinshu*, 94.2429; *Liangshu*, 33.477; and *Xin Tangshu*, 13.369.

46 This was the terrace made famous in a verse by Li Bai entitled "Climbing the Phoenix Terrace in Jingling" 登金陵鳳凰臺; see An Qi 安旗, et al., eds., *Li Bai quanji biannian zhushi* 李白全集編年注釋, 3 vols. (Chengdu: Bashu shushe, 1990), 1:805–11. The storied tower was located in the southwest corner of the city.

47 "To give vent by singing and shouting" translates *shuxiao* 舒嘯; alluding to Tao Qian 陶潛, "Guiqulai xi ci" 歸去來兮辭, *Tao Pengze ji* 陶彭澤集 (BSJJ ed.), 3:2449–2450: "Or climb the eastern hill and let out long whistles;/Or looking on the clear stream, compose a poem" 登東皐以舒嘯，臨清流而賦詩; trans. A. R. Davis, *T'ao Yüan-ming (AD 365–427): His Works and Their Meaning*, 2 vols. (Cambridge: Cambridge University Press, 1983), 1:194.

48 The lines read: "The Three Hills set halfway beyond the blue sky,/Two rivers split White Egret Isle down the middle" 三山半落青天外，二水中分白鷺洲; see An Qi, et al., eds., *Li Bai quanji biannian zhushi*, 1:806.

49 Another reference to Li Bai's poem mentioned above.

50 Witness the printing of the *Fengtai xinsheyin cao chuji* 鳳臺新社吟草初集, edited by Yang Hebin 楊鶴賓 in 1936; see Huang Yinpu, *Guangdong wenxian shumu zhijianlu*, 214. Various notices of the historical Phoenix Terrace and its poetry society are preserved in Zhang Qigan, ed., *Dongguan shilu*, 1:199, 204, 224, 218, 280, 349, and 382.

51 Qu Xiangbang, *Guangdong shihua zhengxubian*, 86.

52 GDWZ, 5:135–36. Luo Tianchi (*zi* Lüxian 履先, *hao* Shihu 石湖, 1686–1765) hailed from Shunde. He was a pupil of the famous classical scholar Hui Shiqi 惠士奇 (1671–1741), the father of the even more renowned Hui Dong 棟 (1697–1758), and was himself a member of a poetry society, the "Southern Fragrance Poetry Society" 南香詩社. Among the members of this poetry club were Su Er 蘇珥 (1699–1767), also from Shunde, Lao Xiaoyu 勞孝輿 and He Mengyao 何夢瑤 (*jinshi* 1730), both from Nanhai. Luo and these three were separately known as the Four Masters from Hui's Gate 惠門四子, referring to their status as former pupils of

Hui Shiqi; see ECCP, 1:356; Lu Ping, *Guangzhou fengwu*, 372. For Luo Tianchi, see GDTZ, 287.15a–15b; GDWZ, 5:133–36. The other three also share the same chapter of the GDTZ: Su Er in 287.18b–19a, Lao Xiaoyu in 287.11a–12a, and He Mengyao in 287.10b–11a. They also appear in the GDWZ; see 5:142 for Su Er, 5:114–15 for He Mengyao, and 5:124–25 for Lao Xiaoyu.

53 Huang Zuo, author of the *Guangzhou renwu zhuan* and his disciples, who were collectively called the "Five Later Masters of the Southern Garden," are treated in Chapter Five below.

54 He Yuechao 何越巢, his son the Oldster of the Southern Pond 南塘翁, and the Oldster's grandson He Yu 何宇 mentioned below are otherwise unknown. Perhaps the son was He Shi 何栻, who was nicknamed "the Old Fisherman of the Southern Pond" 南塘漁父 and who also frequented the Southern Lake. The name of the poetry society he is credited with founding was the "Heart of the Lake Poetry Society" 湖心詩社. It is described in terms reminiscent of the Southern Lake Poetry Society; see *Qingshi jishi*, 2:1003.

55 Literally "Minor Olive" 小欖. The *ganlan* 橄欖, or Chinese olive (*Canarium album* raeusch.), being a product of Guangdong, sometimes served to symbolize the region.

56 An allusion to the Orchid Terrace meeting of Wang Xizhi 王羲之 (321–379 or 307–365).

57 "Elegentiae" 雅 and "Airs of the States" 國風 refer to sections in the ancient Classic of Poetry that embodied different literary and moral virtues; but both strains were considered proper and orthodox.

58 Liang Peilan, *Liuyingtang ji*, 475.

59 Wang Zongyan, *Qu Wengshan nianpu*, 189, 192.

60 Liang Peilan, *Liuyingtang ji*, 475.

61 GDSC, 2:605.

62 Meyer-Fong, *Building Culture in Early Qing Yangzhou*, 58–69 treats these two events in depth.

63 See Jin Zhanlin 金湛霖 (*zi* Zixian 滋軒) from Panyu; GDSC, 2:640.

64 Ibid, 2:417.

65 See Miss Liang Linghui 梁令惠女史 (*zi* Meige 梅格) from Xinhui; ibid, 3:950–51.

66 See Miss Du Lianbi 杜連璧女史 from Sanshui; GDSC, 3:953–54.

67 GDWZ, 3:296.

68 Colin S. C. Hawes provides many insights into the social use of poetry among friends outside of formal poetry club networks; see his *The Social Circulation of Poetry in the Mid-Northern Song: Emotional Energy and Literati Self-Cultivation* (Albany: State University of New York Press, 2005).

69 Liang Peilan, *Liuyingtang ji*, 465.

70 Ibid, 468.

71 Ibid, 470.

72 The influence Liang and his poetry exerted on contemporary Lingnan poets and poetics is treated by Chen Yingchao 陳應潮, "Lun Liang Peilanshi yu Lingnan shitan" 論梁佩蘭詩與嶺南詩壇, *Lishi wenxian yu chuantong wenhua* 4 (1994): 284–92. It is apparent from contemporary sources that Liang was regarded as the leading poet among the several hundred Cantonese literati active during the period, exerting influence even beyond that of either Qu Dajun or Chen Gongyin; ibid, 291.

73 Cited at Huang Foyi, *Guangzhou chengfang zhi*, 5.10b.

74 Ibid, 5.11a.

75 Ibid, 5.9a.

76 Another rare source, the *Yue xiaoji* 粵小記, or *Minor Record of Yue* (cited in Huang Foyi, *Guangzhou chengfang zhi*, 5.11a), records that Chen Zizhuang and his 11 other friends convened a poetry society in the Fuqiu Monastery in language reminiscent of the founding of the Southern Garden Poetry Society; this source clearly mixes up just which poetry society was at question.

77 For this Daoist genie, Fuqiu Gong 浮丘公, see *Lishi zhenxian tidao tongjian* 歷世真仙體道通鑑 (*Zhengtong Daozang* ed.), HY #295, 8:6204.

78 See Chen Shaoru's 陳紹儒 historical essay on this mountain at GDWZ, 3:137.

79 GDXY, 12.355–57. Another short essay on poetry societies in Guangzhou is by Qiu Juchuan 仇巨川 (fl. 17th century), *Yangcheng guchao* 羊城古鈔 (Guangzhou: Guangdong renmin chubanshe, 1993), 207–12. Herein Qiu reviews the Southern Garden, the Fuqiu, the Kelin jingshe, and the Yueshan poetry societies. All of these poetry clubs have been or will be mentioned in the course of the present work.

80 The *Yuexiao ji* (at Huang Foyi, *Guangzhou chengfang zhi*, 5.11a) offers an alternate first precedent for poetry societies in Guangdong: "poetry societies in Yue started with Li Zhongjian 李忠簡 (Maoying) of the Song; by the Ming they were flourishing in our Yue."

81 Wang Jiankui 王漸逵 (1498–1559, *zi* Yongyi 用儀 and Bohong 伯鴻) was from Panyu. He studied the classics under Zhan Ruoshui 湛若水 (1466–1560), and gained his *jinshi* degree in 1518. He served as the Secretary of the Ministry of Justice, but after the fifth in a series of blunt memorials to the throne went unheeded, he retired with the excuse of needing to take care of his family. He authored a number of works on the classics, history, and government, and he was particularly occupied with Neo-Confucian thought in his old age. He was equally active as a poet, and composed several *fu* on local sites, including one to celebrate a trip to Mt. Luofu (GDWZ, 2:368). He was known as the Master of the Green Wisteria 青蘿先生, taken from the hills around where he grew up near Shawan 沙灣. His *Qingluo ji* 青蘿集 is not extant today. The office by which Wang was called here, Grand Master of Splendid Happiness, was an honorary title, granted posthumously (Hucker #3349). For his biography, see GDTZ, 278.22a–22b; a selection of prose is included in GDWZ, 2:358–69. For the Yueshan Poetry Society, see Qiu Juchuan, *Yangcheng guchao*, 208 and Yu Weng, *Yilin conglu*, 163.

82 Lun Yixun 倫以訓 (*zi* Shiyan 式彥) was the second son of probably the most famous Cantonese folk hero of all times, the talented and clever rogue of a literatus, Lun Wenxu 倫文敘 (*zi* Bochou 伯疇) from Nanhai. In 1489 Lun Wenxu earned his *juren* degree by passing the provincial examination; in 1499 he gained first place in both the metropolitan examination and the palace examination. His performance in these exams, especially his ability to think quickly on his feet to defeat his rivals, won him lasting fame back home. Some feel for the notoriety among the Cantonese populace of Lun Wenxu may be gleaned from the following popular novels: *Guicai Lun Wenxu* 鬼才倫文敘 or *The Devilish Talent Lun Wenxu*, ed. He Yancheng 何燕成 (Hong Kong: Xinsheng chubanshe, n.d.) and *Guicai Lun Wenxu quanji* 鬼才倫

文敍全集, or *The Complete Works of that Devilish Talent Lun Wenxu*, ed. Chen Shu 襯叔 (Hong Kong: Xinsheng chubanshe, n.d.). All three of his sons became *jinshi*. First son Yiliang 以諒 (*zi* Yanzhou 彥周) won his provincial examination; Yixun 以訓 his metropolitan examination, and Yishen 以詵 (*zi* Yanqun 彥羣) his palace examination. Father and sons all placing first in their exams and earning *jinshi* degrees was a remarkable feat. Lun Wenxu and Yixun were both *zhuangyuan* 狀元 as they placed first in high examinations, the palace examination for Lun Wenxu and the metropolitan for Yixun (it should be noted that he gained a second place in the palace examination). Qu Dajun memorialized the accomplishments of this family of scholars in his *Guangdong xinyu*, calling them collectively the "four first-place finishers and two pairs of *jinshi*; in examination circles throughout the empire this is the ultimate in fame" 四元雙進士，海內科名之盛; GDXY, 9.282. All four have biographies in GDTZ, 276.15a–18a; selections of their prose are included in GDWZ, 2:141–45, 355–57, 381–83, and 3:149–50. Much of their extant poetry can be found in GDWX, 7:109–42. Lun Yixun's biography does mention his intimate friendship with Wang Jiankui. Lun merits the title of chancellor 祭酒 because he directed the national university in Nanjing.

83 Guo Fei 郭棐 is otherwise unknown. Wang Xuezeng 王學曾 has a short entry in GDTZ, 282.3a–5a. Hailing from Nanhai, he earned his *jinshi* degree in 1578. He served in various provinces around the realm before being summoned to the capital to work in the ministry of rites and imperial secretariat. He seems to have been a forthright official, who more than once offended His Highness with the bluntness of his recommendations. His only compositions were various poetic anthologies. There is no mention of the Fuqiu poetry society in this biography.

84 Chen Zizhuang and the "Twelve Masters off the Southern Garden Poetry" are treated in Chapter Five below. But Qu Dajun seems to be mistaken when he attributes the founding of the Pure Society of the Myrobalan Grove 訶林淨社 to Chen Zizhuang. According to the Qianlong era *Nanhai xianzhi* 南海縣誌 and *Guangzhou fuzhi* 廣州府誌, the society had been founded by Ou Daren, Liang Youyu, and Li Minbiao, et al., three of the Five Later Masters of the Southern Garden; see Huang Foyi, *Guangzhou chengfang zhi*, 3.74b, 81b. It appears then that Chen Zizhuang and his band reconvened the Pure Society, as is clearly stated at *Guangzhou chengfang zhi*, 78b, for the purpose of providing a tranquil environment for the "left-over old men" (*yilao* 遺老) of the Ming, some of whom chose to live within the precincts of the temple as laymen.

85 Ye Shidong is otherwise unknown.

86 For the relationship between *shishe* and *shipai*, see Huang Zhimin, "Mingren shishe zhi yanjiu," 68–85.

87 Hu Yinglin 胡應麟, *Shisou* 詩藪 (Shanghai: Shanghai guji chubanshe, 1958), 341; paraphrased in the *Siku quanshu zongmu tiyao,* 169.4b, in the analysis of the *Chaweng shiji* 槎翁詩集 of Liu Song. Also repeated in Liang Qiqiao 梁啟超, *Shishi* 詩史 (Guangzhou, n.d.), 49–50. All except Liu Song have entries in DMB. For Liu, see his short biography at MS, 137.3957–58; other biographical entries are noted at *Bashijiuzhong Mingdai zhuanji* 八十九種明代傳記, ed. Tian Jizong 田繼綜 (1935; rpt., Shanghai: Shanghai guji chubanshe, 1982), 234. Gao Qi is the subject of a study by Frederick Mote, *The Poet Kao Ch'i 1336–1374* (Princeton: Princeton

University Press, 1962). In Yokota Terutoshi's analysis of early Ming poetical societies, he includes only two from this grouping, those of Gao Qi and Lin Hong, and adds a third of his own choosing, the *Chaling pai* 茶陵派 of Li Dongyang. The latter was rather more of a transitional figure between the early poetry societies and the most famous Ming literary circle, the mid-Ming "Former Seven Ming Masters" 前後七子, as typified by Li Mengyang 李夢陽 (1473 –1529). See Yokota Terutoshi 横田輝俊, "Minsho no shisha" 明初の詩社 *Shinagaku kenkyū* 26 (1961): 39–54; Zhou Yinbin 周寅賓, "Mingdai de Chaling shipai" 明代的茶陵詩派, *Xuelin manlu* 學林漫錄, vol. 10 (Beijing: Zhonghua shuju, 1985), 181–85. Yoshikawa Kōjirō, *Five Hundred Years of Chinese Poetry, 1150–1650*, trans. John Timothy Wixted (Princeton: Princeton University Press, 1989), 120, mentions that poetry societies flourished in Guangdong as well as in Fujian in early Ming times without being more specific. Even though he is a specialist on historical Cantonese literati, Zhou Weimin 周偉民, *Ming-Qing shige* 明清詩歌 (Changchun: Jilin jiaoyu chubanshe, 1995), 59–66 only recognizes three schools of poetry: that of Yue 越 or Zhejiang, that of Wu 吳 or Suzhou, and that of Min 閩 or Fujian. Virtually all poetry societies of the Ming period are treated to some degree in Huang Zhimin, "Mingren shishe zhi yanjiu."

88 The Four Eminences of Wu were Gao Qi, Yang Ji 楊基 (ca. 1334–ca. 1383), Zhang Yu 張羽 (1333–1385), and Xu Ben 徐賁 (1335–1380); all have entries in DMB.

89 The Ten Talents of Minzhong consisted of the group of literati centered around Lin Hong, including Zheng Ding 鄭定, Wang Bao 王褒, Tang Tai 唐泰, Gao Bing 高棅, Wang Gong 王恭, Chen Liang 陳亮, Wang Cheng 王偁, and two disciples of Lin called Zhou Xuan 周玄 and Huang Xuan 黃玄. For the favorable comparison of the poetry of the Five Former Masters with the poetry of the Four Eminences of Wu and the Ten Talents of Min, see the preface (dated 1639) to the reprinting of *Nanyuan wuxiansheng shi* 南園五先生詩 (*Qiaoshan caotang* 樵山草堂 ed.). Li Dechao also agrees with this assessment; see his "Yuedong Nanyuan Shishe ji qianhou wuxiansheng shi" 粵東南園詩社及前後五先生詩, *Huagang wenke xuebao* 16 (1988): 201–22.

90 Cai Yujun 蔡瑜君, *Gao Bing shixue yanjiu* 高棅詩學研究 (Taipei: National Taiwan University, 1990).

91 The 1937 printing of Sun's collected works, the *Sun Xi'anji* 孫西庵集 (*Zimingchenglou congshu* 自明誠樓叢書 ed.; Shunde: Longshi Zhongheyuan, 1934–1937), contains much prefatory matter, including a lengthy biography with fulsome praise from colleagues. Editions of Sun's anthology are evaluated below in the annotations to his biography.

92 For example, I have been unable to find any poems dedicated to a specific *shishe* in the extant poetry of the other four early Ming schools, although some occasional verse does exist that is dedicated to informal socializing.

93 See James Cahill, *Parting at the Shore: Chinese Painting of the Early and Middle Ming Dynasty, 1368–1580* (New York and Tokyo: Weatherhill, 1978), Color Plate 2 for the painting, and pages 24–25 for discussion. Xie was a scholar as well as painter, and served as Yongle's 永樂 (1359–1424) artistic advisor; we may therefore assume that he was very familiar with literati sociality; see Osvald Siren, *A History of Later Chinese Painting*, 2 vols. (New York: Hacker Art Books, 1978), 1:29.

94 GDWZ, 2:1–3.

95 MS, 285.7331–33; GDTZ, 271.20a–26b.

96 DMB, 2:1216–17.

97 The Chinese sources I have consulted, besides GDTZ, 271.20a–26b, include Huang Zuo, *Guangzhou renwu zhuan*, 12.1a–2b; MS, 285.7331–33; and *Gujin tushu jicheng* 古今圖書集成, 79 vols. (Taipei: Dingwen shuju, 1980), 34:1361. W. Pachow mentions several others; *Bashijiuzhong Mingdai zhuanji*, 97 lists 13 sources not referenced by Pachow. See further the references to local gazetteers included in Poon Mingsun, *Guangdong difangzhi zhuanji suoyin*, 2:166, #6330.

98 The *Gujin tushu jicheng* account, as well as the interlinear commentary in the gazetteer, note that "today," i.e. late Qing, Nanhai was under the administrative control of Shunde 順德; hence he could equally be termed a man from Shunde as he is in some biographies. Huang Zuo's *Guangzhou renwu zhuan* adds that he came from the Pingbu 平步 area of Nanhai (12.1a), as does the *Guangdong tongzhi* (Jiajing 嘉靖 ed.), ed. Huang Zuo (Hong Kong: Dadong tushu gongsi, 1977), 59.15a. For a traditional map of Pingbu, see *Shunde xianzhi*, *juan* 2, 45 (a modern reprinting that combines the Qing Xianfeng 咸豐 [1851–1861] and Republican editions); *juan* 23, 674–76 contains the most detailed biography of Sun. The history of the administrative geography of Nanhai is outlined in 3.1a–3a. The natural environment of Nanhai and its human ecology some twenty-five years before Sun Fen's birth are accessible in *Dade Nanhai zhi* (Dade was the period from 1297 to 1308).

99 This phrase, not in the gazetteer, is found in the MS and *Gujin tushu jicheng* biographies.

100 The *Siku* editors evaluate his poetry as being in "the intricate and ornate style left over from the Yuan period; yet his poems were singularly outstanding in the ancient style. Even though his spirit was significant and his structure extraordinary, they did not come up to those of Gao Qi, but were unapproachable by Lin Hong and those associated with him"; SKQS, 169.24b–25a. Critic Deng Qiu 鄧球 assessed his poetry as "heroic and eremitic, sufficient to be considered as following after the ancients"; see *Mingshi jishi* 明詩紀事, 6 vols, ed. Chen Tian 陳田 (Shanghai: Shanghai guji chubanshe, 1993), 1:198. More critical evaluations are included on 198–200, but a better source is the 1937 printing of the 1770 *Sun Xi'anji*; it contains a "Poetic Evaluations" 詩評 section included in a lengthy "Introduction" 卷首, 10a–11b, that was compiled in 1831 by Cantonese literatus Liang Tingnan 梁廷枏. One critic considered his pentasyllabic and heptasyllabic ancient style verse even better than that of Tang poets; "Introduction," 9b. Sun was also particularly noted for his poetical depictions of landscapes, an important component of the Southern Muse; his poem "Descending to Jutang" 下瞿塘 was singled out for special attention in a book treating the development of landscape poetry; see Li Wenchu 李文初, et al., *Zhongguo shanshui shishi* 中國山水詩史 (Guangzhou: Guangdong gaodeng jiaoyu chubanshe, 1991), 344–45.

101 The *Gujin tushu jicheng* version reads *wang* 忘 "forget" instead of the *wang* 妄 "rashly" of the gazetteer, yielding a sense of "he did not forget his associates nor acquaintances."

102 The wording of this sentence is from *Gujin tushu jicheng*.

103 He Zhen was a military leader serving the Mongols who protected the region from the depredations of rebels against the dynasty; see DMB, 1.504, and Qiu Juchuan,

Yangcheng guchao, 350–57 for He Zhen and the surrender of Guangzhou. More biographical particulars are revealed in Chen Zehong, ed., *Guangdong lishi mingren zhuanlüe*, 101–106.

104 The conquest of the south in the name of Zhu Yuanzhang by general Liao Yongzhong is sketched at DMB, 1:909–10. See further, Edward L. Dreyer, "Military Origins of Ming China," in *The Cambridge History of China, Vol. 7: The Ming Dynasty (1368–1644), Part I*, ed. Frederick W. Mote and Denis Twitchett (Cambridge: Cambridge University Press, 1988), 96–98.

105 The Regional Inspector was the governor of the commandery.

106 Huang Zuo, *Guangzhou renwu zhuan*, 12.1b adds the following amplification: "On the basis of Fen's expertise in the *Shijing*, he was one of the highest examinees in the Metropolitan Examination; his essay was selected for discussion. In both the Metropolitan and the Palace Examinations he was set in the front rank and given the degree of Metropolitan Graduate 進士." Huang Yunmei 黃雲眉, *Mingshi kaozheng* 明史考證 (Beijing: Zhonghua shuju, 1985), 7:2227 adds that his *jinshi* degree should be qualified as one that had been earned after having being a prefectural nominee 鄉貢.

107 Additional wording from *Gujin tushu jicheng* and Huang Zuo, *Guangzhou renwu zhuan*.

108 For the great statesman Song Lian and his two notable fellow officials Yue Shaofeng and Zhan Tong, see DMB, 2:1225–31, 2:1641–42, and 1:43–44.

109 For this phonological dictionary, see Li Jinhua 李晉華, *Mingdai chizhuan shukao* 明代勅撰書考, Harvard-Yenching Institute Sinological Index Series, Supplement no. 3 (Beiping: Yanjing University Library, 1932), 11; SKQS, 1.241.

110 This song is not included in the XAJ.

111 The numerous historical gazetteers on Nanjing that I consulted preserve no information on this gate.

112 The last entry in Sun's anthology is "He 'Guiqulai ci,'" or "Matching Rhymes with 'To Return'" (XAJ, 9.8b–9b). It was written when leaving Pingyuan; there must have been another poem with the same title, for Huang Zuo's *Guangzhou renwu zhuan* includes a line from it at this point that does not appear in the one included in XAJ. Sun produced a separately published anthology, no longer extant, entitled *He Tao ji* 和陶集, or *Collection Matching Poems with Tao Qian*, composed entirely of poems in this style.

113 The specific year of this incident is found in Sun's biography composed by Huang Zuo.

114 General Lan Yu (d. 1393) was executed as part of Zhu Yuanzhang's grand design to purge the military of its power; it is said that 15,000 people were executed in conjunction with this purge; see Lan's biography in DMB, 1.788–91, and discussion in *The Cambridge History of China. Vol. 7: The Ming Dynasty (1368–1644), Part I*, 169–172. Cf. Lu Ping 路平, "Nanyuan Qian Wuzi yu Zhu Yuanzhang de wenwang" 南園前五子與朱元璋的文網, in Lu Ping, *Guangzhou fengwu*, 369–71.

115 Zhao Yi 趙翼 (1727–1814), *Gaiyu congkao* 陔餘叢考 (Shanghai: Commercial Press, 1957), 496–97, maintains that Sun did not compose a poem on the spot but rather recited an earlier one written by Jiang Wei 江為 of the Five Dynasties era, who had fallen to a similar fate. Sun's poem, "Improvisation on Facing Execution" 臨形口占,

is preserved in XAJ, 7.44a. Perhaps Sun Fen was imitating an earlier precedent by Xie Lingyun 謝靈運 (385–433), who, although not Cantonese, had been ignominiously executed in exile in Guangzhou after reciting an extempore poem. For this poem, see *Songshu* 宋書, 67.1777, and the translation and analysis by Wu Fusheng, "Composed at Execution: A Look at Three 'Poems Upon Confronting the End' (LINZHONG SHI)," *Early Medieval China* 9 (2003): 105–25. At any rate, after Sun's poem in the *Xi'an ji* is appended a story from the *Mingxing zaji* 明興雜記 which recounts the fanciful tale that the Hongwu emperor asked the supervising official if Sun had left any last words. Upon hearing this poem repeated, he became enraged and asked why the official had not delayed the execution until he reported such a good poem to the throne. Subsequently, the emperor had the official executed. Sun's improvisation was included, along with seven other poems by Sun Fen, in a modern anthology of Cantonese poets, Chen Yongzheng, ed. *Lingnan lidai shixuan* 嶺南歷代詩選 (Guangzhou: Guangdong renmin chubanshe, 1985), 181.

116 These last two lines are from Huang Zuo.

117 Li Zhen from Xinhui 新會, Guangdong, has biographical entries at GDTZ, 271.26b–28a and Huang Zuo, *Guangzhou renwu zhuan*, 13.1a–2a. Seventeen of his prose and poetical pieces are included at GDWZ; the introduction to his selections denies that he was a disciple of Sun Fen, and classifies him instead as a man of late Yuan; GDWZ, 1:159.

118 Following Huang Zuo; GDTZ reads Ansi 安四.

119 Preserved in Song Lian, *Song Wenxian Gong quanji* 宋文憲公全集 (SBCK ed.), 7.14a–14b.

120 Much of the poetry written in the style of Tao Qian and in regulated verse, both constituting one *juan* each, must have been conflated into one *juan* and added to the eight *juan* edition compiled by Li Zhen, resulting in a nine *juan* edition. But in some editions the ninth *juan* consists of prose pieces. And one version evaluated in Huang Yuji 黃虞稷 (1629–1691), *Qianqingtang shumu, fu suoyin* 千頃堂書目(附索引) (Shanghai: Shanghai guji chubanshe, 2001), *juan* 17.454 describes another nine juan edition with one extra juan of pastiche verses "collected from the ancients" plus the *He Tao ji*: 西庵集九卷又孙典籍集句一卷又和陶集. The first extant nine *juan* version was edited by Ye Chuchun 葉初春 (*jinshi* 1580) from Suzhou who was serving as the prefect of Shunde. It was a copy of this version that was printed in the SKQS in 1782. In 1739 Cantonese scholars Ye Fengchun 葉逢春 and Liu Hanyi 劉漢裔 recopied and re-engraved this version. Eighteen years later (1758), Sun Fen's eighth-generation grandson Sun Kangye 孫康業 made a new engraving, with eight *juan* of poetry and one *juan* of prose. But it was not printed in full until 1770 and again in 1777. The 1770 edition was titled *Sun Xi'an ji* 孫西庵集 and includes a biography of Sun composed by the editor. Exemplars of this edition are preserved in the Tōyō Bunka library in Tokyo and the Guangzhou Zhongshan Library. In 1937 this version in eight *juan* (minus the *juan* of prose) was reprinted in the *Zimingchenglou congshu* 自明誠樓叢書 (Shunde: Longshi Zhongheyuan, 1934–1937) and contains much prefatory matter of value, especially an analysis of the filiation history of the various editions and a compilation of poetic evaluations of Sun. It also includes all former prefaces and biographies. An exemplar of this edition is preserved in the Harvard-Yenching library.

A rare ten *juan* version came to light with the publication in 1933 of a catalogue of the rare books contained in the Peiping library; *Guoli Beiping Tushuguan shanben shumu* 國立北平圖書館善本書目 (Guangzhou, 1933), 4.20b. A detailed physical description is contained in a 1987 catalogue, *Beijing Tushuguan guji shanben shumu* 北京圖書館古籍善本書目, 5 vols. (Beijing: Shumu wenxian chubanshe, 1987), 4:2314. Apparently Zhang Xi 張習 (*jinshi* 1469) from Suzhou visited Guangzhou as a retired Assistant Surveillance Commissioner. Already active in republishing the works of several early Ming poets including Yang Ji, Xu Ben, and Gao Qi, his interest was piqued by Sun Fen's works. After he discovered an old edition of XAJ in an old box, he contributed a preface to the movable type edition printed by the local prefect in 1503. This version made its way to Taiwan as one of the national treasures brought over by the KMT in 1949 and was microfilmed by the Library of Congress while the rare books in the National Library of Peiping were housed in Washington for safekeeping during World War Two. Copies of this microfilm are kept at the Library of Congress, the University of Chicago, and the Nanjing Municipal Library. The version, still preserved among the rare books of the Beijing Library, was found to contain a seal from the original Tianyige 天一閣 library of Fan Qin 范欽 (1506–1585).

The most detailed evaluation of the ten *juan* version is *Xuxiu Sikuquanshu tiyao* 續修四庫全書提要 (Taipei: Commercial Press, 1972), *jibu* 集部, 30. The ten *juan* edition contains 90 poems not present in the SKQS edition; eight poems in the received version are missing from the ten *juan* version, and none of the prose pieces contained in the 1770 and 1777 *Sun Xi'an ji* editions are included. A traditional bibliographical account of Sun's poetic works is found at *Shunde xianzhi*, 18.2–4b. For an exhaustive evaluation of the XAJ, see my "Bibliographical Notes on Editions of the *Hsi-an chi*." Paper Presented at the Conference on the Genealogy and Culture of South China, Brigham Young University, Provo, Utah, August 13–15, 1996.

121 Zhao Chun is otherwise unknown. But Huang Yunmei, *Mingshi kaocheng*, 7:2227 suspects that Zhao Chun may have been the Zhao Xun 絢 mentioned by Huang Zuo, *Guangzhou renwu zhuan*, 291 as having composed a biography of Sun.

122 Odd items not included in the other sources are found in *Guangdong tongzhi* (Jiajing 嘉靖 ed.), 59.16b–21b (4:1556–59).

123 The conventional date for the founding of the poetry society is between the years 1355–1356. Thus, the society was formed at the end of the Yuan. As the period of its activity came before the five founding members joined the Ming bureaucracy in various capacities, their society can be characterized as a "left-over" type, being organized by "left-over citizens" 遺民 of a defunct dynasty; nevertheless it still partook of the other two major identifying elements of being centered around a major literary figure and having the purpose of entertainment. For the dating of its founding, see Huang Zhimin, "Mingren shishe zhi yanjiu," 86–89.

124 Luo Tianchi maintains that the Veranda for Screening the Wind was originally the dwelling of Sun Fen; see Luo Tianchi 羅天尺, *Wushan zhilin* 五山志林 (Beijing: Zhonghua shuju, 1985), 50.

125 The event as recorded in Song Lian's biography at MS, 128.3787, seems to be a conflation of similar happenings, for His Highness presented horses to Song Lian on two occasions, once a white horse and once a bay. Both events merited imperial

compositions, which were somehow left out of the modern compilation of Zhu Yuanzhang, *Ming Taizu ji* 明太祖集 (Anhui: Huangshan shushe, 1991), but have been included in *Quan Mingshi* 全明詩, 3 vols. (Shanghai: Shanghai guji chubanshe, 1990–1994), 1:52. Wang Zuo's poem seems to have been occasioned by the second presentation.

126 Wang's composition, entitled "Responding to Imperial Command on the Presentation of a Fine Horse to Prime Minister Song" 應制賜宋承旨馬 is preserved at GZSS, 3.2b.

127 For Liu Sanwu, see DMB, 1:956–58.

128 GZSS, 3; NYQS, 87–96.

129 GZSS, 2; NYQS, 98–117.

130 Li Zhen, a disciple of Sun Fen, wrote a lengthy biographical overview 形狀 on Zhao Jie; see GDWZ, 1:164–65. Wu Jiu 无咎 has a short notice determining Zhao Jie's birth date, something hitherto unknown; see *Yilin conglu*, 58.

131 A modern gazetteer preserves the lore and selected poetry of this mountainous retreat important to many historical Cantonese worthies; see *Xiqiaoshan zhi* 西樵山志 (Guangdong: Guangdong renmin chubanshe, 1992).

132 GZSS, 4; NYQS, 17–20.

133 His fondness for the *Wenxuan* and its author is further illustrated by a later event from his biography: "Once he passed by the tomb of Prince Zhaoming of Liang; he wrote a poem to lament him. Critics said, 'Placing it among the poems of the *Wenxuan*, it almost certainly could not be distinguished for quality'"; GDTZ, 271.26b. This poem, "Passing the Tomb of Prince Zhaoming of Liang" 過梁昭明太子墳墓 is preserved in GZSS, 1.7b–8a; NYQS, 125.

134 GDTZ, 271.24b–25a.

135 Called "Fenghe shengzhi Zhongshan daoyu huoying" 奉和聖制鐘山禱雨穫應, GZSS, 1.16a–b; NYQS, 135.

136 The text of an exorcistic prayer offered at a Hongfan 洪范 Shrine is included in GZSS, 1.9b; NYQS, 127.

137 Included in GZSS, 1; NYQS, 120–57.

138 GZSS, 1.29b–30a; NYQS, 151.

139 GZSS, 1.19b–20a; NYQS, 139–40.

140 "Encountering Zhao Wangzhong in Jinling" 金陵逢趙汪中, GZSS, 2.13b–14a; NYQS, 113.

Chapter 3

1 Andrew H. Plaks effectively encapsulates the early Chinese view of the garden as *locus amoenus*, "a paradise of earthly pleasures," and its later functions as refuge for reflection or retreat for cultivated entertainment; see Plaks, "The Chinese Literary Garden," in *Archetype and Allegory in the "Dream of the Red Chamber"* (Princeton: Princeton University Press, 1976), 146–77. The popularity of garden settings for poetry societies during the transition period between Yuan and Ming is reiterated by Huang Zhimin, "Mingren shishe zhi yanjiu," 41. On the aesthetics of the Chinese garden in general during this period, consult Craig Clunas, *Fruitful Sites: Garden Culture in Ming Dynasty China* (London: Reaktion Books, 1996).

2 QSS, 4:2656.

3 Cf. *Minzhong shizi shi* 閩中十子詩, ed. Yuan Biao 袁表 (*juren* 1558) and Ma Ying 馬熒 (fl. 16th century) (SKQS ed.), 6.1a–1b.

4 See Ellen Johnston Laing, "Real or Ideal: The Problem of the 'Elegant Gathering in the Western Garden' in Chinese Historical and Art Historical Records," *Journal of the American Oriental Society* 88 (1968): 419–35.

5 Studies of the Southern Garden Poetry Society include Wang Zongyan, *Guangdong wenwu congtan*, 1-6; Qu Xiangbang, *Guangdong shihua zhengxubian*, 1–2; and Li Dechao, "Yuedong Nanyuan Shishe ji qianhou wuxiansheng shi," 201–22.

6 Huang Zhimin, "Mingren shishe zhi yanjiu," 19–37.

7 John W. Dardess, *Confucianism and Autocracy* (Berkeley and Los Angeles: University of California Press, 1983), 87 suggests that Confucians faced two intellectual choices at the end of the Yuan dynasty: Yuan loyalism or disloyalism. Perhaps the founding of the Southern Garden Poetry Society at this juncture suggests another option available at the time: avoid making a choice and withdraw from politics to engage in safe socializing in a literary garden.

8 GDXY, 2:470–71 includes a lengthy notice entitled "Famous Gardens" 名園 in which Qu literally boxes the compass as he tours these notable enclaves scattered about the city.

9 Fan Duan'ang, *Yuezhong jianwen*, 29.

10 Luo Tianchi, *Wushan zhilin*, 50. Early inspiration for this name may perhaps be found in Tang times, for the park area surrounding the Xingqing Palace 興慶宮 during the reigns of Zhongzong and Xuanzong was known as the "Southern Inner Park" 南內苑; it had been mentioned in verse by Du Fu. If Sun did indeed recall this loose precedent, then it should be viewed as being part of his poetic effort to identify the early Ming with the early Tang. See D. L. McMullen, "Recollection without Tranquility: Du Fu, the Imperial Gardens, and the State," *Asia Major*, Third Series, 14 (2001), 211.

11 Huang Fuoyi, *Guangzhou chengfang zhi*, 4.36b. Li Dechao, "Yuedong Nanyuan Shishe ji qianhou wuxiansheng shi," 203, corrects the erroneous view that the site was one *li* beyond the city wall. An alternate view, supported by Meng Ziwei 孟子微 at "Nanyuan shiren Ou Daren" 南園詩人歐大任, *Yilin conglu*, 169, holds that the original site is presently occupied by the Southern Garden Restaurant 南園酒家 directly across the Pearl River three miles south in the district today called Nanyuan. Virtually every other authority agrees with Huang.

12 Wang Zongyan, *Guangdong wenwu congtan*, 1. The information about the bookseller is taken from: www.gzlib.gov.cn/gzfw/detail.asp?a_id=777&style=1 (accessed May 29, 2005), the website of the Guangzhou Library. A search of the home page of the Guangzhou Library, www.gzlib.gov.cn/, still yields much data concerning the Southern Garden, but not this particular bit of information.

13 Nine other attendees are listed in Huang Zuo, *Guangzhou renwu zhuan*, 302, and repeated at GZSS, 4.2b. They are Huang Chujin 黃楚金, an administrative aide; Cai Yanghui 蔡養晦, a recruit for office (i.e. "someone nominated by local authorities and summoned to court for possible placement in the officialdom," Hucker #435); Huang Xigong 黃希貢; Huang Xiwen 黃希文; an administrator named Pu Ziwen 蒲子文; an archivist, Huang Yuanshan 黃原善; a *jinshi*, Zhao Anzhong 趙安

中; and Zhao's younger brothers Zhao Cheng 澄, who was an assistant prefect, and Zhao Ne 訥, also a recruit for office. All these participants appear to be low- to mid-level members of the local bureaucracy and were most likely young locals recruited to serve on the staff of magistrates or prefects. It is likely that Huang Xigong and Huang Xiwen were also brothers. None of these eight seem to otherwise appear in the historical record.

14 For instance, Liang Wei 梁韡 (*zi* Wenhuan 文煥, *hao* Ledao 樂道, fl. 1435), met with others in the Southern Garden to write poems to set rhymes, as seen in the title of his own contribution: "A Refined Gathering in the Southern Garden, I Obtained By Turn the 'Pei' Character" 南園雅集，分得陪字. What is interesting about Liang's attendance at the Southern Garden on this particular evening is that separate from this he had joined with other local poets in reconvening the Phoenix Terrance Poetry Society in Dongguan. Apparently some degree of fluidity in socializing in literary circles was possible and probably even common. The first line mentions yet a third poetry club: "The White Poetry Society has come from far beyond the outer walls to meet,/Talented persons gather for a banquet amid the stacks of cyan clouds" 白社偏從郭外開，才人宴集碧雲堆. For this poem, see Zhang Qigan, ed., *Dongguan shilu*, 218.

15 GDXY, 17.471.

16 Alison Hardie, trans., *The Craft of Gardens: Chi Cheng*, with photographs by Zhong Ming (New Haven and London: Yale University Press, 1988), 53. For the location of the Pearl River in relation to the city walls of Guangzhou during the Ming dynasty, see Zeng Zhaoxuan, *Guangzhou lishi dili*, 56–58.

17 According to the *Panyuxian xuzhi* 番禺縣續志, cited in Huang Foyi, *Guangzhou chengfang zhi*, 4.37b.

18 XAJ, 1.2b; NYQS, 31.

19 *Nanbeichaoshi* (XQHS ed.), 1:330; Jean-Pierre Diény, *Les Dix-neuf poèms anciens* (1963; rpt., Paris: Université Paris VII, Centre de Publication Asie Orientale, 1974), 15, 71–77.

20 XAJ, 1.15b. This poem is translated in its entirety in Chapter Four below.

21 Cao Zhi's line reads: "On a clear evening, roaming in the Western Garden" 清夜遊西園; *Chen Siwang ji* 陳思王集 (BSJJ ed.), 2.11a; XQHS, 1:449–50; WX, 20.14b–15a. The introduction to this poem in Cao's collected works reveals that the Duke in question was Cao Zhi's elder brother, Cao Pi 曹丕 (187–226); the setting was a palace in Ye 鄴.

22 Sun must have been especially fond of this term for it appears frequently in his poetic oeuvre. For instance, it is used in the next poem by Sun to be discussed; see also Sun's imitation of an *Nineteen Old poem* that starts out "The florescent moonlight is scattered amid lofty trees" 華月散高樹; XAJ, 1.15b.

23 See *Shiji*, 25.1245. The image reappears in a poem sent by Sun to a good friend from Guangdong: "Sent to Gao Bin" 寄高彬, XAJ, 7.11b.

24 See glosses to *Shijing*, 1e.13a, Mao #25, "Zouyu" 騶虞; Legge, *The Chinese Classics*, 4:37. Sun recycles this term in another poem written on imperial command, so we may safely conclude that its use was a purposeful nod to imperial prestige; see XAJ, 1.11b.

25 On the spread and development of the dominant Chinese culture in Guangdong

throughout history, see Hisayuki Miyakawa, "The Confucianism of South China," in *The Confucian Persuasion*, ed. Arthur F. Wright (Stanford: Stanford University Press, 1960), 21–46.

26 Sitting on mats in the Chinese literary garden was a common trope; see Plaks, *Archetype and Allegory in the "Dream of the Red Chamber,"* 158.

27 For the presence of geishas and musical entertainment at the soirees of most poetry societies, consult the extended treatment by Huang Zhimin, "Mingren shishe zhi yanjiu," 57, 60–67.

28 WX, 4.26b; Knechtges, *Wen xuan*, 1:357.

29 QTS, 1:7–8.

30 Tang Taizong, "Zhijiu zuo feige" 置酒坐飛閣, QTS, 1:12.

31 QTS, 1:2.

32 Especially after 1380, officially directed purges resulted in the deaths of more than 40,000 people, among them Sun Fen. For details, review John D. Langlois, Jr., "The Hung-wu reign, 1368–1398," in *The Cambridge History of China, Vol. 7, Part I*, 140–42; and Ku Chieh-kang, "A Study of Literary Persecution During the Ming Dynasty," trans. L. Carrington Goodrich, *Harvard Journal of Asiatic Studies* 3 (1938): 254–311.

33 In Daoist literature she—or in the plural, her order of spiritual serving maids—is a frequent participant in celestial ceremonies. For instance, she is found among the "spirit brights, attending guards, and jade lads" who make up a courtly retinue described at the *Miyao juefa* 秘要訣法, in *Yunji qiqian* 雲藉七籤, 3 vols. (Taiwan: Ziyu chubanshe, 1973), 2:655a, 657a; and in the "Chronicles of the Heavenly King of the Primal Beginning," *Yuanshi Tianwang ji* 元始天王紀 (*Yunji qiqian*, 3:1381b) she is present at his divine investiture. In a poem by the Tang poet Li Kangcheng 李康成, entitled "Song of the Jade-Flower Genies" 玉華仙子歌, she definitely appears in the plural: "We sight the Jade-Flowers from a distance, but they all conceal their charms" 遙見玉華皆掩嫭; QTS, 6:2129.

34 By "ancient origins" I have in mind the ancient feast at the village altar and the ritual function of astronomer He Zhong 和仲, ordered by Yao to "respectfully feast the setting sun" 寅餞納日 to aid autumn's harvest; *Shangshu*, "Yaotian" 堯典, 2.10a; for an alternate interpretation of this line, see Legge, *The Chinese Classics*, 3:20.

35 For instance, a poem by Wang Zuo characterizes poetry composition at night under the moon as "Linking lines of poetry on the altar of feathered guests" 夜月聯詩羽客壇; GZSS, 3.5a; NYQS, 90. Other Daoist elements in group outings not specifically associated with the Southern Garden appear liberally in the verses of Sun Fen, Li De, and Wang Zuo.

36 See *Liexian zhuan* 列仙傳, HY #294, 2.14b–15a for Lingyang Ziming, and *Lishi zhenxian tidao tongjian* 歷史真仙體道通鑑, HY #295, 4.13b, for Han Zhong.

37 For a dozen national and local holidays celebrated in Guangzhou during imperial times, see GDXY, 9.298–300, "Seasonal holidays in Guangzhou" 廣州時序.

38 XAJ, 3.1b–2a; NYQS, 47–48.

39 XAJ, 8.10a.

40 See XAJ, 8.15a.

41 See, e.g., the commentary at WX, 27.5b.

42 See "Longing for my Studio on Mt. Boyun" 懷白雲山房, XAJ, 5.15b: "My family

lived in Watchet Islet on a hill on the islet"; cf. XAJ, 6.17b. For Mt. Boyun and its resident Cantonese worthies over the ages, see GDXY, 3.80–1.

43 "Sent to Wang Zuo, Supervising Secretary" 寄王給事佐, XAJ, 1.10b; NYQS, 34.

44 "Sent to Wang Yanju" 寄王彥舉, XAJ, 7.12a; NYQS, 78.

45 For Little Jade 小玉 in verse, the *locus classicus* appears to be Bai Juyi's 白居易 poem "The Song of the Rainbow Gown and Feathered Cape" 霓裳羽衣歌, QTS, 13:4971: "The bewitching Little Jade from Wu flies, creating mist,/The voluptuous Xishi of Yue transforms, becoming dust" 吳妖小玉飛作煙, 越艷西施化為土; certain editions of Bai's poems make the identification of Little Jade as Wuwang Fuchai's 吳王夫差 daughter in the commentary. She also makes an appearance in Bai's famous "Song of Everlasting Sorrow" in conjunction with the term Golden Portals, as mentioned in Chapter Two. She appears with a Daoist maiden named Flying Carbuncle 飛瓊 in a verse by the Qing poet from Guangzhou Kuang Lu preserved in GDXY, 12.350 (Kuang Lu is introduced in Chapter Five).

46 XAJ, 1.3a; NYQS, 31.

47 "Probe secluded spots" 幽尋 is a phrase first employed by Luo Binwang 駱賓王 (fl. 640) in his poem "Late in Spring Roaming the Ancient Hills of Kaidaolin with Senior Scribe Li" 春晚從李長史游開道林古山: "Probing secluded spots in a gully that is the ultimate in seclusion,/Sight-seeing in spring we climb a spring terrace" 幽尋極幽壑，春望陟春臺; see QTS, 3:854.

48 "Recruited" 招攜 recalls pleasurable outings on hilltop gardens: "As for notable gents of talent, whenever frolicking and feasting took place on hilltop gardens, they were always recruited, grasping bows and reciting poems" 至於才名之士。。。每山園游燕必招攜，執射賦詩; *Beiqishu* 北齊書, "Wenxiangdi ji" 文襄帝紀, 3.31–32.

49 Officials are represented by the term "floral hairpins" 華簪; these were fancy hairpins used to pin caps of office onto the hair of the high officials; by extension it serves to denote these honorable officials themselves. Sima Guang 司馬光 (1019–1086) has a verse that illustrates this very well: "In life one honors fulfilling one's intents,/Why long for a floral hairpin?" 人生貴適意，何必慕華簪; see "Seeing Off Mr. Wu Geng" 送吳耿先生, QSS, 9:6092.

50 The locution *difanjin* 滌煩襟 is most often used metaphorically for "wash away my vexed depression"; see for instance Wang Bo 王勃 (649–676), "Touring the Buddhist Temple Three Enlightenment Monastery" 游梵宇三覺寺, at QTS, 3:675. But here Sun cleverly uses it literally to describe the muggy condition of the Cantonese summer.

51 "Seasonal rain" 澍雨 is another possible patriotic nod to the beneficence of Ming Taizu, for it portended imperial grace. For this use, see Wang Yucheng 王禹偁 (Song dynasty), "Memorial Expressing Gratitude for Issuing the Imperial Rites" 謝降御禮表; *Quan Songwen* 全宋文, 50 vols. (Sichuan: Bashu shushe, 1989), 4:296.

52 The phrase "sunk into oblivion" 銷沉 recalls some lines by Du Mu 杜牧 (803–852) in his "Ascending the Leyou Plateau" 登樂游原: "Across the long stretches of empty eerie space, a solitary bird is swallowed up,/Over ten thousand years of antiquity, all has passed into oblivion at this point" 長空澹澹孤鳥沒，萬古銷沉向此中; QTS, 16:5954.

53 Using the phrase "drink with abandon" 痛飲 is an adroit way to borrow what appears to be irresponsible behavior to elevate oneself and one's drinking buddies

into the category of "notable gents" 名士, for it derives from the *Shishuo xinyu* 世說新語, 5.198 (ZZJC ed.), "Rendan" 任誕: "A notable gent does not necessarily have to be an extraordinary one; as long as he would frequently drink with abandon when at leisure, and be thoroughly familiar with the 'Lisao,' then he could be called a notable gent."

54 XAJ, 1.6a; NYQS, 33.

Chapter 4

1 See Huang Zhe at GZSS, 1.30a; NYQS, 151: "The flowers blooming in the upper park sets parrots,/The green grass in the Southern Garden makes the francolins cry" 花開上苑啼鸚鵡，草綠南園泣鷓鴣. Zhao Jie at NYQS, 20, closes his poem with the hope that after the rain clears up his buddies will meet him at the Southern Garden for a drink. This particular poem is not found in GZSS but was included in Zhu Yizun 朱彝尊, ed., *Mingshi zong* 明詩綜 (Taibei: Shijie shuju, 1962), 11.28a.

2 GZSS, 2.5b; NYQS, 103.

3 That Li De conceived his poem in Cantonese rather than Early Mandarin *guanhua* is based on the fact that few of his rhymes share the same groups 攝 of either the Song dynasty rime tables or the dictionary of ca. 1333, the *Zhongyuan yinyun* 中原音韻.

4 Wang Zongyan, *Qu Wengshan nianpu*, 32.

5 Liang Peilan, *Liuyingtang ji*, 402. For a similar poem by Qu Dajun set at Fuqiu, see *Wengshan shiwai*, 6.31b.

6 This grotto was located on Mt. Luofu.

7 Qu Dajun, *Wengshan shiwai*, 13.42a.

8 GDSC, 2:480.

9 This is a quote from *The Heart of Perfect Wisdom Sutra, Prajñāpāramitā Hṛdaya Sūtra* 般若波羅蜜多心經, in *Taishū shinshū Daizōkyō* 大正新修大藏經, ed. Takakusu Junjirō 高楠順次郎 and Watanabe Kaigyoku 渡邊海旭 (Tokyo: Taishō Issaikyō Kankōkai, 1924–1934), vol. T08, No. 251.

10 See GDSC, 2:686. For more lore connecting butterflies with Daoism in Guangdong, see the *fu* on butterflies by Li Suiqiu, GDWZ, 4:313–14.

11 GDSC, 2:398.

12 Schafer, *The Vermilion Bird*, 87.

13 GDSC, 1:390.

14 According to the *Liji*, 14.14a, "Yueling" 月令, the east wind is the spring wind.

15 GDSC, 1:390.

16 GZSS, 2.7a–7b; NYQS, 105.

17 GZSS, 2.13b; NYQS, 113.

18 XAJ, 10 *juan* ed., 3.2a; XAJ, 1.15b. The title in the ten *juan* edition erroneously writes *xiao* 霄 "empyrean" for *yan* 宴 "banquet."

19 *Shijing* 詩經, 11a.1a, 1a.1a.

20 XAJ, 10 *juan* ed., 8.10b–11a.

21 "Primal Dragon" 元龍 refers to Chen Deng 陳登 of the Wei Kingdom who was known for his "heroic valor" and his military and civil aspirations; see *Sanguozhi* 三國志, 7.229–30.

22 An ancient song from Chu that came to symbolize highbrow literature and cultivated pastimes. See Song Yu 宋玉, "Responding to the King of Chu's Queries" 對楚王問,

WX, 45.1.

23 GDSC, 2:505.

24 It is likely that at least Liang's friend, Chen Gongyin, met at the Southern Garden. In 1660 Chen lived in isolation as one of the "Five Masters of the Northern Field." All of them were from Shunde 順德, Guangdong, and swore not to serve the new dynasty. One member, He Feng 何絳 (*zi* Buxie 不偕, 1627–1712) recorded in verse "Gathering at the Southern Garden Shrine to the Five Masters" 集南園五先生祠; Wen Runeng 溫汝能, comp., *Yuedong shihai* 粵東詩海, 3 vols. (Guangzhou: Zhongshan Daxue, 1999), 2:1083.

25 Liang Peilan, *Liuyingtang ji*, 51–52.

26 I take the word "leisurely" *xian* 閑 as an error for "closed" *bi* 閉, per a suggestion of Paul W. Kroll.

27 The "oarsman's song" 棹歌 is an allusion to Han Wudi's "Lyrics of the Autumn Wind" 秋風辭: "With flutes singing and drums sounding, we break forth in an oarsman's song,/Our delight has peaked, yet sorrowful sentiments abound" 簫鼓鳴兮發棹歌，歡樂極兮哀情多. See XQHS, 1:94.

28 Huang Zhimin, "Mingren shishe zhi yanjiu," 55.

29 GZSS, 2.4a–4b; NYQS, 101–02.

30 Huang Zhe, "Wang Yanju's Porch for Listening to the Rain" 王彥舉聽雨軒, GZSS, 1.19b–20a; NYQS, 139–40.

31 XAJ, 4.5a.

Chapter 5

1 Recently reprinted in 1990 with NYQS.

2 MS, 287.7366. Li Shixing was also possibly a student of Huang.

3 None of them have individual entries in DMB but are mentioned in the biography of Huang Zuo at DMB, 1:671. For another modern assessment of Huang, see Chen Zehong, ed., *Guangdong lishi mingren zhuanlüe*, 150–55. The main sources for their biographies are GDTZ, 280.4b–12a, and the individual biographies in NYHS. Other notices in various Cantonese gazetteers may be traced in Poon Ming-sun, *Guangdong difangzhi zhuanji suoyin*. Short introductions to Ou Daren and Li Minbiao are also found in MS, 287.7366; a more substantial entry on Liang Youyu is located at MS, 287.7378. Ou Daren is the subject of a modern biographical epitome by Meng Yuwei 孟于微 in *Yilin congtan*, 169–71. See also Chen Zehong, ed., *Guangdong lishi mingren zhuanlüe*, 176–84 for these Five Later Masters.

4 See Huang Yinpu, *Guangdong wenxian shumu zhijianlu*, 149. GDWZ, 3:341–55 records 25 prose items, and *Mingshi jishi*, 4:1935–1941 includes samples of his poetry. His "complete works" is exhaustively analyzed at *Shunde xianzhi*, 18.13a–18a.

5 Yan Song was a corrupt court official who worked his way from a Junior Compiler to Grand Preceptor of the Heir Apparent by ingratiating himself with the emperor; see MS, 308.7914–21. His attempted recruitment of Liang Youyu does not appear in any of Liang's traditional biographies but is mentioned in the modern introduction to Liang in NYHS, 163.

6 See GDWZ, 3:198–204 for eight of his prefaces, and *Mingshi jishi*, 4:1902–1906 for his poetry.

7 Cf. Huang Yinpu, *Guangdong wenxian shumu zhijianlu*, 149. For his necrology, see Ou Biyuan 歐必元, "Li Gong Minbiao zhuan" 黎公民表傳, GDWZ, 4:381. See GDWZ, 3:97–101 for three *fu* pieces, three records, and one preface, and *Mingshi jishi*, 4:1949–1956 for some poems.

8 See *Mingshi jishi*, 4:1970–1973.

9 Ibid, 4:1974.

10 GDTZ, 280.7b–8a.

11 Ibid.

12 Huang Foyi, *Guangzhou chengfang zhi*, 4.36b.

13 NYHS, 204.

14 "Irrigation pond" 滮池 as used by Zuo Si in his "Weidu fu"; WX, 6.10b, is quite a change in status from the sparkling lotus pond that used to grace the Southern Garden. This term was originally found in the *Shijing*, 15b.15b, Mao #229, "Baihua" 白華: "A rippling pond flows to the north, inundating the rice fields" 滮池北流，浸彼稻田; cf. Legge's translation at *The Chinese Classics*, 4:416.

15 Writing poetry in the style of Wei and Jin was one characterization of his poetic approach mentioned in Sun's GDTZ biography.

16 "Primordial Chaos" 草昧 is an image drawn from the *Yijing*, 1.28b, "Zhun" 屯, and refers to the formless and vacant chaos that prevailed before heaven and earth were divided. Here it refers to the state of letters in Guangzhou before Sun Fen came on the scene.

17 "Fragrant lord" 靈荃 is an allusion to the "Lisao" 離騷; see *Chuci buzhu*, 1.7b, commentary of Wang Yi 王逸: "The *quan* 荃 is an aromatic plant; it alludes to the lord."

18 Alluding to events in the *Zhuangzi*, "Xiaoyao you" 逍遙游; see *Zhuangzi jishi*, 1.1–3.

19 Yangyue 揚粵 was an old name of the Yue region; see *Hanshu*, "Xinan Yi liang-Yue Chaoxian zhuan" 西南夷兩粵朝鮮傳, 95.3847.

20 "The Nine Obscurities" 九玄 were the nine levels of heaven; see Ge Hong 葛洪, *Baopuzi* 抱朴子 (ZZJC ed.), "Renmming" 任命, 9.135.

21 Dong Shao 董紹, *zi* Xingyun 興運 (fl. A.D. 500), was a famous official high in the favor of the emperors of the Northern Wei. Prefiguring the later role of Wang Zuo, Dong Shao was particularly noted for his editorial skills in managing the continuous flow of documents to and from the throne; see his biography at *Weishu*, 79.1758. I have been unable to identity one Xiuju 修矩.

22 Both lines allude to Huang's employment in the Hanlin bureau at Nanjing, where he became one of Zhu Yuanzhang's favorites and often attended His Highness on various outings, including trips to Bell Mountain, i.e. Mt. Zhong 鐘山.

23 Probably an allusion to Huang's meritorious service as magistrate among the people at a time of disorder.

24 Referring to a story in *Zhuangzi*: a carpenter, noted for his skill in wielding his hatchet which would whirl like the wind, mourned his plasterer friend. Zhuangzi compares his own sense of loss at the death of his sophist friend Huizi to the loss felt by the carpenter for the plasterer. The relevant conclusion is: "'It's true that I was once able to slice like that—but the material I worked on has been dead these many years.' Since you died, Master Hui, I have had no material to work on. There's no one I can to talk to any more." Translation by Burton Watson, *The Complete Works of*

Chuang Tzu (New York: Columbia University Press, 1968), 269; *Zhuangzi jishi*, 24:365.

25 These last two lines compare Huang Zhe's poetry to that of the archetypical poet of the south, Qu Yuan.

26 Literally, while still "a chrysalis."

27 Referring to his fondness for exploring Luoyang and its environs and recording his impressions in verse.

28 "Friendly instructor" 友教 was one of the minor classes of Confucius' disciples; see *Shiji*, 121.3116. Here it refers to Li De's status as a student of Neo-Confucianism.

29 Yunmeng was the great marsh around Lake Dongting 洞庭湖. Here it refers to an incident involving the ancient poet Song Yu 宋玉 (ca. 290 B.C.–ca. 223 B.C.). King Xiang of Chu 楚襄王 (r. 298 B.C.–263 B.C.) once led a group of poets to climb the Yangyun Terrace 陽雲 to view the countryside around Yunmeng and versify. Song Yu was awarded fields around Yunmeng for his prize-winning minor *fu* poem; see QSGW, 1:72.

30 Guayan was the former capital of the old state of Qin during the Spring and Autumn period, north of modern Xiaoyi in Shanxi. Its use here refers to an incident in the *Zuozhuan*. In the autumn of 593 B.C., the Marquis of Qin 秦侯 awarded one Shibo 士伯 the district of Guayan for his part in wresting territory from the Di tribes; ever after, this allusion refers to a large reward. See *Zuozhuan*, "Xuangong 15th year," 24.12a–12b; Legge, *The Chinese Classics*, 5:329.

31 This alludes to an episode in the life of Ruan Ji 阮籍 (210–263), who went to consult with one Sun Deng concerning the Daoist arts of cultivation; after no response, Ruan whistled and left. When halfway up the mountain slope, he heard the sound of a simurgh's whistle echoing around the valley. It turned out that Sun had whistled in response; see *Jinshu*, 49.1362.

32 An allusion to a story in *Hou Hanshu*, 53.1744, where Huang Xian, the son of a lowly cow veterinarian, came to exceed the reputation of the famous veterinarian Dai Liang 戴良.

33 Mt. Yu is one-half of the old name of Guangzhou, Panyu, and was one *li* southwest of Guangzhou.

34 Mt. Xiqiao in Nanhai, along with Mt. Luofu, is the most renowned mountain in southern Guangdong; it is known for its miraculous and beautiful scenery; see GDXY, 3.97. Consult further *Xiqiaoshan zhi* for a detailed description.

35 A bow and banner were traditional gifts used to recruit worthies in ancient China, the bow being used in the case of knights and the banner in the case of grandees; see *Zuozhuan*, "Zhao gong 20th year," 49.14a. The pair later became a common trope for the recruitment of worthy gentlemen.

36 An allusion to a line in Tao Qian's fifth "Drinking Wine" poem: "When the heart is remote, the place becomes like it" 心遠地自偏; trans. A. R. Davis, *T'ao Yüan-ming (AD 365–427): His Works and Their Meaning*, 1:96.

37 Chaisang was the home region of Tao Qian near modern Jiujiang 九江 in Jiangxi.

38 A mountain range near Jiankang Nanjing where Tao Hongjing 陶弘景 (456–536) practiced alchemy.

39 The two "Tao" were Tao Qian and Tao Hongjing. Zhao Jie could not have been compared to better historical hermits than these two "Tao," the former the most

upright poet of his times and the latter a reclusive alchemist.

40 GDTZ, 280.5b.

41 Huang Foyi, *Guangzhou chengfang zhi*, 4.36b.

42 Ibid.

43 As at NYHS, 270, 317, 357–60. For the Later Seven Masters, see MS, 287.7378, including a short biographical epitome of Liang Youyu.

44 The Yueshan shishe had been founded by Wang Jiankui 王漸逵 and Lun Yixun 倫以訓, as mentioned in Chapter Two.

45 This is the reasoned assertion of Wang Zongyan, *Guangdong wenwu congtan*, 2 and Huang Zhimin, "Mingren shishe zhi yanjiu," 69.

46 NYHS, 395.

47 Wang Zongyan, *Guangdong wenwu congtan*, 2.

48 NYHS, 273.

49 NYHS, 247. The Lord of Canghai was Lin Weiqiao 林維喬; the others, equally little known, were Kuang Ziqian 鄺子乾, Liang Gongrui 梁公瑞, Pan Ganzhou 潘干周, and Pan Shaocheng 潘少承. Another poem of nostalgia dedicated to this group from the "ancient garden" by Ou Daren was composed in Zhengzhou; see NYHS, 271. Yet another mention of the garden in found on 282.

50 NYHS, 320.

51 See NYHS, 400; another poem by Liang on the White Society is found on 382. Huang Yinpu, *Guangdong wenxian shumu zhijianlu*, 284 lists a work that is perhaps related to this very poetry society, a "Baishe gao" 白社稿 in 14 *juan*. It was compiled by Dong Xian 董暹 and published by Li Xueyuan 李學元 at Guangzhou in 1628.

52 Consult Liang Youyu, NYHS, 351, 355, and 3 poems at 433, and Li Minbiao, NYHS, 451.

53 See Miles, "Celebrating the Yu Fan Shrine," 43.

54 *Yilin conglu*, 164.

55 Wang Zongyan, writing as Yu An, at ibid. Zhu's sojourn in Guangdong is noted at ECCP, 1:182. The entries for the poetry of the five "later" masters (except for Li Shixing) are in Zhu Yizun, *Mingshi zong*, scattered throughout *juan* 51, 52, and 53. All five are anthologized in *Mingshi jishi*, 4:1902–06 (Liang); 1935–41 (Ou); 1949–56 (Li); 1970–73 (Wu); and 1974 (Li).

56 *Yilin conglu*, 163.

57 Ibid.

58 A three-foot sword is the tool wielded by a great man to establish a great cause, as Liu Bang did when he founded the Han; see *Shiji*, 8.321; *Hanshu*, 1b.79.

59 The two reign periods of 713–742 and 767–780 covered the end of the so-called "High Tang" era, when poetry was at its height, and the start of the Middle Tang.

60 The envoy of Liu Bang who persuaded Zhao Tuo to submit to Han in 200 B.C.; *Shiji*, 113.2967.

61 A young Han emissary who was murdered in Guangzhou while still in his twenties after successfully persuading the king of Nanyue to submit to Han. A noted man of letters, he had been one of the "disciples of the erudites" 博士弟子; *Shiji*, 113.2972. He has a short biography at *Hanshu*, 64b.2814–821.

62 That is, the exam that confers the *jinshi* degree.

63 GDXY, 12.355–6.

64 Ou Biyuan, "Li Minbiao zhuan," GDWZ, 4:381.
65 Liang Youyu mentions a poetry gathering to versify on Mt. Fuqiu, presumably with this same poetry society; see NYHS, 408.
66 Ou Biyuan, "Jia Yupu gong zhuan," GDWZ, 4:379.
67 GDXY, 12.357.
68 GDXY, 17.471.
69 Yi Hangguang, *Yu Jing shixuan*, 183.
70 See NYHS, 678, 679.
71 MS, 287.7366.
72 GDXY, 12.355.
73 Both the latter two have biographies in *Guangdong wenwu*; see Yan Xuxin 顏虛心, "Mingshi Chen Bangyanzhuan pangzheng," 551–87 and Mai Shaolin 麥少麟, "Minzu yingxiong Zhang Jiayu" 民族英雄張家玉, *Guangdong wenwu*, 588–611. Short introductions to Zhang Jiayu and Chen Bangyan are by Struve, *The Ming-Qing Conflict*, 292–95. For an introduction to the intellectual environment in the late Ming-early Qing interface, see Chen Zuwu 陳祖武, "Cong Yuan Chonghuan dao Qu Dajun: Mingmo Qingchu de Hua'nan zhishijie" 從袁崇煥到屈大均明末清初的華南知識界, in *Mingmo Qingchu Hua'nan diqu lishiwenwu gongye yantaohui lunwenji*, 287–96 and Lynn A. Struve, "Ambivalence and Action: Some Frustrated Scholars of the K'ang-hsi Period," in *From Ming to Ch'ing: Conquest, Region, and Continuity in Seventeenth-Century China*, ed. Jonathan D. Spence and John E. Wills, Jr. (New Haven and London: Yale University Press, 1979), 321–65. The biographies of Chen Zizhuang, Zhang Jiayu, and Chen Bangyan, along with those of Qu Dajun and Chen Gongyin, figure prominently in Huang Haizhang's modern compilation, *Mingmo Guangdong kang Qing shiren pingzhuan*.
74 For Chen Zizhuang's life, see the anonymous 14-page necrology included in Chen's *Libu zonggao* 黎部總稿 (*Guangdong congshu* ed.; Shanghai: Commercial Press, 1946); GDTZ, 284.25a–29b; Li Jian'er 李健兒, "Chen Zizhuang nianpu" 陳子壯年譜, in *Guangdong wenwu*, 516–50, and J.C. Yang in ECCP, 1:101–02. The necrology includes two portraits of Chen. Lynn Struve, in *The Cambridge History of China, Vol. 7: The Ming Dynasty (1368–1644), Part I*, 679–81, sets the historical background to the Manchu invasion of Guangdong; a concise synopsis of the roles of both Chen Zizhuang and Chen Pangyan in the attempt to retake Guangzhou from the Manchus is Frederic Wakeman Jr., *The Great Enterprise: The Manchu Reconstruction of Imperial Order in Seventeenth-Century China*, 2 vols. (Berkeley: University of California Press, 1985), 2:760–62 (N.b.: the "Zi" of Zizhuang is written with the wrong graph in Wakeman's index).
75 Huang Yinpu, *Guangdong wenxian shumu zhijianlu*, 143. For his poetry, see *Mingshi jishi*, 5:2952–55; Zhu Yizun, *Mingshi zong*, 77.8b–9a. A short selection of his prose, including the preface to the reprinting of *Nanyuan wuxiansheng shi*, is contained in GDWZ, 4:249–58.
76 GDXY, 17.471.
77 The twelve members are introduced briefly in Li Jian'er, "Chen Zizhuang nianpu," 529–30.
78 For Li, see GDTZ, 284.3a–4b. His poetics are treated at *Mingshi jishi*, 5:2944–48; forty-two prose pieces, including 11 *fu* and numerous essays, are presented in

GDWZ, 4:285–317. A modern assessment is Lau Kin-ming 劉健明, "Li Suiqiu de shengping ji qi zhenglun" 黎遂球的生平與其政論, in *Mingmo Qingchu Hua'nan diqu lishiwenwu gongye yantaohui lunwenji*, 171–78.

79 For Zhang and Wu, see ECCP, 1:52–53; 2:882–83.

80 On Li Suiqiu's victory in the Yellow Peony Association, see Huang Zhimin, "Mingren shishe zhi yanjiu," 59; *Yilin congtan*, 165, and especially the notice in *Yilin congtan* by Zhang Mu 章木 devoted to Li's "Yellow Peony Poems," 171–74. Qu Dajun also provided welcome details at GDXY, 12.350. For a recent assessment, see Yasushi Oki, "The Yellow Peony Party." Paper presented at the Annual Meeting of the Association for Asian Studies, Chicago, Illinois, March 23, 2002.

81 Li composed a *fu* on this garden dedicated to Zheng that is included in GDWZ, 4:315–16 and *Qingshi jishi*, 4:760.

82 For Kuang, see GDTZ, 285.26a–27b; GDWZ, 4:464–69. His poetry is treated in GDXY, 12.350–51, *Mingshi jishi*, 5:2948, and *Qingshi jishi*, 1:147–54. His collection of poetry, called *Qiaoya* 嶠雅, is evaluated by Wang Yongfu 王永福, "*Qiaoya* jiaozhu shuping"《嶠雅》校注述評, *Guji zhengli yanjiu tongxun* 4 (1990): 12–13. A work of prose, the *Chiya* 赤雅, focused on subjects of prime importance for the Southern Muse, for among the local oddities were the hills and streams of home; see *Qingshi jishi*, 1:147. This work seems to be largely preserved in the GDWX, 4:601–720.

83 *Qingshi jishi*, 1:147 includes this incident in a short biographical snippet. Later on in this work, Zhu Yizun, Wang Shizhen, Quan Zuwang, and others are quoted at great length about this romantic episode. The two zithers were the Southern Wind 南風, an antique from the court of Song Lizong 理宗 (1125–1260), and the even more ancient "Platform of Green Gauze" 綠綺臺, manufactured during the first Tang reign period of Wude 武德 (618–627). An elderly Manchu trooper fished out the latter zither and sold it in the market where it was purchased by one Ye Longwen 葉龍文 for one hundred catties of silver. Ye often showed it to his comrade Qu Dajun, who, inspired through such tactile contact with his lamented friend, versified on the zither. The zither later came into the possession of Zhang Jingxiu, who built a special room to house it in his famous Ke Garden 可園 in Dongguan. It was last publicly displayed in Hong Kong during World War Two. For more on this famous event and the history of this zither, see Xu Xu, *Lingnan gujinlu*, 232–33.

84 GDXY, 12.350 details Kuang's participation in the Yellow Peony Poetry Competition. He may have earned a reputation for eccentricity, but he was an important poet, for the new poetic style inaugurated by Ou Daxiang known as the Eastern Yue school 東粵派 was first blazed by Kuang; see *Qingshi jishi*, 1:148.

85 Li Jian'er, "Chen Zizhuang nianpu," 519. For a short biography and evaluation of Chen Zisheng's literary talents, see Chen Yongzheng, *Lingnan wenxueshi*, 248–50.

86 Li Jian'er, "Chen Zizhuang nianpu," 529.

87 The famous hermit-poet Tao Qian used to live in Chaisang, as seen above; the peach font is another obvious allusion to Tao Qian.

88 Li Jian'er, "Chen Zizhuang nianpu," 529.

89 GDWZ, 4:325–26; *Mingshi jishi*, 6:3263.

90 See GDTZ, 297.8b–9, GDWZ, 4: 125–38, and *Mingshi jishi*, 4:2235.

91 For his biography, see GDTZ 277.15a–15b; three prose pieces are included in

GDWZ, 4:317–20.

92 Other works are listed in the short biographical notice included at GDWZ, 4:317.

93 *Qingshi jishi*, 1:148.

94 GDWZ, 4:237–38.

95 GDWX, 7:507; Li Jian'er amplifies this statement into "He entertained himself through wine and poetry"; "Chen Zizhuang nianpu," 529.

96 GDWX, 7:509.

97 Ibid, 7:510.

98 Ou Zhuyu, in GDWX , 7:504.

99 Li Jian'er, "Chen Zizhuang nianpu," 527. A nicely detailed biographical study of her is by Huang Yuting 黃宇庭, in *Yilin conglu*, 120–29; see also the short notice in Qiu Juchuan, *Yangcheng guchao*, 543–46. A convenient entrée into the world of cultivated courtesans of late imperial China is Grace S. Fong, "Writing from a Side Room of Her Own: The Literary Vocation of Concubines in Ming-Qing China," in *Hsiang Lectures on Chinese Poetry*, vol. 1 (Montreal: Centre for East Asian Research, McGill University, 2001), 41–63. The enthusiastic welcome for female poets on the part of male poets of the Ming and Qing dynasties is treated by Kang-I Sun Chang, "Gender and Canonicity: Ming-Qing Women Poets in the Eyes of the Male Literati," in *Hsiang Lectures on Chinese Poetry*, vol. 1, 1–18. For the image of the cultivated courtesan during the Ming-Qing transition, see Wai-Yee Li, "The Late Ming Courtesan: Invention of a Cultural Ideal," in *Writing Women in Late Imperial China*, ed. Ellen Widmer and Kang-I Sun Chang (Stanford: Stanford University Press, 1997), 46–73.

100 Her portrait is reproduced in Li Jian'er, "Chen Zizhuang nianpu," 528. The *ci* by Xu Yushan is entitled "A Small Portrait of Zhang Qiaoqian Holding a Zither" 張喬倩抱琴小像; *Yuedong cichao*, "Xu Yushan," 2a–2b. This painting and notices of other lost paintings and specimens of calligraphy by the members of the Southern Garden during its Qing manifestations is the subject of a nostalgic retrospect by Wang Qiuwei 王秋達, "Nanyuan mohen" 南園墨痕, *Yijing* 21 (1937):15–18. It also sums up most of what is known of Zhang Qiao. This article was kindly brought to my attention by Mr. Qin Huanming, who also graciously supplied a copy.

101 Chen Yongzheng, *Lingnan lidai shixuan*, 271.

102 *Yuedong cichao*, "Zhang Qiao," 1b–2a.

103 Chen Yongzheng, *Lingnan lidai cixuan*, 55.

104 *Yuedong cichao*, "Zhang Qiao," 1a.

105 Li Jian'er, "Chen Zihuang nianpu," 527. Four of her *ci* poems are preserved in the *Yuedong cichao* listed under her name; two of them are included, with annotations, in Chen Yongzheng, ed., *Lingnan lidai cixuan*, 53–55.

106 Li Jian'er, "Chen Zizhuang nianpu," 528. For a physical description of the grave, see *Guangzhoushi wenwu zhi*, 137–38.

107 *Yuedong cichao*, "Huang Qinsong," 23b–24a. Several other poems dedicated to her are included in Li Jian'er, "Chen Zizhuang nianpu," 527–29.

108 Huang Yinpu, *Guangdong wenxian shumu zhijianlu*, 202. Li Suiqiu's preface to this compilation is included in GDWX , 4:785–86.

109 See Li Suiqiu, "Taking my seat on the third day of the third month with all members celebrating the lustration rites while meeting as a society in the Southern Garden, with rhymes delimited" 三月三日同諸公社文集南園禊祓即席限韻; Wen

Runeng, *Yuedong shihai*, 2:894–95.

110 GDWZ, 4:254; NYQS, 11–12.

111 Wang Zongyan, *Guangdong wenwu congkan*, 4.

112 Qu Xiangbang, *Guangdong shihua zhengxubian*, 99.

113 From a poem entitled "The Southern Garden," *Yuedong shihai*, 3:1331. Page 1333 preserves a poem that records a meeting of a poetry society in the garden, presumably that of his contemporary Chen Zizhuang.

114 Xiao Chi, *The Chinese Garden as Lyric Enclave: A Generic Study of The Story of the Stone* (Ann Arbor: Center for Chinese Studies, The University of Michigan, 2001), 31.

115 Ibid, 42. Zhang Erqiao used the locution "mountain man" in a poem examined above. For another example of mountain men and a Cantonese poetry society, see a poem by Liang Youyu: "Delighting in the Two Mountain Men Liang and Li Joining Our Poetry Society" 喜梁，李二山人入社; NYHS, 400–401; the poetry society in question is not identified. See further ibid, 407, 434, 435, and Li Shixing at 637.

116 Li Jian'er, "Chen Zizhuang nianpu," 520.

117 Ibid. For the implications of being associated with this reformist party during Wei Zhongxian's reign of terror, see Charles O. Hucker, "The Tung-lin Movement of the Late Ming Period," in *Chinese Thought and Institutions*, ed. John K. Fairbank (1957; rpt., Chicago and London: University of Chicago Press, 1973), 132–62, and Jerry Dennerline, chapter 2, "The Tung-lin Party in Action: From Loyal Opposition to Loyalism," in *The Chia-Ting Loyalists: Confucian Leadership and Social Change in Seventeenth-Century China* (New Haven and London: Yale University Press, 1981), 43–68.

118 See William S. Atwell, "From Education to Politics: The Fu She," in *The Unfolding of Neo-Confucianism*, ed. Wm. Theodore de Bary (New York and London: Columbia University Press, 1985), 333–67, and the biography of founder of the Fushe, Zhang Pu 張溥 (*zi* Tianru 天如, *hao* Ximing 西銘, 1602–1641), at ECCP, 1:52–53.

119 The same membership list is reproduced, along with biographical epitomes, in Wu Shanjia 吳山嘉, *Fushe xingshi zhuanlüe* 復社姓氏傳略 (*Haiwangcun guji congkan* 海王村古籍叢刊 ed.; Guangzhou: Zhongguo shudian, 1990). Members from Guangdong are included at 9.1a–4b. The original *Fushe xingshi lu* 復社姓氏錄 by Wu's fifth generation grandfather, Wu Fujiu 吳福久, is appended to this work, with Guangdong members appearing on 38a–b.

120 Li Jian'er, "Chen Zizhuang nianpu," 529, basing himself on the poetical preface by Ou Zhuyu as noted above.

121 GDWZ, 4:254. Xie Xingyao 謝興堯, the chief editor of the semi-monthly literary magazine *Yijing* 逸經, introduces an article on the Southern Garden by Wang Qiuwei 王秋逵,"Nanyuan mohen" 南園墨痕, with the assertion that Chen Zizhuang's late-Ming early-Qing version of the poetry club shared the same substantial political nature as the Fushe and the Jishe 幾社 of North China. Xie's editorial comments are at *Yijing* 21 (1937): 2. The article is on pages 15–18 .

122 Susan Naquin and Evelyn S. Rawski, *Chinese Society in the Eighteenth Century* (New Haven and London: Yale University Press, 1987), 71.

123 Kale, *French Salons.*

124 Benjamin Elman, "The Social Roles of Literati in Early to Mid-Ch'ing," in *The*

Cambridge History of China. Vol. 9. Part One: The Ch'ing Empire to 1800, ed. Willard J. Peterson (Cambridge: Cambridge University Press, 2002), 399.

125 *Goudang* 鉤黨 is a term of hoary provenance traceable to *Hou Hanshu*, 8.330, "Lingdi ji" 靈帝紀. It refers to the formation of a faction or party at court by high-ranking ministers; cf. *Hou Hanshu*, 64.2110 and 65.2136 for two other typical examples. For a Cantonese view of party politics starting with the Han, see Che Tengfang 車騰芳 (*juren* 1720), "On Party Politics" 黨錮論; GDWZ, 5:66.

126 Li Jian'er, "Chen Zizhuang nianpu," 521.

127 Meyer-Fong, *Building Culture in Early Qing Yangzhou*, 31.

128 Ibid, 4.

129 GDWX , 7:503–11.

130 Ibid, 7:503–04.

131 Meyer-Fong, *Building Culture in Early Qing Yangzhou*, 34.

132 This poem is found at XAJ, 8.1a–9a. Wang Zhaoyun, *zi* Zixia 子霞, was originally a geisha from Qiantang; she first met Su Shi when she was twelve, and stayed with him some 20 years. See Xu Xu, *Lingnan gujinlu*, 70–71; on 72–74 Xu savors Sun Fen's pastiche poetic compilation.

133 GDWX, 7:488; He Feng's ten poems are found on 484–89. A short biography is on 457–58. Five prose pieces and 31 poems from his collected works are included on 453–91.

134 One Ouyang Shao 歐陽韶 (*zi* Xiaoxing 笑杏), an educationalist from Shunde active in poetic circles during the Republican era, composed a set of ten poems matching rhymes with his earlier and very famous co-regionalist from Shunde, Chen Gongyin; see GDSC, 3:945–48.

135 "He Tao Zhengjun yinjiu ershishou" 和陶征君飲酒二十首, NYHS, 456–62.

136 GDWX, 7:511. The White Lotus Society was founded by Huiyuan 惠遠 (334–419) and other monks at Donglin Monastery 東林寺 on Mt. Lu 廬山 to reach enlightenment through chanting and meditation.

137 I.e. the era of the "Seven Masters of Jian'an," including Wang Can; it was the last reign period of the Eastern Han dynasty (199–220).

138 Xu Gan 徐幹 (171–217), one of the so-called Seven Masters of the Jian'an Era, is here referred to by his *zi*, Weichang 偉長.

139 I take the geographic name Cangwu as emblematic of Lingnan as a whole.

140 GDWX, 7:505.

Chapter 6

1 "A refined gathering at the Southern Garden, deciding on a visit to the Little Ridge Monastery; selected first was the Superior Man from the Han River, who obtained the 'year' character" 雅集南園訂游小嶺寺先東漢川上人得年字, Wen Runeng, comp., *Yuedong shihai*, 3:1386–87.

2 Qu Xiangbang, *Guangdong shihua zhengxubian*, 99.

3 Ibid.

4 Huang Yu, ed., *Lidai mingren ru Yue shixuan*, 369.

5 Indicating that Guangdong was able to establish its own poetic school, inspired no doubt by the natural wonders of the locale.

6 The gist of both lines is that even though a poet such as Zhang Jiuling is no longer

present, the poetic elegance traceable in the south back to Qu Yuan is still present in the region.

7 Wen Runeng, comp., *Yuedong shihai*, 3:1440–41.

8 Ibid, 3:1460.

9 Ibid, 3:1489.

10 The term "fraternity of brothers" 棣蕚 first appears at *Jinshu*, 55.1525, where it refers to friends whose natures are completely compatible.

11 Zhong Ganquan 鍾淦泉 and Yang Baolin 楊寶霖, eds., *Humen lidai shixuan* 虎門歷代詩選 (Guangzhou: Guangdong jiaoyu chubanshe, 2004), 11.403.

12 Ye You (*zi* Chaonan 巢南, *hao* Shucheng 黍成) was from Panyu. He was most noted for socializing with celebrities from around the country; see a short biography at GDSC, 1:163.

13 Ibid, 1:165.

14 This term alludes to the wise rules of King Wen and the Duke of Zhou during the early Zhou period, according to the "Great Preface" to the *Book of Poetry*: "The 'Zhounan' and 'Shaonan' sections show the path of the Orthodox Beginning and are the foundation of royal transformation" 周南召南正始之道，王化之基; *Shijing*, 1a.18b. Through metonymy, Orthodox Beginning also refers to the elegant and orthodox poetry of the *Shijing*.

15 The author is punning on Li Erqiao's *hao*, "Two Qiao Li," and perhaps suggesting a trip to Xiqiao.

16 GDWZ, 5:232.

17 A general introduction to Li Jian is presented by Xian Yuqing 冼玉清 in *Yilin conglu*, 230–32; his relationship with Yuan Mei is given deeper treatment on 232–34. Li's poetics, including a short collection of *yuefu*, are addressed by Yi Ding 一丁, *Yilin conglu*, 185–87. A long dedication to a local temple by Li is preserved in GDWZ, 5:232.

18 Wang Zongyan, *Guangdong wenwu congtan*, 4.

19 For a sketch of Zhangs's life, consult Li Mangui, in ECCP, 1:58–59; for a chronology and introduction to his thought and poetics, see Wang Songtao 汪松濤, "Zhang Weiping nianbiao jianbian" 張維屏年表簡編, *Guji zhengli yanjiu tongxun* 3 (1988): 16–20; "Zhang Weiping sixiang ji shiwen tese lüelun" 張維屏思想及詩文特色略論, *Guji zhengli yanjiu tongxun* 6 (1992): 6–12. Zhang's public profile in Guangzhou during the decades preceding and following the Opium Wars may be followed in Polachek, *The Inner Opium War*, *passim*.

20 Yang Guozhen, "Zailun Xuannan shishe yu Lin Zexu," 150.

21 Wang Songtao 汪松濤, ed., *Zhang Nanshan quanji* 張南山全集 (Guangzhou: Guangdong gaodeng jiaoyu, 1993). For Zhang's poetics, see *Qingshi jishi*, 14:9447–74; twenty prose pieces are included in GDWZ, 5:416–25.

22 Cf. ECCP, 1:58; GDWZ, 5:366–68, 310–17 for these two worthies. All three were anthologized in the 1842 compilation *Yuedong Sanzi shichao* 粵東三子詩鈔, 14 *juan* (described in Huang Yinpu, *Guangdong wenxian shumu zhijianlu*, 203). Huang has the further distinction of having painted the picture of the Sea of Learning reproduced in Rong Zhaozu 容肇祖, "Xuehai tang kao" 學海堂考, *Lingnan xuebao* 3 (1934): 1–147. Xu Xinfu, *Guangdong cangshu jishishi*, 181 devotes a poem to Huang and his notable "Ridge Sea Library" 嶺海樓, which "preserved the virtue of the

ages…invigorating the Southern Garden"; a short biographical notice on Huang is also included.

23 Miles, "Celebrating the Yu Fan Shrine," 38. Weng Fanggang served in Guangdong as Commissioner of Education for seven years from 1764–1771. A specialist on paleography, he compiled one work relevant to Guangzhou, the *Yuedong jinshilue* 粵東金石略, 12 *juan*, printed in 1771. This work is examined by Xu Xu, *Lingnan gujinlu*, 153–54. For Weng's life and career, see ECCP, 2:856–58.

24 Miles, "Celebrating the Yu Fan Shrine," 50–52, describes the building of this mountain resort and some of the participants. Huang's second son, Huang Zhaowen 黃照文 (*zi* Shilin 世臨), who unfortunately died young, provides a brief poetic description of the exquisite natural surroundings in GDSC, 1:243; of much greater depth is Zhang Weiping's "Spring of Clouds Song," included in *Qingshi jishi*, 14:9460–461.

25 On Huang's ancestry, see Guan Lin 管林, "Huang Peifang de jiashi, shengping he zhuzuo" 黃培芳的家世，生平和著作, *Guji zhengli yanjiu tongxun* 7 (1992): 13–16.

26 See DMB, 1:672.

27 Xu Xinfu, *Guangdong cangshu jishishi*, 181. Xu also dedicated a verse to Huang Zuo's *Baoshulou*; see ibid, 137.

28 The name "Meditation on Tang Worthies" 唐賢三昧 of Huang's anthology seems to have been inspired by a phrase from his friend Zhang Weiping, for in Zhang's poetic evaluation of Chen Gongyin he credited his poetic success to having "meditated on the men of Tang" 唐人三昧; earlier Wang Shizhen had coined this phrase and had singled out several of Chen's verses as all representing "fine lines from Tang worthies" 唐賢佳句; *Qingshi jishi*, 2:882, 880.

29 Guan Lin, "Huang Peifang de jiashi," 16.

30 Ibid, 16.

31 Xu Xinfu, *Guangdong cangshu jishishi*, 181.

32 This particular *ci* tune was popular for the purpose of celebrating Guangzhou; witness Qiu Fengjia's effort, entitled "Yue Wang tai," *Lingyun hairilou shichao*, 235; see also Li Zifu 李子黼 (Qing), "Longing for the Past at the King of Yue Terrace," *Yuedong cichao*, "Li Changrong" 李長榮, 1b–2a.

33 *Yuedong cichao*, 2a–b.

34 "The Hundred Clans of the Yue" anciently inhabited the regions south of the middle stretches of the Yangzi River all the way down to the watershed of the Pearl River. Consult He Guangyue, *Baiyue yuanliushi*, 1–20 and Erica Brindley, "Barbarians or Not? Ethnicity and Changing Conceptions of the Ancient Yue (Viet) Peoples, ca. 400–50 BC," *Asia Major*, Third Series, 16 (2003): 1–32.

35 Yang Pu was a general under Han Wudi who conquered Nanyue; his title was the "Admiral of the Towered-ships" 樓船將軍; see *Shiji*, 113.2975.

36 Referring to the last ruler of the Southern Han, Liu Chang 劉鋹 (r. 959–971).

37 The "Calling Bells" 呼鑾 imperial roadway was built on Mt. Yuexiu by Liu Yan 劉龑 (r. 917–941), the first emperor of the Southern Han dynasty; Huang Foyi, *Guangzhou chengfang zhi*, 2.1b.

38 Emperor Liu Chang used to host an annual Red Cloud Banquet in the Glorious Florescence Park 昌華苑 to celebrate the lichee; see Miles, "Rewriting the Southern Han," 49.

39 *Yuedong cichao*, "Yangcheng huaigu," 1b–2a.
40 The legendary sage king Yao.
41 Nanjiao was another term for Jiaozhi 交趾, ancient name of the region of Vietnam; see GDXY, 2:30.
42 According to ancient lore, the sun rises from below the Fusang tree, as in *Chuci*, 2.16b, "Shaosiming" 少司命.
43 The Terrace for Reverencing Han 朝漢臺 was constructed on a hillock outside the northern gate of Guangzhou. It was purpose-built to welcome the Han emissary Lu Jia as an expression of loyalty to the Chinese throne; see GDXY, 17.461.
44 Referring to the visit of the Han emissary Lu Jia.
45 Indicating Zhao Tuo's pacifist attitudes after surrender; the Law of the West is the power of Buddhism. "Trays" 盤 symbolized amnesty or relief from taxes, as those who had to pay tribute or taxes, placed on trays, were allowed to put them away.
46 The same staff of surrender was brandished by the king of Southern Han when he surrendered to the conquering Song dynasty, as described in the *Songshi*, 481.13929, "Nanhan shijia" 南漢世家.
47 For Clear Canal 清濠, see *Yuan Dade Nanhaizhi canben*, 8.54.
48 Huang Foyi, *Guangzhou chengfang zhi*, 4.36a confirms the connection between the "Quarter of the Assembled Worthies" 聚賢坊 and the original site of the Southern Garden.
49 Zhang Weiping 張維平, *Zhang Nanshan quanji* (1857; Guangzhou), "Songxin shilu" 松心詩錄, 6.1a.
50 Zhang Weiping, *Zhang Nanshan quanji*, "Huadi ji" 花地集, 33b–34a.
51 Huang Foyi, *Guangzhou chengfang zhi*, 4.36a–36b, 38b.
52 Ibid, 4.41B. In a similar vein, Luo Tianchi reveals in a poem that one Su Errui 蘇二瑞 lived in the Southern Garden for a time, establishing his own Southern Garden Studio 書舍; *Yuedong shihai*, 3:1495.
53 *Qingshi jishi*, 7:3885.
54 *Yuedong cichao*, "Huang Qinsong," 23a.
55 "Comrades in drinking" refers to paired wine cups.
56 "Black Pearls" 驪珠 is another name for the fruit longan, *Euphoria longan*. But here it refers to "precious poems," alluding to *Zhuangzi,* "Lieyukou" 列禦寇, *Zhuangzi jishi*, 32.459.
57 "Privately cultivated" 私淑 alludes to Mencius, who said, "Although I could not be a disciple of Confucius himself, I have endeavored to cultivate my virtue by means of others who were." *Mengzi* 孟子, 8a.12b, trans. Legge, *The Chinese Classics*, 2:328.
58 Ruan Yuan's *nianpu*, compiled by Zhang Jian 張鑑 and other disciples of Ruan Yuan and first published between 1850 and 1851, only mentions the site of the Wenyuan Academy; Zhang Jian, *Ruan Yuan nianpu* 阮元年譜 (Beijing: Zhonghua shuju, 1995), 132. A new, exhaustively annotated edition adds nothing new; Wang Zhangtao 王章濤, *Ruan Yuan nianpu* (Hefei: Huangshan shushe, 2003), 672. Stephen B. Miles accepts the Wenlan Academy location; *The Sea of Learning: Mobility and Identity in Nineteenth-Century Guangzhou*, Harvard East Asian monographs, no. 269 (Cambridge and London: Harvard University Asia Center, 2006), 94. Rong Zhaozu, "Xuehai tang kao," 17 states that the Southern Garden was considered for the permanent site of the new academy, but it was ultimately rejected,

as was the site of the Wenlan Academy and one next to the Haizhuang Monastery 海幢寺 south of the Pearl River. None of the four major collections of studies, essays, and poetry produced at the academy, the *Xuehai tang zhi* 學海堂志 and the three installations of the *Xuehai tang ji* 集, numbers one, two, and three, touch on this issue except one short entry at *Xuehai tang zhi*, 6b, where it mentions the three possibilities cited above. This entry is, in fact, the source of Rong Zhaozu's statement. These collections are all found in Zhao Suosheng 趙所生 and Xue Zhengxing 薛正興, eds., *Zhongguo lidai shuyuan zhi* 中國歷代書院志, 16 vols. (Nanjing: Jiangsu jiaoyu chubanshe, 1995), vols. 3, 13, and 14.

59 For Ruan Yuan, in addition to his *nianpu*, see ECCP, 1:399–402 and the recent biographies by Betty Peh-T'i Wei, *Ruan Yuan, 1764–1849. The Life and Work of a Major Scholar-Official in Nineteenth-Century China before the Opium War* (Hong Kong: Hong Kong University Press, 2006); Wang Zhangtao 王章濤, *Ruan Yuan pingzhuan* 阮元評傳 (Yangzhou: Guangling shushe, 2004); and Chen Juyuan 陳居淵, *Jiao Xun, Ruan Yuan pingzhuan* 焦循阮元評傳, *Zhongguo sixiangjiao pingzhuan congshu* 中國思想家評傳叢書 (Nanjing: Nanjing Daxue chubanshe, 2006). Ruan's role in founding the Sea of Learning is studied in depth by Stephen B. Miles, *The Sea of Learning*, and Rong Zhaozu, "Xuehai tang kao." See also Yu Weng 于翁, "Ruan Yuan yu Xuehai tang" 阮元與學海堂, in *Yilin conglu*, 131–35, and Benjamin A. Elman, "The Hsüeh-Hai T'ang and the Rise of New Text Scholarship in Canton," *Ch'ing-shih Wen-t'i* 4 (Dec. 1979): 51–82. He Guohua's 何國華 short epitome, "Qingdai Lingnan de gaodeng xuefu—Guangdong Xuehai tang" 清代嶺南的高等學府廣東學海堂, *Guangdong shizhi* 2 (1994): 51–52, provides welcome details from the point of view of the "specialized students" 專科生: the course of study was three years, with four semesters per year. Ten students were recruited for the first year, but later on classes averaged 10 to 20 students per term. Scholarships were provided, and papers on the classics and poetry compositions were expected to be handed in within one day to monitors for the assignment of the grades of A, B, etc. According to a personal communication from Stephen Miles, most students at the Sea of Learning simply composed examination essays and poems and turned them in to a designated site on a designated day. Biographical notices of some 327 students who studied at the Sea of Learning in some capacity are found in Rong Zhaozu, "Xuehai tang kao," 60–139; for the works published by the Sea of Learning, see 140–47, and Huang Yinpu, *Guangdong wenxian shumu zhijianlu*, 285–88.

60 Huang Foyi, *Guangzhou chengfang zhi*, 1.70a. For the largest academy, see Liang Tingnan 梁廷枏, *Yuexiu shuyuanzhi* 粵秀書院志, in *Zhongguo lidai shuyuanzhi* 中國歷代書院志, vol. 3 (Nanjing: Jiangsu jiaoyu chubanshe, 1995).

61 Miles, "Rewriting the Southern Han," 54.

62 Ruan considered the site somewhat "low-lying and narrow" 湫隘; Rong Zhaozu, "Xuehai tang kao," 17. This reason is entirely understandable, for way back in 1380 Zhu Liangzu 朱亮祖, the Marquis of Yongjia 永嘉侯 (d. 1380), gave a similar reason—"low and narrow" 低隘—for proposing to connect the old part of Guangzhou with two other towns to form a new, more habitable city. This new administrative unit became known as the "Inner City" 內城 or "Old City" 舊城; see Huang Foyi, *Guangzhou chengfang zhi*, 1.22b.

63 Translated by Benjamin A. Elman, "The Hsueh-Hai T'ang and the Rise of New Text

Scholarship in Canton," 59. The name "Clear Spring" that appears in the next line is another possible allusion to the Southern Garden if it refers to the Clear Canal 清濠 of Zhang Weiping.

64 *Yuedong cichao*, "Chen Lanpu," 4a. Chen Li was from Panyu; after studies in the Yangcheng and Yuexiu academies, he entered the Sea of Learning in 1834. From 1833 until 1852, he failed in seven separate bids for his *jinshi* degree in the capital and afterwards devoted himself to education and private scholarship. He sought help from Zhang Weiping on how to write poetry and became accomplished not only in this art, but his calligraphy was also subject to local praise. Since he used to study in the eastern chamber of his grandfather's house, he came to call himself Mr. Eastern Villa 東塾先生. During five years of advanced work at the Sea of Learning he devoted himself to philological study and began to publish. Eventually his works grew to some 116 individual items encompassing the fields of philology, history, geography, phonology, and the like. He began to teach at the Sea of Learning in 1840, staying there for 27 years. He and his many students came to form what was known as the Dongshu school. Chen's most important work is the *Dongshu dushu ji* 東塾讀書記. In 1857 the Sea of Learning was damaged by cannon fire during the second Opium War; Chen and his family took refuge in a small village in Nanhai. He returned to the newly reopened Sea of Learning in 1860 and continued the fertile studies in many fields that earned him the reputation of polymath. For Chen's life and numerous intellectual interests, see ECCP, 1:90–92; Rong Zhaozu, "Xuehai tang kao," 40–41, and most exhaustively, Wang Zongyan 汪宗衍, "Chen Dongshu xiansheng nianpu" 陳東塾先生年譜, *Lingnan xuebao* 4 (1935): 55–118. More convenient is Chen Zehong, *Guangdong lishi mingren zhuanlüe*, 357–66. Chen's attainments as a classical scholar are epitomized in Xinzhong Yao, ed., *RoutledgeCurzon Encyclopedia of Confucianism*, 2 vols. (London and New York: RoutledgeCurzon, 2003), 1:45 (where Chen Li is erroneously called Chen Feng). Four of his prose pieces are included in GDWZ, 5:483–511. From the perspective of some modern Chinese historians, Chen Li as well as Jian Zhaoliang's teacher Zhu Ciqi are best known for being "patriotric thinkers" rather than classical scholars and teachers; see Jiang Zuyuan and Fang Zhiqin, eds., *Jianming Guangdongshi*, 452–54.

65 *Yuedong cichao*, "Wu Shihua," 9a. See Rong Zhaozu, "Xuehai tang kao," 26–27 for a short biographical notice on Wu; 16 prose works are preserved in GDWZ, 5:323–33. See also Miles, "Rewriting the Southern Han," 67–68.

66 Rong Zhaozu, "Xuehai tang kao," 31, 35.

67 Wang Zongyan, *Guangdong wenwu congtan*, 4.

68 GDSC, 2:461.

69 "Dreams of cranes" 鶴夢 are lofty aspirations that transcend mundane concerns. Witness a poem by Sikong Tu 司空圖 (837–908) in QTS, 19:7289.

70 Jiang Fan 江藩, *Jiang Fan ji* 江藩集 (Shanghai: Shanghai shiji chuban gufen youxian gongsi, Shanghai guji chubanshe, 2006), 121–22.

71 *Xuehai tang ji*, 13.1a–b, in Zhao Suosheng and Xue Zhengxing, eds., *Zhongguo lidai shuyuan zhi*. For Chen, see Rong Zhaozu, "Xuehai tang kao," 102.

72 Miles, "Rewriting the Southern Han," 58–65 treats the subject of poetry devoted to the Southern Han by Sea of Learning members.

73 Ibid, 58.

74 Ibid.

75 Yuedong cichao, "Chen Lanpu," 1b–2a.

76 "Poet's walking stick" 吟筇 recalls a distich from the Yuan poet Yuan Shiyuan's 袁士元 offering "Seeing off Xin Fuzhong to Stay at the Longxiang Jiqingsi" 送信孚中住龍翔集慶寺: "Probing secluded spots, returning again to roam on Mt. Tiantong,/ On a path amid ten-thousand pines I lean on my poet's walking stick" 尋幽近復游天童，萬松徑裏支吟筇; Gu Sili 顧嗣立, ed., *Yuanshixuan* 元詩選, 4 vols. (Shanghai: Shanghai guji chubanshe, 1993), 2:281.

77 A "Yellow Dwelling" 黃屋 is a royal palace; see *Weishu*, 5.92. Here it refers to Zhao Tuo's royal compound in Guangzhou.

78 "Boat People rain and Man barbarian winds" 蛋雨蠻風 is a phrase from Su Shi; see his "Fully Blossoming Plums Beneath the Pine Wind Kiosk" 松風亭下梅花盛開"; QSS, 14.9506.

79 *Yuedong cichao*, "Chen Lanpu," 2a. Making a "league with gulls" 鷗盟 means to live in solitude as in a line by Li Dongyang: "Angling for seaside stones, I am distant through my league with gulls" 海邊釣石鷗盟遠; *Li Dongyang ji*, 1:379.

80 Wang Zongyan, *Guangdong wenwu congtan*, 4.

81 Xu Yingheng 許應鑅, comp., *Ji Nan yuan erzi shichao* 寄南園二子詩鈔, 1874; recorded in Huang Yinpu, *Guangdong wenxian shumu zhijianlu*, 203. I thank Stephen Miles for identifying Ji as the name of a garden owned by the Rong family and popular as a site for literary gatherings in the 1840s and 1850s.

82 Wang Zongyan, *Guangdong wenwu congtan*, 4 describes the buildings on the periphery of the Southern Garden that were demolished for the printing house building project, including the shrine to Wen Tianxiang; he also mentions the new constructions such as the Ten Peaks Veranda that figures in one of the poems translated in this chapter. A long list of works printed by this publishing house is contained in Huang Yinpu, *Guangdong wenxian shumu zhijianlu*, 295–309. Much poetry on the Guangya Academy and the historical background to its founding are included in Xu Xinfu, *Guangdong cangshu jishishi*, 202–10.

83 For Zhang Zhidong and his administrative and academic activities in Guangzhou, see William Ayers, *Chang Chih-tung and Educational Reform in China*, Harvard East Asian Series, 54 (Cambridge, Massachusetts: Harvard University Press, 1971), 58–60; see also ECCP, 1:27–32. A physical description of the Guangya shuyuan and a short historical narrative is found in *Guangzhoushi wenwu zhi,* 178–79.

84 Xu Xinfu, *Guangdong cangshu jishishi*, 206; GDSC, 3:750. Also recorded in Chen Pan 陳槃, "*Guangdong lidai shichao* bielu" 廣東歷代詩鈔別錄, *Dalu zazhi* 69, no. 13 (1984): 48.

85 These refer to two notable libraries during the late Qing period, the One Hundred Song Editions in One Shop 百宋一廛 library of Huang Peilie 黃丕烈 (1763–1825) in Suzhou and the One Thousand Yuan Editions on Ten Carts 千元十駕 library of Wu Qian 吳騫 (1733–1813) in Haining. The derivation of the latter name was due to Huang's precedent; see ECCP, 1:341.

86 Qu Xiangbang, *Guangdong shihua zhengxubian*, 1. *Qingshi jishi*, 18:12887 preserves an earlier version of the remarks by Qu Xiangbang.

87 The Ten Talents of the Dali period were a group of poetic gallants gathered around

Li Yuzhong 李虞仲 during the Dali reign period (766–780): "During the midst of the Dali reign, he versified in writing and chanted to match rhymes with Han Xiang, Qian Qi, and Lu Lun, et al.; their fame spread throughout the capital"; *Jiu Tangshu*, 113.4266. The same passage goes on to recount how they frequently attended banquets hosted by Princess Shengping 昇平 (the eldest daughter of Daizong 代宗, r. 762–779), who had cultivated literary taste and enjoyed the company of poets. One poetic game is recorded as follows: "At each convivial banquet they would versify while the princess listened from behind curtains. She awarded those who produced good poems with one hundred pieces of fine silk." According to *Jiu Tangshu*, 118.4383, they were the subject of contemporary painters. In all, the other members of the Ten Talents were Lu Lun 盧綸, Ji Zhongfu 吉中孚, Han Xiang 韓翃, Qian Qi 錢起, Sikong Shu 司空曙, Miao Fa 苗發, Cui Dong 崔峒, Di Wei 耿湋, Xiahou Shen 夏侯審, and Li Duan 李端. (The listing enumerated at *Xin Tangshu*, 203.128 does not include the name of Li Yuzhong.)

88 This is an allusion to some lines by Du Fu, who wrote about visiting the country estate of one General He: "I do not recognize the road to the south pond,/But today I know the Fifth Bridge,/Where a famous garden is hard by the green river" 不識南塘路，今知第五橋，名園依綠水; QTS, 7:2397.

89 Meng Ziwei 孟子微, in *Yilin congtan*, 169.

90 Biographical details of Liang Dingfen and Huang Jie will be introduced below. Of the remaining members, the most important in terms of the impact exerted on Cantonese belles-lettres is Wu Daorong. He hailed from Panyu. After earning his *jinshi* degree in 1880, he was assigned to the Hanlin Academy as an Editor, but he did not enjoy the bureaucratic context of his work—temperamentally he was more at home as an educator. He subsequently resigned and returned to Guangzhou where he worked in various private academies, including serving as a monitor at the Xuehai tang; Rong Zhaozu, "Xuehai tang kao," 60. The preface to Wu's anthology *Dan'an wencun* erroneously states that Wu studied at the Sea of Learning in 1901, a strange course of action for a *jinshi* degree holder! After more than twenty years in educational leadership, he turned back to editorial work and devoted the remainder of his life to local history. After the revolution, he was put in charge of compiling a new edition of the gazetteer on Panyu; it was finally completed and printed in 1931 as the *Panyuxian xuzhi* 番禺縣續志, 44 *juan*. He compiled the important anthology *Guangdong wenzheng* 廣東文徵 in 240 *juan,* containing more than 3,000 separate pieces, and also wrote short biographical notices of the more than 700 authors included, published separately as the *Guangdong wenzheng zuozhe kao* 廣東文徵作者考. The modern edition produced by the Hong Kong Chinese University Press in 1973 combines the two works, prefacing the biographical notices at the head of the selections of each author. His individual prose pieces are preserved in the *Dan'an wencun*; two biographical notices are included in this collection. Incidentally, the original edition of the biographical notices to the *Guangdong wenzheng* was printed, appropriately enough, on the site of the original Southern Garden Poetry Society by the Zhongshan Library in 1958.

The other five members of the Southern Garden Poetry Society at this time were Wang Zhaoquan 汪兆銓, Yao Yun 姚筠, Li Qilong 李啓隆, Shen Zetang 沈澤棠, and Wen Su 溫肅. Wang Zhaoquan (*zi* Xinbo 莘伯) was from Panyu; he gained his *juren* degree in 1885. He served as an instructor at the Sea of Learning and was esteemed by Chen Li. After the revolution he presided over the Teaching Loyalty School 教忠學校 as principal for over ten years, then died of complications due to alcohol. He left two anthologies of his belletristic works, the *Xingmozhai shiji* 惺默齋詩集 and the *Changchuxuan cigao* 萇楚軒詞稿; see GDWZ, 6:284–86 for one *fu* and one prose piece. Yao Yun (*zi* Xiexue 嶰雪, *hao* Junqing 俊卿) was from Panyu and became a *juren* during the Tongzhi 同治 reign (1861–1875). He served as Director of the Sea of Learning, but he was most known for his accomplishments as a landscape painter; see GDSC, 1:357 for three poems lamenting the past at the Terrace of the King of Song 宋王台 in Hong Kong. Li Qilong (*zi* Xiangwen 襄文, also Liu'an 留菴) was from Panyu and noted for his landscape painting; see GDSC, 1:393. Shen Zetang (*zi* Zhilin 芷鄰), himself from Panyu, also earned his *juren* degree during the Tongzhi era. He was a prose writer of distinction, as well as a renowned calligrapher in the *kaishu* style. His works include the *Xiaomoweige shichao* 小摩圍閣詩鈔, the *Chan'anci* 懺菴詞, and the *Chan'an suibi* 懺菴隨筆. Wen Su (*zi* Yifu 毅夫) was from Shunde. He gained his *jinshi* degree during the Guangxu 光緒 reign (1875–1909) and was appointed to be an Imperial Scribe. His anthology reflects the posthumous title he was awarded, the *Anthology of Transmitted Works of the Cultured and Virtuous Duke Wen, Wen Wenjiegong yiji* 溫文節公遺集. Three poems are preserved at GDSC, 3:414, including a poem of historical interest recording his feeling upon the renovation of the grave of Chen Gongyin.

91 Wang Zongyan, *Guangdong wenwu congtan*, 154, 85–87.

92 Chen Yongzheng 陳永正, ed., *Lingnan lidai shixuan*, 859–61.

93 An allusion to *Shijing*, 15b.1a, Mao #225, "Durenshi" 都人士 (The Men of the Capital). A *taili* 臺笠 was a cap made of the unidentified *tai* plant; but according to Mao what was made was a cloak. Regardless, based on the Little Preface, Legge characterizes this poem as "Praise of the ladies and gentlemen of a former time for the simplicity of their dress, the correctness of their deportment, and the elegance of their speech", Legge, *The Chinese Classics*, 4:409.

94 The name of Mao #225, alluded to in the previous line.

95 Or "chant songs from the 'elegentiae' section of the *Book of Poetry*." Given Liang Dingfen's royalist leanings, it is likely that Huang was alluding to the appearance of this phrase in *Suishu* 隋書, 13.297, where it indicated music used in the sacrifices.

96 "Surveying" 俯仰 the affairs of a generation is one privilege of like-minded friends when they gather, as noted in the "Preface to the Lan Tingxu Gathering" 蘭亭序 of Wang Xizhi 王羲之; see *Wang Youjun ji* 王右軍集 (BSJJ ed.), 3:2241–2282 (2.41b), *Jinshu*, 80.2099.

97 Liao Jingzeng (*zi* Bolu 伯魯) came from Nanhai. He studied at both the Sea of Learning and the Guangya Academies. He was an educationalist, teaching in higher education and working in both the provincial gazetteer compilation office and as an Archivist at the provincial library. His numerous works include the *Chunqiu tongyi* 春秋通義, *Genlu shihua* 艮盧詩話, and *Yueshi biaowei* 粵詩表微; he also edited the *Guangya shuyuan zhi* 廣雅書院志. See GDSC, 3:774–76 for five poems.

98 Ibid, 3:775.

99 These two ancient Chu songs are synonymous with highbrow art and literature, as was evident above in the case of "White Snow" in a poem by Sun Fen dedicated to

Wang Zuo.

100 The winners and selected poems are included in Wang Zongyan, *Guangdong wenwu congtan*, 5–6.

101 Ibid, 5. He is otherwise unknown. This poem, along with the second and third place entries on this same theme, are also preserved in GDSC, 3:690.

102 Wang Zongyan, *Guangdong wenwu congtan*, 5–6.

103 Ibid.

104 *Qingshi jishi*, 18:12887.

105 Liu Sifen 劉斯奮, ed., *Huang Jie shixuan* 黃節詩選 (Guangzhou: Guangdong renmin chubanshe, 1993), 56.

106 Personal insights into the character and literary talent of Liang Dingfen are provided by fellow tutor Reginald F. Johnston, *Twilight in the Forbidden City* (London: Victor Gollancz, 1934), 187–90.

107 For a short biography, see GDWZ, 6:229; numerous prose works are found on 229–36. His life and works are subjected to fuller treatment by Xu Xinfu, *Guangdong cangshu jishishi*, 196–98.

108 This Confucian master was from Shunde and had studied with Kang Youwei's 康有為 (1858–1927) own master Zhu Ciqi 朱次琦 (1807–1882). Jian collected the scattered remnants of Zhu's writings and published them in 1897 along with a *nianpu* of his master under the title of *Zhu Jiujiang xiansheng ji* 朱九江先生集. Other than this, Jian's main claim to fame was his lifelong devotion to classical studies and the simple frugality of his lifestyle; he also won some renown for his calligraphy.

109 Howard L. Boorman and Richard C. Howard, eds., *Biographical Dictionary of Republican China*, 5 vols. (New York and London: Columbia University Press, 1968), 2:187. In addition to Huang Jie's biography on this page, see 4:218 for works by and about Huang. For the broader intellectual and political environment of Huang's youthful political activities, see Charlotte Furth, "Intellectual Change: From the Reform Movement to the May Fourth Movement, 1895–1920," in *The Cambridge History of China. Vol. 12. Republican China,* ed. John K. Fairbank (Cambridge: Cambridge University Press, 1983), 354–61.

110 See the *nianpu* appended to Liu Sifen, ed., *Huang Jie shixuan*, 314–21. For his attainments in traditional literary pursuits, see Xu Xinfu, *Guangdong cangshu jishishi*, 234–37.

111 Ibid, 3.

112 Ibid, 56.

113 Meyer-Fang, *Building Culture in Early Qing Yangzhou*, 33.

114 Liu Sifen, ed., *Huang Jie shixuan*, 317.

115 Ibid, 317.

116 Ibid, 26.

117 GDSC, 2:792. Ren Shixi (*zi* Muchen 穆臣), from Panyu, had been a tribute student. He left an anthology called the *Lianyin shichao* 蓮隱詩鈔.

118 "Ashes of the apocalypse" 劫灰 is Buddhist, signifying the ashes caused by the fires that destroy each cosmic cycle. It was a favorite element of Qiu Fengjia's poetic diction, perhaps because he shared the same gloomy outlook on the state of China at this juncture in her fortunes. On Qiu's use of this term, see my "Cong Lingnan

shifeng kan Qiu Fengjia de Guangdong shi" 從嶺南詩風看丘逢甲的廣東詩 (Poetizing the Local in Qiu Fengjia's Verses on Guangdong), in *Qiu Fengjia, Qiu Niantai fuzi ji qi shidai xueshu yantaohui* 丘逢甲，丘念台父子及其時代學術研討會 (Taizhong: Fengjia University, 1999), 3–18.

119 *Yilin conglu*, 163.

120 Ibid, 164; Huang Foyi, *Guangzhou chengfang zhi*, 4.37b.

121 All listed in ibid.

122 Wang Deming, "Lun Songdai de shishe," 68.

123 Xiao Chi, *The Chinese Garden as Lyric Enclave*, 47, n. 14. The same intellectual trends isolated by Xiao Chi that developed at the beginning of the Qing may be said to have been regenerated at its collapse: the call for a return to pragmatic statecraft, the appeal for ritualistic ethics, and an upsurge of Han culturalism; see the discussion at ibid, 47ff.

124 Martin Kern cites the work of eminent students of ritual to support his reading of Mao #209, "Chuci" 楚茨, as a performance text normative in the formation of ritual sacrifice. These specialists include Catherine Bell, Walter Burkert, and Edmund Leach. For their work, see Kern, "*Shi Jing* Songs As Performance Texts: A Case Study of 'Chu Ci' (Thorny Caltrop)," 55, n. 23. Along with "social solidarity," another key term, this time borrowed by Kern from the Egyptologist Jan Assmann, is "ritual coherence"; it "refers to ritual as the key factor to bring about cultural continuity" (65, n. 68). Especially noteworthy here is Kern's discussion on 66–68 entitled "The Cultural Memory."

125 Ibid, 67.

Chapter 7

1 Peter Brown, *Augustine of Hippo* (NY: Dorset Press, 1967), 289.

2 Jiang Zuyuan and Fang Zhiqin, eds., *Jianming Guangdongshi*, 573; see 572–74 for a summary of Qiu's contributions to education in Guangdong.

3 For his life, see Xu Bodong 徐博東 and Huang Zhiping 黃志萍, *Qiu Fengjiazhuan* 丘逢甲傳 (Beijing: Shishi chubanshe, 1987); Wu Hongcong 吳宏聰 and Li Hongsheng 李鴻生, eds., *Qiu Fengjia yanjiu* 丘逢甲研究 (Guangdong: Guangdong renmin chubanshe, 1986); and ECCP, 1:171–72. His surname was originally written 丘; but the Yongzheng emperor (r. 1723–1740) issued a mandate requiring this surname be written with the so-called "ear" radical, thus yielding 邱. Qiu himself insisted on the original orthography. After the fall of the Qing, Qiu sent a letter to his clan members requesting that they all "take off their ears"; see Xu Xu, *Lingnan gujinlu*, 318–19.

4 See Wu, preface to Qiu Fengjia, *Canghaijun gengxu Luofu youcao* 滄海君庚戌羅浮游草, or *Draft Poems on Roaming around Luofu on Day Gengxu by the Lord of Watchet Sea*, printed by Wu Daorong, 1910, and Qu Xiangbang, *Guangdong shihua zhengxubian*, 49.

5 Qiu Fengjia, *Lingyun hairilou shichao*, 271–72.

6 Ibid, 221.

7 Literally, to rain heavily enough to raise "krakens and dragons."

8 Qiu Fengjia, *Lingyun hairilou shichao*, 218.

9 Ibid, 222.

10 The river is described through hyperbole as a "sea."
11 Qiu Fengjia, *Lingyun hairilou shichao*, 274–75.
12 Ibid, 274.
13 See Honey, "Cong Lingnan shifeng kan Qiu Fengjia de Guangdong shi."
14 Yi Moqing is otherwise unknown.
15 "To grasp the bull's ear" 執牛耳 is to preside over a meeting. It derives from the ancient practice of cutting off the ear of a bull to provide blood for anointing the covenants of the feudal princes; see *Zuozhuan*, 60.12a, Duke Ai, 17th Year; Legge, *The Chinese Classics*, 5:851. Here it seems to refer to be the winner of the poetry games.
16 Qiu Fengjia, *Lingyun hairilou shichao*, 275. Two poems by Qiu's contemporary Hu Yisheng 胡毅生 (*hao* Suizhai 隋齋) that mourn Zhang Qiao at her gravesite are preserved in GDSC, 2:552; they do not, however, mention her connection to the Southern Garden.
17 Poem Eight dedicated to the monk Seng Tong'an contains the wording of "ashes of disaster"; see GDWX, 7:511.
18 Ibid, 7:508. Probably the most effective use of this term with regard to Cantonese poetics and the tragic particulars of historical change is by Lun Ming 倫明 (d. 1942) who wrote: "How often have I heard that the Watchet Sea has experienced a great upheaval" 幾聞滄海變滄桑; GDSC, 2:624.
19 For Qiu's poetic diction, see Honey, "Cong Lingnan shifeng kan Qiu Fengjia de Guangdong shi."
20 Qiu's own interlinear note indicates that this variety of willow in Guangdong does not produce flowers.
21 This line refers to the Jin period gallant from Luoyang Xie An 謝安 (320–385). He was gifted at chanting student's ditties in the Luoyang style but was afflicted with a defect in his nose that made his voice nasal. In order to imitate his popular chants, others would cover their noses while chanting; see *Jinshu*, 79.2076.
22 See QTS, 11:4117.
23 An Qi, *Li Bai quanji biannian zhushi*, 1:806.
24 Qiu Fengjia, *Lingyun hairilou shichao*, 275.
25 GDSC, 2:482.
26 If we credit Luo Genshen with merely comparing the two poetry societies, then our understanding of this line would be: "Beneath the flowers there were zithers and goblets at our Southern Garden-type meetings."
27 The reference to the Northern Song likely refers to the use made by cultivated literati of the vacated pleasure grounds of the temporary palace built on this site by the Southern Han, newly conquered by the Northern Song.
28 *Yuedong cichao*, "Zhang Qiao," 1a.
29 See the poem by Chen Jingji, one of the founders of the Phoenix Terrace Poetry Society, in Zhang Qigan, ed., *Dongguan shilu*, 126.
30 Witness the biographical entry by Wu Daorong, GDSC, 2:541–42, and Xu Xinfu, *Guangdong cangshu jishishi*, 240–42. For his poetics, see Chen Yongzheng, ed., *Lingnan wenxueshi*, 824–27.
31 Published in *Guangdong wenwu*, 53–70.
32 *Guangdong wenwu*, 903.

33 Ibid, 910.
34 Ibid, 906. A related motivation was perhaps just idle reading in his garden, for "Reading books and brewing wine are best for dispensing sorrow" 讀書釀酒最消愁, 910.
35 Ibid, 904.
36 The nine sacred mountains.
37 Ibid, 905.
38 "Virtuous brilliance" 休明 is traceable to *Zuozhuan*, 21.16b, Duke Xuan 3rd year, where it refers to the virtue and brilliance of the state tripods. This image of tripods lends poetical support to the political legitimacy of Guangdong.
39 *Guangdong wenwu*, 911.
40 Ibid, 908.
41 Ibid, 913.
42 Ibid, 908, 916.
43 Ibid, 912.
44 Ibid, 914, 910, 912.
45 Ibid, 910.
46 Ibid, 910, 915.
47 Ibid, 915.
48 GDSC, 3:846, editorial preface. In addition to "having the reputation" of being the Five Modern Masters, other verbs used by Wu Daorong were even more forceful: they were "classed as" 目 the Modern Masters and "were called" 稱 the Modern Masters; see 842, 833.
49 Sometimes Yu 余 is written 餘
50 Biographical notes to each master except for Zeng Xiying are included in GDSC, 3:842–46.
51 Ibid, 3:857.
52 *Zhuanke nianli* 篆刻年歷, accessed at www.candc.com.tw/sealbank/ZR7610.htm-5k on December 20, 2005. (As the above link is no longer working, the same quote may be accessed now at http://sealbank.net/M3MainFind.asp?LM=3&L1=7&L2=71&L3=030&LS=&SRCHTXT=WS&SK=US771030&PN=0&PNRN=0.)
53 GDSC, 3:843–44.
54 A "treasured stele" is a stone tablet with a Buddhist inscription.
55 Ruoye 若耶 was the name of the stream besides which Xishi 西施 "rinsed" 浣 silken garments when she was discovered and recruited into the service of Fuchai, the king of Wu 吳王夫差.
56 See ibid, 3:927.
57 GDSC, 2:858.
58 For the members of this poetry society, see the notes appended to Su Baohe's 蘇寶盉 "Liaoshe shizhong ji" 聊社詩鐘集; ibid, 2:757–58.
59 Ibid, 2:847.
60 Fan Pang 范滂 was an official of the Later Han who expressed the "ambition to cleanse and purify the world" 澄清天下之志. Upright and incorruptible, he submitted fearless memorials to the throne that resulted in numerous personal attacks; he was ultimately imprisoned and executed. See his biography at *Hou Hanshu*, 67.2203–208.

61 Han Wo 韓握 (844–923) won repute as a poet and statesman who steadfastly remained loyal to the Tang in its final decade; see Beth Upton in *The Indiana Companion to Traditional Chinese Literature*, 395–96.

62 Referring to the surrender of the Japanese that concluded World War Two.

63 GDSC, 3:933–35.

64 The "Garden of Fine Arts" 藝苑 refers to literary circles in Guangzhou; for the *locus classicus*, see *Songshu*, 43.1339.

65 This is an allusion to an incident in Yang Fu's life when auspicious snow fell on his residence, which was south across the Pearl River in the Henan 河南 district; see GDXY, 2:42; Lu Ping, *Guangzhou fengwu*, 345–46.

66 "Subsidiary *qi*" 間氣 was the type of *qi* that formed ministers, for according to the commentary of Song Jun 宋均 to the *Chunqiu weiyan Kongtu* 春秋緯演孔圖, "Orthodox *qi* forms emperors, subsidiary qi forms ministers" 正氣為帝，間氣為臣; cited at Zhang Qiyun 張其昀, ed., *Zhongwen dacidian* 中文大辭典, 12 vols. (1962–1968; rpt., Taipei: Zhongguo Wenhua Daxue, 1973), 9:968 (written as 閒氣).

67 Hai Rui 海瑞 (*zi* Ruxian 汝賢, *hao* Gangfeng 剛峰, 1513–1587) was a native of Hainan Island who became a fearless champion of justice for the people; he became renowned throughout the realm for his integrity. He was spared execution for sending a blistering memorial to the throne criticizing Shizong 世宗 (r. 1521–1567) only because of the emperor's sudden death. After his own death he became celebrated in folk literature and legend; he was the subject of an opera written by Wu Han ca. 1961. See the lengthy treatment of DMB, 1:474–79.

68 Zhao Jie died on shipboard in Nanchang; Wang Zhe was executed in Shandong.

69 1522 to 1566.

70 The phrase "troubles and uncertainties" 艱虞 is an allusion to the upheaval that occurred at the end of the Song dynasty (420–477); see Ren Fang 任昉, "Wang Wenxian jixu" 王文憲集序, WX, 46.34b.

71 Referring to Chen Zizhuang and the Twelve Masters of the Southern Garden.

72 This lake, formally called the "Lake for Looking in the Mirror" 照鏡湖, was fifty *li* northwest of Panyu.

73 The course of Feng Minchang 馮敏昌 (*zi* Boqiu 伯求, *hao* Yushan 魚山, 1747–1806) through the examination field was sponsored by the famous scholar-official Weng Fanggang 翁方綱 (1733–1818). Feng served in a variety of official posts around the country, but he spent more time in retirement in Guangzhou than anywhere. Late in life he directed several local academies, the Yuehua 粵華 and Yuexiu Academies. As a poet he was known as the leading member of the Three Masters of Lingnan 嶺南三子, along with Zhang Jinfang 張錦芳 (*zi* Canfu 粲夫, *hao* Yaofang 葯房 Huatian 花田, 1747–1792) and Hu Yichang 胡亦常(*zi* Tongqian 同謙 Shifu 豕甫 Shipu 豕浦, 1743–1773). Feng was also ranked with Li Jian and two others as the Four Great Calligraphers from Lingnan 嶺南四大書家 of mid-Qing. For the biographies of all Three Masters of Lingnan, see Chen Zehong, ed., *Guangdong lishi mingren zhuanlüe*, 269–76.

74 This refers to the style of poetry adopted by Feng from his mentor Weng Fanggang that stressed the "substance" 肌理 of a poem instead of the "spiritual harmony" 神韻 as advocated by Wang Shizhen. This style came to characterize Lingnan poetics of the time.

75 Song Xiang 宋湘 (*zi* Huanxiang 焕襄, *hao* Zhiwan 芷灣, 1757–1826) was the next leading poet in the line of succession from Feng Minchang and Li Jian. In fact, one critic praised him as the best poet in Guangdong since Qu Dajun; Chen Zehong, *Guangdong lishi mingren zhuanlüe*, 288. He was equally skilled as a painter and calligraphist. He was born in Meixian 梅縣 and studied at the Yuexiu Academy, but it took a fourth attempt before he passed his *jinshi* exam at age 43. In 1801 he assumed the post of director of the Fenghu Academy in Huizhou 豐湖書院, where Su Shi had lived in exile for three years. In 1803 he began to teach at the Yuexiu Academy, and socialized with Feng Minchang. He began a nine-year stint in Beijing in 1804, working in the Hanlin yuan but frequently traveling around the country to administer provincial exams. While in Beijing, he feasted and frolicked with such literary luminaries as Weng Fanggang. Starting in 1813 he spent the next 8 years as a local magistrate in Yunnan before returning to Beijing; he died on the road the next year. His collected works are called *Hongxing shanfang ji* 紅杏山房集, 13 *juan*. See GDWZ, 5:271–72; *Qingshi jishi*, 12:8163–184; Chen Zehong, *Guangdong lidai mingren zhuanlüe*, 283–88.

76 In this line of verse, Sheng alludes to an alternate name of the group, the Seven Masters of the Poetry Altar 七子詩壇; see Chen Zehong, *Guangdong lidai mingren zhuanlüe*, 290.

77 An allusion to the *Shijing*, 4a.3b, Mao# 65, "Shuli" 黍離, preface: "An officer describes his melancholy and reflections on seeing the desolation of the old capital of Chow"; Legge, *The Chinese Classics*, 4:110; the ruins of the ancestral temple had all become overgrown with millet.

78 Referring to Chen Li.

79 Yu Shimei 于式枚 (1859–1915) was the private secretary of Li Hongzhang 李鴻章 (1823–1901), serving on his staff from 1885 to 1899. He was a member of the Chinese embassies in Germany, England, and the US. In 1910 he was appointed vice-president of the Board of Civil Appointments; see *Qingshigao*, 443.12444. His official career may be pieced together in *Qingshigao*, 196, *passim*. He was the third highest editor of the *Qingshigao*, serving as Chief Examiner. As the vice-minister of the Court of State Ceremonial, Yu was dispatched to Guangdong to manage educational affairs, then was appointed as superintendent of training. Wen Tingshi 文廷式 (1856–1904) was a high official who earned the displeasure of the Empress Dowager by defending Emperor Dezong against her and Li Hongzhang's attempted coup. He was consequently demoted in 1896. When she finally overthrew the emperor in 1898, Wen's life was in real danger, so he fled to Japan. It is not known when he was in Guangdong. For his life, see ECCP, 2:855–56.

80 These were the last two reign periods of the Qing dynasty, Guangxu (r. 1875–1909) and Xuantong (r. 1909–1912).

81 The canal was presumably the Clear Canal.

82 Mirror Lake, as seen above.

83 According to an interlineal note, this Buddhist building was a site where left–over citizens of the Ming gathered.

84 An interlinear note states that this refers to receiving a publication from the literary society in Macao.

85 An allusion to *Shiji*, 7.333; when Xiang Yu 項羽 was besieged by his nemesis Liu Bang,

the founder of the Han dynasty, he was shocked to hear so many songs of his native Chu being sung by the besieging forces; this revealed that among the encircling forces were many newly absorbed troops from Chu that had formerly fought for him, greatly swelling the ranks of the enemy. This saying then means to be encircled on every side by difficulties; in this case, it refers to the Japanese occupation of Guangzhou.

86 The ancient sage king Shun is referred to via one of his prominent features: he was reputed to have double pupils; see *Shiji*, 1.31.

87 Referring to Chen's 3,000 poems on Cantonese poetic history.

88 *Zhong* 鐘 and *lü* 呂 were ancient musical pitches; the fabulous Zouyu beast was reputed to walk accompanied by their sounds; see Kong Yingda's commentary to *Shijing*, 13.10b, Mao #11, "Lin zhi zhi" 麟支趾. Here they represent the orthodox sounds of music as poetry.

89 See, for instance, a line from Kang Youwei's poem "Climbing the Terrace of the King of Yue in Autumn" 秋登越王臺: "Three thousand disasters—how often have we experienced reincarnation?" 三千劫幾歷輪回; *Qingshi jishi*, 20:13887. The "left-over citizen" of the Qing, Ren Shixi, also used this term in his poem on the sacrifice in the Southern Garden noted above in Chapter Six. As a final example, witness Huang Jushi 黄居石, a "left-over citizen" of the Ming: "In which places have the ashes of disaster sunk into the waters of academy ponds?" 何處劫灰沉泮水; *Qingshi jishi*, 2:1179. Given the fact that the Pantang 泮塘 area of Guangzhou used to be the site of the Sunken Evening Lake 沉夜湖, an equally plausible rendering of the line above could read: "Where are the ashes of disaster in the 'sunken pond'?" For this lake to the west of Mt. Yuexiu, see Lu Ping, *Guangzhou fengwu*, 237.

90 From his *Ming yiminshi* 明遺民詩, cited at *Qingshi jishi*, 1:532. "Ban" and "Dang" were poems in the *Shijing* that betoken corrupt officials and the resultant ruin; see *Shijing*, 17d.14b–21b and 18a.1a–7b, Mao #s 254 and 255, Legge, *The Chinese Classics*, 4:499–504, 505–510.

91 *Qingshi jishi*, 1:536.

92 Ibid, 2:863.

93 Ibid, 2:1003. He Shi was introduced in Chapter Two.

94 Zhang's essay is called "'Shuli' jiang wei Guofeng ban" 黍離降為國風辨; GDWZ, 5:419–420. The only other *Shijing* poem to be singled out for individual treatment among the essays included in the *Guangdong wenzheng* is Mao #1, "Guanju"; see 5:418.

95 Huang Yu, ed., *Lidai mingren ru Yue shixuan*, 395. Hang Shijun stayed in Guangzhou for two years, from 1753–1755, directing the Yuexiu Academy; several of his poems on Guangzhou composed during his short stay are included in the *Lidai mingren ru Yue shixuan*, 391–96; for his life and bibliography, see ECCP, 1:276–77.

96 I.e. the kapok tree.

Abbreviations

BSJJ	Han-Wei Liuchao baisan mingjia ji
DMB	Dictionary of Ming Biography
ECCP	Eminent Chinese of the Ch'ing Period
GDSC	Guangdong lidai shichao
GDTZ	Guangdong tongzhi
GDWX	Guangdong wenxian
GDWZ	Guangdong wenzheng
GDXY	Guangdong xinyu
GZSS	Guangzhou sixiansheng shi
HY	Daozang zimu yinde (Harvard-Yenching catalogue)
MS	Mingshi
NYHS	Nanyuan houwu xiansheng shi
NYQS	Nanyuan qianwu xiansheng shi
QSGW	Quan Shanggu Sandai Qin Han Sanguo Liuchaowen
QSS	Quan Songshi
QTS	Quan Tangshi
SBCK	Sibu congkan
SKQS	Siku quanshu
WX	Zengbu liuchenzhu wenxuan
XAJ	Xi'an ji
XQHS	Xian-Qin, Han, Wei, Jin Nanbeichao shi
ZZJC	Xinbian Zhuzi jicheng

Bibliography

An Qi 安旗, et al., eds. *Li Bai quanji biannian zhushi* 李白全集編年注釋. 3 vols. Chengdu: Bashu shushe, 1990.

Anderson, Benedict. *Imagined Communities: Reflections on the Origin and Spread of Nationalism*. 1983. Rpt., London: Verso, 1991.

Andrews, Corey. *Literary Nationalism in Eighteenth-Century Scottish Club Poetry*. Studies in British Literature, vol. 82. Lewiston, Queenston, and Lampeter: The Edwin Mellen Press, 2004.

Atwell, William S. "From Education to Politics: The Fu She." In *The Unfolding of Neo-Confucianism*, ed. Wm. Theodore de Bary. New York and London: Columbia University Press, 1985, 333–67.

Ayers, William. *Chang Chih-tung and Educational Reform in China*. Harvard East Asian Series, 54. Cambridge, Massachusetts: Harvard University Press, 1971.

Balazs, Etienne and Yves Hervouet, eds. *A Sung Bibliography*. Hong Kong: The Chinese University Press, 1978.

Bashijiuzhong Mingdai zhuanji 八十九種明代傳記. Ed. Tian Jizong 田繼綜. 1935. Rpt., Shanghai: Shanghai guji chubanshe, 1982.

Beijing tushuguan guji shanben shumu 北京圖書館古籍善本書目. 5 vols. Beijing: Shumu wenxian chubanshe, 1987.

Bishop, Carl Whiting. "Long-Houses and Dragon-Boats." *Antiquity* 12 (1938): 411–24.

Boorman, Howard L. and Richard C. Howard, eds. *Biographical Dictionary of Republican China*. 5 vols. New York and London: Columbia University Press, 1968.

Brindley, Erica. "Barbarians or Not? Ethnicity and Changing Conceptions of the Ancient Yue (Viet) Peoples, ca. 400–50 BC." *Asia Major*, Third Series, 16 (2003): 1–32.

Brown, Peter. *Augustine of Hippo*. New York: Dorset Press, 1967.

Cahill, James. *Parting at the Shore: Chinese Painting of the Early and Middle Ming Dynasty, 1368–1580*. New York and Tokyo: Weatherhill, 1978.

Cai, Yujun 蔡瑜君. *Gao Bing shixue yanjiu* 高棅詩學研究. Taipei: National Taiwan University, 1990.

Cambridge History of China, The, Vol. 7: The Ming Dynasty (1368–1644), Part I. Ed. Frederick W. Mote and Denis Twitchett. Cambridge: Cambridge University Press, 1988.

Cambridge History of English Literature, The. 15 vols. Cambridge: Cambridge University Press, 1963.

Canghai yizhu 滄海遺珠. (SKQS ed.), *juan* 570.

Cao, Pi 曹丕. *Wei Wendi ji* 魏文帝集. (BSJJ ed.), 2:945–1028.

Cao, Zhi 曹植. *Chen Siwang ji* 陳思王集. (BSJJ ed.), 2:1029–158.

Chang, Kang-I Sun. "Gender and Canonicity: Ming-Qing Women Poets in the Eyes of the Male Literati." In *Hsiang Lectures on Chinese Poetry*, vol. 1. Montreal: Centre for East Asian Research, McGill University, 2001, 1–18.

Chen, Baozhen 陳寶珍. "Zhang Jiuling yanjiu ziliao suoyin" 張九齡研究資料索引. *Guji zhengli yanjiu tongxun* 3 (1988): 10–11.

Chen, Fenghuai 陳封懷, ed. *Guangdong zhiwuzhi* 廣東植物志. Guangdong: Guangdong guji chubanshe, 1987.

Chen, Gongyin 陳恭尹. *Dulutang ji* 獨漉堂集. Guangzhou: Zhongshan Daxue chubanshe, 1988.

Chen, Juyuan 陳居淵. *Jiao Xun, Ruan Yuan pingzhuan* 焦循阮元評傳. *Zhongguo sixiangjiao pingzhuan congshu* 中國思想家評傳叢書. Nanjing: Nanjing Daxue chubanshe, 2006.

Chen, Lian 陳璉. *Luofuzhi* 羅浮志. 10 *juan.* (*Lingnan yishu* 嶺南遺書 ed.). N.p: Nanhai Wushi, [1831].

Chen, Pan 陳槃. "Guangdong lidai shichao bielu" 廣東歷代詩鈔別錄. *Dalu zazhi* 69, no. 13 (1984): 1–62.

Chen, Yan 陳衍. *Yuanshi jishi* 元詩紀事. 2 vols. Shanghai: Shanghai guji chubanshe, 1987.

Chen, Yingchao 陳應潮. "Lun Liang Peilanshi yu Lingnan shitan" 論梁佩蘭詩與嶺南詩壇. *Lishi wenxian yu chuantong wenhua* 4 (1994): 284–92.

Chen, Yongzheng 陳永正, ed. *Lingnan lidai shixuan* 嶺南歷代詩選. Guangzhou: Guangdong renmin chubanshe, 1985.

———. *Lingnan lidai cixuan* 嶺南歷代詞選. Guangzhou: Guangdong renmin chubanshe, 1993.

———. *Lingnan wenxueshi* 嶺南文學史. Guangzhou: Guangdong gaodeng jiaoyu chubanshe, 1993.

Chen, Zehong 陳澤泓, ed. *Guangdong lishi mingren zhuanlüe* 廣東歷史名人傳略. Guangzhou: Guangdong renmin chubanshe, 1998.

Chen, Zizhuang 陳子壯. *Libu zonggao* 黎部總稿. (*Guangdong congshu* ed.). Shanghai: Commercial Press, 1946.

Chen, Zuwu 陳祖武. "Cong Yuan Chonghuan dao Qu Dajun: Mingmo Qingchu de Hua'nan zhishijie" 從袁崇煥到屈大均明末清初的華南知識界. In *Mingmo Qingchu Hua'nan diqu lishiwenwu gongye yantaohui lunwenji*, 287–96.

Chinese Scholar's Studio: Artistic Life in the Late Ming Period, The. An Exhibition from the Shanghai Museum. Ed. Chu-Tsing Li and James C. Y. Watt. New York and London: Thames and Hudson, in conjunction with The Asia Society Galleries, 1987.

Chuci buzhu 楚辭補註. Taipei: Yiwen yinshuguan, 1981.

Clunas, Craig. *Fruitful Sites: Garden Culture in Ming Dynasty China*. London: Reaktion Books, 1996.

Cohen, Paul. *History in Three Keys: The Boxers as Event, Experience, and Myth*. New York: Columbia University Press, 1997.

Congshu jicheng chubian 叢書集成初編. Shanghai: Commercial Press, 1936.

Connerton, Paul. *How Societies Remember*. Cambridge: Cambridge University Press, 1989.

Curtis, Lewis P. and Harmon W. Liebert. *Esto Perpetua: The Club of Dr. Samuel Johnson and His Friends, 1764–1784*. N.p.: Archon Press-The Shoestring Press, 1963.

Dade Nanhai zhi 大德南海志. Comp. Chen Dazhen 陳大震. In *Song-Yuan fangzhi congkan* 宋元方志叢刊, 8 vols. Beijing: Zhonghua shuju, 1990.

Daozang zimu yinde 道藏子目引得. *Combined Indexes to the Authors and Titles of Books in Two Collections of Taoist Literature*. Ed. Weng Dujian 翁獨健. Harvard-Yenching Institute Sinological Index Series, no. 25. 1935. Rpt., Taipei: Chengwen, 1966.

Dardess, John W. *Confucianism and Autocracy*. Berkeley and Los Angeles: University of California Press, 1983.

Davis, A. R. *T'ao Yüan-ming (AD 365–427): His Works and Their Meaning*. 2 vols. Cambridge: Cambridge University Press, 1983.

Deng, Zhicheng 鄧之誠. *Qingshi jishi chubian* 清詩紀事初編. 2 vols. Hong Kong: Zhonghua shuju, 1976.

Dennerline, Jerry. *The Chia-Ting Loyalists: Confucian Leadership and Social Change in Seventeenth-Century China*. New Haven and London: Yale University Press, 1981.

Dictionary of Ming Biography. 2 vols. Ed. L. Carrington Goodrich and Chaoying Fang. New York: Columbia University Press, 1976.

Diény, Jean-Pierre. *Les Dix-neuf poèms anciens*. 1963. Rpt., Paris: Université Paris VII, Centre de Publication Asie Orientale, 1974.

Dongguan xianzhi 東莞縣志. Comp. Huang Shipei 黃時沛. 46 *juan*. N.p.: Jiaqing 3 (1798).

Dreyer, Edward L. "Military Origins of Ming China." In *The Cambridge History of China, Vol. 7: The Ming Dynasty (1368–1644), Part I*, 58–106.

Elman, Benjamin A. "The Hsüeh-Hai T'ang and the Rise of New Text Scholarship in Canton." *Ch'ing-shih Wen-t'i* 4 (Dec. 1979): 51–82.

———. "The Social Roles of Literati in Early to Mid-Ch'ing." In *The Cambridge History of China. Vol. 9. Part One: The Ch'ing Empire to 1800*, ed. Willard J. Peterson. Cambridge: Cambridge University Press, 2002, 360–427.

Eminent Chinese of the Ch'ing Period (1644–1912). 2 vols. Ed. Arthur Hummel. Washington D.C.: United States Printing Office, 1943.

Fan, Duan'ang 范端昂. *Yuezhong jianwen* 粵中見聞. Guangzhou: Guangdong gaodeng jiaoyu chubanshe, 1988.

Feng, Erkang 馮爾康. "Qingchu Guangdongren yu Jiangsu" 清初廣東人與江蘇. In *Mingmo Qingchu Hua'nan diqu lishiwenwu gongye yantaohui lunwenji*, 75–83.

Fifer, Charles N., ed. *The Correspondence of James Boswell with Certain Members of the Club*. New York and Toronto: McGraw Hill, 1976.

Fong, Grace S. "Writing from a Side Room of Her Own: The Literary Vocation of Concubines in Ming-Qing China." In *Hsiang Lectures on Chinese Poetry*, vol. 1. Montreal: Centre for East Asian Research, McGill University, 2001, 41–63.

Furth, Charlotte. "Intellectual Change: From the Reform Movement to the May Fourth Movement, 1895–1920." In *The Cambridge History of China. Vol. 12. Republican China*, ed. John K. Fairbank. Cambridge: Cambridge University Press, 1983, 322–405.

Ge, Hong 葛洪. *Baopuzi* 抱朴子. (ZZJC ed.).

Geil, William Edgar. *Eighteen Capitals of China*. London: Constable, 1911.

Gong, Pengcheng 龔鵬程. *Jiangxi shishe zongpai yanjiu* 江西詩社宗派研究. Taipei: Wen, shi, zhe chubanshe, 1983.

Goodrich, L. Carrington. *The Literary Inquisition of Ch'ien-Lung*. 1935. Rpt., New York: Paragon, 1966.

Gu, Sili 顧嗣立, ed. *Yuanshixuan* 元詩選. 4 vols. Shanghai: Shanghai guji chubanshe, 1993.

Gu, Xueyi 顧學郜, ed. *Bai Juyi ji* 白居易集. 4 vols. Beijing: Zhonghua shuju, 1979.

Guan, Lin 管林. "Huang Peifang de jiashi, shengping he zhuzuo" 黃培芳的家世，生平和著作. *Guji zhengli yanjiu tongxun* 7 (1992): 13–16.

Guangdong lidai shichao 廣東歷代詩鈔. 3 vols. Ed. Yu Shaofan 余少颿. *Nengren shuyuan congshu* 能仁書院叢書. Hong Kong: Nengren shuyuan, 1980.

Guangdong tongzhi 廣東通志. (Jiajing 嘉靖 ed.). Ed. Huang Zuo 黃佐. Hong Kong: Dadong tushu gongsi, 1977.

Guangdong tongzhi 廣東通志. Comp. Ruan Yuan 阮元. 1864.

Guangdong wenwu 廣東文物. 1937. Rpt., Shanghai: Shanghai shuju, 1990.

Guangdong wenxian 廣東文獻. 8 vols. Comp. Luo Xuepeng 羅學鵬. (*Luoshi Chunhuitang* 羅氏春暉堂 ed.). 1864. Rpt., Jiangsu: Guangling guji keyinshe, 1994.

Guangdong wenxuan 廣東文選. Comp. Qu Dajun 屈大均. (*Siku jinhuishu congkan* ed.). Bejing: Beijing chubanshe, 1997.

Guangdong wenzheng 廣東文徵. 5 vols. Hong Kong: Xianggang Zhongwen Daxue, 1973.

Guangdong xinyu 廣東新語. 2 vols. Comp. Qu Dajun 屈大均. Beijing: Zhonghua shuju, 1985.

Guangdongsheng Zhongshan Tushuguan 廣東省中山圖書館, comp. *Guancang Guangdong difangzhi mulu* 館藏廣東地方誌目錄. Guangzhou: Guangdongsheng Zhongshan Tushuguan lishi wenxianbu, 1986.

Guangzhou sixiansheng shi 廣州四先生詩. (SKQS *zhenben* ed.).

Guangzhoushi wenwu zhi 廣州市文物志. Guangzhou: Lingnan meishu chubanshe, 1990.

Guicai Lun Wenxu 鬼才倫文敍. Ed. He Yancheng 何燕成. Guangdong: Guangdong gaodeng jiaoyu chubanshe, 1994.

Guicai Lun Wenxu quanji 鬼才倫文敍全集. Ed. Chen Shu 襯叔. Hong Kong: Xinsheng chubanshe, n.d.

Gujin tushu jicheng 古今圖書集成. 79 vols. Taipei: Dingwen shuju, 1980.

Guo, Jianxun 郭建勳. *Yijing duben* 易經讀本. Taipei: Sanmin shuju, 2004.

Guoli Beiping tushuguan shanben shumu 國立北平圖書館善本書目. Guangzhou, 1933.

Han-Wei Liuchao baisan mingjia ji 漢魏六朝百三名家集. 6 vols. Taipei: Wenjin chubanshe, 1979.

Hardie, Alison, trans. *The Craft of Gardens: Chi Cheng*. With photographs by Zhong Ming. New Haven and London: Yale University Press, 1988.

Hawes, Colin S. C. *The Social Circulation of Poetry in the Mid-Northern Song: Emotional Energy and Literati Self-Cultivation*. Albany: State University of New York Press, 2005.

Hawkes, David. *The Story of the Stone, vol 2: The Crab-Flower Club*. Harmondsworth, England: Penguin Books, 1977.

———. *The Songs of the South: An Ancient Chinese Anthology of Poems by Qu Yuan and Other Poets*. Harmondsworth, England and New York: Penguin Books, 1985.

He, Ge'en 何格恩. "Zhang Jiuling nianpu" 張九齡年譜. *Lingnan xuebao* 4, no. 1 (1935): 1–21.

———. "Zhang Jiuling zhi zhengzhi shenghuo" 張九齡之政治生活. *Lingnan xuebao* 4, no. 1 (1935): 22–46.

———. "Zhang Qujiang shiwen shiji biannniankao" 張曲江詩文事跡篇年考. In *Guangdong wenwu*, 444–515.

He, Guangyue 何光岳. *Baiyue yuanliushi* 百越源流史. Nanchang: Jiangxi jiaoyu chubanshe, 1989.

He, Guohua 何國華. "Lingnan zuizao xueshu zhuzuo—Yang Fu *Yiwu zhi*" 嶺南最早學術著作楊浮異物志. *Guji zhengli yanjiu tongxun* 10 (1994): 17.

———. "Qingdai Lingnan de gaodeng xuefu—Guangdong Xuehai tang" 清代嶺南的高等學府廣東學海堂. *Guangdong shizhi* 2 (1994): 51–52.

Hershatter, Gail, et al., eds. *Remapping China: Fissures in Historical Terrain*. Stanford: Stanford University Press, 1996.

Ho, Wai-Kam. "Late Ming Literati: Their Social and Cultural Ambience." In *The Chinese Scholar's Studio*, 23–36.

Honey, David B. "The Southern Muse: Some Cantonese Men of Letters." Paper presented at the Annual Meeting of the Western Branch of the American Oriental Society, Boulder, Colorado, October 2, 1992.

———. "Bibliographical Notes on Editions of the *Hsi-an chi*." Paper Presented at the Genealogy and Culture of South China, Brigham Young University, Provo, Utah, August 13–15, 1996.

———. "The Southern Garden Poetry Society" 南園詩社. In *Lingnan wenhua xin tanjiu lunwenji*, 251–60.

———. "Cong Lingnan shifeng kan Qiu Fengjia de Guangdong shi" 從嶺南詩風看丘逢甲的廣東詩 (Poetizing the Local in Qiu Fengjia's Verses on Guangdong). In *Qiu Fengjia, Qiu Niantai fuzi ji qi shidai xueshu yantaohui* 丘逢甲，丘念台父子及其時代學術研討會. Taizhong: Fengjia University, 1999, 3–18.

Hu, Shouwei 胡守為. "Zaoqi Daojiao yu Lingnan de guanxi" 早期道教與嶺南的關係. In *Lingnan wenhua xin tanjiu lunwenji*, 111–20.

Hu, Yinglin 胡應麟. *Shisou* 詩藪. Shanghai: Shanghai guji chubanshe, 1958.

Huang, Baohua 黃寶華. "*Jiangxi shishe zongpaitu* de xieding yu *Jiangxi shipai* zongji de kanxing"《江西詩社宗派圖》的寫定與《江西詩派》總集的刊行. *Wenxue yichan* 1999, issue 6, 68–69.

Huang, Foyi 黃佛頤. *Guangzhou chengfang zhi* 廣州城坊志. Yangzhou: Guangling guji keyinshe, 1991.

Huang, Haizhang 黃海章. *Mingmo Guangdong kang Qing shiren pingzhuan* 明末廣東抗清詩人評傳. Guangdong: Guangdong renmin chubanshe, 1987.

Huang, Yinpu 黃蔭普. *Guangdong wenxian shumu zhijianlu* 廣東文獻書目知見錄. Hong Kong: Chongwen shudian, 1972.

Huang, Yu 黃雨. *Lidai mingren ru Yue shixuan* 歷代名人入粵詩選. Guangdong: Guangdong renmin chubanshe, 1980.

Huang, Yuji 黃虞稷. *Qianqingtang shumu, fu suoyin* 千頃堂書目(附索引). Shanghai: Shanghai guji chubanshe, 2001.

Huang, Yunmei 黃雲眉. *Mingshi kaozheng* 明史考證. Beijing: Zhonghua shuju, 1985.

Huang, Zhimin 黃志民. "Mingren shishe zhi yanjiu" 明代詩社之研究. Master's Thesis, Zhengzhi University (Taiwan), 1972.

Huang, Zuo 黃佐. *Guangzhou renwu zhuan* 廣州人物傳. Guangdong: Guangdong gaodeng jiaoyu chubanshe, 1991.

Hucker, Charles O. "The Tung-lin Movement of the Late Ming Period." In *Chinese Thought and Institutions*, ed. John K. Fairbank. 1957. Rpt., Chicago and London: University of Chicago Press, 1973, 132–62.

———. *A Dictionary of Official Titles in Imperial China*. Stanford: Stanford University Press, 1985.

Hui'an xiansheng Zhuwengong ji 晦庵先生朱文公集. 2 vols. (SBCK ed.).

Iriya, Yoshitaka 入矢義高. *Mindai shibun* 明代詩文. Tōkyō: Chikuma shobō, 1978.

Jiang, Fan 江藩. *Jiang Fan ji* 江藩集. Shanghai: Shanghai shiji chuban gufen youxian gongsi, Shanghai guji chubanshe, 2006.

Jiang, Zuyuan 蔣祖緣 and Fang Zhiqin 方志欽, eds. *Jianming Guangdongshi* 簡明廣東史. Guangzhou: Guangdong renmin chubanshe, 1987.

Johnston, Reginald F. *Twilight in the Forbidden City*. London: Victor Gollancz, 1934.

Kale, Steven. *French Salons: High Society and Political Sociability from the Old Regime to the Revolution of 1848*. Baltimore: Johns Hopkins University Press, 2004.

Kaltenmark, Max. "Le Dompteur des flots." *Han Hiue* 3 (1948): 1–112.

Kern, Martin. "*Shi Jing* Songs As Performance Texts: A Case Study of 'Chu Ci' (Thorny Caltrop)." *Early China* 25 (2000): 49–111.

Knechtges, David R. *Wen xuan, or Selections of Refined Literature*. 3 vols. Princeton: Princeton University Press, 1982–1996.

Kramers, R. P. *K'ung Tsu Chia Yü* 孔子家語. *The School Sayings of Confucius*. Leiden: E.J. Brill, 1950.

Kroll, Paul. "The Memories of Lu Chao-lin." *Journal of the American Oriental Society* 109 (1989): 581–92.

Ku, Chieh-kang (Gu Jiegang). "A Study of Literary Persecution During the Ming Dynasty." Trans. L. Carrington Goodrich. *Harvard Journal of Asiatic Studies* 3 (1938): 254–311.

Lai, Xinxia 來新夏. "Qu Dajun yu *Guangdong xinyu*" 屈大均與廣東新語. In *Lingnan wenhua xin tanjiu lunwenji*, 127–31.

Laing, Ellen Johnston. "Real or Ideal: The Problem of the 'Elegant Gathering in the Western Garden' in Chinese Historical and Art Historical Records." *Journal of the American Oriental Society* 88 (1968): 419–35.

Langlois, John D. Jr. "The Hung-wu reign, 1368–1398." In *The Cambridge History of China, Vol. 7, Part I,* 107–81.

Lau, Kin-ming (Liu Jianming) 劉健明. "Li Suiqiu de shengping jiqi zhenglun" 黎遂球的生平與其政論. In *Mingmo Qingchu Hua'nan diqu lishiwenwu gongye yantaohui lunwenji,* 171–78.

Legge, James. *Li Chi: Book of Rites*. 2 vols. New Hyde Park, N.Y.: University Books, [1967].

———. *The Chinese Classics*. 5 vols. 1861–1893. Rpt., Hong Kong: Hong Kong University Press, 1970.

Levy, Howard S. *Translations from Po Chü-i's Collected Works*. 2 vols. New York: Paragon Book Reprint Corp., 1971.

Li, Chu-Tsing. "The Literati Life." In *The Chinese Scholar's Studio*, 37–51.

Li, Dechao 李德超. "Yuedong Nanyuan Shishe ji qianhou wuxiansheng shi" 粵東南園詩社及前後五先生詩. *Huagang wenke xuebao* 16 (1988): 201–22.

———. "Guangdong zhi zhongyi shige chugao" 廣東之忠義詩歌初稿. In *Lingnan wenhua xin tanjiu lunwenji,* 7–13.

———. *Lingnan shishigao* 嶺南詩史稿. Taipei: Fayansi chubanshe, 1998.

Li, Dongyang 李東陽. *Li Dongyang ji* 李東陽集. 3 vols. Changsha: Yuelu shushe chubanshe, 1984.

Li, Huilin. *Nanfang caomu zhuang. A Fourth Century Flora of Southeast Asia.* Hong Kong: The Chinese University Press, 1979.

Li, Jian'er. "Chen Zizhuang nianpu" 陳子莊年譜. In *Guangdong wenwu,* 516–50.

Li, Jinhua 李晉華. *Mingdai chizhuan shukao* 明代勅撰書考. Harvard-Yenching Institute Sinological Index Series, Supplement no. 3. Beiping: Yanjing University Library, 1932.

Li, Wai-Yee. "The Late Ming Courtesan: Invention of a Cultural Ideal." In *Writing Women in Late Imperial China,* ed. Ellen Widmer and Kang-I Sun Chang. Stanford: Stanford University Press, 1997, 46–73.

Li, Wenchu 李文初, et al. *Zhongguo shanshui shishi* 中國山水詩史. Guangzhou: Guangdong gaodeng jiaoyu chubanshe, 1991.

Liang, Peilan 梁佩蘭. *Liuyingtang ji* 六瑩堂集. Guangzhou: Zhongshan Daxue chubanshe, 1992.

Liang, Qichao 梁啟超. *Shishi* 詩史. Guangzhou, n.d.

Liang, Tingnan 梁廷枏. *Yuexiu shuyuanzhi* 粵秀書院志. In *Zhongguo lidai shuyuanzhi* 中國歷代書院志, vol. 3. Nanjing: Jiangsu jiaoyu chubanshe, 1995.

Liexian zhuan 列仙傳. (*Zhengtong Daozang* 正統道藏 ed.), HY #294, 8:6111–6129.

Lingnan wenhua xin tanjiu lunwenji 嶺南文化新探究論文集. Ed. Lin Tianwei 林天蔚. Hong Kong: Xiandai jiaoyu yanjiushe, 1996.

Lishi zhenxian tidao tongjian 歷世真仙體道通鑑. (*Zhengtong Daozang* 正統道藏 ed.), HY #295, 8:6163–6542; 9:6543–6636.

Lissarrague, Francois. *The Aesthetics of the Greek Banquet: Images of Wine and Ritual.* Trans. Andrew Szegedy-Maszak. Princeton: Princeton University Press, 1990.

Liu, Can 劉燦. "Daojia yu Lingnan fangzhi xiaoshuo" 道家與嶺南方志小說. *Lishi wenxian yu chuantong wenhua* 2 (1992): 252–67.

Liu, Sifen 劉斯奮, ed. *Huang Jie shixuan* 黃節詩選. Guangzhou: Guangdong renmin chubanshe, 1993.

Liu, Sifen and Zhou Xifu 周錫輹, eds. *Lingnan sanjia shixuan* 嶺南三家詩選. Guangdong: Guangdong renmin chubanshe, 1980.

Liu, Zuomei 柳作梅. "Qu Dajun *Guangdong xinyu* de lishi beijing" 屈大均《廣東新語》的歷史背景. *Guangdong wenxian* 5 (1976): 16–21.

Lo, Hsiang-lin (Luo Xianglin) 羅香林. "Song Wangtai yu Song ji zhi haishang xingchao" 宋王臺與宋際之海上行朝. *Journal of Oriental Studies* 3 (1956):185–217.

———. *Tangdai Guangzhou Guangxiaosi yu Zhong-Yin jiaotong zhi guanxi* 唐代光孝寺與中印交通之關係. Hong Kong: Zhongguo xueshe, 1960.

———. "The Southward Expansion of Chinese Civilization and the Advancement of Learning in Kwangtung Province." In *Symposium on Historical, Archaeological and Linguistic Studies on Southern China, Southeast Asia, and the Hong Kong Region,* ed. F. S. Drake. Hong Kong: University of Hong Kong, 1967, 139–49.

Lu, Ping 路平. *Guangzhou fengwu* 廣州風物. Guangdong: Guangdong keji, 1991.

Luo, Tianchi 羅天尺. *Wushan zhilin* 五山志林. Beijing: Zhonghua shuju, 1985.

Luo, Zhufeng 羅竹風, ed. *Hanyu dacidian* 漢語大詞典. 12 vols. Shanghai: Hanyu dacidian chubanshe, 1989.

Mai, Shaolin 麥少麟. "Minzu yingxiong Zhang Jiayu" 民族英雄張家玉. In *Guangdong wenwu*, 588–611.

Mai, Yinghao 麥英豪. "Guangzhoucheng shijian niandaikao" 廣州城始建年代考. In *Yangcheng wenwu bowu yanjiu*, 64–75.

Mather, Richard. *Shih-shuo Hsin-yü. A New Account of Tales of the World.* 2nd ed. Ann Arbor: Center for Chinese Studies, University of Michigan, 2002.

McMullen, D. L. "Recollection without Tranquility: Du Fu, the Imperial Gardens, and the State." *Asia Major*, Third Series, 14 (2001): 189–252.

Meng, Ziwei 孟子微. "Nanyuan shiren Ou Daren" 南園詩人歐大任. In *Yilin conglu* 藝林叢錄, vol. 3. 1962. Rpt., Hong Kong: Commercial Press, 1975, 169–71.

Meyer-Fong, Tobie. *Building Culture in Early Qing Yangzhou.* Stanford: Stanford University Press, 2003.

Miles, Steven B. "Rewriting the Southern Han (917–971): The Production of Local Culture in Nineteenth-Century Guangzhou." *Harvard Journal of Asiatic Studies* 62 (2002): 39–75.

———. "Celebrating the Yu Fan Shrine: Literary Networks and Local Identity in Early Nineteenth-Century Guangzhou." *Late Imperial China* 25, no. 2 (December 2004): 33–73.

———. *The Sea of Learning: Mobility and Identity in Nineteenth-Century Guangzhou.* Harvard East Asian monographs, no. 269. Cambridge, Massachusetts and London: Harvard University Asia Center, 2006.

Mingmo Qingchu Hua'nan diqu lishiwenwu gongye yantaohui lunwen ji 明末清初華南地區歷史文物功業研討會論文集. Ed. Law Ping-min 羅炳綿 and Lau Kin-ming 劉健明. Hong Kong: History Department, Chinese University of Hong Kong, 1993.

Mingshi jishi 明詩紀事. 6 vols. Ed. Chen Tian 陳田. Shanghai: Shanghai guji chubanshe, 1993.

Minzhong shizi shi 閩中十子詩. Ed. Yuan Biao 袁表 and Ma Ying 馬熒. (SKQS ed.).

Miyakawa, Hisayuki. "The Confucianism of South China." In *The Confucian Persuasion*, ed. Arthur F. Wright. Stanford: Stanford University Press, 1960, 21–46.

Mote, Frederick. *The Poet Kao Ch'i.* Princeton: Princeton University Press, 1962.

Nanyuan houwu xiansheng shi 南園後五先生詩. Guangzhou: Zhongshan Daxue chubanshe, 1990.

Nanyuan qianwu xiansheng shi 南園前五先生詩. Printed with *Nanyuan houwu xiansheng shi.*

Naquin, Susan and Evelyn S. Rawski. *Chinese Society in the Eighteenth Century.* New Haven and London: Yale University Press, 1987.

Nelson, J. Walter. "The Literary Club and Gregarious Males." Paper presented to the South Central Society for Eighteenth-Century Studies, 17th Annual Meeting, Lubbock, Texas, Feb. 14, 1992.

Netolitzky, Almut. *Das Ling-wai tai-ta von Chou Ch'ü-fei. Eine landeskunde Südchinas aus dem 12. Jahrhundert.* Wiesbaden: Franz Steiner, 1977.

Nienhauser, William H. Jr., ed. *The Indiana Companion to Traditional Chinese Literature*. Bloomington: Indiana University Press, 1986.

———, et al., trans. *The Grand Scribe's Records, Vol 1. The Basic Annals of Pre-Han China*. Bloomington and Indianapolis: Indiana University Press, 1994.

Oki, Yasushi. "The Yellow Peony Party." Paper presented at the Annual Meeting of the Association for Asian Studies, Chicago, Illinois, March 23, 2002.

Ouyang, Guang 歐陽光. "Yumen shiluo de qunti: lun Yuanchu yimin shishe jian yu Wang Deming xiansheng shangque" 鬱懣失落的群體：論元初遺民詩社兼與王德明先生商榷. *Wenxue yichan*, 1993, issue 4: 83–89.

———. "Yuequan yinshe zuozhe kaolüe" 月泉吟社作者考略. *Wenxian* 1 (1993).

———. "Yuequan yinshe zuozhe xukao" 月泉吟社作者續考. *Wenxian* 3 (1994): 232–45.

———. *Song-Yuan shishe yanjiu conggao* 宋元詩社研究叢稿. Guangzhou: Guangdong gaodeng jiaoyu chubanshe, 1996.

Owen, Stephen. *Remembrance: The Experience of the Past in Classical Chinese Literature*. Cambridge, Massachusetts: Harvard University Press, 1986.

Pease, Jonathan O. "Lin-ch'uan and Fen-ning: Kiangsi Locales and Kiangsi Writers during the Sung." *Asia Major*, Third series, 4 (1991): 39–85.

Plaks, Andrew H. *Archetype and Allegory in the "Dream of the Red Chamber."* Princeton: Princeton University Press, 1976.

Polachek, James M. *The Inner Opium War*. Harvard East Asian Monographs, 151. Cambridge, Massachusetts: The Council on East Asian Studies, Harvard University, 1992.

Poon, Ming-sun (Pan Mingshen) 潘銘燊. *Guangdong difangzhi zhuanji suoyin* 廣東地方志傳記索引. 2 vols. Hong Kong: Zhongwen Daxue chubanshe, 1989.

Qin, Huanming 秦環明. "Lü Benzhong *Jiangxi shishe zongpaitu* chuangzuo shijian kaobian" 呂本中「江西詩社宗派圖」創作時間考辨. *Wenjiao ziliao*, 1989, issue 6: 91–97.

Qingshi jishi 清詩紀事. 22 vols. Ed. Qian Zhonglian 錢仲聯, et al. Jiangsu: Jiangsu guji chubanshe, 1987–1989.

Qiu, Fengjia 丘峰甲. *Canghaijun gengxu Luofuyoucao* 滄海君庚戌羅浮游草. Printed by Wu Daorong, 1910.

———. *Lingyun huirilou shichao* 嶺雲海日樓詩鈔. Shanghai: Shanghai guji chubanshe, 1982.

Qiu, Jiang 仇江, ed. *Lingnan lidai wenxuan* 嶺南歷代文選. Guangzhou: Guangdong renmin chubanshe, 1993.

Qiu, Juchuan 仇巨川. *Yangcheng guchao* 羊城古鈔. Guangzhou: Guangdong renmin chubanshe, 1993.

Qu, Dajun 屈大均. *Wengshan shiwai* 翁山詩外. (*Xuxiu siku quanshu* ed.).

———. *Wengshan wenwai* 翁山文外. Beijing: Wenwu chubanshe, 1982.

Qu, Xiangbang 屈向邦. *Guangdong shihua zhengxubian* 廣東詩話政續編. Hong Kong: Longmen shudian, 1964.

Quan Mingshi 全明詩. 3 vols. Shanghai: Shanghai guji chubanshe, 1990–1994.

Quan Shanggu Sandai Qin-Han Sanguo Liuchaowen 全上古三代秦漢三國六朝文. 4 vols. 1958. Rpt., Beijing: Zhonghua shuju, 1987.

Quan Songshi 全宋詩. 5 vols. Beijing: Beijing University Press, 1991.

Quan Songwen 全宋文. 50 vols. Sichuan: Bashu shushe, 1988.

Quan Tangshi 全唐詩. 25 vols. Beijng: Zhonghua shuju, 1979.

Raylor, Timothy. *Cavaliers, Clubs, and Literary Culture: Sir John Mennes, James Smith, and the Order of Fancy*. Newark: University of Delaware Press; London and Toronto: Associate University Presses, 1994.

Robinet, Isabelle. *Taoism. Growth of a Religion*. Trans. Phyllis Brooks. Stanford: Stanford University Press, 1997.

Rong, Zhaozu 容肇祖. "Xuehai tang kao" 學海堂考. *Lingnan xuebao* 3 (1934): 1–147.

Schafer, Edward H. "Li Kang: A Rhapsody on the Banyon Tree." *Oriens* 6 (1955): 344–53.

———. "A Fourteenth Century Gazeteer of Canton." In *Oriente Poliano*, ed. Étienne Balazs, et al. Rome: Istituto italiano per il Medio e Estremo Oriente, 1957, 67–93.

———. *The Vermilion Bird: T'ang Images of the South*. Berkeley and Los Angeles: University of California Press, 1967.

Schipper, K. M. *Index du Yunji Qiqian: Project Tao-Tsang*. Publications de l'Ecole Française d'Extreme-Orient, no. 131. 2 vols. Paris: L'Ecole Française d'Extreme-Orient, 1981–1982.

Shao, Yaonian 邵堯年. "The Kapok of Guangdong" 廣東木棉樹. *Lingnan xuebao* 2, no. 1 (1931): 77–83.

Shisanjing zhushu 十三經注疏. *Thirteen Classics* ed. Taipei: Yiwen Yinshuguan, 1981.

Shunde xianzhi 順德縣誌. Guangzhou: Zhongshan Daxue chubanshe, 1993.

Sibu congkan 四部叢刊. Shanghai: Commercial Press, 1929–1936.

Siku quanshu zhenben 四庫全書珍本. 1933–35. Rpt., Taipei: Commercial Press, 1982–85.

Siku quanshu zongmu tiyao 四庫全書總目提要. Taipei: Hanjing wenhua shiye youxian gongsi, 1981.

Siren, Osvald. *A History of Later Chinese Painting*. 2 vols. New York: Hacker Art Books, 1978.

Song, Lian 宋濂. *Song Wenxian Gong quanji* 宋文憲公全集. (SBCK ed.).

Soushen houji 搜神後記. Beijing: Zhonghua shudian, 1981.

Soymié, Michel. "Le Lo-Feou Chan: Etude de geographie religieuse." *Bulletin de L'École Française d'Extrême-Orient* (BEFEO) 48 (1956): 1–139.

Struve, Lynn A. "Ambivalence and Action: Some Frustrated Scholars of the K'ang-hsi Period." In *From Ming to Ch'ing: Conquest, Region, and Continuity in Seventeenth-Century China*, ed. Jonathan D. Spence and John E. Wills, Jr. New Haven and London: Yale University Press, 1979, 321–65.

———. "The Southern Ming." In *The Cambridge History of China, Vol. 7: The Ming Dynasty (1368–1644), Part I*, 641–725.

———. *The Ming-Qing Conflict, 1610–1683: A Historiography and Source Guide*. Association for Asian Studies, Monograph and Occasional Paper Series, no. 56. Ann Arbor: Association of Asian Studies, 1998.

Su, Shi 蘇軾. *Dongpo shiji fenlei* 東坡詩集分類. (SBCK ed.).

Sun, Fen 孫蕡. *Sun Xi'an ji* 孫西庵集. (*Zimingchenglou congshu* 自明誠樓叢書 ed.). Shunde: Longshi Zhongheyuan 龍氏中和園, 1934–1937.

———. *Xi'an ji* 西庵集. (SKQS ed.).

———. *Xi'an ji* 西庵集. 10 *juan* ed. 1503. Nanjing Municiple Library. Microfilm #2152.

Sun, Jing'an 孫靜庵. *Ming yiminlu* 明遺民錄. Hangzhou: Zhejiang guji chubanshe, 1985.

Sutton, Donald S. "A Case of Literary Piety: The Ma Yuan Cult from High-Tang to High-Qing." *Chinese Literature: Essays, Articles, Reviews* 11 (1989): 79–114.

Taishō shinshū Daizōkyō 大正新修大藏經. Ed. Takakusu Junjirō 高楠順次郎 and Watanabe Kaikyoku 渡邊海旭. Tōkyō: Taishō Issaikyō Kankōkai, 1924–1934.

Tao, Qian 陶潛. *Tao Pengze ji* 陶彭澤集. (BSJJ ed.), 3:2439–2496.

Taylor, Keith Weller. *The Birth of Vietnam*. Berkeley, Los Angeles, and Oxford: University of California Press, 1983.

Thrower, S. L. *Hong Kong Trees*. Hong Kong: Urban Council, 1988.

Tsang, Yat-man (Zeng Yimin) 曾一民. "Guangzhou Zhao Tuo gucheng kao" 廣州趙佗古城考. *Guangdong wenxian* 8, no. 21 (1978): 30–38.

Turner, J. A. *Kwang Tung or Five Years in South China*. 1894. Rpt., Hong Kong: Oxford University Press, 1984.

Wakeman, Frederic, Jr. *The Great Enterprise: The Manchu Reconstruction of Imperial Order in Seventeenth-Century China*. 2 vols. Berkeley: University of California Press, 1985.

Walden, Beryl M. and Shiu Ying Hu. *Wild Flowers of South China and Hong Kong*, Part 2. Hong Kong: All Noble Co., 1987.

Walton, Linda. "Southern Sung Academies and the Construction of Sacred Space." In *Landscape, Culture, and Power in Chinese Society*, ed. Wen-hsin Yeh. China Research Monograph, Center for Chinese Studies. Berkeley: Institute of East Asian Studies, University of California, 1998, 23–51.

Wang, Deming 王德明. "Lun Songdai de shishe" 論宋代的詩社. *Wenxuan yichan* 6 (1992): 66–72.

Wang, Qiuwei 王秋達. "Nanyuan mohen" 南園墨痕. *Yijing* 逸經 21 (1937): 15–18.

Wang, Songtao 汪松濤. "Zhang Weiping nianbiao jianbian" 張維屏年表簡編. *Guji zhengli yanjiu tongxun* 3 (1988): 16–20.

———. "Zhang Weiping sixiang ji shiwen tese lüelun" 張維屏思想及詩文特色略論. *Guji zhengli yanjiu tongxun* 6 (1992): 6–12.

———. *Zhang Nanshan quanji* 張南山全集. 2 vols. Guangzhou: Guangdong gaodeng jiaoyu chubanshe, 1993.

Wang, Xizhi 王羲之. *Wang Youjun ji* 王右軍集. (BSJJ ed.), 3:2241–282.

Wang, Yongfu 王永福. "*Qiaoya* jiaozhu shuping"《嶠雅》校注述評. *Guji zhengli yanjiu tongxun* 4 (1990): 12–13.

Wang, Zhangtao 王章濤. *Ruan Yuan nianpu* 阮元年譜. Hefei: Huangshan shushe, 2003.

———. *Ruan Yuan pingzhuan* 阮元評傳. Yangzhou: Guangling shushe, 2004.

Wang, Zongyan 汪宗衍. "Chen Dongshu xiansheng nianpu" 陳東塾先生年譜. *Lingnan xuebao* 4 (1935): 55–118.

———. *Qu Wengshan xiansheng nianpu* 屈翁山先生年譜. Macao: Yujin shuwu, 1970.

———. *Guangdong wenwu congtan* 廣東文物叢談. Kowloon: Zhonghua shuju, 1974.

Ware, James R. *Alchemy, Medicine, and Religion in the China of A.D. 320: The Nei P'ien of Ko Hung*. 1966. Rpt., New York: Dover Publications, 1981.

Watson, Burton. *The Complete Works of Chuang Tzu*. New York: Columbia University Press, 1968.

Wei, Betty Peh-T'i. *Ruan Yuan, 1764–1849. The Life and Work of a Major Scholar-Official in Nineteenth-Century China before the Opium War*. Hong Kong: Hong Kong University Press, 2006.

Wen, Runeng 溫汝能, comp. *Yuedong shihai* 粵東詩海. 3 vols. Guangzhou: Zhongshan Daxue, 1999.

Wenyuan yinghua 文苑英華. 6 vols. Ed. Li Fang 李昉, et al. Beijing: Zhonghua shuju, 1966.

Wong, Siu-kit. *Notes on Poetry from the Ginger Studio*. Hong Kong: The Chinese University Press, 1987.

Wu, Daorong 吳道鎔, comp. *Panyuxian xuzhi* 番禺縣續志. N.p., 1911.

———. *Dan'an wencun* 澹盦文存. Jindai Zhongguo shiliao congkan xubian 近代中國史料叢刊繼編, No. 20. Taipei: Wenhai chubanshe, 1975.

Wu, Fusheng. "Composed at Execution: A Look at Three 'Poems Upon Confronting the End' (LINZHONG SHI)." *Early Medieval China* 9 (2003): 105–25.

Wu, Hongcong 吳宏聰 and Li Hongsheng 李鴻生, eds. *Qiu Fengjia yanjiu* 丘逢甲研究. Guangdong: Guangdong renmin chubanshe, 1986.

Wu, Shanjia 吳山嘉. *Fushe xingshi zhuanlüe* 復社姓氏傳略. (*Haiwangcun guji congkan* 海王村古籍叢刊 ed.). Guangzhou: Zhongguo shudian, 1990.

Xi-Han Nanyuewang mu 西漢南越王墓. 2 vols. Beijing: wenwu chubanshe, 1991.

Xian-Qin, Han, Wei, Jin Nanbeichao shi 先秦漢魏晉南北朝詩. 3 vols. Ed. Lu Qinli 逯欽立. Beijing: Zhonghua shuju, 1983.

Xiao, Chi. *The Chinese Garden as Lyric Enclave: A Generic Study of The Story of the Stone*. Ann Arbor: Center for Chinese Studies, The University of Michigan, 2001.

Xie, Fuya 謝扶雅. "Guangxiaosi yu Liuzu Huineng" 光孝寺與六祖慧能. *Lingnan xuebao* 4, no. 1 (1935): 175–201.

Xinbian Zhuzi jicheng 新編諸子集成. 8 vols. Taipei: World Book Company, 1983.

Xiqiaoshan zhi 西樵山志. Guangzhou: Guangdong renmin chubanshe, 1992.

Xu, Bodong 徐博東 and Huang Zhiping 黃志萍. *Qiu Fengjiazhuan* 丘逢甲傳. Beijing: Shishi chubanshe, 1987.

Xu, Xinfu 徐信符. *Guangdong cangshu jishihi* 廣東藏書紀事詩. Jindai Zhongguo shiliao congkan xubian 近代中國史料叢刊續編, No. 20. Taipei: Wenhai chubanshe, 1975.

Xu, Xu 徐續. *Lingnan gujinlu* 嶺南古今錄. Hong Kong: Shanghai shuju, 1984.

Xuxiu Sikuquanshu tiyao 續修四庫全書提要. Taipei: Commercial Press, 1972.

Yan, Xuxin 顏虛心. "Mingshi Chen Bangyanzhuan pangzheng" 明史陳邦彥傳旁證. In *Guangdong wenwu,* 551–87.

Yang, Baolin 楊寶霖, ed. *Keyuan Zhangshi jiazu shiwen ji* 可園張氏家族詩文集. Dongguan: Dongguanshi zhengxie wenshi ziliao weiyuanhui chuban, 2003.

Yang, Guozhen 楊國楨. "Zailun Xuannan shishe yu Lin Zexu" 再論宣南詩社與林則徐. *Zhuanghua wenshi luncong* 13 (1980): 149–58.

Yang, Zhihua 楊芷華. "Wenxi cungao zuozhe Li Maoying shengping kaolüe" 文溪存稿作者李昴英生平考略. *Lishi wenxian yu chuantong wenhua* 1 (1992): 147–65.

———. "Li Maoying nianpu" 李昴英年普. *Lishi wenxian yu chuangtong wenhua* 4 (1994): 181–224.

Yangcheng wenwu bowu yanjiu 羊城文物博物研究. Guangzhou: Guangdong renmin chubanshe, 1993.

Yao, Xinzhong, ed. *RoutledgeCurzon Encyclopedia of Confucianism*. 2 vols. London and New York: RoutledgeCurzon, 2003.

Yi, Hangguang 易行廣, ed. *Yu Jing shixuan* 余靖詩選. Guilin: Lijiang chubanshe, 1993.

Yilin conglu 藝林叢錄. 1962. Rpt., Hong Kong: Commercial Press, 1975.

Yokota, Terutoshi 横田輝俊. "Minsho no shisha" 明初の詩社. *Shinagaku kenkyū* 26 (1961): 39–54.

Yoshikawa, Kōjirō 吉川幸次郎. "Sung Poetry in Canton." In *Symposium on Historical, Archaeological and Linguistic Studies on Southern China, Southeast Asia, and the Hong Kong Region*, ed. F. S. Drake. Hong Kong: University of Hong Kong, 1967, 135–36.

———. *Five Hundred Years of Chinese Poetry, 1150–1650*. Trans. John Timothy Wixted. Princeton: Princeton University Press, 1989.

Yu, Pauline. *The Reading of Imagery in the Chinese Poetic Tradition*. Princeton: Princeton University Press, 1987.

Yu, Weng 于翁. "Ruan Yuan yu Xuehai tang" 阮元與學海堂. In *Yilin conglu*, 131–35.

Yuan Dade Nanhaizhi canben (fu jiyi) 元大德南海志殘本(附輯佚). Guangzhou: Guangdong renmin chubanshe, 1991.

Yuan, Zhongren 袁鐘仁. "Zhongwai xuezhe zhongshi de *Lingwai daida*" 中外學者重視的嶺外待答. *Lishi wenxian yu chuantong wenhua* (1994): 170–80.

Yue shisanjia ji 粵十三家集 (*Anthology of the Thirteen Masters of Yue*). Ed. Wu Yuanwei 伍元薇. (*Shixuexuan* 詩雪軒 ed.). 1845.

Yuedong cichao 粵東詞鈔. Comp. Xu Yubin 許玉彬. 1849. Rpt., Macao, 1965.

Yueshi souyi 粵詩蒐遺. Comp. Huang Zigao 黃子高. (*Lingnan yishu* 嶺南遺書 ed.). Nanhai Wushi, [1831].

Yunji qiqian 雲藉七籤. 3 vols. Taiwan: Ziyu chubanshe, 1973.

Zeng, Zhaoxuan 曾昭璇. *Guangzhou lishi dili* 廣州歷史地理. Guangzhou: Guangdong renmin chubanshe, 1991.

Zengbu liuchenzhu Wenxuan 增補六臣註文選. Taipei: Huazheng shuju, 1980.

Zhang, Jian 張鑑. *Ruan Yuan nianpu* 阮元年譜. Beijing: Zhonghua shuju, 1995.

Zhang, Jiuling 張九齡. *Qujiang Zhang xiansheng wenji* 曲江張先生文集. (SBCK ed.).

Zhang, Qigan 張其淦. *Dongguan shilu* 東莞詩祿, vol. 1. Dongguan: Dongguanshi zhengxie wenshiziliao weiyuanhui, 2001.

Zhang, Qiyun 張其昀, ed. *Zhongwen dacidian* 中文大辭典. 12 vols. 1962–1968. Rpt., Taipei: Zhongguo Wenhua Daxue, 1973.

Zhang, Weiping 張維平. *Zhang Nanshan quanji* 張南山全集. Guangzhou, 1857.

Zhao, Suosheng 趙所生 and Xue Zhengxing 薛正興, eds. *Zhongguo lidai shuyuan zhi* 中國歷代書院志. 16 vols. Nanjing: Jiangsu jiaoyu chubanshe, 1995.

Zhao, Yi 趙翼. *Gaiyu congkao* 陔餘叢考. Shanghai: Commercial Press, 1957.

Zhao, Yongji 趙永紀, ed. *Qingdai xueshu cidian* 清代學術辭典. Beijing: Xueyuan chubanshe, 2004.

Zhong, Ganquan 鍾淦泉 and Yang Baolin 楊寶霖, eds. *Humen lidai shixuan* 虎門歷代詩選. Guangzhou: Guangdong jiaoyu chubanshe, 2004.

Zhou, Weimin 周偉民. *Ming-Qing shige* 明清詩歌. Changchun: Jilin jiaoyu chubanshe, 1995.

Zhou, Yinbin 周寅賓. "Mingdai de Chaling shipai" 明代的茶陵勢派. *Xuelin manlu* 學林漫錄 10 (1985): 181–85.

Zhu, Jincheng 朱金城. *Bai Juyi nianpu* 白居易年譜. Shanghai: Shanghai guji chubanshe, 1982.

Zhu, Yizun 朱彝尊, ed. *Mingshi zong* 明詩綜. Taipei: Shijie shuju, 1962.

Zhu, Yuanzhang 朱元璋. *Ming Taizu ji* 明太祖集. Anhui: Huangshan shushe, 1991.

Zhuanke nianli 篆刻年歷. Accessed at www.candc.com.tw/sealbank/ZR7610.htm-5k. (As the above link is no longer working, the same quote may be accessed now at http://sealbank.net/M3MainFind.asp?LM=3&L1=7&L2=71&L3=030&LS=&SRCHTXT=WS&SK=US771030&PN=0&PNRN=0).

Index